children,
families
and violence

of related interest

Child Protection, Domestic Violence and Parental Substance Misuse
Family Experiences and Effective Practice
Hedy Cleaver, Don Nicholson, Sukey Tarr and Deborah Cleaver
ISBN 978 1 84310 582 4

Young Children's Rights
Exploring Beliefs, Principles and Practice
2nd edition
Priscilla Alderson
Foreword by Mary John
ISBN 978 1 84310 599 2
Children in Charge series

Conduct Disorder and Offending Behaviour in Young People
Findings from Research
Kristin Liabø and Joanna Richardson
ISBN 978 1 84310 508 4

Domestic Violence and Child Protection
Directions for Good Practice
Edited by Cathy Humphreys and Nicky Stanley
ISBN 978 1 84310 276 2

Children Who Commit Acts of Serious Interpersonal Violence
Messages for Best Practice
Edited by Ann Hagell and Renuka Jeyarajah-Dent
ISBN 978 1 84310 384 4

Understanding Attachment and Attachment Disorders
Theory, Evidence and Practice
Vivien Prior and Danya Glaser
ISBN 978 1 84310 245 8

Developing Advocacy for Children and Young People
Current Issues in Research, Policy and Practice
Edited by Christine M. Oliver and Jane Dalrymple
Foreword by Cherie Booth QC
ISBN 978 1 84310 596 1

Making an Impact
Children and Domestic Violence—A Reader
2nd edition
Marianne Hester, Chris Pearson and Nicola Harwin
With Hilary Abrahams
ISBN 978 1 84310 157 4

children, families
and violence

CHALLENGES FOR CHILDREN'S RIGHTS

Katherine Covell and R. Brian Howe

Jessica Kingsley Publishers
London and Philadelphia

This book is dedicated to all the children who took part in the *UN Secretary General's Global Study on Violence Against Children*. Their understanding and ideals are our hope for the future.

CONTENTS

CHAPTER 1
Introduction   9

CHAPTER 2
Neurological Underpinnings   30

CHAPTER 3
Parenting Styles   63

CHAPTER 4
Violence in the Family   95

CHAPTER 5
Policy Interventions   129

CHAPTER 6
Cultural Contexts   183

CHAPTER 7
Respecting Children's Rights   228

REFERENCES   241
SUBJECT INDEX   279
AUTHOR INDEX   283

CHAPTER 1

INTRODUCTION

Violence is a cycle. We see our parents being violent and then we do violent things and then our kids will do violent things.[1]

We first met Adam on the day he was released from prison.[2] He was 19 years old. He spoke compellingly about his childhood and his hopes for the future of his own child. Adam, a victim of prolonged emotional and physical abuse, was born into a violent household. Predictably, like many others in similar situations, his developmental path led him into the care of the child welfare services, numerous foster homes and group homes, juvenile detention centers, and eventually adult prison. Adam's main concern on the day we met him was caring for his son for whom he now had sole custody. Adam was aware that he needed support and that he needed parenting education. He did not want to repeat the cycle of violence he had experienced.

But there was no help available. In fact, he told us, the waiting list for parenting classes was so long that his son would likely be in school well before help was offered. His son, an 11-month-old who had spent his early life with his drug-addicted mother and then in foster care, was in great need of a supportive family environment. Adam was anxious to do his best for his son. But with little education, few job skills, no family support, and little experience with positive family life, his prospects for a successful outcome are quite dim. And so the cycle continues. It is a cycle of dysfunction, of violence, and of the violation

---

1   This and all subsequent epigraphs are from children who participated in the United Nations Global Study on Violence Against Children, North American Region (Covell 2006).

2   Adam's full name is omitted to protect his and his son's privacy.

of children's fundamental human rights. It is a cycle, we believe, that can be significantly lessened only with respect for the rights of the child.

The purpose of this book is to examine from a children's rights perspective the risk factors for the raising of violent children. Violence through childhood is not spontaneous. Like Adam, children are raised to become violent in poorly functioning families and child-unfriendly environments. They may be exposed to toxic substances *in utero*, to maltreatment in infancy, and to domestic violence or parental criminality as they grow. Each of these risk factors is empirically linked with the development of antisocial and aggressive behaviors, and each reflects a violation of children's rights. The pervasiveness of these risk factors in children's lives is connected to the policies and cultures in which they are being raised. Cultures and policies that are friendly to children and work to advance their rights lessen the likelihood that children are put at risk of a pathway into aggressive and violent behavior. Respecting the rights of every child would do much to shift the balance between risk and protective factors and, as a result, reduce the incidence and severity of childhood violence.

THE PROBLEM OF VIOLENCE

There has been significant attention to the problem of violence among children and youth over the past few decades. A number of high-profile acts of violence during the 1990s, particularly the Bulger case in England and school killings in North America,[3] have attracted public outcry and demands for more action and more punitive

---

3   Two-year-old Jamie Bulger was killed by two ten-year-old boys in Liverpool in 1993. On 24 March 1998, four students and one teacher were killed at Westside Middle School, Jonesboro, Arkansas by students aged 13 and 11 years. On 24 April 1998, a 14-year-old student killed a teacher at James W. Parker Middle School in Edinboro, Pennsylvania. On 19 May 1998, a student was killed by another, aged 18 years, in the parking lot at Lincoln County High School, Fayetteville, Tennessee. Two students were killed by a 15-year-old (whose parents were then found shot) in the cafeteria at Thurston High School, Springfield, Oregon, on 21 May 1998. Fourteen students (including the two killers, aged 17 and 18 years) and one teacher were killed on 20 April 1999 at Columbine High School in Littleton, Colorado. On April 28, 1999, one student was killed in the first fatal high school shooting in Canada in 20 years. A 14-year-

responses to violent children. Over the same time period, there has been accumulating empirical evidence in North America, Europe, and Australia of an increased incidence of early adversity in children's rearing environments, aggressive children, and violent youth (e.g. Colman 2003; Heide 2003; Maughan *et al.* 2004; Mullis *et al.* 2004; Pridemore 2002).

The findings of the *United Nations Secretary General's Study on Violence Against Children* (2007) emphasize the importance of lessening the adversity in children's lives if we are to stop raising violent children. In extraordinarily large numbers around the globe, children are the victims of maltreatment. Children are living in families in which they are exposed to intimate partner violence and are beaten, sexually abused, and even killed. Despite an almost global commitment to securing the rights of the child, the majority of the world's children, the report notes, are without adequate protections from violence. As long as this continues, we can expect children to grow up with antisocial, aggressive, and criminally violent behaviors.

As will be discussed in this book, there are clear and compelling links among early adversity, childhood aggression, and subsequent criminal violence (e.g. Farrington 2000; Sutton *et al.* 1999). Inappropriate aggressiveness in early childhood tends to be highly stable and resistant to modification (Broidy *et al.* 2003; Shaw *et al.* 2003). It is a strong predictor of juvenile arrests and adult violent criminal offending (Stewart, Simons and Conger 2002). The link between early aggression and subsequent offending has been demonstrated in a wide number of countries including Canada, the United States, the United Kingdom, Sweden, Finland, and New Zealand (Huesmann, Eron and Dubow 2002). The link is clear and strong whether it is assessed by self-reports or through official crime statistics (Herrenkohl *et al.* 2003). Despite such evidence, and the obvious costs of violence to the individual and society, little has been done to systematically address the sources of violent behavior. Interventions, when they do

---

old student killed another at W.R. Myers High School in Taber, Alberta. On 19 November 1999, a 12-year-old student killed a 13-year-old in the lobby of Deming Middle School in Deming, New Mexico. Of course such killings did not end in the 1990s. Since the early 2000s, there have been at least 11 school shootings, resulting in 32 deaths, by those under age 18 years in the US.

occur, are usually reactive and too late in the child's development to be effective.

Responses to violent children typically are punitive, consistent with the demands of many of the public. But punitive responses to the problem of violent children are not effective. In schools, commonly used strategies such as expulsions, suspensions, and zero-tolerance policies have had little if any impact on reducing violence among school children (Dill 1998; Ierley and Claassen-Wilson 2003; McCann 2002). And in juvenile justice systems, policies of longer incarceration have been shown to be ineffective and potentially harmful (Dishion, McCord and Poulin 1999; MacKenzie, Wilson and Kidder 2001). As Kenneth Dodge and his colleagues have pointed out (Dodge, Dishion and Lansford 2006), institutionalizing antisocial youth with their deviant peers, a common response to violent adolescents, merely exacerbates existing problems. So it is critical that a focus be on early prevention and proactive approaches. A children's rights approach provides such a focus. Before describing what a children's rights approach entails, we will explain how we define violent children, why we are focussing on families, and why it is important to consider families in their social contexts.

DEFINING VIOLENT CHILDREN

Consistent with the United Nations Convention on the Rights of the Child (the Convention), we use the term "children" here to refer to all persons under the age of 18 years. As in *UN Secretary General's Study on Violence Against Children* (2007), and as in the Convention (Article 19), we define "violence" very broadly here as behaviors that attempt to harm or result in injury. These include the following three fundamental types of behaviors. One type is disruptive antisocial aggressive behaviors, such as bullying, that impair the child's daily functioning, and impair or threaten the development and maintenance of healthy social relationships. A second are the clinical designations of Oppositional Defiant Disorder, essentially recurring defiant disobedient and hostile behavior, and Conduct Disorder which describes "repetitive and persistent patterns of behavior in which the basic rights of others or major age-appropriate societal norms or rules are violated" (American Psychiatric Association 2000, p.93). The third is criminal violence, including assault, sexual assault, and homicide. These three types tend to be developmentally linked. Criminal violence most often is an outcome of developmentally inappropriate early aggression (Boots and Heide 2006; Heide 2003).

Our purpose here is to demonstrate that the violation of children's rights is a major contributor to the early onset aggressive behavior pattern that is associated with these three types of violent outcomes. We first note that some physical aggression in early childhood is developmentally normal and not of concern. As Richard Tremblay has emphasized, it is important to differentiate between developmentally appropriate aggression, from which children learn to regulate their behavior, and age-inappropriate or excessive levels of aggression (Tremblay 2006; Tremblay *et al.* 1999). Developmentally appropriate physical aggression peaks around age two. It lessens as language skills develop and with appropriate socialization. Young children who display abnormally high levels of aggression, or who fail to regulate their aggressive behaviors in early childhood, are on a developmental pathway that predicts subsequent violence and the intergenerational transmission of that violence. Such children are said to be on a life-course persistent path (Moffitt 1993). Typically they have neuropsychological impairments and experience family adversities. The aggressive behaviors start early because of the neuropsychological impairments. These impairments also heighten the child's vulnerability to the family adversities they experience. The pattern of aggressive behavior, in consequence, becomes self-perpetuating.

FOCUSSING ON FAMILIES

At this time, we have enough knowledge from the fields of behavioral science and developmental neuroscience to identify and address many of the factors that place the child at risk for becoming violent. In much of the literature on violent children, attention is given to problems in the child's school and community. We do not discount the value of such focus. However, it is our contention that families are the key setting. The developmental period at which the risk is greatest, and preventive intervention most important, is from the prenatal stage through the first three years of life. At this time, there is both the greatest vulnerability for maladaptive development and the greatest neurodevelopmental plasticity (Shonkoff and Phillips 2000). Developmental pathways can still be modified later, but neural plasticity lessens with increasing age.

With the compelling and consistent data implicating family characteristics and practices in the raising of violent children, and with the emphasis on the early critical period of development in mind, a time when the child's development is most directly influenced by the family, we focus on family factors that can be prevented or modified by early intervention. In essence, children most at risk for early onset aggression and violence are those who experience neuropsychological and parenting deficits (Hill 2002). The neuropsychological deficits impair the child's capacity to regulate emotion, control impulses, experience empathy, and acquire the skills needed for social competence (Herrenkohl *et al.* 2003; van Goozen *et al.* 2007). These deficits may be, and often are, caused by maternal alcohol and tobacco use during pregnancy (Harris, Rice and Lalumiere 2001). The parenting deficits describe inappropriate socialization practices such as harsh punishment, neglect and abuse, and parent characteristics such as criminality, substance abuse, and mental health problems (Gelfand and Drew 2003; Stewart *et al.* 2002; Wolff and McCall Smith 2001).

The likelihood of a child becoming violent is predictable by the number of risk factors in the child's early development (Whitaker, Orzol and Kahn 2006). Children who are exposed to both neuropsychological and socialization risk factors are at greatest developmental vulnerability to violence (Gelfand and Drew 2003; Harris *et al.* 2001; Shonkoff and Phillips 2000). Depending on their severity and chronicity, cumulative risk factors may be manifest in less serious forms of violence such as anger expressed at school (Fryxell 2000), more serious forms of violence such as sexual assault (Starzyk and Marshall 2003), or in the most serious form of violence—homicide (Boots and Heide 2006; Dolan and Smith 2001; Shumaker and Prinz 2000; Wolff and McCall Smith 2001). A recent study is illustrative. In his assessment of 50 juveniles aged 12 to 17 years who were convicted of crimes such as murder, assault, and armed robbery, Beyer (2006) noted the commonality among them of a history of physical and sexual abuse, and the decision-making and emotion regulation difficulties that are associated with neuropsychological deficits.

It would be remiss not to acknowledge a role of genetic influences on the development of violent behavior. Researchers have concluded that as much as 60 to 65 percent of population variation in aggressive antisocial behavior results from genetic influences (Tackett *et al.* 2005). However, the extent to which a genetic predisposition to violence is expressed will vary with the child's rearing environment (Bakermans-Kranenburg and van Ijzendoorn 2007). The potential for a genetic predisposition to violence to be expressed can be significantly minimized if the environment of rearing respects the rights of the child to be free from abuse and neglect, and to be reared by supportive democratic parents. Conversely, the likelihood that the genetic predisposition will be expressed in violence increases with the level of adversity, or rights violations, in the child's environment. The child subjected to abuse, neglect, inappropriate parenting, domestic violence, and antisocial parents may be highly likely to realize his or her genetic potential for violence (Nilsson *et al.* 2005). Unfortunately, children with a genetic predisposition for violence often are born into adverse rearing environments. Antisocial parents are less likely to be effective parents (Rutter, Giller and Hagel 1998), and problems such as parental substance abuse, domestic violence, child abuse, and poor mental health tend to co-exist (Harris *et al.* 2001; Whitaker, Orzol and Kahn 2006).

Temperament is a heritable trait that also should be considered. Some infants are simply more difficult to care for. Thomas, Chess and Birch (1968) noted that infants tend to vary on responsiveness to novelty, dominant mood, and regularity of sleeping and feeding. Infants with "easy temperaments" are undisturbed by novelty, they usually are content, and they sleep and feed regularly. "Difficult" infants are distressed easily by novelty, predominantly irritable and hard to soothe, and have irregular sleeping and feeding patterns. The assumption has been that difficult infants are likely to elicit negative responses from their caregivers that in turn will make them more difficult and set the stage for subsequent behavior problems. However, this assumption has discounted the importance of gene—environment interaction. Researchers generally have found that parents' perceptions of infant temperament often are different from objective assessments; they tend to be affected by parental psychological functioning and by a priori expectations of the child (Hill 2002).

Not surprisingly, it is parental response to the infant and the quality of parenting that determine whether an infant with a difficult temperament will subsequently display antisocial aggressive behaviors.

It may be important at this point to note that we are aware of the role of the child's peers in the persistence of violence. Peer influence, however, is limited. Aggressive behavior patterns are formed in early childhood; they later become entrenched through peer interactions usually when children start attending school. Aggressive children tend to be rejected by their prosocial peers and so come together in mutually reinforcing antisocial peer groups that support violence (Catalano and Hawkins 1996; Fergusson and Horwood 1996; Patterson and Yoerger 1999). The influence of peers, then, is in the maintenance of violence, rather than its initiation. There is one exception that should be recognized. Through adolescence, peer groups may encourage aggressive antisocial behaviors among previously prosocial children. This, however, most often reflects developmentally normal experimentation with identity and attempts to distance oneself from one's parents. It is behavior that is less serious and it is temporary (Erikson 1968; Moffitt 1993).

We also wish to emphasize here that we do not *blame* parents for the raising of violent children. Nonetheless, the power of parenting cannot be ignored. Parents' socialization practices have the strongest empirical support of influences on the development of violence (Tolan, Gorman-Smith and Henry 2003). In addition to contributing to how heritable traits are expressed, as summarized above, parenting moderates the relation between exposure to community violence and child outcomes (Proctor 2006; Stewart *et al.* 2002). Parenting also affects the extent to which children are likely to imitate media violence (Kearney 2003). That said, we realize that parents and families are as healthy and effective as the communities and cultures within which they are embedded. In recognition of the rights of their children, families should be provided with the support and assistance they need to ensure that every child is raised in a healthy manner, free from all forms of violence.

PUTTING CHILDREN AND FAMILIES IN CONTEXT

Implied in much of the research on the etiology of violent children is the need to provide and build protective factors that bolster the environment in which the child is being raised. Protective factors are ones that work to reduce the influence of risk factors and that involve interventions to prevent children from entering a pathway into violence. They are needed to provide children and families with supports that improve such things as prenatal health, parenting practices, and parents' mental health status. Effective protective factors, then, must also function to reduce parental substance abuse, violence, and criminality. Protective factors can come in many forms but critically important are supports through strong family policies and child-friendly cultures that deeply value children and that demonstrate this value through respect for the rights of the child.

As such, a particularly useful framework for our analysis is the ecological approach first described by Uri Bronfenbrenner three decades ago (1977, 1979). The ecological framework describes the reciprocal influences between individuals and the totality of their environments. Bronfenbrenner describes the individual as embedded in a series of systems each of which has increasingly less direct influence on the development of the individual, but influence nonetheless. The systems approach was developed further by Cicchetti and Lynch (1993). Their ecological-transactional model similarly recognizes that the development of the individual is influenced by both proximal and direct factors (e.g. the child's mother and family) and distal and indirect factors (e.g. the community and cultural values). The model acknowledges the importance of the child's neuropsychological status in contributing to her developmental pathway, and acknowledges that she will be influenced by her family, her community, her government policies, and her culture.

As Shonkoff and Phillips (2000) explain, the ecological model describes well the current beliefs about the interaction between nature and nurture. How the child responds to his environments varies with the child's nature. For example, whether the child has a genetic predisposition to violence, a difficult temperament, or neuropsychological deficits will affect how the child responds to stressful circumstances. But nurture is as important. The influence of nurture is seen in the contexts of the child's rearing. How she is reared will vary with the practices and beliefs of her family and her culture. Is she being raised by a substance-abusing parent with a criminal history who believes in corporal punishment? Is the culture child-friendly or indifferent or hostile to children? Are there sufficient supports and government funding for policies dealing with families and children? Are children valued as rights-respecting individuals, or are they seen as parental property? And nature and nurture will dynamically interact with reciprocal influence through development. Children are active participants in their development; they affect their environments and are affected by them.

A helpful illustration of how the model explains the reciprocal influences on development is seen in William Pridemore's interesting analysis of transitional Russia. Since the dissolution of the Soviet Union, there have been profound social, economic, and cultural changes in Russia (2002). The economic uncertainty and strain that have accompanied these changes, and the decreases in funding for social services, have contributed to a drop in marriage rates, a very large increase in divorce rates, and a staggering 50 percent increase in infants born to unwed mothers. By 1996, 23 percent of all births in Russia were to unwed mothers living in stressful conditions. In turn, Russia has seen a significant increase in rates of child abuse and neglect, at-risk youth, and violent crime. Social changes at the macrosystem or cultural level have had a profound effect on parenting practices and the health and lives of individual children. The difficulties these children are manifesting will have further impact on Russia's social and economic functioning. The cycle of violence and dysfunction is perpetuated by its consequences.

TAKING A CHILDREN'S RIGHTS PERSPECTIVE

There are empirical, legal, and philosophical reasons why we believe that taking a children's rights perspective is a particularly useful approach to explaining how children are at risk of developing violent behaviors. The children's rights perspective we take here is one that embraces the Convention on the Rights of the Child, an international treaty that was unanimously approved by the General Assembly of the United Nations in 1989. It is our contention that there is a connection between the raising of violent children and the denial or compromising of their rights, as defined in the Convention.

Despite whatever shortcomings it may have, the Convention is a valuable moral and legal instrument for promoting the well-being of children because it provides a clear and systematic statement on the rights of children, and on the obligations of countries to provide for and respect the rights of children. It is a positive force for children because it officially elevates the status of children to persons with rights, and it puts to rest traditional and lingering assumptions about children as the property of their parents or as vulnerable not-yets in need of the protection of the paternalistic state (Hart 1991; Howe and Covell 2005; Verhellen 1994).

The Convention has been ratified by virtually all countries of the world, making it the most widely and quickly ratified convention in world history. Only the United States and Somalia have yet to ratify the Convention. Such widespread agreement is important because it reflects an almost global consensus on what childhood should be, and an almost global commitment to make policies, laws, and practices consistent with the provisions of the Convention. By ratifying the Convention, countries officially are agreeing to the principle that children are neither parental property nor noble causes, but worthy persons with rights of their own that are independent of their parents or the state (Knutsson 1997). Countries are agreeing that it is children who are the claim holders, who have fundamental rights as individual persons, and that it is parents, adults, and state authorities who are the duty-bearers, who have obligations for providing for those rights (Freeman 1996; Howe 2001; Verhellen 1994).

The rights in the Convention can be summarized in three categories: (1) rights of provision (provision of health care, education, economic welfare), (2) rights of protection (protection from abuse, neglect, violence, exploitation), and (3) rights of participation (rights to have access to information and to have a voice in decisions affecting the child) (Hammarberg 1990). The guiding principles of the Convention can also be summarized as three: (1) non-discrimination (Article 2), where children are to be protected from all forms of discrimination, (2) the best interests of the child (Article 3), where a primary consideration in all actions concerning children is their best interests, and (3) participation (Article 12), where children have the right to be heard and their views given weight in accord with their age and maturity (Hill and Tisdall 1997).

What is also emphasized in the Convention is the critical importance of families in the lives of children and of the obligations of parents to children and of governments to both parents and children. In the Convention's preamble, reference is made to the family as "the fundamental group of society and the natural environment for the growth and well-being of all its members and particularly children." Under Article 5, parents and legal guardians have the obligation to provide "appropriate direction and guidance in the exercise by the child of [his/her] rights" and, under Article 18, parents have as "their basic concern" the best interests of the child. Furthermore, under various articles of the Convention, governments have the obligation to assist parents in advancing the best interests of the child, should this be required. Governments are obligated to do this in general terms (Article 18.2), and in the specific areas of childcare (Article 18.3), care for children with disabilities (Article 23), health care (Article 24), and provision of an adequate standard of living (Article 27). Because parents periodically need help and because a positive nurturing environment is so important for children, it is expected that governments will provide support for families and policies friendly to children.

An important linkage between the rights of children and their healthy development has been empirically demonstrated (Covell and Howe 2001a; Flekkoy and Kaufman 1997; Waterston and Goldhagen 2006). As will be shown throughout this book, when the rights of children are violated or compromised, children are put at risk of unhealthy development, including entry into a pathway of antisocial and violent behavior. The violation of children's rights has a more profound impact than is often thought. It adversely affects not only the emotional and psychological health of children, but also their neurological development and long-term well-being. The problem is deep and the consequence is serious. Our analysis shows that when children's development is compromised through a violation of their rights, especially in their early years, they are put at risk of antisocial and violent behavior that is likely to continue into later childhood and adulthood. This is a serious problem for the children affected and it is obviously also a serious problem for society. So it is important, we contend, that the rights of the child be respected and secured through strong healthy families and through child-friendly policies and cultures that support and nurture strong families.

When fully implemented, the Convention serves as a powerful protective factor against the risk factors for the raising of violent children. This is most obvious when considering Article 19 and the child's right to be protected against all forms of violence. Violence breeds violence. But it is also apparent with respect to other rights. When children's provision rights are respected and when governments fulfill their obligations to assist parents in providing a positive nurturing environment for children, the risk of raising violent children is diminished significantly. Stress impairs parenting. Similarly, in articles dealing with participation, when children are respected and their voices heard, when they are parented democratically, the risk of violence is diminished. Finally, when the Convention's central principle is put into effect and the best interests of children are aggressively pursued, the likelihood of raising violent children is greatly reduced. As will be demonstrated later in this book, the more consistent with the Convention a country's policies are, the less violent the children.

The Convention is an especially important force for children because it is a legally binding piece of international law. In 1959, the Universal Declaration of the Rights of the Child was adopted by the United Nations and agreed to by virtually all countries of the world. But this was a declaration of moral ideals, not a legally binding international treaty. The Convention, however, is in a different category. It is a legally binding treaty (Doek 1992; Verhellen 1994). By ratifying the Convention, a state party to the Convention has agreed to implement the articles of the treaty (if not already implemented) and to ensure that its laws, policies, and practices are in compliance. Under Article 4, countries "shall undertake all appropriate legislative, administrative, and other measures for the implementation of the rights recognized in the present Convention." To be sure, there may be difficulties with implementation due to a shortage of resources. But as required by Article 4, countries "shall undertake such measures to the maximum extent of their available resources…" In essence, although countries may encounter economic or other difficulties, they are responsible over time for the progressive implementation of the provision, protection, and participation rights of children.

The system of enforcing the Convention is far from perfect. But it is a force for prodding governments into action that did not previously exist. Under the system, countries make a report to an expert United Nations committee—the UN Committee on the Rights of the Child—every five years. A country documents how well it has been complying with the Convention, what measures it has taken to implement the various articles of the Convention, and what problems have been encountered. The UN Committee then reviews the country's report, along with shadow reports from child advocacy organizations, and then issues a report back to the country—called "concluding observations"—where it notes progress and shortcomings. The shadow reports are an important part of the monitoring process because they provide alternative information and serve as a check and balance to country reports. On the basis of the information, the Committee makes recommendations for improvements where needed. The countries are then expected to improve their performance, although they are not legally obligated to act on the recommendations. The Convention ultimately is enforced through the court of public opinion and on the basis of moral and political pressure. A country typically does not want to be embarrassed by criticism that it does not honor its commitments. Although the Convention may not be hard law, it has force because it is legally binding. A country cannot respond to criticism simply by saying that it is not bound by the Convention. Through the reporting and monitoring process, a country is under pressure—insufficient though it may be—to demonstrate that it has made progress. Some pressure is better than no pressure in lessening the risks for children.

In addition to the legal obligations, there is a philosophical reason for taking the rights of the child seriously. As Martin Luther King (1963) reminded us in his famous "Letter from Birmingham Jail", there is an important difference between just and unjust laws. When laws are just, we have an obligation to obey them. But when they are unjust, we may resist. According to Michael Freeman (1992), what makes laws and policies on children's rights just, is that they are in accord with fundamental principles of justice. Using John Rawls' theory of justice and applying it to children, Freeman makes the persuasive case that children's rights should be seen as part of the first principle of justice, the principle that equal rights should come before all else in a just society. If reasonable persons were to deliberate on principles of justice for a future society they would be part of, and if they knew they could end up in a disadvantaged or worse-off position, they would embrace the principle of equal basic rights not only for adults but also for children. Knowing that they could end up as vulnerable children at risk of serious harm, they would want to incorporate children's rights into the first principle of justice—not the principle of parental rights—so that they could be protected against forces that otherwise could do them harm. This would include protection from the risk factors for childhood violence. For Freeman, children's rights are a vital means not only of protecting children but also of showing them fundamental respect. "To accord rights is to respect dignity: to deny rights is to cast doubt on humanity and on integrity" (Freeman 2007, p.7).

There are, of course, perspectives other than children's rights. A parents' rights perspective is one that puts the welfare of children completely, or almost completely, into the hands of parents. But it no longer is taken seriously. In the words of Freeman (2007, p.10), "it is only one stage on from conceptualizing children as the property of their parents." A more serious perspective is one that emphasizes the importance of providing for the basic needs of children if not by parents then by the state. Here, problems such as childhood violence can be more seriously addressed. However, a needs perspective does not have the same legitimacy or power to improve children's lives as does a rights perspective (Collins, Pearson and Delany 2002).

A needs perspective is a paternalistic or welfare approach in which children, as objects of pity, are the passive recipients of others' benevolence. In this approach, children's needs are identified, a hierarchy of their importance is determined, and policies and practices are implemented to supply children with their most pressing needs. Although needs are recognized as valid claims, obligations to meet those needs are motivated only by moral or charitable considerations. Children, for example, have a need to be protected from risk factors, such as being abused by their parents, and society has a duty to protect them in the interests of their welfare. Because the needs approach focusses on dealing with the overt manifestations or proximal causes of problems, a typical response has been to establish child protection agencies to respond to incidents of abuse as best they can. There is little proactive or preventive action. A needs perspective does not recognize its target group as bearers of rights. Children are to be protected from parental maltreatment not because they have rights but because governments have an obligation to look after their welfare. Their welfare will be attended to where, when, and how a government sees fit.

Among the many advantages of a children's rights perspective, five stand out. First is the recognition that each and every child is a bearer of rights, a claim-holder of rights that are inalienable. A child can neither give up nor lose his or her rights regardless of behavior, family context, or parental wishes. Rights to protection from maltreatment, then, must be extended to all children in all circumstances. It is not enough to institute programming for identified at-risk children or to react to those whose abuse comes to the attention of welfare or justice agencies. The aim is not simply to provide for the general welfare of children. It is to provide for the rights of every single child.

Second is the explicit recognition in the Convention of the obligations of those who can be held accountable and against whom a claim can be made. Thus, as described above, there are legal—rather than only moral—obligations to work for the betterment of children and to respect and protect the rights of the child. In fact, in some countries such as Belgium, the Convention is self-executing; that is, its effect is immediate upon ratification and it can be invoked in a court of law (Alen and Pas 1996; Verhellen 1996). However, regardless of whether the Convention is immediately or progressively incorporated into domestic law, it obligates respect for the rights of the child among all levels of government, in civil society, and especially among those who directly interact with children. A claim based on rights and incorporated into law is more compelling than a claim based simply on needs.

Third is the recognition that the rights of the Convention are indivisible. Rights cannot be prioritized and considered in hierarchical order. This does not require that in efforts to improve children's lives it is necessary to target all rights at the same time. However, it does require considering the possibility that focussing on a particular right or target group may affect others. Connected with this requirement is the responsibility to undertake child impact assessments of new or amended laws, policies, and budgets (Sylwander 2001). What effect will government actions have on respecting the rights of the child? Will outcomes of planned expenditures, or laws or policies, be in the best interests of the child? Will the rights of all children be affected? Have the views of children been included? These are the types of questions addressed in child impact assessments. The Committee on the Rights of the Child has recommended that all governments that have ratified the Convention undertake child impact assessments in all their decisions affecting children. And, of course, follow-up evaluations of the effects of action are important to future laws, policies, and budgets.

Fourth, and especially important in our context, is the recognition of the need to be proactive by addressing the distal as well as proximal causes of rights violations. Unlike needs approaches to policy and practice, rights approaches not only focus on the overt and immediate manifestations of problems, but also examine and address the underlying sources of problems (Collins *et al.* 2002). In considering the rapidity of child development and the possible consequences of rights violations, it is not enough to react to the infringement of a child's rights. It is important to effect polices and programming that prevent infringements. For example, instead of reacting to abuse only after there has been significant evidence of it, supports and education programs for parents should be in place to prevent or at least lessen the incidence of abuse. And preventive interventions should always be evidence-based. Child impact assessments, together with existing research in the social sciences, can provide an excellent foundation for proactive programming.

Finally, the criterion of success is more stringent. From a needs perspective, success is determined in terms of the proportion of children whose circumstances are improved. For example, if widespread parent education was instituted and was shown to have an effect on reducing rates of corporal punishment by 50 percent, it likely would be considered successful. From a rights perspective, success is measured by consistency with the three principles of the Convention. First, under the principle of the best interests of the child, interventions such as parent education or legal reforms would be required to show concomitant improvements in other areas of rights. For example, it is possible that a legal ban on corporal punishment may increase permissive parenting. Parents may believe they can no longer discipline their children. It would be important, then, that the ban be accompanied with parent education to increase the use of non-violent and positive socialization strategies. Second, under the principle of participation, success would require that policy changes or interventions were made with input from children, or from the chosen representatives of children. The design of parent education programs would take into account the experiences, thoughts, and feelings of children, and of their advocates. Third, under the principle of nondiscrimination, success would mean that changes benefit *every* child. The 50 percent reduction in the use of corporal punishment would not be considered adequate. It would be necessary to identify obstacles to change (e.g. by age, gender, ethnicity, religion, geographic area), how discriminatory practices (if any) are being sustained, and what is being done to address them. Every child has equal rights to protection from abuse and violence. Every child matters.

OVERVIEW OF THIS BOOK

The first part of the book deals with risk factors for the child in families. In Chapter 2 we discuss the rights-violating toxic substances and experiences that wire the brain in ways that predispose the child to violent behaviors. After summarizing the current knowledge about relevant neural development, we describe the links between fetal exposure to tobacco and alcohol and later aggressive and criminally violent behaviors. We then examine the importance of the quality of the early infant–caregiver relationship through the critical first year of the infant's life. During this developmental stage, inappropriate caregiver responding reflected in an insecure attachment relationship predisposes the child to a number of developmental difficulties including poor social relationships, childhood conduct disorders, and adolescent and adult interpersonal violence.

Our focus in Chapter 3 is on parenting strategies that are associated with the development of violence in children. We first examine general parenting styles, identifying that which is most consistent with the Convention, and that which is associated with childhood relational and physical aggression. Of particular concern from the child rights perspective are hostile, rejecting, and coercive parenting styles. In particular, the use of corporal punishment as a socialization strategy is shown to be strongly associated with the development of violence in the child across time and culture. We then review child abuse and neglect. These parenting behaviors are among the most egregious violations of children's rights and are strongly linked with the development of violence in their child victims. A history of maltreatment is a common factor among children who display violent behaviors, from schoolyard bullying to homicide. The chapter ends with a discussion of the underlying neural processes that are affected by rights-inconsistent parenting and their role in affecting the child's reasoning skills and behavior.

In Chapter 4, we examine ways in which parents inadvertently model violence to their children. High rates of exposure to intimate partner violence are reported by many nations in the *World Report on Violence Against Children* (United Nations 2006), and in the social science research. Children imitate their parents' violence in their relationships with others, their peers, and their pets. Parental criminality is associated with poor parenting and poor family functioning. It is also clear in the literature that parental criminality is a strong predictor of the development of aggressive and antisocial behavior in children. Studies of the children of incarcerated parents provide compelling evidence here. Parents who abuse substances are also modeling violence. Although genetics may play a role in the intergenerational concordance of substance abuse, parental use and the inadequate parenting behaviors that accompany substance use, are strong predictors of violent children. Finally we discuss maternal depression. Whereas not a direct model of violent behaviors, maternal depression, particularly postpartum depression, is associated with inadequate parenting, and is found to be predictive of childhood conduct disorders. We find that disadvantage, adversity, and stress tend to cluster in particular families, but that provision of protective factors can significantly lessen the likelihood of the child's developmental pathway being characterized by violence. These are discussed in the second part of the book.

The second part of the book deals with policies and cultures as risk factors for childhood violence. In Chapter 5, we examine the risk factor of weak child and family policies that fail to provide programs and sufficient support for families and children in the areas of childcare, income assistance, child health, child welfare, and early childhood prevention programs such as parent education. Comparisons are made between relatively child-friendly policies in the Nordic countries (Norway, Sweden, Finland, Denmark, and Iceland) and the relatively unfriendly policies in North America (the United States and Canada), and between friendly and unfriendly policies within North America. The comparisons show that where policies are relatively less friendly to children, as in much of North America, there is a greater degree of childhood and youth violence. Conversely, where they are friendlier to children, as in the Nordic countries, there is a lesser degree of violence. Our analysis shows that where the Convention on the Rights of the Child is less fully implemented, and where child and family policies are relatively weak and limited in scope, the raising of violent children is made more likely.

In Chapter 6, we focus on the risk factor of political cultures that work against the building of child-friendly policies. We find that behind policies that are unfriendly to children are political cultures that are unfriendly to children. Such child-unfriendly cultures inhibit the implementation of the Convention and prevent the development of strong policies and supports for families and children. Again, comparisons are made between political cultures in the Nordic countries and ones in North America, and between ones within North America. The comparisons show that where cultures are relatively unfriendly to children because of beliefs in individualism, individual responsibility, and children as not-yets or parental property, as in much of North America, policies are relatively weak and childhood violence more in evidence. Conversely, where cultures are friendlier to children because of beliefs in a positive role for government, social responsibility, and children as bearers of rights, as in the Nordic countries, policies are much stronger and childhood violence is less of a problem.

Throughout the book, we refer to a wide number of countries to illustrate points. But in Chapters 5 and 6 we give particular attention to a comparison between North America and the Nordic nations. These nations make good candidates for comparative analysis. They are similar in general terms—all are Western liberal democracies and economically advanced states—but are different in terms of policy directions and political cultures. In addition, there are many comparative data on them from research studies and sources such as the Organization of Economic Cooperation and Development. A reason that we give attention to variations within the United States and Canada is that both have federal systems of government where states and provinces have major responsibility for child and family policy. The variations among the states and provinces make them highly useful for comparative study. We appreciate that there are many nuances and many differences between the United States and Canada and among the Nordic nations that we do not cover. Our goal, however, is not to deal with all the nuances and qualifications but to illustrate the overarching connection between what goes on in the family and what goes on in child and family policies and in political cultures.

In the final chapter, we offer some thoughts on the challenges faced and on the changes needed to lessen the incidence of violence against children and thereby violent children. In keeping with the recommendations from the *World Report on Violence Against Children* (United Nations 2006), we focus on the provision of education. Education is an important means of promoting child-friendly cultures and respect for children's rights. By education, we refer not simply to education about the value of early prevention and family supports. We refer also to education that elevates the status of children as bearers of independent rights, and education that is gained through experience with respecting children's rights. Over time, such education is expected to impel public pressure and support for stronger and more rights-consistent child and family policies. With these changes in place, risk factors for the raising of violent children are expected to be significantly reduced.

CHAPTER 2

NEUROLOGICAL UNDERPINNINGS

Parents have to get away from the drugs and alcohol and focus on their children. They need to think of their children, not themselves.

The child who made this comment was explaining what parents could do to prevent their children becoming violent. He is right. His comment reflects well the evidence demonstrating that the use of alcohol or tobacco during pregnancy, and inadequate attention to the infant, are risk factors for wiring the brain in ways that predispose the child to violence. In this chapter, after considering the relevance of the Convention on the Rights of the Child to the fetus, we summarize the neurodevelopmental consequences of maternal tobacco and alcohol use during pregnancy, and of inadequate parenting through the first year of life.

FETAL RIGHTS?

The developmental pathway of the child reflects a continuous interaction between genetic potential and experience, nature and nurture. Traditionally, it was assumed that experience, or nurture, was for the most part an important developmental influence after birth. But this assumption appears to be false. Increasingly, we are learning the importance of prenatal experiences in influencing developmental outcomes. We know that "the importance of cellular environments free of disruptive elements through all stages of prenatal development is paralleled by the importance of an enriched positive environment for the infant and the toddler" (Levitt, Reinoso and Jones 1998, p.183). We are comfortable advocating for a healthy postnatal environment. Ensuring a healthy prenatal environment, however, has been problematic. Discussions of fetal rights or fetal health have been difficult to keep separate from the abortion issue and from women's rights. As a result, there is neither a convention on fetal rights nor an agreement on when childhood begins.

One of the more difficult questions for the framers of the Convention on the Rights of the Child concerned the definition of a child. It was relatively easy to define the upper age of the child. In Article 1, it is stated that a child is every person under the age of 18 years, unless the law of a nation grants majority at an earlier age. But when does a child begin to be a child? Should rights be granted at conception or at birth? With potential signatories to the Convention holding quite different positions on the attainment of personhood and abortion rights, the minimum age was a very controversial issue (Cantwell 1992). A compromise was needed. To obtain a consensus, the framers decided that in the legally binding text of the Convention, there would be no mention of a minimum age. This would allow signatories to decide in accordance with their national beliefs whether childhood begins at conception, the age of viability, or at birth. Nonetheless, there was realization of, and agreement on, the importance of the prenatal environment to the health and well-being of the child. It was decided to recognize this in the legally non-binding preamble to the Convention. The preamble states that the child "needs special safeguards and care, including appropriate protection, both before as well as after birth." The hope was that this would be enough to promote the importance of prenatal care without prohibiting abortion, and thus be acceptable across nations. In addition, obligating signatories in Article 24(d) to provide prenatal health care for mothers reinforced the importance of the prenatal period.

There is, of course, an inextricable link between pre- and postnatal health. As will be described in this chapter, the child whose prenatal health is compromised by toxic substances such as tobacco and alcohol may never have a chance to realize his or her rights through childhood. Thus it is reasonable to assume that once there has been a decision to take a pregnancy to term, there should be protections extended to the fetus. To be consistent with Article 19 (protection from abuse), Article 33 (protection from harmful sub-stances), and Article 24 (provision of the highest attainable health care) in particular, the fetus should be protected from exposure to toxic substances and any form of maltreatment that poses a threat to the healthy development of the child. But these protections are not legally obligated under the Convention. Without them, the child at birth may be predisposed toward the development of violence.

The brain continues to develop rapidly through the first years of life and it is particularly important to healthy brain development that early parenting be sensitive to the infant's needs such that a relationship of trust develops between the infant and the primary caregiver. The Convention is explicit in Article 18 about the state's obligation to assist the parent with child-rearing. The reduction of poverty and the accessibility of childcare would do much to lessen the stress that impairs effective parenting. The care of an infant can be challenging under the best of circumstances. Poverty can make it overwhelming. Articles 26 and 27 of the Convention describe the child's right to social security and a reasonable standard of living. The provision of high-quality childcare as needed by parents, and required in Article 18, would also do much to lessen stress and thereby improve early parenting. As discussed elsewhere (Covell and Howe 2001a), it is stressful for parents who wish to continue employment to be unable to do so because of a lack of appropriate childcare for the infant. It is equally stressful for those who wish to parent their newborn, but must return to the labor force for financial reasons.

Over the past few years there has been a lot of rhetoric about the importance of the early years. Recognition, however, does not always mean action. We now have very compelling evidence from neuroscience and from many studies of the effects of adverse prenatal and early childhood experiences. Brain growth and organization are highly vulnerable to environmental adversity. The effects may be permanent.

WIRING THE BRAIN FOR VIOLENCE

The vulnerability of the brain to toxic experiences and substances is due in large part to the complexity and rapidity of early neuronal growth and differentiation. The wiring of the prenatal brain starts with the development and migration of brain cells to the areas where they will function, proceeds with the embellishments of nerve cells, the neurons, and then the formations of connections between the nerve cells (Shonkoff and Phillips 2000). Throughout the process, networks are sculpted as neural pathways fine-tune perception, attention, cognition, and socio-emotional functioning. If the environment is toxic, the developing neurons are likely to establish and maintain aberrant connections. With the exception of genetic problems, it is the environment, the ultimate architect of the brain, that determines whether the neural networks will promote or impede the brain's ability for selective attention, appropriate information processing, emotion and behavior regulation (Joseph 1999). It is a process of clockwork precision that remains highly vulnerable throughout the first few years of life. Brain development is most rapid and dramatic through the prenatal period, but continues apace in the first few years of life. Functional maturity of the stress-regulating neural systems is not achieved in children until the fourth year of life (van Goozen et al. 2007).

Through the first four years of life, the maturation of the brain is characterized by both regressive and progressive processes (De Bellis 2005). Initially, in utero, the brain overproduces nerve cells that are interconnected in complex ways. Largely through the first four years of life, although continuing somewhat through adolescence, there is a selective pruning or elimination of some of these neurons. During the same developmental period, there are increases in neuron size and synapses (the axonal connections among the neurons). In essence, as with shrubs, the pruning of some branches promotes the healthy growth of others. Myelination of the axons is also increasing during this time. Myelin is a fatty substance that insulates the axon and allows speedier transmission of messages among neurons. But the early neural connections are not stable; they are use-dependent, with the result that growth and differentiation can go awry in adverse environmental circumstances.

The exact nature and processes by which neural disruptions occur is the subject of considerable research at this time. Debra Niehoff (2003) provides a very eloquent description of the link between environment and brain structure. Chemical messengers, the neurotransmitters, transmit the "latest news" among neurons. This communication triggers a sequence of biochemical reactions that ultimately activate target proteins that have the power to alter cell behavior. Whereas some make temporary adjustments, others make lasting changes to genes to alter the levels of proteins encoded by those genes. "Thanks to their meddling," Niehoff writes, "a transaction that began outside the cell with a diffusion of a chemical signal concludes on the inside with a physical record of the conversation…that changes the way the neuron responds to subsequent inputs" (p.237). Thus the biochemical changes that initiate from experience continually update neural circuitry, and in its responding, the brain is altered. Changes in neural circuitries regulating emotion, cognition, and responses to stress are associated with, or predict, aggression.

De Bellis (2005; De Bellis *et al.* 2002) believes that abnormal brain development occurs in response to stress through one or more of the following processes: (1) accelerated loss of neurons, (2) delays in myelination, (3) abnormalities in developmentally appropriate pruning, and (4) inhibition of neurogenesis (growth of new neurons). Profound and lasting neurobehavioral consequences appear to result from these changes in brain circuits and systems (Anda *et al.* 2006). For example, accelerated loss of neurons is believed to impair the development of cognitive functioning and the ability to integrate information (Watts-English *et al.* 2006); certain abnormalities in pruning may reduce children's capacity for emotion regulation (Creeden 2004); and impaired neurogenesis is associated with deficits in memory and learning and with depression (Dawson *et al.* 2003; Watts-English *et al.* 2006).

Over the past decade, we have learned much from neuroscientists about the neural mechanisms that are associated with violent behavior. Neurodevelopmental research with children remains in its infancy, and largely informed by rodent and non-human primate research (Gunnar *et al.* 2006; van Goozen *et al.* 2007). Nonetheless, studies of early stress on the neurobiological systems of clinical populations of children (van Goozen *et al.* 2007), adult violent offenders, and aggressive psychiatric patients (Bufkin and Luttrell 2005; Retz *et al.* 2004) provide data that are consistent with the predictions based on animal studies. It is well beyond the scope of this book to detail the evidence for a neurobiological basis for violence: an excellent summary is provided by Stephanie van Goozen and her colleagues (2007). We will, however, briefly summarize some of the existing knowledge as it helps explain the importance of an early environment free from the rights violations of exposure to substances and experiences that are toxic to the developing brain. Much of this knowledge has been gained recently with advances in technology.

Technological developments have improved our capacity for examining neural structures and functioning. As a result we have been allowed greater understanding of the neural circuitry that appears to underlie faulty emotion regulation and violent behaviors. As Jana Bufkin and Vickie Luttrell (2005) detail, the new functional and structural brain imaging techniques, such as single-photon emission computed tomography (SPECT), positon emission tomography (PET), magnetic resonance imaging (MRI), and functional magnetic resonance imaging (fMRI), have allowed the viewing of the brain in action and the identifying of areas of dysfunction. But our knowledge, especially of children, is far from complete. This technology is not easily used with children, especially infants and young children. For example, functional imaging can only be used with older children. Structural imaging requires lying still for periods of time—time so long that it would not be possible for children without medicating them. And since it would be unethical to startle children to measure the neural reaction to being startled, these measures are limited to assessments of cortisol (an indicator of stress) in the child's urine or saliva (Gunnar et al. 2006). Despite such limitations, there is some consensus in the literature of the neural basis of violence. We first consider the animal research.

Experiments with rats have provided compelling evidence that brain development varies significantly with early parental care (Chapillon et al. 2002). For example, if experimenters disrupt the mother's care of her offspring, the stress system of the pups is affected (Denenberg 1999). Overall, the research shows that gene expression is regulated and neural systems are shaped in accord with the quality of early caregiving (Levine 2005). Megan Gunnar and her colleagues (2006) point out that birth occurs in the rat when the brain is significantly less mature than is the brain of the full-term infant. What has been learned from rodent research, then, may be most applicable to human prenatal and early postnatal development. In that case, rodent research tells us that adverse early environmental influences may be expected to affect the development of neural systems and gene expression. In humans, this is evidenced in recent studies of adults showing that those who carry the low activity form of the MAO gene and who also have been reared in adverse environments are at significantly increased risk of aggression (van Goozen et al. 2007). Monoamine Oxidase (MAO) is a class of enzymes that catabolize, or break down, serotonin, dopamine, and noradrenaline (these cause physical changes that prepare the body for "flight or fight"). Low MAO activity increases the risk of Conduct Disorder (De Bellis 2005), and has been found in males with early onset aggression (Eklund, Alm and Klinteberg 2005), and in adult males incarcerated for homicide, assault, or violent robbery (Skondras et al. 2004). Importantly, however, there is little evidence that low levels of MAO affect aggression in the absence of early maltreatment or other chronic adversity (De Bellis 2005; Foley et al. 2004).

Experiments with non-human primates have demonstrated neurobehavioral effects of early maternal stress that are similar to those that have been found with rodents (e.g. Coe, Lulbach and Schneider 2002; Schneider et al. 1998). The importance of appropriate postnatal caregiving has been highlighted in non-human primate research. The pioneering work of Harry Harlow is well known. Harlow separated infant monkeys from their mothers and raised them with wire or terry-cloth mother surrogates. The effect of maternal deprivation on the development of infant monkeys was manifest in a range of subsequent severe developmental difficulties, including inappropriate dominance and aggressive reactions (Harlow, Harlow and Suomi 1971). These infants were demonstrating severe stress reactions. It is interesting to note that the non-human primate experiments show that the neural systems of infants are similarly affected when stress is manipulated in the mother. For example, Leonard Rosenblum and his colleagues (Rosenblum and Andrews 1994; Rosenblum et al. 1994) created stress conditions by varying foraging demands for mothers. The infants, who were not directly affected by the unpredictable food resources, nevertheless evidenced high levels of stress hormones and developed into less socially competent adults than those whose mothers were not stressed. Effectively, like human mothers, those who were stressed became less psychologically available to their offspring, thus affecting the neural development of the infants.

The animal research cannot be translated directly to children, although there may be many similar associations between stress and compromised brain development. The main difference, and a most important one, is that of timing. In the child, the period of vulnerability to neural damage is much longer than it is in rats or non-human primates (Gunnar *et al.* 2006). It begins early in the prenatal period and extends into childhood. How the brain develops reflects an elaborate and continuous interplay between gene activity and environmental influences.

The significant vulnerability of the brain to toxic substances and experiences through this early period of development is particularly evident in studies examining high-risk pregnancies. As suggested by the animal studies, experience seems to have its greatest impact early (Dawson, Ashman and Carver 2000; Huizink, Mulder and Buitelaar 2004). When maternal health status is compromised during pregnancy, there is a risk for impaired central nervous system (CNS) functioning in the infant (Beck and Shaw 2005). Studies of infants born to mothers with high-risk pregnancies due to such factors as smoking or alcohol or drug use (Lundy *et al.* 1999), or maternal stress and anxiety (Gunnar *et al.* 2006), show the infants to have impaired, or aberrant, brain development. Similarly, abnormal brain development is found among infants whose first year or so of life is in adverse parenting environments characterized by neglect, abuse, and poor-quality parenting (van Goozen *et al.* 2007). As Stephanie van Goozen and her colleagues (van Goozen *et al.* 2007) explain, the initial prenatal disruptions in neurobiological functioning (which may also involve genetic factors) disrupt subsequent emotional and cognitive functioning. In turn these disruptions effect further disruptions at the neural level.

The strong relation between environmental experience and early brain development was dramatically demonstrated in an interesting experimental study with preterm infants. Heidelise and colleagues (2004) were concerned about the potential effects of the typical neonatal intensive care unit (ICU) on the rapidly developing brain of the premature newborn. Their experiment involved 30 medically healthy low-risk preterm infants (28–33 weeks' gestation), 16 of whom were provided individualized developmentally supportive caregiving by specialists and by their parents. The parents were taught how to cradle and comfort the infant through stressful procedures, to provide restful skin-to-skin contact for prolonged periods, and to personalize the infant's sleeping area. The differences at two weeks and nine months (corrected age) between the experimental group infants and those provided the standard ICU care were quite dramatic. The experimental group showed significantly better neurobehavioral functioning and more mature brain structure; the differences included areas of the brain responsible for motor system function, responsiveness, state-stability and self-regulation.

The research to date suggests the serotonin system, the hypothalamic–pituitary–adrenal (HPA) axis, and the limbic system are particularly vulnerable to early adverse experiences in ways that predispose the child to become violent. Interconnections among these indicate that dysregulation in one will evoke some dysregulation of all. Each will be discussed in turn.

The neurotransmitter serotonin (5-HT) modulates physiological and emotional functioning in the CNS. Serotonin influences an extensive variety of psychological processes including memory, learning, mood, sexual behavior, and aggression (van Goozen *et al.* 2007; Watts-English *et al.* 2006). Among its many tasks, the serotonergic system mediates the interaction between the prefrontal cortex and the amygdala in the limbic system. These structures play a key role in interpreting social cues and in regulating emotion. They communicate to determine threat and appropriate responses to that threat. Dysfunction in either structure, or in the serotonergic system that is their primary means of communication, may result in misperceived threat or faulty regulation of negative emotion (Bufkin and Luttrell 2005). The faulty processing of social cues may dispose the child to aggression through the misperception of threat, and the difficulty with emotion regulation may increase the probability of an inappropriately aggressive response to that perceived threat. Dysregulation of the serotonin system is associated with difficulties with mood regulation and with elevated risk of aggression (Watts-English *et al.* 2006).

Serotonin, which is activated by stress (De Bellis 2005), is the most extensively documented neurotransmitter implicated in the development of aggression. As Shonkoff and Phillips (2000) point out, it is highly unlikely that serotonin is the only neurotransmitter involved in aggression. There is, for example, some evidence for the involvement of dopaminergic systems especially in impulsive aggression and more serious forms of violence (Retz *et al.* 2003). Nonetheless, the neurotransmitter serotonin is one of the most widely distributed neurotransmitter systems in the brain, and there is significant evidence of its involvement in aggression. Diminished serotonergic function is believed to disinhibit displays of aggression. Disruptions in the functioning of the serotonin system have been associated with violent behaviors among adults (Retz *et al.* 2004), and the extent of impairment of the system appears to predict the severity of violence (van Goozen *et al.* 2007). Low serotonin levels also are strongly related to behavior disorders in childhood (Bufkin and Luttrell 2005).

When the transmission of serotonin is disrupted, cortisol reactivity is also impaired (van Goozen and Fairchild 2006). The HPA axis regulates the brain's neuroendocrine response to stress. When stimulated, the hypothalamus secretes corticotropin-releasing hormone (CRH) that in turn stimulates the pituitary gland to secrete andrenocorticotropic hormone (ACTH). The release of ACTH then causes the release of the stress hormone cortisol which helps prepare the body to cope with difficult circumstances. Cortisol also acts on the hypothalamus to inhibit the further release of CRH. The HPA axis then works on a feedback loop system that is designed to regulate levels of alertness, arousal, and apprehension. Disruptions to the system can cause a prolonged state of hyper-arousal.

There is significant evidence that the functioning of the HPA axis is affected by adverse early rearing conditions, especially neglect and abuse (Bremner and Vermetten 2001; van Goozen and Fairchild 2006; van Goozen *et al.* 2007). This is especially so until the end of the first year of life (Gunnar *et al.* 2006). Levels of stress are indicated by the concentration and secretion of cortisol. Van Goozen and her colleagues (2007) report there is increasing evidence that low levels of cortisol are predictive, rather than correlative, of aggression in childhood. Interestingly, they also report that cortisol may be involved in the intergenerational transmission of aggression. One reason for this assertion is that basal glucocorticoid concentrations are somewhat, albeit not entirely, heritable. A second reason is an observed relation between cortisol concentrations in children and antisocial personality symptoms in their parents (van Goozen *et al.* 2007). The diminished basal cortisol levels, or difficulties with HPA axis activation in response to stress, may contribute to aggression in children by making them oversensitive to stressful or fearful events while at the same time rendering them unable to fully comprehend or experience the negative consequences of their aggressive behaviors (van Goozen *et al.* 2007). In fact, the HPA axis is implicated in a number of childhood behavior disorders that are associated with difficulty with mood and behavior regulation (Mash and Wolfe 1999).

The limbic system describes a set of interconnected structures that are particularly important in emotion regulation and memory. Two important components of the limbic system are the amygdala and the hippocampus. As noted previously, the amygdala plays a key role in interpreting emotion cues and in the ability to regulate negative emotion (Bufkin and Luttrell 2005). The primary task of the amygdala is to filter and interpret incoming sensory information in the context of survival and emotional needs, to determine the emotional value of social stimuli and then to initiate appropriate responses (Teicher 2002). In situations perceived to be emergencies, the amygdala relies on first impressions to determine rapid responding (Niehoff 2003). It is not surprising, then, that the disruptions to amygdala function are associated with inappropriate aggressive and sexual behaviors and with impulsive violence (Teicher *et al.* 2003). Neither it is surprising that children who are diagnosed with early onset aggression show deficits in amygdala functioning (van Goozen *et al.* 2007). The hippocampus is especially vulnerable to stress because it plays a critical role in encoding and retrieving episodic memory (memory of experiences), and it has a much higher density of receptors for cortisol than most of the brain (Teicher 2002). In addition, the hippocampus continues to develop postnatally, growing new neurons into adulthood. Stress, however, inhibits this growth (Anda *et al.* 2006). Together, the amygdala and the hippocampus determine how experiences are understood, stored as information in long-term memory, retrieved and used as the context for determining behaviors. Antisocial and violent behaviors resulting from adverse experiences such as child abuse are attributed, in part, to dysfunction of these limbic system components (Teicher 2002).

What such findings from neuroscience highlight is that in the absence of a healthy prenatal and early postnatal environment, a child may be neurologically predisposed for violence in ways that make her behavior very resistant to change. As Martin Teicher explains, "Society reaps what it sows in the way it nurtures its children. Stress sculpts the brain to exhibit various antisocial, though adaptive behaviors...stress can set off a ripple of hormonal changes that permanently wire the child's brain to cope with a malevolent world" (Teicher 2002, p.76). The wiring of the brain is such that only contemporaneous circumstances are of relevance. It does not assume a better future. Adverse experiences such as prenatal exposure to toxins such as tobacco or alcohol or early inappropriate parenting may have enduring neurodevelopmental consequences.

PRENATAL EXPOSURE TO TOBACCO

Rates of smoking generally have been going down in Western industrialized countries, especially in those countries where advanced tobacco control policies have been adopted. However, three patterns of smoking described by the World Health Organization (2002a) indicate concern for fetal exposure. First, they report that the reductions in tobacco use among Western countries have been offset by large increases in cigarette smoking elsewhere. Eastern Europe provides an illustration. Smoking prevalence rates among young women in the former East Germany increased from 27 percent in 1993 to 47 percent in 1997 (Cnattingius 2004). Second, in most areas, the World Health Organization finds that there is an inverse relation between smoking and income. Rates of smoking are three times higher among the poorest citizens than among the most affluent. In the United States, for example, smoking prevalence is the highest among those living below the poverty line (Cnattingius 2004). Third, across regions, the World Health Organization reports that smoking by young adult women has either increased or remained stable, and that smoking rates among teenaged girls are increasing. The extent of the problem here is reflected in a recent study of pregnant teens (average age 18 years) in the UK—a country whose smoking rate is lower than many (Delpisheh et al. 2006). Almost one half of the teens in this study (46.2%) had smoked during the pregnancy.

Smoking intervention strategies during pregnancy have shown very limited success (Cnattingius 2004). Women with low levels of education, low age at onset of smoking and heavy use of cigarettes, and those who are exposed to environmental tobacco smoke are the most likely to continue to smoke through their pregnancy (Cnattingius 2004). These data tell us that infants born into environments most likely to be adverse because of poverty, and/or single, young, or poorly educated mothers, are the infants who also are the most likely to have been exposed to cigarette smoke during fetal development.

Many of the health outcomes of fetal exposure to maternal smoking have been well documented: they include miscarriage, placental complications, stillbirth, preterm birth, and low birth weight (Cnattingius 2004; Delpisheh et al. 2006). In addition, there is growing evidence that fetal exposure to tobacco smoke poses a very real threat to the neurological integrity of the child in ways that predispose the child to violence. The observed effects are likely a function of the constituents of tobacco smoke that limit oxygen and nutrient supply to the fetus, and alter cells, enzymes, and DNA (Perera et al. 2005). And as Michael Monuteaux and his colleagues have summarized (2006), studies suggest a direct effect of nicotine on the fetal serotonin and dopaminergic systems as well as brain cell growth and DNA and RNA synthesis. Perhaps most compelling are animal studies that show prenatal nicotine exposure to be associated not only with structural damage in the brain, but also with brain cell death (Roy, Seidler and Slotkin 2002; Roy et al. 1998). In essence, although we are far from definitive knowledge about the effects of tobacco smoke on the development of the fetal central nervous system, the data to date show fairly strong evidence that prenatal exposure affects neural systems and structures in ways that are predictive of aggressive behavior.

An increasing body of research is identifying a link between fetal exposure to tobacco smoke and increased risk of persistent and serious disruptive behavior disorders (reviews are provided in Ernst, Moolchan and Robinson 2001, and in Wakschlag et al. 2002). These behavior problems show very early onset and life-course persistence. In a rare assessment of the behavior of toddlers whose mothers smoked during pregnancy, Lauren Wakschlag and her colleagues (Wakschlag et al. 2006) reported significantly higher rates of

disruptive behavior problems among those who were exposed to tobacco smoke. Compared with their non-exposed peers, these toddlers
displayed increased levels of stubborn defiance, aggression, and low
social competence including fundamental difficulties responding to
or initiating social contact with their mothers. And interestingly, at
around the age two years, when the normal developmental pattern
among toddlers is a plateau or decrease in aggression the tobacco-
exposed toddlers showed increases in aggressive behaviors. In fact,
the researchers report that by the age of two, the atypical aggressive
behaviors were at clinically significant levels.

Similar findings were obtained in a prospective cohort study of the
prevalence, stability, and predictors of clinically significant behavior
problems in preterm low birth-weight infants (Gray, Indurkhya and
McCormick 2004). Behavior problems were assessed when the children were three, five and eight years of age. Among the significant
predictors of clinically significant behavior problems was maternal
cigarette smoking during pregnancy. (Other predictors were maternal
distress at 40 weeks and ethnicity.) In fact, the odds of clinically significant behavior problems at each age were 57 percent higher in children whose mothers had smoked during pregnancy compared with
children whose mothers had not smoked. There were no effects of
birth weight or neonatal health on behavior problems. These findings
are consistent with others in providing strong support for a connection between fetal tobacco exposure and neurological damage.

That there is a neural-level explanation for the observed association between maternal prenatal smoking and subsequent child aggressive behaviors is supported by the nature and consistency of the
research data, especially the specificity and dose-dependency of the
effects observed. A specificity of association between maternal prenatal smoking (MPS) and child aggression is seen in two areas. First,
researchers have found that MPS is associated with adolescent antisocial aggressive behaviors, but not with other aspects of maladjustment
or mental health (Fergusson, Woodward and Horwood 1998). Second, and very important in our context, is the finding that MPS is
significantly related to life-course persistent aggressive offending
(measured as those who had arrest histories both before and after age
18 years), but not to adolescent-limited offending (measured as those
whose arrest histories were only prior to age 18 years) (Brennan,

Grekin and Mednick 1999). A dose-dependent relation between MPS and outcomes was demonstrated in a study of an Australian cohort of over 5000 children (Williams *et al.* 1998). Maternal smoking behavior was assessed pre-pregnancy, early pregnancy, and late pregnancy, and again when the child was aged five years. Behavior problems were also assessed at age five years. The findings showed a clear relation between the extent of fetal tobacco exposure and the rates of subsequent behavior problems. The higher the rates of behavior problems, the higher the levels of smoking had been reported by the mother. Perhaps even more dramatic are the demonstrations of dose-dependent findings (e.g. Brennan *et al.* 1999).

In an exemplary longitudinal study, Patricia Brennan and her colleagues assessed the smoking behavior of over 4000 pregnant women in Denmark, and the arrest histories of their sons when they were 34 years of age. The study's validity is seen in its following four characteristics. First is that the sample was population based rather than a clinical subset. Second, maternal smoking behaviors were assessed concurrently rather than retroactively (and at a time where there was much less, if any, social stigma associated with smoking). Third, potentially related perinatal risk factors were recorded by obstetricians and pediatric neurologists rather than by the researchers. Fourth was their use of objective measures of violence—arrest for violent crime. Using the Danish National Criminal Registry, violent crime was operationalized as arrests for murder, attempted murder, robbery, rape, and assault. Their analyses demonstrated a significant link between the number of cigarettes smoked daily by the mothers during the third trimester of their pregnancy, and their sons' involvement in violent crime.

It is important to note that the findings of an association between MPS and aggressiveness in childhood or violence in adulthood generally are obtained independent of a range of potential confounds including maternal age, socioeconomic status, marital status, mental health status, prenatal or perinatal complications. Studies in Sweden (Hook, Cederblad and Berg 2006), New Zealand (Fergusson *et al.* 1998), the Netherlands (Batstra, Hadders-Algra and Neelman 2003), and the US (Brennan *et al.* 1999; Brennan *et al.* 2002; Wakschlag *et al.* 2006) consistently report obtaining a significant association between MPS and aggressiveness when possible confounds are controlled for.

For example, maternal smoking and stress often are comorbid. However, MPS has an effect on child behavior that is independent of the effect of maternal stress (Rodriquez and Bohlin 2005). One recent exception is found in a study examining MPS and conduct disorder in childhood and adolescence (Monuteaux *et al.* 2006). Here, an association between MPS and aggressive behaviors was seen only for those living in low socioeconomic circumstances. These data may result from methodological differences between the Monuteaux *et al.* (2006) study and the others summarized above. One major methodological difference is seen in the use of categorical rather than continuous variables; these may affect statistical power and alter the outcomes of analyses. Whereas most researchers have assessed relations between numbers of cigarettes smoked and outcomes, Monuteaux and his colleagues categorized mothers into non-, light, or heavy smokers. Similarly they dichotomized socioeconomic status on the basis of a median split into low or high, and restricted the measure of behavior to a subset of DSM-IV symptoms of conduct disorder, omitting juvenile arrest histories. Nonetheless, there is general consensus in the research that MPS is associated with offspring violence.

An area of research in which there is somewhat less agreement is that of gender. The majority of studies examining the effects of MPS exclusively have assessed outcomes in male offspring. Where girls have been included, the findings are somewhat inconsistent. Some researchers report an association between MPS and conduct disorder in males but not females (Wakschlag and Hans 2002; Weissman *et al.* 1999); others report an association that is stronger for males than females (Fergusson *et al.* 1998); and yet others report no difference by gender in behavioral outcomes of MPS (Gibson, Piquero and Tibbetts 2000; Hook *et al.* 2006; Maughan *et al.* 2001; Orlebeke, Knol and Verhulst 1997; Wakschlag *et al.* 2006). And different from each of these are the findings of Brennan and her colleagues (2002) in which the overall association between MPS and aggressive behaviors is observed among both males and females, but in females, the association appears to be mediated by substance abuse. In light of the specificity and dose-dependency of effects, and the animal studies, it would seem most plausible that the gender differences obtained may reflect the different outcome measures or target ages used by different researchers. It is noteworthy that the general child health effects noted as a result of MPS—for example low birth weight and its attendant problems of respiratory, metabolic, and learning difficulties—are not gender specific, and that MPS is a key predictor of serious behavior problems in preterm low birth weight infants (Gray *et al.* 2004; Hook *et al.* 2006; Perera *et al.* 2005). It is noteworthy also that interventions that are found to reduce disruptive behaviors in young children are ineffective among children who have a history of fetal exposure to tobacco smoke (Vuijk *et al.* 2006); this strengthens the probability that there has been permanent neurological damage.

In summary, there is sufficient evidence of a link between MPS and childhood behavior problems and adult criminal offending to identify MPS as a denial of a child's right to healthy and positive development. It is a rights violation that is eminently preventable.

FETAL ALCOHOL EXPOSURE

Young women who are not planning to become pregnant are unlikely to be concerned about the pregnancy-related risks of drinking, even if they are aware of them. Unfortunately, many pregnancies are unplanned and damage to the critical cell division and migration of the early gestation period may have happened before there is awareness of pregnancy. This is of concern given that binge drinking appears to be on the increase among young women (e.g. Floyd *et al.* 2007). Children who experience prenatal exposure to alcohol are unlikely to fully realize their rights. They have not been protected against exposure to a harmful substance; they have not been provided with the necessities for attaining health, and neurological damage may preclude the meaningful exercise of their participation rights. Clinical and research evidence converge to describe fetal alcohol exposure as producing a generalized deficit in complex processing, especially of social information. It is a deficit that results from the neurodevelopmental toxicity of alcohol, and it is a deficit that is manifest in serious and persistent behavior problems (Kodituwakku 2007).

The effects of prenatal alcohol exposure have been known since at least the 1970s when fetal alcohol syndrome (FAS) formally was first described (Jones and Smith 1973). Some three decades later, we have reports of alcohol use through pregnancy, and of children whose development is compromised as a result. Such reports have been made in North America (Clarren *et al.* 2001; Masotti *et al.* 2006), Europe (May *et al.* 2006), Russia (Miller *et al.* 2006), and the UK (Jones *et al.* 2006). Of particular concern are reports of higher rates of binge drinking in North American Aboriginal communities (Masotti *et al.* 2006), and among youth in the United Kingdom (Jones *et al.* 2006). It is especially egregious that we see reports of increased binge drinking among young woman accompanied by concerns about the health, economic, and social impact of binge drinking, but with no mention of the potential harm to a developing fetus (Jones *et al.* 2006). In fact, there is evidence to indicate that drinking alcohol during pregnancy is not even recognized as a health risk in Australia (O'Leary 2004), or in Europe (Room 2005), despite numerous studies showing functioning deficits in children exposed to alcohol prenatally (e.g. Autti-Ramo 2000; Steinhausen and Spohr 1998). Similarly in Russia, where the annual consumption of alcohol is among the highest in the world, there is little awareness, or acknowledgment, of the adverse developmental effects on the child of alcohol use during pregnancy (Miller *et al.* 2006). With the exception of the US, each of these countries has ratified the Convention. Not only does the Convention require that the best interests of the child be given a primary consideration in decision-making, it also specifies that signatories are to ensure appropriate prenatal health, develop preventive health care for children, and ensure that parents have access to education that supports the healthy development of children. These countries it would seem are failing to fulfill their Convention obligations. In turn, many children are being denied their rights, and being placed at risk for impulsive violence.

Alcohol is a neurodevelopmental toxin. It causes neuronal damage and cell loss in the fetal brain (Wattendorf, Usaf and Muenke 2005). Fetal alcohol spectrum disorder (FASD) is the umbrella term now used to describe the range of alcohol-related developmental deficits that result from maternal consumption of alcohol during pregnancy. Fetal alcohol syndrome (FAS) is the most severe and clinically recognizable outcome of fetal exposure to alcohol (Wattendorf *et al.* 2005). It is evident in facial anomalies including a thin upper lip, flat nasal bridge, upturned nose, and epicanthal folds (eyelid skin). Less visible, but arguably more important, is the functional and structural damage to the CNS. At the other end of the range of outcomes is what used to be labeled fetal alcohol effect (FAE) or alcohol-related birth defects (ARBD). These labels have been replaced with alcohol-related neurodevelopmental disorder (ARND) (Masotti *et al.* 2006). Children with ARND are unlikely to exhibit the facial malformations, but they do have significant CNS impairment.

Since the identification of FAS, it has been quite clear that the primary effect of alcohol on the fetus is on the developing brain (Jones *et al.* 2006). So for the past three decades, there have been efforts to identify the specific brain structures and mechanisms that are affected by prenatal exposure to alcohol and the neurobehavioral characteristics of FASD. To date, the hippocampus and the dopamine system have received the most attention. Rafael Galindo and his colleagues (Galindo, Zamudio and Valenzuela 2005) have described the adverse effects of alcohol on hippocampal formation, effects that account for observed deficits in learning and memory. Their experimental work with rats demonstrates that alcohol affects neuronal activity in ways that lead to abnormal synapse maturation, and, or neuronal death in the developing hippocampus. The research findings of Choong and Shen (2004) suggest alcohol has a major deleterious effect on dopamine neurons; this work helps explain the neural underpinnings of hyperactivity and attention deficits that are observed in children with FASD. These animal studies are helpful in explaining how alcohol affects the brain and may eventually facilitate the use of pharmacological interventions that reduce symptoms. The behavioral manifestations of CNS impairment at this point in time, however, remain lifelong and the damage to brain structures and functioning appear to be permanent (Galindo *et al.* 2005).

In the absence of facial dysmorphology, the neonatal indicators of prenatal exposure to alcohol are a maternal history of drinking, and infant irritability, high-pitched crying, disturbed sleep, and feeding difficulties. These infant conditions are likely to elicit negative responses from caregivers, adding to an already unfavorable rearing environment (O'Connor 1996). Children born to mothers who consume alcohol during pregnancy may be faced with the multiple risks associated with inappropriate parenting, especially if their mothers have substance abuse problems (Conners *et al.* 2004).

During the first year of life, impairments to cognitive and social development become increasingly apparent (Autti-Ramo and Granstrom 1996). By early childhood, children with FASD are characterized by their persistent hyperactivity, attention deficits, social difficulties, information processing difficulties, and conduct disorder; they evidence a wide range of serious behavioral and emotional problems (Bailey *et al.* 2004; Steinhausen and Spohr 1998). Although children with FASD may look somewhat like those with attention-deficit hyperactivity disorder (ADHD) in their behavioral difficulties and impulsivity, unlike those with ADHD, FASD children lack guilt, are cruel to others, and are more likely to lie and steal (Nash *et al.* 2006). The lack of guilt, together with the other observed social deficits among FASD children, suggests that they are at particular risk of interpersonal violence (Pardini 2006).

Studies with school children consistently find that children exposed to alcohol prenatally show higher rates of disruptive behavior disorders at home and at school (Delaney-Black *et al.* 2000; Kodituwakku *et al.* 2006; May *et al.* 2006; Sood *et al.* 2001). The extent or seriousness of these disorders varies with the extent of alcohol exposure; however, they are evident even with low levels of exposure (Sood *et al.* 2001). Especially illustrative is a study conducted at the School of Medicine at Wayne State University (Sood *et al.* 2001). The researchers assessed maternal alcohol, cigarette, and illicit drug use prospectively, during pregnancy and postnatally, and subsequent child outcomes among a sample comprising 501 mothers and their six- to seven-year-old children who were attending a university-based maternity clinic. To assess the dose-dependent effects of alcohol, mothers were categorized on the basis of their reported pregnancy consumption into three groups: no alcohol, low alcohol (less 0.3 fl. oz absolute alcohol per day), and moderate to heavy (0.3 fl oz or more per day). Interestingly, fewer than 25 percent of the sample reported no alcohol consumption during the pregnancy, and a surprisingly large 13 percent admitted to moderate or heavy usage. To assess child behavioral outcomes, the Achenbach Child Behavior Checklist, the most common assessment of childhood behavior problems, was used. On this measure, the higher the obtained score, the more the problem behaviors. Their analyses showed that even low fetal exposure to alcohol resulted in significantly higher scores on measures of behavior problems that are aggressive and delinquent in nature. Such findings are consistent with animal studies in which it is found that even one episode of consuming the equivalent of two drinks during pregnancy can result in the loss of fetal brain cells (Olney 2004). The greater the prenatal exposure, however, the higher were the problem behavior scores. The more alcohol exposure the child experiences during prenatal development, the greater the likelihood of neural damage and, in consequence, of aggressive behaviors.

By adolescence, poor judgment, distractibility and difficulty perceiving social cues are the hallmarks of FASD (Habbick *et al.* 1996; Steinhausen 1996). Common also is involvement in the youth criminal justice system (Fast and Conry 2004). The disruptive behavior problems of childhood become increasingly problematic through adolescence. The behavioral, intellectual, social, and cognitive neurological deficits associated with FASD, increase vulnerability to criminal involvement, and make it difficult for those affected to adhere to system requirements and regulations. The ease with which others can manipulate children with FASD, and the difficulties these children have understanding the link between action and consequence, make them particularly susceptible to peer influence during adolescence. Adding to their difficulties and the likelihood of criminal involvement is the frequent comorbidity of substance abuse disorders (Fast and Conry 2004). How these factors interact is exemplified well in an example provided by Diane Fast and Julianne Conry of the British Columbia Children's Hospital in Canada. The example describes a case where a youth with FASD committed an armed robbery while under the influence of a cousin and of alcohol consumption. The judge concluded that "were it not for his streetwise cousin urging him on, Mr Williams would not likely have committed the armed robbery" (Fast and Conry 2004, p.163). The researchers concluded that the violent act was caused by a combination of the youth's poor judgment resulting from neural damage due to prenatal alcohol exposure, and the concurrent influence of his alcohol use.

That same characteristic poor judgment, manipulability, and substance use, may well also result in the intergenerational transmission of children with FASD, particularly since there appears to be a genetic predisposition to problem drinking (Mulligan *et al.* 2003). But as Daniel Wattendorf (Wattendorf *et al.* 2005) said, FASD is not hereditary. It is entirely the result of maternal alcohol consumption during pregnancy.

Not all children who are prenatally exposed to alcohol will show symptoms of FASD. The variations in outcomes have been attributed to the chronicity of maternal drinking through the pregnancy, the amount consumed, the stage of pregnancy at which alcohol is consumed, and maternal metabolism (Spohr 1996). Additional maternal risk factors for giving birth to a child with FASD also have been identified: these include older maternal age, poor nutritional status, ethnic minority status, and low socioeconomic status (Floyd *et al.* 2005). Nonetheless, it has not been possible to identify any safe stage of pregnancy, any safe amount of alcohol consumption during pregnancy, or any maternal characteristics that protect against alcohol's adverse effects on fetal brain development. What we can say is that the more alcohol the mother consumes while pregnant, the greater the risk to her child. That said, it is important to emphasize that FASD can and does occur in children born to any woman who drinks alcohol while pregnant (Floyd *et al.* 2005). Since there is no evidence at all to suggest any benefits of alcohol consumption on fetal development, the best interests principle of the Convention obligates avoidance of all alcohol during a pregnancy.

One intervention approach that is promising is described by Louise Floyd and her colleagues (2007). Their success may well be due to their targeting of both risky drinking (binge drinking) and risky sexual behavior (ineffective contraception) among women aged 18 to 44 (average age 30). The intervention itself was brief: four counseling sessions and one contraception consultation. Nonetheless it appeared relatively successful. Follow-up measures indicated binge drinking had dropped from 30 episodes in three months to seven episodes in the past three months at the nine-month follow-up, and effective contraceptive use showed a steady increase from 45.8 percent to 56.3 percent. Considerable progress is still needed, but the intervention does indicate that lessened fetal exposure to alcohol is possible, even among high-risk women.

Maternal use of alcohol through pregnancy does not, of course, always occur in the absence of other risks to the health of the developing fetal brain. For example, in the population-based study described earlier in this chapter (Sood *et al.* 2001), prenatal alcohol exposure was associated with prenatal exposure to cocaine and cigarette smoking. Each of these substances is toxic to the fetus. Each has an independent effect on the developing CNS, but the overall effect will be additive. And increasing the child's propensity for life-course persistent aggression is the typical environment into which children who are prenatally exposed to neurodevelopmental toxins are born. These children all too often are raised in abusive family environments (Fast and Conry 2004), in which the effects of poor early parenting will interact with the neurodevelopmental consequences of fetal substance exposure. The result will be an increased tendency to early onset aggressive behavior disorders. The brain is still developing.

EARLY PARENTING: THE ATTACHMENT RELATIONSHIP

The early relationship or the "attachment" that develops between the infant and primary caregiver is the foundation upon which all social relationships are built. The quality of attachment determines an individual's expectations for self and others, the processing of social cues, emotion regulation, and social interactions. Poor quality of attachment has been identified as a risk factor in the development of disruptive behavior disorders in childhood, and for psychopathology and violent criminality in adolescence and adulthood. Like alcohol and tobacco, disrupted attachment relationships are neurodevelopmental toxins.

When we use the term "attachment", we are referring to the quality of the dyadic relationship between the infant and the primary caregiver—this usually has been and continues to be the infant's mother. Effectively, then, the research information that is available describes the quality of the relationship between the mother and her infant. This relationship is built over the first year of life as the infant and mother get to know each other. The infant gets to learn her mother's face, voice, smell; what behaviors elicit her attention, and how dependably she responds. The mother gets to learn her infant's sleeping and feeding needs and patterns, to interpret the infant's cries, and to find what comforts her infant. The quality of the attachment relationship that develops is primarily dependent on caregiver behaviors. This is why it is so important to provide supports to parents as described in the Convention, and especially in Articles 18, 26, and 27, as noted earlier. Such supports would facilitate the caregiver behaviors that underlie the development of a positive attachment relationship.

Some infants are more difficult to "read" and some are more difficult to care for. There is little evidence, however, that the infant's temperament influences the quality of the attachment relationship, although interactions between temperament and attachment are found to affect child behavior (Guttmann-Steinmetz and Crowell 2006). Attachment quality appears to be relatively independent not only of the child's temperament, but also of other genetic influences and family contextual variables. The evidence for other genetic factors has been slim. There is some evidence of genetic influences on quality of attachment, but the environment of rearing plays the key role (Bakermans-Kranenburg and van Ijzendoorn 2007). The findings of a recent study of attachment quality in monozygotic (identical) twins are illustrative (Constantino *et al.* 2006). This well-controlled study examined the attachment quality of reared-together female monozygotic twins and their female non-twin siblings. The data indicate strongly that the major contributor to attachment quality is shared environmental influences, not genetic ones. And, interestingly, in the consideration of environmental influences, there appears to be no effect of the marital relationship, including spousal violence, on the quality of the attachment between parent and child (Bolen 2005; Sternberg *et al.* 2005).

One of the most robust findings in developmental psychology is the importance of a good attachment relationship. The earliest conceptualization of the attachment construct is seen in the writings of the neo-Freudian psychologist, Erik Erikson (1968). Erikson theorized that the most important developmental task of infancy was to establish a sense of trust. The child's sense of trust in his caregiver and the world around her were seen as the necessary foundation for healthy development. Without that trust, Erikson argued, the child would grow up with a poor sense of self and be vulnerable to negative developmental outcomes throughout the lifespan. The sense of trust, as described by Erikson, underlies what has become known as secure attachment.

Attachment theory was formulated by John Bowlby based on his observations of a link between early maternal deprivation and subsequent juvenile delinquencies (Bowlby 1969, 1973). Using an evolutionary framework, Bowlby described attachment as an innate biological system that, in balance with exploratory behaviors, promotes caregiver proximity-seeking behaviors in the infant, especially under stressful circumstances. Its goal is survival. As they are an evolutionarily programmed mechanism, infant proximity-seeking behaviors will emerge regardless of caregiver responses. All infants are "attached." It is the quality of that attachment that is important and it is caregiver responses that will determine the quality. When the caregiver responds appropriately, that is in a sensitive and contingent manner, the infant will develop a secure attachment. The infant will have the sense of trust that Erikson talked about. The infant will learn that comfort and support are readily available when she is distressed; that all her needs will be met; that her caregiver is dependable. In fact, we might say that when caregivers are contingent in their responses to their infant's cues, they are respecting the child's earliest participation rights. The infant is communicating her wishes to be held, changed, fed, or otherwise comforted—having a voice in matters that affect her. When the caregiver is ignoring, rejecting, or unpredictable, then the infant will develop an insecure attachment; the infant can count on neither caregiver availability nor comfort when she is stressed. The infant has a sense of distrust in the world around her.

Subtypes of insecure attachment have been identified. Mary Ainsworth and her colleagues (Ainsworth *et al.* 1978) developed the "Strange Situation" laboratory task in which stress is manipulated to assess attachment quality. The assessment is usually made around the age of one year when the attachment relationship is at its initial peak of development. The infant and mother initially are together in a room with toys. The stress manipulation comprises two brief separations of the infant from the mother (or primary caregiver) while the infant is playing with the toys. The infant's reunion behavior when the mother returns reflects the quality of attachment. Using the Strange Situation measure, the following differences in reunion behavior are found. Securely attached infants seem to miss their caregiver upon separation, but do not display distress; they greet her upon reunion and quickly return to play. Their behavior is reflecting their trust in her availability. Two types of insecure attachment have been identified based on reunion behaviors. Avoidant attachment, now associated with rejecting parenting, describes infants who show little distress on separation and actively avoid or ignore the caregiver on reunion. Ambivalent attachment, associated with inconsistent parenting, describes infants who are highly distressed by separation and seek contact on reunion but are not comforted by that contact. Since these initial categorizations, a third type of insecure attachment has been identified to describe those who display some avoidant and some ambivalent behaviors. This type has been referred to as avoidant/ambivalent or as disorganized/disoriented attachment (Main and Hesse 1990). It is seen most often in infants who have experienced parental maltreatment; children whose evolutionarily programmed source of comfort is also a source of fear.

During the development of the attachment relationship, infants (unconsciously) adapt their behavior in accord with caregiver response, and in accord with the developing sense of self as worthy and deserving or the antithesis thereof. A child with a secure attachment sees the self as worthy of love and capable of obtaining positive attention. The positive relationship she experiences with her mother generalizes to relationships with others, and promotes positive social skills. The work of Judy Dunn (e.g. 2004) illustrates well the importance of secure attachment to positive sibling and peer relationships. An insecurely attached child understands the self to be unworthy of love and positive attention, and sees others as unpredictable or hostile. With an underlying fear of rejection, or anticipation of hostility, it is hard for the insecurely attached child to develop positive relationships or develop good social skills. In fact, Bowlby believed that these different caregiving-related outcomes were important because of their predictions for later development and adjustment.

The attachment classifications have important implications for the development of the child's emotion regulation skills. When the securely attached infant learns that she can regulate proximity to the caregiver as needed, she is learning that she can effectively manage her feelings of fear, anxiety, or distress. She learns, over time, when to express distress and when to inhibit it. The situation is very different for insecurely attached children. When the primary caregiver does not respond to the infant's distress, the infant has a build-up of negative emotion—that of the initial distress-causing situation and that elicited by the unresponsive caregiver. Insecure–avoidant infants are thought to learn to suppress their emotions as indicated by their reunion behavior in the Strange Situation, and as reflected in elevated heart rate and cortisol levels despite apparent calmness (Guttmann-Steinmetz and Crowell 2006). Insecure–ambivalent infants display an antithetical pattern. They express high levels of anger and anxiety, again as indicated in the Strange Situation paradigm, and have tremendous difficulty calming down. It is as though they have learned that unless they continue to express high levels of distress, they will be ignored (Guttmann-Steinmetz and Crowell 2006). These difficulties with emotion regulation have profound implications for subsequent interpersonal functioning and interpersonal violence.

The quality of early attachment provides a template of the social world that influences how individuals think, act, and react. It is a template that most often in the literature is referred to as the child's internal working model. It is a model that consists of views of self and expectations of others that are used to organize, interpret, and predict behaviors (Bowlby 1989). The internal working model provides a base for perception, feelings, and behaviors, in all subsequent relationships, and explains the stability of attachment quality in determining relationships across the lifespan (Moreira *et al.* 2003). It is the child's blueprint of the social world. That there is a neurobiological basis for that blueprint is now agreed upon. Its exact nature remains speculative.

As noted earlier, most studies assessing the neurobiology of social behaviors have used animals. Again in the study of the attachment, experiments with rodents have been informative. They have demonstrated a key role of the neuropeptide oxytocin in the expression of maternal behaviors, stress, and feeding behaviors (Mayes, Swain and Leckman 2005). For example, high levels of licking and grooming by mothers of infant rats is correlated with high levels of oxytocin receptor binding in adulthood and with increased maternal care to their own offspring. Where there has been research with humans, the findings suggest a role for oxytocin in responses to stress, in affiliative behaviors, and in number of developmental difficulties characterized by social attachment dysfunction (Bartz and Hollander 2006). Oxytocin, acting on the limbic structures, is strongly implicated in neural mechanisms that are believed to underlie the formation and expression of attachment (Bartz and Hollander 2006; Beech and Mitchell 2005). Interestingly, orphanage or socially deprived children show very low levels of oxytocin (Carter 2005). They also tend to have difficulty trusting others and poor quality of attachment (Dunn 2004). And there is a suggestion of a neural-level inter-generational transmission of attachment quality. As Guttmann-Steinmetz and Crowell (2006) summarize, there are a number of studies that demonstrate the continuity of attachment quality from infancy into adulthood, and the link between maternal attachment status, and caregiving behaviors. Mothers who themselves have a history of insecure attachment, fail to sufficiently cuddle, talk to, smile at, contingently feed, change, and bathe their infants (the human equivalent of the rat's licking and grooming). They are thought to behave that way, at least in part, because they have oxytocin dysfunction (Beech and Mitchell 2005). The capacity to form social bonds or to manage stressful experiences (two key aspects of early parenting) is reduced by low levels of oxytocin (Carter 2005). In turn, the lack of appropriate caregiving the infant receives will dysregulate the infant's oxytocin system. The ongoing interaction between neural and social/maternal deficits is manifest in an insecure attachment that most likely will be lifelong in its effects on relationships.

Over the next decade, our knowledge of the neural underpinnings of attachment may well become much more than speculative. No doubt we will learn more about the role of oxytocin and its interactions with serotonin and dopamine levels, cortisol and so forth. Oxytocin may continue to be identified as the critical hormone in interpersonal attachments; it may also be implicated in antisocial behaviors. Regardless, it is clear from the animal and human research to date that difficulties with social relationships stem from early caregiving experiences. Poor caregiving experiences appear to cause biochemical changes whose effects are seen in social and relational difficulties from early childhood into adulthood. Insecure attachment is a well-documented risk factor for the development of behavior problems in childhood and adolescence, and for adult relationship violence. Since Bowlby's initial work, much evidence has emerged to support his theory.

Early studies examining attachment quality and behavior demonstrate that compared with their insecurely attached peers, infants and toddlers with secure attachments display more sociability, more effective emotion regulation, and greater compliance with maternal requests (e.g. Bretherton 1985; Richters and Waters 1991; Thompson 1999). Infants with insecure attachments have less effective emotion regulation, tend to be angry, and have difficulty with social relationships (Thompson 1999). Far from being compliant, insecurely attached infants are oppositional and aggressive to their mothers (Frankel and Bates 1990), and as their social interactions expand outward from the family, they are more aggressive, hostile and impulsive with others (Greenberg 1999). It is as though these infants are adopting a defensive stance and developing coercive behavior patterns to cope with the social world as they see it—a world that is hostile, untrustworthy, or unpredictable. Such expectations and behaviors tend to be self-reinforcing. Positive relationships with adults and with peers become increasingly unlikely (Starzyk and Marshall 2003).

By preschool, there is a link between the quality of attachment and the quality of peer friendships (Dunn 2004). Children with secure attachment classifications tend to be more prosocial and experience more social success. In contrast, children with an insecure attachment classification experience peer rejection and show high levels of aggression and disruptive behavior disorders (e.g. Greenberg *et al.* 1991; Shaw *et al.* 1996; Speltz, DeKlyen and Greenberg 1999; Wood *et al.*'s 2004). Moreover, the peer rejection combined with the antisocial behaviors elicits further peer rejection (Wood, Cowan and Baker 2002). It is worth noting here that the Wood *et al.* (2004) data do indicate a causal relation among attachment quality and aggression and rejection. Other researchers also have found that attachment quality does tend to predict peer acceptance or rejection through the elementary school years (Cassidy *et al.* 1996; Cohn 1990; Shulman, Elicker and Sroufe 1994).

Attachment quality continues to be an influence on behavior problems in middle childhood. A recent innovative study of attachment and behavior problems in middle childhood replicates previous data, and demonstrates the robustness of findings (Moss *et al.* 2006). Unlike others, this study used children as reporters of their own behaviors—an interesting example of respect for children's participation rights. Attachment classifications were measured at age six years when children were just starting formal schooling. Behavior problems were assessed two years later through teacher, parent, and child reports. There was general consensus among reporters of a link between attachment classification and disruptive behavior disorders.

Insecure attachment is also thought to be a primary contributor to conduct disorders and delinquencies among adolescents (Allen, Moore and Kuperminc 1997; Keiley 2002; McElhaney *et al.* 2006; Rosenstein and Horowitz 1996). Substantial stability in attachment security has been identified across adolescence (Allen *et al.* 2004). With a history of defiance and hostility, of low compliance with parental requests, and of poor social skills and peer rejection, the insecurely attached adolescent will have difficulty developing a positive sense of self and autonomy—the key developmental tasks of the adolescent period. And importantly, the insecurely attached adolescent may have difficulty forming healthy intimate relationships.

As part of a 26-year longitudinal study, Glenn Roisman and his colleagues (2005) tested Bowlby's suggestion that early attachment quality, mediated by the child's internal working model, would be recapitulated in romantic relationships. Attachment classifications had been recorded on their sample during infancy through the use of the Strange Situation. At age 20, as young adults, they were asked to evaluate their current romantic relationships using the Current Relationship Interview. This interview protocol asks for respondents to describe and evaluate such aspects of the relationship as separation episodes, instances of perceived rejection, and experiences with care-seeking. The quality of the current relationship was strongly associated with the quality of maternal attachment measured in infancy. Where there are very serious relationship difficulties, some attachment theorists have suggested a link between early attachment quality and juvenile psychopathy, violence in intimate relationships, and adult sexual offending.

Insecure attachment has been identified as one precursor of the hallmark emotional detachment and interpersonal insensitivity of the psychopath (Saltaris 2002). Psychopaths are noted for being among the most violent, persistent, and most likely to recidivate of all criminal offenders (Forth and Burke 1998; Harris, Rice and Cormier 1991; Newman, Schmitt and Voss 1997; Serin, Peters and Barbaree 1990). These characteristics have been noted among adolescents. Psychopathic adolescents are significantly different from non-psychopathic antisocial adolescents in age of onset of behavior problems, the seriousness of their offenses, the violence of the offences and their recidivism rates (Forth and Burke 1998). Christina Saltaris (2002) provides a developmental analysis of the role of attachment quality in psychopathy. She notes that "the emotional detachment displayed by psychopathic individuals is so fundamental and pervasive that it is likely to originate in the first few months of life, and that it is relatively independent of later inadequacies in the rearing environment" (p.733). The core of her explanation of the attachment basis of psychopathy is as follows.

The use of the attachment construct to explain an absence of concern for others that typically is displayed by juvenile offenders has a history that goes back to Bowlby. Recall that Bowlby initially was interested in explaining the early maternal precursors of juvenile offending. The internal working model of the insecurely attached child—that others, like the self, are unworthy, unconcerned, undependable, and untrustworthy—can result in emotional callousness. One developmental outcome of this, the lack of affective bonds with peers, parents or authority figures, can lead to a lack of identification with, or rejection of, the social and moral order. Empirical support for this assertion is seen in data demonstrating links between (extremely) insecure attachment and (1) violent interpersonal crime such as rape and murder, (2) personality disturbances such as narcissism and sadism, and (3) an inability to understand or care about the impact of violence on the victim. Saltaris' explanation of the link between insecure attachment and violent offending is consistent with Dustin Pardini's (2006) description of the emotional and behavioral underpinnings of severe violent delinquency.

Violent behavior in intimate relationships also has been conceptualized as stemming from early insecure attachment. Higher rates of insecure attachment are found in those who perpetrate violence against romantic or sexual partners (Chapple 2003; Magdol et al. 1998). Consistent with the observed outcomes of insecure attachment, males who perpetrate violence against their partners appear to be anticipating rejection: they are found to be more threatened by their partner's independence, to feel relatively powerless in the relationship, and to have difficulty expressing their needs (Babcock et al. 1993; Berns, Jacobson and Gottman 1999; Ehrensaft and Vivian 1999). Fear of rejection or abandonment appears to result in over-controlling behavior towards a partner (Bogaerts, Vanheule and Declercq 2005). Sexual violence is of particular concern.

The link between attachment security and sexual relationships has been explained well (Ward, Hudson and Marshall 1996). The self-worth and positive expectations of others that characterize the securely attached person result in successful interpersonal strategies that lead to high levels of intimacy and satisfaction in close adult relationships. In contrast, insecure attachment leads to a need to maintain independence and invulnerability, pursuing and perceiving sexual activity as a means to a sense of self-worth, or avoiding closeness because of fear of rejection. Each of these has implications for sexual offending, Ward further suggests that the combination of poor adult intimate relationships, and the history of insecure attachment make the individual highly vulnerable to sexually offending against children (Ward and Siegert 2002).

Compared with non-offenders, sexual offenders, especially those who offend against children, do show less secure attachment histories (Bogaerts *et al.* 2005). However, analyses of convicted child molesters with personality disorders suggest that the link between sexual offending against children and attachment quality may be personality disorders (Bogaerts *et al.* 2005). Nonetheless, as the researchers noted in their study, the most striking factor differentiating the child molesters from the control group was their recollection of their mother as uncaring.

Overall, the attachment literature demonstrates a pathway leading from insecure attachment quality in infancy, to early onset aggression, childhood conduct disorders, and adolescent and adult interpersonal violence. It is, of course, extremely unlikely that there is such a clear and simple developmental path. As Mark Chaffin and other members of the American Psychological Association Section on Child Maltreatment have argued, we must be cautious not to oversimplify or exaggerate the outcomes of insecure attachment (Chaffin *et al.* 2006). Insecure attachment most likely is one risk factor among many that predict violence. It is possible that attachment quality predisposes the child to aggressive or violent behaviors independent of other risk factors because of its effect on neural development. And it is highly likely that attachment quality interacts with other factors in the child's environment of rearing in determining the extent to which aggression is expressed. The association between early attachment insecurity and later severe relational and behavioral problems may be better understood by taking into account the typical parent or family characteristics observed among insecurely attached children.

Attachment difficulties most often are seen in children who are being raised in stressful circumstances. Insecurely attached children are found in families where there is evidence of domestic violence (Dankoski *et al.* 2006; Starzyk and Marshall 2003), where mothers suffer mental illness or depression, and where the family is living in poverty (McCartney *et al.* 2004). The stress placed on parents in these circumstances makes it difficult for them to display the sensitive responding needed for the development of secure attachment. For example, whereas poverty is itself not a risk factor for insecure attachment, mothers with economic stress behave less responsively to their children (Raikes and Thompson 2005). Stressful living conditions make effective parenting very difficult. The cumulative risk model would suggest that each of these factors would have an additive or interactive effect on increasing the likelihood that the child will display violent behavior.

Insecure attachment is, nonetheless, a risk factor for violence as is prenatal exposure to the neurodevelopmental toxins of nicotine and alcohol. We may not have certainty on the mechanisms by which children are affected, and we cannot predict with certainty which children will be affected, or to what extent their development will be impaired. But we can say with assurance that any substance or experience that compromises the health and developmental capacity of the child is a denial of the child's rights. We are, therefore, obligated to make every effort to prevent conditions that result in insecure attachment or prenatal exposure to toxic substances. Respecting children's Convention rights would do much to lessen the stressful circumstances that are associated with the development of insecure attachment.

Under the Convention, countries are responsible for assisting parents with their child-rearing responsibilities. As will be discussed in Chapter 5, the provision of such programs as home visitation, parent education, and childcare is associated with lower rates of child violence. Getting the wiring right the first time is always easier than trying to fix it later.

CHAPTER 3

PARENTING STYLES

*Parents need to encourage their kids, support them, spend time
with them, tell them they love them. Parents should not be
allowed to hit their children, that is violence and things will only
get worse.*

Children appear to be well aware of the effects of parental neglect,
emotional abuse, and violence. More general public awareness may
follow from the recent global study on violence against children. In
recognition of the extent of violence against children, in 2001, the
United Nations General Assembly asked the UN Secretary General
to conduct a global study of violence against children. The final
report, released in 2007 (*United Nations Secretary General's Study on
Violence Against Children* 2007) demonstrates that violence in the
home is a common and serious problem worldwide. In the United
States and Canada, for example, the family is the primary setting for
violence for children, and parents are most frequently its perpetrators
(Covell 2005). In direct contravention of the Convention, children
experience physical abuse, emotional abuse, sexual abuse, and
neglect in the home. And as seen in the continued, although lessening,
allowance of corporal punishment in many countries that have
ratified the Convention, legal protections against violence remain
inadequate. Moreover, as seen in the high rates of child deaths from
abuse, child protection services remain inadequate. Many children
remain at risk of experiencing violence and of becoming violent.

The focus of this chapter is on parenting practices that are associated with the development of violence among children. After first
examining general parenting styles, we discuss the outcomes

associated with parental use of corporal punishment and abuse. The consistency of findings in outcomes of the various forms of parental maltreatment implicate involvement of underlying neural processes that are reflected in social information processing deficits. We end this chapter with a discussion of these deficits among aggressive children with a history of poor or abusive parenting.

The Convention, as described in Article 19, requires that strong laws and policies be in place to protect *all* children from *all* forms of physical or mental injury, abuse, neglect, and exploitation. In addition, the child's right to be protected from sexual abuse is described in Article 34. There is tacit acknowledgment of the challenges faced by parents living in poverty or other stressful circumstances that increase the likelihood of abuse or neglect. Article 27 of the Convention obligates countries to take measures to assist parents to ensure "a standard of living adequate for the child's physical, mental, spiritual, moral and social development," and Article 18.2 requires that states "render appropriate assistance to parents and legal guardians in the performance of their child-rearing responsibilities." The Convention does not address the issue of corporal punishment directly except in Article 28 which requires that school discipline be "consistent with the child's human dignity." However, the UN Committee on the Rights of the Child repeatedly has criticized the continued use of corporal punishment in the home, stressing that corporal punishment is incompatible with the Convention (Committee on the Rights of the Child 1994, 2003). In the absence of protections and supports against abuse and neglect, children are at risk of developing violent behaviors.

THE IMPORTANCE OF POSITIVE PARENTING

There is evidence that maltreatment in early childhood can have significant structural and functional consequences for neuro-development (Anda *et al.* 2006; De Bellis *et al.* 2002). As described in the previous chapter, although the period of most rapid brain growth is prenatal and perinatal, the brain continues to mature after birth. Child maltreatment is associated with alterations in the neurobiological systems that are highly involved in brain maturation: these affect learning and memory, emotion regulation, and behavior

(Teicher *et al.* 2003; Watts-English *et al.* 2006). The nature of the changes is evidenced in two ways. MRI brain scans show differences in brain structure between children who have been maltreated compared with their peers who have not been maltreated (De Bellis *et al.* 2002; Watts-English *et al.* 2006). In addition, myelination is delayed in children who have been neglected or exposed to the chronic stress of abuse (De Bellis 2005). More obvious are the manifestations of the altered brain structure seen in a range of emotional and behavioral difficulties such as impulsivity and aggressive antisocial behavior (Creeden 2004).

Poor parenting practices consistently have been identified as a risk factor for the development of aggressive antisocial behavior (Arthur 2005; Bosmans *et al.* 2006; Casas *et al.* 2006; Roelofs *et al.* 2006). Poor parenting practices are not only seen in abuse and neglect. They are seen also in parental hostility and rejection, inconsistency and lack of involvement, and in the use of excess control and punitiveness. There is a large body of data demonstrating that children who experience poor parenting, who feel rejected, have punitive parents, experience corporal punishment, and are under-socialized, are children at risk for early onset life-course persistent behavior problems (e.g. Farrington 1994, 1995; Loeber and Hay 1997; Maccoby 2000; Scott 1998).

Positive parenting comprises high levels of warmth and acceptance, socialization through inductive reasoning and modeling of desired behaviors, and the promotion of autonomy through the systematic provision of age-appropriate choices. Positive parenting is consistent with the Convention: research demonstrates it to be in the best interests of every child. Positive parenting has been identified as a major protective factor for children being raised in difficult circumstances such as with low-income single mothers in poor inner-city neighborhoods (e.g. Jackson *et al.* 2000; Koblinsky, Kuvalanka and Randolph 2006; McGroder 2000). Where such children have experienced parental support, warmth, and positive socialization strategies, they show greater social competence, social maturity, school performance, and, importantly, significantly fewer behavior problems than do their less positively parented peers. Positive parenting has also been suggested to moderate the influence of impaired fetal brain development on the development of behavior disorders (Morrell and Murray 2003).

Parenting practices tend, to some extent, to be associated with family circumstances. Children being reared by young parents, in single-parent homes, or in poverty, are less likely to experience positive parenting, and are more likely to evidence behavior problems. As reported by Susan Dahinten, Jennifer Shapka, and Doug Willms (2007), studies generally demonstrate a link between adolescent mothering and the emergence and persistence of behavior problems. For example, a 20-year longitudinal study of adolescent mothers and their children in New Zealand demonstrated a strong link between maternal age and violent offending in their children during late adolescence into early adulthood. Single-parent status (usually single motherhood) also has been linked with poor parenting practices and aggressive antisocial behaviors among children (e.g. Antecol and Bedard 2007; Dahinten *et al.* 2007; Flouri and Buchanan 2002). Children raised in poor families are at heightened risk of developing behavior problems (Koblinsky *et al.* 2006). There is significant evidence demonstrating that poverty, and its related stresses from chronic adverse conditions, increases the likelihood of a reactive socialization style in which harsh physical punishment is used (McLoyd 1998). Of course, these characteristics tend to co-occur. For the most part, adolescent mothers tend to be unmarried and poor (Dahinten *et al.* 2007). But not all children of poor, unmarried young mothers are antisocial, aggressive, or violent. And some children from wealthy two-parent homes become antisocial, aggressive, or violent. Parenting is a powerful determinant of outcomes across family circumstances.

PARENTING STYLES

The most well-known and researched parenting styles are those described by Diana Baumrind initially in 1967 (Baumrind 1967, 1971). The three styles she described, authoritative, authoritarian, and permissive, vary in their combination of demanding and responsive parental behaviors. The authoritative or democratic, as it has been called, is the one that is most consistent with the Convention. It is the only style of parenting that is consistent with the Convention principles of best interests and participation. The demanding behaviors of the democratic parent are the setting and enforcement of age-appropriate limits, expectations for age-appropriate maturity, and the monitoring and supervision of the child. In terms of responsiveness, democratic parents are affectionate and supportive, they recognize the child's achievements, and they maintain involvement in their children's social and academic development. Democratic parents encourage their children to express their views in matters that affect them and they encourage their children to explore options in decision-making. Socialization is focussed on proactive teaching, modeling, and reward. Inductive reasoning is used for discipline. In essence, this is exemplar positive parenting.

Authoritarian and permissive categories describe less positive parenting styles. Authoritarian parents tend to have excessive and inflexible demands for obedience and behavioral standards. Children's talents, interests, strengths, and weaknesses are not well accommodated. Children usually are not respected as autonomous bearers of rights, and typically they are denied expression of opinion. Discipline tends to be harsh. Power assertion, especially corporal punishment, is its key characteristic. Permissive parents, either indulgent or indifferent, have few demands or expectations for behavior. Their children often are left to follow their impulses; socialization and discipline are infrequent or inconsistent. Child misbehaviors often are simply ignored.

Considerable evidence supports the existence of the three types of parenting and their link to child outcomes. Our focus here is on authoritarian parenting as it frequently has been demonstrated to be a path to aggression and violence. The outcomes associated with democratic and permissive parenting are first summarized. Democratic parenting styles consistently are found to be associated with optimum social, academic, and behavioral outcomes. The outcomes have been summarized well by Nadia Sorkhabi (2005). Democratic parenting "has been found to provide children with the experiential basis for optimally balancing agency (characterized by self-assertion, self-reliance, and prudential self-interest) with communion (characterized by prosocial engagement, cooperation, and moral concern for others' interests)" (Sorkhabi 2005, p.552). The children of democratic parents show high levels of self-esteem, self-reliance, self-control, and social maturity, and few behavior problems. In adolescence, compared with those raised by authoritarian or permissive parents, children of democratic parents show more prosocial peer group selection, greater self-control, less risk-taking, good conflict resolution abilities, and very low levels of interpersonal conflict or violence (Covell and Howe 2001a). Permissive and authoritarian parenting styles, in contrast, consistently have been associated with behavior problems, especially physical aggression, from early childhood to adolescence (McKee *et al.* 2004).

Parents who fail to adequately socialize their children may be unwittingly teaching their children that any behavior is acceptable. When permissive parents ignore the natural tendency of the toddler to be aggressive, when they neither correct the child nor teach him the importance of non-aggressive interactions, they are reinforcing the child's aggressive behaviors and increasing the likelihood that they will continue. Further reinforcement in toddlerhood is provided by the consequences of aggression, which at that age is usually instrumental. Through aggression, the child obtains the toy or treat she wanted. Aggressive interactions then become part of the child's social interactive repertoire. As Casas *et al.* (2006) cite, studies have found maternal permissiveness to be a major predictor of childhood physical aggression. Nonetheless, authoritarian parenting is the most strongly linked parenting style to early onset life-course persistent behavior problems, and to adult criminal behaviors (Huesmann *et al.* 2002).

In their study of relational and physical aggression, Juan Casas and his colleagues (Casas *et al.* 2006) explain the links between parenting style and childhood aggression. Relational and physical aggression are distinguished by the type of harm they incur. Physical aggression does harm through actual or threatened physical harm; it includes pushing, hitting, or threatening to beat up another child. Relational aggression does harm by damaging a relationship; it includes social exclusion and rumor-spreading. Typically, physical aggression is seen more often in boys, and relational aggression is seen more often in girls. However, both are seen most frequently among children with authoritarian parents. Authoritarian parents, through their use of power-assertive discipline techniques are teaching the acceptability of aggression, especially as an effective means of resolving interpersonal conflict. In addition, the hostility and psychological control that are part of authoritarian parenting are teaching relational aggression. Essentially, Casas and his colleagues (2006) are suggesting that children are generalizing to other relationships what they have learned from their parents—power assertion and psychological control are appropriate and effective interpersonal strategies. Their own study of preschoolers confirms their suggestion. Two dimensions of authoritarian parenting seem to be particularly associated with aggression in children: parental rejection and parental hostility.

Underlying authoritarian parenting, with its lack of warmth and support, and its demands for the child to adhere to some absolute standard, is a fundamental rejection of the individual child. Parental rejection is a major predictor not only of aggressive behaviors, but also of their severity (Roelofs *et al.* 2006; Rohner and Britner 2002). In contrast, parental acceptance is associated with prosocial behavior and positive peer relationships (Rohner and Britner 2002). The power of parental rejection has been demonstrated very clearly in the work of Ronald Rohner and his colleagues at the Center for the Study of Parental Acceptance and Rejection at the University of Connecticut. Their work indicates that parental rejection plays a major role in the development of various behavior problems including clinically significant conduct disorder and juvenile offending. Their review of studies in various countries implicates parental rejection as the key precursor to behavior problems such as non-compliance, hostility, aggression, and cruelty, across a range of cultures. They cite empirical evidence from the following countries: Bahrain, China, Croatia, England, Finland, India, Japan, Norway, Pakistan, and the United States. And within the United States, evidence for a link between parental rejection and behavior problems is provided for various ethnocultural subgroups including African-Americans, Chinese Americans, European Americans, and Hispanic Americans. The robustness of findings is reinforced by the consistency of the association over time, across a variety of research designs, and by parental rejection being significantly associated with behavior problems after factors such as family conflict, structure, and socioeconomic status are controlled for (Rohner and Britner 2002). Not surprisingly, it would appear that the need for parental love and acceptance is universal (Khaleque and Rohner 2002). Among the consequences of an unmet need for parental acceptance are hostility, aggression, low self-esteem, and a negative world-view (Khaleque and Rohner 2002). These findings are consistent with Maslow's needs theory (1970) and Bowlby's attachment theory (1982).

One expression of parental rejection is seen in hostile parenting. Hostile parenting describes parenting behavior that is harsh, angry, controlling, disapproving, and rejecting (Brannigan *et al.* 2002; Scaramella and Conger 2003). There is considerable research in which hostile parenting is an identified risk factor for disruptive and problem behaviors in children (Scaramella and Conger 2003). In an interesting and comprehensive study of the etiology of juvenile offending, for example, the parenting styles and childhood behaviors were assessed in a population sample of over 13,000 children aged 4 to 11 years (Brannigan *et al.* 2002). The contextual variables of family dysfunction, structure, social support, and socioeconomic status also were considered. The findings showed some effect of family structure on child outcomes. Independent of other factors, however, hostile parenting was a significant contributor to misconduct (destruction of property, stealing, lying, cheating, and vandalism) and aggression (defiance, fighting, kicking, biting, hitting) at every age across childhood. Haskett and Willoughby (2006) suggest that hostile parenting may affect the child's social information processing in much the same way as insecure attachment, adding to the child's internal working model of the social world as hostile. Social information processing theory (to be discussed further in this chapter) suggests that children who experience hostile parenting will tend to be hypervigilant to hostile cues and attribute hostile intent to others (Dodge *et al.* 1986). An angry coercive style of social interaction, one characterized by attempts to manipulate or control another person's behavior in an angry and aggressive manner, may then be adopted.

Coercive control is a core aspect of hostile parenting. Coercive parenting describes parent–child interactions that are characterized by the use of coercive control tactics during discipline (Patterson 1982; Patterson, Reid and Dishion 1998). It is most often evidenced in discipline episodes in which both the child and the parent attempt to control the other's behaviors through the use of intimidating, angry, or hostile strategies such as demands and threats. Coercive interaction cycles develop through mutual reinforcement. To reduce oppositional or non-compliant behavior, parents give in to children's demands, and to reduce tensions, they may ignore children's aggressive behaviors. Coercive parenting teaches aggression and antisocial behavior through reinforcing the child's use of coercive tactics. The child learns the value of demands, aggression, and intimidation for maintaining relationships, and dealing with conflict. It is a lesson that the child uses for peer relationships in school, dating relationships in later adolescence, and adult interpersonal relationships. There is considerable evidence to support Patterson's coercion model. Coercive parenting is a strong predictive of antisocial aggressive behaviors among children and adolescents (Bor and Sanders 2004; George, Herman and Ostrander 2006). And interventions that reduce coercive parenting also reduce the antisocial behavior of children (Barber 2004). Early coercive parenting is seen as a distal cause of adult psychological abuse and domestic violence (Schwartz *et al.* 2006). It is highly likely that it is coercive parenting that accounts, at least in part, for the observed intergenerational continuity of hostile parenting (Scaramella and Conger 2003).

It is worth noting that the association between Baumrind's parenting types and child outcomes consistently has been found across time and culture and with both male and female children (Covell and Howe 2001a). Democratic parenting is associated with positive outcomes in a wide variety of cultures including the United States, Australia, Argentina, China, Hong Kong, Pakistan, and Scotland (Steinberg 2001). Especially compelling are the findings from a recent comprehensive review of studies examining Baumrind's parenting typology and child outcomes that were undertaken in collectivist cultures in which interdependence is valued, and individualistic cultures in which independence is valued (Sorkhabi 2005). Two important commonalities emerged from the review. One is that children and adolescents across cultures interpret authoritarian parenting behaviors in the same way. Adolescents in collectivist cultures, like their peers in individualistic cultures, perceive authoritarian parents' lack of warmth, lack of autonomy and support, and their high levels of control, as undesirable and hostile. They do not, as some had suggested previously, see these behaviors as a necessary part of the preservation of order, harmony, or similar cultural values (Sorkhabi 2005). The second commonality across cultures follows from this. Authoritarian parenting is associated with the same negative developmental outcomes across cultures. In particular, authoritarian parenting in any culture appears to produce aggressive children. It may well be that a primary reason for the robustness of the findings is a result of the use of corporal punishment by authoritarian parents.

CORPORAL PUNISHMENT

Parents who emphasize control, who have attitudes that devalue their children, and who expect immediate child compliance, are those most likely to use corporal punishment (Gershoff 2002). There would appear to be many such parents. Despite the almost global ratification of the Convention, the expressed concerns of the UN Committee on the Rights of the Child, and an increasing number of countries legally banning the use of corporal punishment, the reported prevalence rates of its use remain alarmingly high. Ateah and Durrant (2005) report the following prevalence estimates: Canada 51 percent, Greece 61 percent, Northern Ireland 87 percent, United States 60 to 90 percent, and approximately 90 percent in Hong Kong, New Zealand, and the United Kingdom. The use of corporal punishment sometimes starts very early in the child's life and tends to stabilize across childhood (Vittrup, Holden and Buck 2006). Phillips and Alderson (2003) report that in the United Kingdom more than half of all infants have been hit before reaching their first birthday, and three-quarters before their second birthday. In the United States between 29 and 50 percent of parents admit to researchers that they have hit their 12-month-old (Vittrup *et al.* 2006). And sometimes, corporal punishment is a lot more than a slap on the buttocks. In their study of recalled corporal punishment among American university students, Bower-Russa, Knutson and Winebarger (2001) report that 21 percent met the objective criteria for having been severely physically punished in their childhood.

Reported country prevalence rates provide only general patterns of the use of corporal punishment. They may be misleading. First, there are regional variations in the use of corporal punishment within countries (Covell 2005). For example, in Canada, in the province of Quebec, 22 percent of parents report using corporal punishment whereas in the province of Alberta, 60 percent report its use. And although the overall rates of reported use of corporal punishment in the US are very high, at least one state, Minnesota, has attempted to put restrictions on its use. Second, estimates are usually based on parent reports and therefore subject to recall error and to concerns with social desirability (Durrant *et al.* 2004). Third is the related concern of method of reporting: some researchers have asked parents through interviews and some through surveys, and some in person and some by telephone. Under-reporting is more likely in some of these methods, for example in-person interviews, than in others, for example, anonymous surveys (Durrant *et al.* 2004). Finally, there is variation in what is meant by corporal punishment, and parents' beliefs about what constitutes a slap or a hit or spanking can be very different. Elizabeth Gershoff (2002) notes that parents may understand spanking to consist of one slap on a child's buttocks, or repeated slaps with a hand, or slaps with an object. Researchers do not always precisely define their terms. Moreover, researchers rarely include concomitant parent behaviors such as yelling, humiliating, or making threats that may magnify the effects of corporal punishment (Gershoff 2002). Nonetheless, consistent reports of parental use of corporal punishment (especially by mothers) and of negative outcomes of its use permeate the child-rearing literature.

In the following discussion, we consider corporal punishment to be on a continuum of physically power assertive whose other end is abuse. It has been suggested that there are no real distinctions between physical abuse and corporal punishment in terms of force, parental intent, or extent of injury (Durrant *et al.* 2004). This may well be true. We consider corporal punishment separately here, however, since in the literature it is seen as the major risk factor for abuse, rather than as abuse itself (Trocme *et al.* 2001). For the most part, the literature shows tacit agreement with Straus' definition of corporal punishment as "the use of physical force with the intention of causing a child to experience pain but not injury for the purposes of correction or control of the child's behavior" (Straus 1994, p.4). The intention, of course, is misguided, and the results are antithetical to those desired. The child's behavior is neither corrected nor controlled. The child learns aggression and violence.

There are four primary ways in which children learn to be aggressive or violent when their parents use corporal punishment to "correct and control." One is by providing a model of aggression as problem-solving. Bandura's (1973) observational learning theory implies that when parents use corporal punishment on their children, they are teaching their children that aggression is an appropriate and effective means of expressing one's displeasure at another's behavior, and of controlling others. And as Gershoff (2002) points out, parental aggressiveness is highly likely to be imitated because children tend to imitate aggressive models, and because children are prone to imitate their parents. It is particularly ironic that the most frequent reason parents use corporal punishment is to stop child aggressive behavior (Gershoff 2002).

A second means to teaching aggression through corporal punishment is by focussing the child's attention on the consequences of the behavior rather than the behavior itself. Parents who primarily respond to misconduct with corporal punishment are inhibiting the development of the child's internal controls. The child is not told why the behavior is inappropriate, or its effects on others, or how to make reparation. Corporal punishment does not teach the child how to behave; it does little to promote the internalization of moral or socially acceptable standards for behavior. Rather, corporal punishment teaches the child that certain behaviors, if noticed, elicit punishment. As a result, the child learns to evaluate the consequences of misconduct in terms of the likelihood of discovery and punishment, rather than harm to others (Swinford *et al.* 2000). Aggression is fine, the child learns, if the punisher is absent. Adam, to whom you were introduced at the beginning of this book, made a cogent observation about his prison mates. Those who feel bad about their behavior, he told us, you can help. But those who only feel bad about being caught, are beyond help.

A third means, based on social control theory, is related (Gershoff 2002). Socialization strategies are assumed to be a major determinant of the development of self-control. Children who do not internalize values and standards of behavior tend not to develop good self-control. Those with low self-control tend to make behavioral choices that focus on immediate gratification. Low self-control, then, is expected to predispose the child toward aggressive behaviors, or to criminal behaviors in an older child, because long-term costs and effects on others are not considered.

The fourth means to aggression stems from the effect of corporal punishment on the parent–child relationship. As noted in the previous chapter, a positive parent–child relationship characterized by trust elicits compliance. When a parent uses corporal punishment, the child may feel pain, anger, fear, and distress (Gershoff 2002). These negative emotions can lead the child to ignore or avoid the parent, or can evoke retaliatory aggression (Berkowitz 1983; Snyder and Patterson 1986). The damage to the parent–child relationship wrought by these negative emotions, and their behavioral consequences, undermines the parent's ability to elicit compliance from the child. The more the child associates the parent with pain, the more the child avoids the parent, the less the child trusts the parent, the less compliant the child will become. How these mechanisms interact in their effect is not clear in the literature. It is clear, however, that the parental use of corporal punishment has a profound impact on the development and maintenance of aggressive behaviors.

Much of the research examining the developmental effects of parental use of corporal punishment has been focussed on the behavioral outcomes of aggression. Researchers examining parenting socialization styles and child outcomes from the 1950s to the present consistently have demonstrated a relation between the use of corporal punishment and increased levels of aggression (Covell and Howe 2001a). Corporal punishment has been associated with increased aggression in childhood, with both peer and sibling aggression, with elevated levels of aggression in adolescence, and with aggression or violence in romantic relationships in adolescence and adulthood (Durrant et al. 2004; Gershoff 2002). Studies that have examined the etiology of criminal antisocial and violent behaviors have identified parental use of corporal punishment as a childhood predictor of subsequent offending (Gershoff 2002). A brief examination of some typical studies is illustrative.

Roy Herrenkohl and his colleagues (Herrenkohl, Egolf and Herrenkohl 1997) conducted a 16-year longitudinal study whose goal was to identify early indications of adolescent problem behaviors. They assessed the quality of mother–child relationships, the mother's discipline style, and evidence of abuse and neglect, as well as aggressive behaviors among 457 children, starting in 1976/7, when the children were in preschool. In 1990–2, when the children were in adolescence, their aggressive behaviors were assessed. The incidents of aggressive behaviors measured were as follows: being involved in a gang fight, hitting their parents, hitting people at work, hitting with the intent of injuring or killing someone, committing sexual assault, and threatening someone in order to get money or possessions. The data analysis demonstrated that it was maternal use of corporal punishment while the child was of preschool age that predicted the aggressive behaviors of adolescence. The data also provide strong support for the assertion that corporal punishment is a cause of aggression. Whereas there were no differences in the reported levels of aggression at the preschool age, by adolescence there was a strong relation between the severity of corporal punishment experienced and aggressive behaviors displayed. In particular, the more severe the corporal punishment received during the preschool years, the higher the level of physical assaults committed during later adolescence.

Eamon and Mulder (2005) also identified parental use of corporal punishment to be an indicator of behavior problems. These researchers examined the predictors of antisocial aggressive behaviors among Latino adolescents aged 10 to 14 years. In the US, Latino adolescents often face multiple risks including having single mothers, living in poverty, and living in disadvantaged neighborhoods. Taking the ecological systems perspective, the researchers assessed sociodemographic variables and the broader social environment as well as parenting practices to determine predictors of antisocial outcomes in adolescence. Antisocial outcomes measured included the aggressive behaviors of cruelty, bullying and meanness (measured separately), poor relations with teachers, non-compliance, lack of concern for others, and destruction of property. The findings were clear. When compared with their equally disadvantaged, but less harshly disciplined peers, the adolescents whose mothers had used corporal punishment as a discipline strategy were three times more likely to exhibit antisocial aggressive behaviors and poor interpersonal functioning

The effects of early corporal punishment are as clearly in evidence in adult relationships. Consistently over time, studies have demonstrated that experiencing corporal punishment as a child, regardless of its severity, is a significant predictor of violence against a partner in late adolescence and adulthood (Caesar 1988; Downs *et al.* 1992; Lavoie *et al.* 2002; Sigelman, Berry and Wiles 1984; Simons, Lin and Gordon 1998; Straus and Kaufman-Kantor 1994; Straus and Yodanis 1996; Swinford *et al.* 2000). The study by Steven Swinford and his colleagues (2000) exemplifies the findings. They used data from a longitudinal study of a representative sample of 942 adolescents between the ages of 12 and 19, who had been followed since 1982. An impressive 721 were available for re-interview in 1992/3. Those in a couple relationship, married, cohabitating, or dating (608 of the 721) were interviewed to examine possible links among experiencing harsh corporal punishment in childhood, problem behaviors in adolescence, and perpetrating violence against a partner in adulthood. Harsh physical punishment was defined as being hit with closed fist or object, spanked with belt or strap, thrown against a wall, and physically injured. It was found that harsh physical punishment had direct effects on problem behaviors, which in turn affected the perpetration of violence against a partner. These data confirm previous suggestions that children who are the victims of corporal punishment generalize their learning about aggressive behavior such that they develop a general pattern of antisocial behavior whose hallmark characteristic is violence against others.

There have been some suggestions in the literature that the link between corporal punishment and negative outcomes would not be seen in cultures where its use is more commonly accepted (Gershoff 2002). More recent analyses suggest that although the effects of corporal punishment vary across cultures, in all cultures parental use of corporal punishment is associated with child aggression. And there is little likelihood that it is the child aggression that causes the corporal punishment. Researchers from the US, Hong Kong, Sweden, Italy, Thailand, and India examined whether cultural norms for corporal punishment moderate the link between mother's use of corporal punishment and child outcomes (Lansford *et al.* 2005). They conducted interviews with 336 mother–child dyads, whose children ranged from 6 to 17 years old, in China, India, Italy, Kenya, the Phillipines, and Thailand. The countries were chosen to represent differences in the following: predominant religion, ideology, child welfare legislation, and the extent to which the culture was characterized by an individualistic or collectivist orientation. Each of these dimensions has been associated with parenting practices. Corporal punishment in this research was defined as spanking, slapping, grabbing, shaking, and beating up. Consistent with the researchers' expectations, the countries differed in the reported use and normativeness of corporal punishment. Mothers in Thailand (predominantly Buddhist) reported the least use of corporal punishment, whereas those in Kenya (with a history of harsh physical discipline) reported the most. Also as hypothesized, more frequent use of corporal punishment was less strongly associated with child aggression (fighting and bullying) when it was perceived to be the cultural norm, but the association remained. In fact, in all countries, greater use of corporal punishment was associated with child aggression. These findings are consistent with Rohner's (1986) acceptance–rejection theory, and with the findings of Sorkhabi (2005) discussed above. Children's perception of parental rejection is a powerful determinant of behavior. And cultural norms, ideologies, or religions do not fully override the rejection children feel when they are parented in an authoritarian manner and punished physically. Despite these essentially uniform negative responses to receiving corporal punishment, there remains around a 30 percent transgenerational persistence rate in the use of corporal punishment (Bower-Russa *et al.* 2001).

There is a pattern of transgenerational beliefs about parenting style, including the appropriateness of corporal punishment (Gershoff 2002). An international study of university students sheds light on this transgenerational transmission. Attitudes supportive of the use of corporal punishment are primarily a function of a personal history of being a recipient of corporal punishment, and being in a culture in which its use is accepted (Douglas 2006). It is this belief in the acceptability of hitting children that increases the likelihood of parental use of corporal punishment (Ateah and Durrant 2005; Bower-Russa *et al.* 2001; Vittrup *et al.* 2006). Ateah and Durrant (2005) examined the hypothesized distal causes (history of receiving and approval of its use) and proximal causes of corporal punishment (type of child misconduct, attribution of misconduct, and parent's mood) with a sample of 110 mothers with three-year-old children. Approval of the use of corporal punishment was the strongest predictor of its use. Other research shows that the more strongly parents approve of physical punishment, the more harshly they administer it (Durrant *et al.* 2004). But where does this approval come from when children feel rejected in response to corporal punishment?

The literature would seem to suggest that a key problem is that children seem to feel that they deserve the punishment they receive. This is strongly suggested by the findings of a study of 18- to 20-year-old university students in the United States (Bower-Russa *et al.* 2001). Twenty-one percent of the students met the objective criteria for having been severely physically punished during their childhood. Most of these students saw this punishment as normal rather than excessively harsh. What was most illuminating in their data was that students were least likely to consider an act abusive if it was an act they had experienced themselves. Such acts included being hit with an object such as a strap or a belt. This failure to see these parental behaviors as abusive no doubt provides some psychological comfort to the recipients of them, but at the same time it seems to indicate acceptance of potentially injurious disciplinary behaviors. These findings highlight the importance of children everywhere, and their parents, being aware of children's Convention rights and the link between respect for their rights and healthy development. To date, most countries have done little to inform their citizens of children's rights (Howe and Covell 2005). Continued use of corporal punishment across generations implies transmission of risk for aggression among cohorts of children. It also means children at risk for abuse.

The primary risk factor for child physical abuse is parental use of corporal punishment (Covell 2005). There has been a long history of reports showing that parents who have physically abused their children frequently have done so in the context of an episode of corporal punishment (Coontz and Martin 1988; Gil 1970; Kadushin and Martin 1981; Trocme *et al.* 2001). In a national study in Canada, for example, more than 10,000 substantiated cases of child physical abuse (more than two-thirds of all substantiated cases) had taken place within the context of corporal punishment (Trocme *et al.* 2001). In another Canadian study it was found that children who received what many believe to be minor acts of corporal punishment, such as pinching, or spanking, were seven times more likely to experience more injurious forms of corporal punishment, such as kicking, or being hit with an object, compared with children whose parents did not use corporal punishment (Clement *et al.* 2000 cited in Durrant *et al.* 2004). As the vice-chair of the UN Committee on the Rights of the Child said "The line between physical punishment or what is termed 'reasonable chastisement' and abuse or actual physical and mental harm is too fine for the practice to be retained without exposing children to danger of real damage. The use of excessive force and the occurrence of accidental injury is a prevalent reality" (Karp 1999). Part of that "real damage" is elevating the child's risk of a social-interactional style characterized by aggression or violence.

CHILD ABUSE

Child abuse suffers from the same definitional difficulties that led to a commonly used description of pornography as "I'll know it when I see it." There are a variety of legal definitions of abuse and neglect that are used to determine child welfare interventions and custody decisions, and there are psychiatric definitions of physical and sexual abuse and neglect in the *Diagnostic and Statistical Manual of Mental Disorders* (American Psychiatric Association 2000). Researchers do not necessarily adhere to any of these definitions.

As noted above, it has been argued that corporal punishment is indistinguishable from physical abuse (Durrant *et al.* 2004). However, most researchers use a history of physical injury (which may or may not be related to corporal punishment) as their definition of physical abuse (e.g. Bowlus *et al.* 2003; Ehrensaft *et al.* 2003; Jaffee *et al.* 2004). Child physical abuse generally refers to acts such as shaking, hitting, kicking, throwing against walls or doors, and burning with objects such as cigarettes or irons. Definitions of abuse typically do not include physical injury to the child's genitalia or the rectum that are caused by sexual abuse. Nor do definitions usually include the emotional abuse that is, at least in our opinion, an inevitable concomitant of all forms of abuse.

Child sexual abuse most often involves acts in which there is completed or attempted forced sexual activity. It may also include sexual exploitation including involvement in prostitution or the making of pornography (Covell 2005). Child emotional abuse has a very broad definition. It subsumes verbal abuse, threat, humiliation, and neglect. It may also include rejecting, isolating, corrupting, and placing excess pressure on the child (Hamarman and Bernet 2000). Increasingly emotional abuse has come to include exposure to domestic violence which itself has an ever-widening definition. In Canada at this time, for example, exposure to domestic violence includes the child's seeing evidence of injury caused by the violence regardless of whether the child witnessed the actual violence. The emotional impact on children of witnessing violence between their parents should not be underestimated. However, we see this form of abuse as different from the direct attacks on the child that define other forms of child abuse. As such we discuss exposure to violence between parents in the next chapter. Neglect, unlike other forms of abuse, generally describes chronic failure to act rather than inappropriate actions. This includes emotional abuse. Failure to provide for the physical, medical, educational, and psychological needs of children, failure to supervise that results in child injury, permitting criminal behavior, and abandonment are the acts of omission that describe neglect (Hildyard and Wolfe 2002).

Despite the varying definitions and despite the various *foci* of child maltreatment research, some including one type of abuse, some two, and some all, there have been consistent findings of an association between childhood maltreatment and later violent behavior.

SEXUAL ABUSE

Sexual abuse, the least often documented type of abuse but the most clearly defined, is the most researched (Chaffin 2006). Victims of childhood sexual abuse are at heightened risk for many psychological disorders, for interpersonal hostility and aggression, and for sexual offending in adolescence and adulthood (Denov 2004; Roberts *et al.* 2004; Salter *et al.* 2003). The outcomes are most severe where the abuse has continued over time, involved penetration, and where the perpetrator is a member of the child's family. In fact, the dose-dependent nature of the association between chronicity of abuse and severity of outcome is such that it clearly indicates a cause and effect relation (Roberts *et al.* 2004). Although there is some evidence suggesting that the deleterious effects of sexual abuse are more pronounced when there is a history of multiple types of abuse (Walrath *et al.* 2006), childhood sexual abuse has been shown to have unique effects that are independent of the existence of other adversities in the child's life (Roberts *et al.* 2004).

Much of the research on the effects of childhood sexual abuse is concerned with its intergenerational transmission. Being a victim of sexual abuse frequently is identified as a key risk factor for becoming an abuser, particularly among males (e.g. Glasser *et al.* 2001; Hummel *et al.* 2000; Langstrom, Grann and Lindblad 2000; Salter *et al.* 2003). Recent data indicate that childhood sexual abuse of females also has long-term consequences for the next generation through its effects on parenting. A number of researchers have implicated childhood sexual abuse as a risk factor for impaired parenting among women. Of particular concern is that it is the parenting behaviors that are associated with physical abuse that seem to be affected. Mothers who have history of childhood sexual abuse are more likely to use corporal punishment (Banyard, Williams and Siegel 2003; Cole *et al.* 1992), and are more likely to have unrealistic expectations of their children (Cross 2001). Corporal punishment and unrealistic expectations of children's development are strong predictors of physically abusive parenting.

Susan Mapp (2006) examined the relation between being a victim of childhood sexual abuse and subsequent harsh parenting. Her data demonstrate that the effects of sexual abuse in childhood on parenting capacity in adulthood are moderated by three factors. The woman's level of depression and her locus of control were two predictive factors. The third and likely related factor was how well the woman had been able to cope with her history of abuse. Such findings underscore the importance of therapeutic interventions with child victims of sexual abuse. The Convention, in Article 39, requires states to "promote physical and psychological recovery and social reintegration of a child victim of any form of neglect, exploitation or abuse..." In fact we should not expect any individual to recover fully from the effects of childhood sexual abuse without effective therapy.

The provision of therapeutic interventions requires first recognizing that sexual abuse is a problem that poses a serious threat to the healthy development of the child. Whereas such recognition has been the case for female victims of male perpetrators, there is little evidence that female perpetrators and their male victims are given the same attention. The research generally indicates somewhat more severe outcomes for male victims of female perpetrators of sexual abuse (Salter *et al.* 2003). Studies of female perpetrators, however, are few. The reason for this has been explained well by Myriam Denov (2001, 2004). Building on a scant literature, Denov (2001) has shown that professionals, including police and psychiatrists, view the sexual abuse of children by women to be less harmful than sexual abuse by men. The evidence stands in sharp contrast to this view. In Denov's study of male and female victims of sexual abuse perpetrated by a female (mostly family members), harmful outcomes were reported. The average age of onset of the abuse was fve years, and the average duration was six years. As adults, both the male and female victims reported long-term difficulties with substance abuse, self-injurious behavior, rage and anger, and relationship problems. Twenty-nine percent of her sample (males and females) also admitted to sexually abusing children themselves. The difficulties were particularly pronounced, however, for the male victims. They reported that they felt humiliated and needed to compensate for their perceived weakness. As one of her respondents explained: "I studied martial arts, I boxed competitively. I was a really tough kid... By age 12 I was already trafficking and pulling break and enters... It was this distorted idea of what it means to be a man" (Denov 2001, p.1149). And the relationship difficulties experienced are exemplified in the comments of another of the males in the study: "As a man, I'm supposed to be the powerful one...I'm always supposed to have the upper hand" (p.1149).

Denov (2001) calls the failure to acknowledge the harm done by female perpetrators of sexual abuse a "culture of denial." It is also a denial of children's rights. Every child should be protected from abuse, and every child who is abused should receive understanding and assistance with recovery. As Denov (2004) notes, there are four deleterious outcomes that stem from a denial of harm done by female perpetrators of sexual abuse. First, there will be delays of referral to social services. Second, and in consequence, there will be a delay in the provision of therapeutic interventions. Third, where there is denial of consequence, disclosure is much more difficult. Disclosure is of course particularly difficult for male victims in a culture that tends to have difficulty conceiving of a male as a victim of a female.

The fourth outcome is that female perpetrators may continue to have access to children. High-profile cases in the North American media highlight some of Denov's findings.

In the United States, over the past few years, there have been many examples of female schoolteachers charged with the sexual abuse of their students. A brief internet search will list an astonishing number of cases. Too often, even with convictions, sentences are light, and the impact not taken seriously. Many jokes and comments have been made that it is every young boy's dream to have sex with his teacher. The child is seen as lucky rather than as a victim. Probation has been a common response. Among the most publicized, and an exemplar of cases, is that of schoolteacher Debra LaFave in 2004. According to the media, the judge declared her "too pretty to go to jail" despite being convicted of having sex on more than one occasion with a 14-year-old boy. As Denov (2004) stated, professionals tend to alter their perceptions of the female sex offender and her abusive behavior to conform to the culturally acceptable notions of female behavior. Such judicial attitudes are highly discriminatory to young boys, and very much against the Convention's Article 2 principle of non-discrimination.

NEGLECT

A lack of consensus on definitions of abuse is especially apparent in the area of neglect. This may be one reason why, although it is the most frequently documented type of abuse, neglect is also the least researched (Hildyard and Wolfe 2002; Theodore, Runyan and Chang 2007; Tyler, Allison and Winsler 2006). Neglect, the lack of parental care and nurturance, usually starts early, is chronic, and is strongly associated with developmental deficits in all areas of growth (Hildyard and Wolfe 2002). Most studies of neglect use its broadest definition, an overall failure of parental care and attention.

Early studies of institutionalized infants and children provided dramatic evidence of the effects of neglect. Initially the observations were of high death rates among infants (Chapin 1917). As basic conditions improved, death rates decreased. However, it was clear that those who lived past infancy, in addition to health problems, had severe problems with social interaction, emotion regulation, and behavior (Spitz 1945). Since then, where there has been research examining the effects of early neglect, the findings have been similar. The developmental effects have been summarized by Kathryn Hildyard and David Wolfe (2002). In addition to health problems, from infancy through adolescence, children who are neglected show poor impulse control; difficulties with emotion regulation; poor self-worth; non-compliant, oppositional, and aggressive behaviors; and poor peer relationships. By late adolescence and into early adulthood, children with a history of neglect are at risk for running away, criminal offending, and violent criminal behaviors.

In a study of adolescent detainees in Atlanta, Georgia, emotional neglect was not only found to be related to their offending behavior, but also to the likelihood of recidivism (Kingree, Phan and Thompson 2003). The extent to which these outcomes are seen will, of course, depend on the age of the child at the onset of neglect, the duration and the severity of the neglect. The studies of children adopted from the Romanian orphanages under the dictatorship of Nicolae Ceausescu provide evidence of this. The length of time spent in the orphanages, in which all forms of neglect were extreme and pervasive, determined the extent of the children's subsequent social, emotional, and behavioral deficits (De Bellis 2005).

Michael De Bellis (2005) has suggested that the observed effects of neglect on child development result from adverse brain development. Basing his work on comparative studies of maternal deprivation in rats and monkeys, he has been examining the effects of neglect on the developing biological stress response systems. De Bellis is a leader in the new field of developmental traumatology, an area of study that synthesizes knowledge from developmental psychopathology, developmental neuroscience, and stress and trauma research. It seems likely that his work will be a catalyst for further investigation into the effects of neglect.

PHYSICAL ABUSE

Like sexual abuse and neglect, a history of physical abuse has been consistently linked with aggressive and antisocial behavior. From preschool age through to late adolescence, children who have been physically abused tend to show high rates of aggression; uncooperative, disruptive, and oppositional behaviors; and elevated risk of delinquency, and violent criminal offending in adulthood (Egeland *et al.* 2002; Hildyard and Wolfe 2002; Jaffee *et al.* 2004; Kolko 2002). Childhood physical abuse by mothers to their sons, also has been linked with an increased likelihood of adult partner violence (Holmes and Sammel 2005).

Questions have been raised about the nature of the observed link between the physical abuse of children and violence in adulthood. Is there some sort of genetic transmission of aggressivity that accounts for both the physical abuse and the violence, or does the physical abuse actually cause the antisocial aggressive behavior? Sara Jaffee and her colleagues addressed this question in a well-designed and comprehensive study of 1116 twin pairs and their parents (Jaffee *et al.* 2004). Parents reported on the physical maltreatment of each child by the age of five years, and both parents and teachers reported on the child's aggressivity when the child was five and seven years old. As in the corporal punishment research, their findings provide compelling evidence of a causal relation between physical abuse and the development of aggression. In their study physical maltreatment prospectively predicted antisocial behaviors in a dose-dependent relation, and the effects of physical maltreatment remained significant after controlling for the parents' history of antisocial behavior. The researchers conclude that the intergenerational cycle of violence could be broken and rates of violence reduced if the physical maltreatment of children stopped. Unfortunately, official statistics of child maltreatment are high, and parental reports suggest that the reality is even higher (e.g. Theodore *et al.* 2005). Moreover, most assessments of child maltreatment suggest that it is unusual for a child to be subjected to only one type. Most children who are abused experience multiple types of maltreatment (Walrath *et al.* 2006).

CHILD MALTREATMENT

Much of the published research on child abuse has used the umbrella term of "child maltreatment," and examined the effects of more than one type of abuse. Most frequent are physical abuse and neglect since they most often tend to co-occur (Chaffin 2006). Children who are abused and neglected are at elevated risk for seriously impaired psychological, social, and behavioral development (Zielinski and Bradshaw 2006). Antisocial and aggressive behavior, criminal behavior, dating and partner violence are among the outcomes of childhood maltreatment (Huefner *et al.* 2007; Kingree *et al.* 2003; Wolfe *et al.* 2004; Zielinski and Bradshaw 2006).

The chronicity of the maltreatment is a key factor in determining the extent of its negative outcomes. It is an especially important consideration since much maltreatment persists over a considerable period of the child's early life. Researchers assessing the effects of the chronicity of maltreatment have defined chronicity on a continuum from one to 14 years of age, and as with studies of single types of abuse, have noted a dose-dependent relation between maltreatment and the extent of consequent behavior problems (Ethier, Lemelin and Lacharite 2004). Chronicity of maltreatment predicts high levels of aggression reported by children's peers and teachers, and even by the children themselves (Bolger and Patterson 2001; Ethier *et al.* 2004; Manly, Cicchetti and Barnett 1994). Moreover, in some cases, the aggressiveness is at clinically significant levels (Ethier *et al.* 2004). There are indications in the research that early interventions that significantly lessen the maltreatment, and thereby its chronicity, can have an impact on lessening the associated aggression in childhood. Without interventions, chronically maltreated children may be on a developmental pathway that will lead them to relationship violence in adolescence and adulthood. And violent behavior to a romantic partner appears to be very resistant to treatment (Dunford 2000).

Child maltreatment has been identified as an especially strong predictor of later interpersonal violence. Victims of childhood maltreatment are especially at risk of becoming adolescent and adult perpetrators of intimate partner violence (Huefner *et al.* 2007; Wolfe *et al.* 2004). Dating violence in both its more mild form of insults, threats, and intimidation, and its more severe form of physical and sexual assault, is quite prevalent in mid-adolescence (Wolfe *et al.* 2004). It is particularly prevalent among adolescents with a history of maltreatment. And perhaps surprisingly, adolescent girls are found to perpetrate dating violence as frequently as do adolescent males (Chase, Treboux and O'Leary 2002; Halpern *et al.* 2001).

In a one-year study of 1317 high school students aged 14 to 19 years, child maltreatment and the perpetration of dating violence were assessed for boys and girls (Wolfe *et al.* 2004). The adolescents' history of maltreatment (all forms of abuse) and dating behaviors were assessed in addition to three hypothesized mediating factors: trauma symptoms (e.g. anger, anxiety, stress, assumed to stem from childhood maltreatment), attitudes justifying dating violence, and empathy/self-efficacy with dating partner. Data were collected at two times, one year apart. Given the rapidity of partner change among this age group, this allowed for assessment of a more general pattern of dating behavior than would be possible with a one-time measure. A one-time measure may limit information to the properties of a particular couple. Only one of the three mediating factors predicted the pattern of dating violence over time, that of trauma symptoms. However, within that, there was a gender difference. Trauma symptoms were a significant predictor of dating violence over time for boys. But for girls, it was specifically trauma-related anger that was a significant mediator between childhood maltreatment and dating violence over time. Girls with high levels of trauma-related anger were likely to show increases in the perpetration of dating violence over the year of the study. This physical expression of anger in relationships is likely to continue. In a 20-year longitudinal study of the inter-generational transmission of partner violence, a history of maltreatment, in particular of physical injury by a caregiver, directly increased the likelihood of violent conflict resolution strategies with a partner (Ehrensaft *et al.* 2003).

The extreme manifestation of a history of maltreatment is evidenced in children who kill. Almost three decades ago, Farrington and West (1981) provided evidence of a significant association between a history of severe maltreatment in childhood and the commission of violent crime in adolescence and adulthood. Since then there has been growing concern about children who commit homicides. The concern has been especially great in the United States where rates of homicides by children, although still low, have been increasing since the 1980s (Heide 2003; Shumaker and Prinz 2000). [We note here that in the US, while adult homicide rates have been dropping overall, the homicide rate of children, especially of infants and usually by their parents, has been increasing (Pritchard and Butler 2003).] It is a concern that is played out in media reporting of high-profile murder cases such as those of Jamie Bulger in England and Reena

Virk in Canada (described in Chapter 4). And perhaps even greater concern is elicited by the sensationalistic, extensive, and frequent media coverage of cases where young people kill their parents. The case of Lyle and Eric Menendez in California is illustrative. The Menendez brothers were convicted of the 1989 murder of their parents, Jose and Kitty. As noted by Boots and Heide (2006), the trials were extensively covered, dominating television reporting and print media headlines for many years. It is a concern that is reflected also in a growing research literature in which efforts are made to identify the factors associated with youth homicide. Why do children murder?

First, as many researchers have noted (e.g. Heide 2003), younger murderers, especially those younger than age nine or ten, are not cognitively mature enough to understand that death is irreversible. There are also too few of them to allow analysis of causes. The literature, then, for the most part, deals with children between the ages of 10 and 18 years. It is also the case that much of the research has focussed on boys who kill. Where there has been analysis of girls who kill, the indications are that girls are more likely than boys to kill family members or to use accomplices to kill family members (Heide 2003). The findings, then, are based primarily on male preadolescent and adolescent children. Researchers have found a variety of personality characteristics, mood disorders, levels of psychopathy and intellectual functioning among such children who have been convicted of murder (e.g. Heide 2003; Walsh, Beyer and Petee 2001). However, what holds greater predictive power than any of these, and the commonality among cases, is a history of abuse (Davis 2003; Kelly and Totten 2002; Walsh et al. 2001; Wolff and McCall Smith 2001). Children who kill tend to have a long history of severe and multiple maltreatment. This is particularly apparent in cases where the child has killed a parent.

The media reported that the Menendez brothers killed their parents to obtain freedom and money. However, court records show a long history of very hostile parenting, emotional abuse, and exposure to spousal violence. In addition, the boys' behaviors suggest the possibility of serious psychological problems and/or sexual abuse. There was significant evidence of difficulties at school, of bed-wetting (at age 14), and of the type of age-inappropriate sexual behavior that often is associated with a history of childhood sexual abuse.

Denise Boots and Kathleen Heide (2006) undertook a content analysis of 226 incidents of parricide (killing of a parent) that had been presented in the media. Analyzing the 43 percent of these cases in which the perpetrator was identified as younger than 18 years of age, they found that a long-standing history of abuse and multiple types of abuse were the common factors in the backgrounds of those convicted of parricide. In the words of Walsh and his colleagues (2001), a history of severe and multiple maltreatment by a parent is "a diagnostic marker of dangerousness" (p.391).

Overall, the data demonstrate quite clearly that children who are poorly parented are at risk for becoming violent. Children who are parented in an authoritarian manner, who are rejected or treated with hostility; children who are physically punished, children who are sexually abused, neglected, or physically abused, are all at risk for developing poor social and problem-solving skills. Depending on factors such as severity and chronicity, the social and problem-solving skills deficits tend to be manifest in physical and relational aggression from early childhood through adulthood in ways that disrupt or preclude healthy peer relationships, intimate partner relationships, and parenting behaviors. For some, the deficits will lead to violent criminal offending. The consistency of findings across types of poor parenting and maltreatment implicates underlying neural processes. The child's basic capacity for emotion and behavioral regulation, and for social information processing, appears to be affected.

SOCIAL INFORMATION PROCESSING

It has been suggested that the most deleterious effect of childhood maltreatment is seen in the child's deficits in social information processing (Dodge, Bates and Petit 1990). There is significant evidence for this assertion. As discussed, poor and abusive parenting is associated with neurological impairments in systems that are involved in emotion regulation, learning, and memory. Inappropriate parenting also is related to early onset life-course persistent aggressive antisocial behaviors. Stable patterns of social judgments and behaviors extend to adulthood (Fontaine 2006). Social information processing may well be the link between the child's rearing experiences, neurological integrity, and behavioral patterns. Social information processing develops early and has a major impact on the child's social behaviors. Maladaptive social information processing reflects deficits with emotion regulation and memory, and predicts antisocial aggressive behaviors.

The child's neurological status places constraints on the child's ability to develop effective social information skills. In addition, how children initially learn to understand social information depends on what they have observed in the family, and what kinds of behaviors they have been reinforced for (Bandura 1986). When parents use coercive tactics or corporal punishment, when they neglect, reject, or abuse the child, the child's processing of social information will be affected. It is unlikely that the child will learn how to interpret social behaviors in anything but a negative way, and in consequence, the child must be expected to have difficulty responding to others appropriately. In essence, experiences in the family that are hostile, aggressive, and conflictful will result in aggression-prone social information processing (Losel, Bliesener and Bender 2007).

Social information processing theory regards the child as an active interpreter of social information. Like a computer, data are input, processing occurs in accord with programming and memory, and there is selected output. When in a social situation such as playing with another child, behaviors—especially in response to ambiguous situations such as being knocked over—are determined after a non-conscious progression through discrete information processing steps. The six steps in the process, proposed by Kenneth Dodge and his colleagues (Crick and Dodge 1994; Dodge et al. 1990; Dodge and Schwartz 1997), are as follows. First, social information cues are encoded. Second, the cues are interpreted to attribute causality and intent. Third, goals of the interaction are identified to determine what would be in the child's best interests. Fourth, possible responses to achieve the goal are generated. Fifth, the possible goals are evaluated in terms of their likelihood of achieving the desired goal, and one is selected. Sixth, the selected response is acted upon. It is a decision-making protocol in which maladaptive processing at any step may lead to aggressive behavior. Specific deficits at each stage that are related to aggressive behavior have been identified (Lansford et al. 2006). At the input stage, the primary deficits are excess attention to hostile cues, and the attribution of hostile, rather than benign, intent ("He knocked me over to hurt me because he's mean"). At the processing stage, there tends to be a focus on the selection of instrumental (e.g. to obtain something for self) rather than interpersonal goals (e.g. to maintain a friendship), and the generation of a high proportion of possible responses that are aggressive ("I'll show him I'm stronger than he is, I can knock him over, push him and punch his face"). Finally, the output—the selected and acted upon response—is aggressive ("I'll punch his nose"). This pattern has been shown repeatedly, especially with boys.

When compared with their non-aggressive peers, aggressive boys have been found to have more maladaptive processing in all six steps. When aggressive boys encode situational cues, they encode more aggression-relevant information, and remember more aggression-relevant details of the situation (Losel *et al.* 2007). When interpreting the cues, they attribute more hostile intent to the other's behavior. In identifying a goal, aggressive boys are egocentric and often antisocial. Aggressive boys, more frequently than others, explain their responses as attempts to get even, get revenge, to dominate, or control the interaction: maintaining friendship is not a response goal (Losel *et al.* 2007; Nas, de Castro and Koops 2005). Again, in the fourth stage when possible responses are being generated, aggressive boys are hostile and antisocial in what they access. In the evaluation and selection of a response, aggressive boys anticipate positive consequences from aggression. The final action, then, is aggressive (Nas *et al.* 2005). Recent research suggests that the strongest link between social information processing deficits and aggressive behavior stems from difficulties with the fourth stage in which the child is retrieving possible responses from memory (Losel *et al.* 2007). This is really not surprising. Since most of the children will have histories of some form of abuse, they must also be expected to have an internal working model of the social world as hostile. The anticipation of hostility, the attribution of hostility, and the experience of hostility must be expected to bias what is stored in memory.

In some research a distinction has been made between subtypes of aggression and social information processing. For example, Fontaine (2006) reports findings that reactively aggressive children (those who respond to social cues with aggression) have more difficulties with encoding cues and generating non-aggressive responses. Children who are proactively aggressive (those such as bullies who use aggression to achieve a goal) have more difficulty with the latter stages of the social information processing sequence. Bullies show very high positive evaluations of aggression, and are most likely to see aggression as an appropriate means to achieve their (instrumental) goals. Whether these differences can be accounted for by variations in histories of maltreatment is not clear in the research. However, that aggressive children have a history of maltreatment, and that they have difficulty with social information processing, is clear.

Although the focus of the social information processing model is cognitive, difficulty with emotion regulation is an integral aspect of both biased attributions and aggressive behaviors (de Castro *et al.* 2005). And difficulty with emotion regulation consistently has been identified as stemming from poor and inadequate or abusive parenting (e.g. Teicher *et al.* 2003; Watts-English *et al.* 2006). To study the emotional aspects of social information processing, de Castro *et al.* (2005) compared 7- to 13-year-old boys who had aggressive behavior problems, with a group of non-aggressive boys. Using the model described above, the researchers found the expected pattern of differences between the aggressive and comparison boys at each stage of processing, and they found emotion differences. Their data demonstrated that the aggressive boys expressed more hostility, more anger, more happiness, and less guilt than the comparison group. The aggressive boys also described less adaptive emotion regulation strategies than did their non-aggressive peers.

In essence, the findings from the social information processing research with boys demonstrate quite clearly that the choices, feelings, and behaviors are a direct reflection of the child's socialization history. Social information processing also is a strong predictor of future aggression and violence, especially violent and sexual offending (e.g. Hanson and Harris 2000). It is noteworthy that similar maladaptive patterns of social information processing are found for physical aggression, verbal aggression, and violent criminal offenses (Losel *et al.* 2007). Whether the same pattern holds for girls has not been established. It has been suggested that one reason females show lower rates of violent crime is due to their superior social information processing skills. Two explanations are offered for the gender difference in social information processing. One is that female infants and young children are less vulnerable than are males to neurological damage because of their earlier brain maturation. The second is that boys and girls are differentially socialized by parents in ways that advantage the development of effective social information processing among girls (Bennet, Farrington and Huesmann 2005). This is an intriguing idea, but one with very limited support at this time.

Lansford and her colleagues (Lansford *et al.* 2006) assessed the social information processing patterns of 576 male and female children when they were in kindergarten, and when they were in grades 3, 8, and 11. On the basis of their responses to vignettes, the children were categorized into four groups: no social processing problems, early onset problems, later onset, and pervasive problems. Gender was significantly associated with social information processing style in kindergarten and grade 11. Only at those ages were girls less likely than boys to display maladaptive processing. Moreover, overriding the effect of gender was ethnicity. At all times of measure, except grade 11, African-American children were more likely to display social information processing deficits. This ethnic group also is over-represented in behavior problems and in living in high-risk family circumstances as will be referred to in Chapter 5.

Perhaps what is most useful about the Lansford study is the demonstration that social information processing can be assessed while children are in kindergarten. This allows the identification of children who need, and have a right to, intervention. There is evidence that altering the child's style of social information processing can lessen aggressive behaviors (Lansford *et al.* 2006), and thereby lessen the likelihood of affiliation with deviant peers through school. What has been shown to be particularly effective are interventions that focus both on improving the child's cognition and improving the parenting that the child is receiving at home (Bennet *et al.* 2005). Such interventions need to occur early before full brain maturation.

Parents need to be given support and provided education on how to socialize their children without hostility, without corporal punishment, and without any form of abuse. Only when children's rights to positive parenting and protection from abuse are realized, will the cycle of interpersonal violence be reduced.

CHAPTER 4

VIOLENCE IN THE FAMILY

*Adults try to blame the video games and the internet. I think
you learn more from your parents. Witnessing violence teaches
you violence and makes you hate.*

Many children who took part in the focus groups held as part of the
United Nations Secretary-General's Study on Violence Against Children
expressed their beliefs about the hypocrisy of adults (Covell 2006). In
particular the children expressed their frustration at the modeling of
violence by their parents. Parents, they said, hit their children; they
yell at each other, and they take out their distress on their children.
Then, they said, when they see their children acting aggressively, they
blame the media. Parents, the young people said, need to take responsibility for their children's violent behavior. Children learn violence
from their parents. Their observations are astute and empirically
supported in the research literature. The focus of this chapter is on
children's exposure to intimate partner violence and the frequently
comorbid risk factors of parental substance abuse, criminality, and
mental health problems: each is a risk factor for the intergenerational
transmission of violence in families.

The Convention on the Rights of the Child recognizes the family
as the natural environment for raising children. In the preamble, it is
specified that for optimum development children "should grow up in
a family environment, in an atmosphere of happiness, love and understanding." Article 18 states that parents "have the primary responsibility for the upbringing and development of the child. The best
interests of the child will be their basic concern." Being aware that this
is not always the case, the Convention requires there be legislation to
protect children from all forms of maltreatment as described in the

previous chapter. The Convention states that parents should be provided assistance as needed to help them fulfill their parenting responsibilities.

In a partial step towards consistency with the Convention's obligations, many jurisdictions now have expanded their definitions of child abuse and neglect to include the child being exposed, directly or indirectly, to parental violence (e.g. Edleson, Gassman-Pines and Hill 2006). This means that children exposed to parental violence in the home can be referred to child protection services, and that their parents can be held to account for failure to protect their children. However, the capacity of policy-makers to effect appropriate interventions and treatments has been seriously hampered by a number of factors including the politicization of domestic violence.

In the first chapter of this book, we pointed out that taking a rights-based approach to programs and policies requires that they be evidence-based. It is of course necessary that the evidence be available. When social scientists undertake their research in biased ways, when ideology is given primacy over objectivity, then evidence is lacking. Biased research guided by stereotyped beliefs about men and women is especially pervasive in studies that have examined the effect on children of violence between their parents. Until recently, the term "domestic violence" generally has referred to male perpetrators of violence against women. It has rarely included female perpetrators of violence against men, or violence in same-sex relationships. And rarely has the term included violence against children. Yet community statistics indicate that perpetration rates of partner violence are approximately equal by men and women (although women are more likely to suffer serious injury), that partner violence occurs in same-sex relationships as well as heterosexual ones, and that rates of violence against children, especially by their mothers, are the highest of all rates of family, or "domestic" violence. For example, in both the United States and Canada, the chance of being a victim of family homicide is greatest in the first year of life (Covell 2005).

The more recently adopted label of "intimate partner violence" may be an improvement in that it more accurately reflects the focus on the couple. In addition it is a more inclusive term allowing for violence between same-sex partners and unmarried partners. Nonetheless, many researchers continue to focus only on male-perpetrated violence against women, thus perpetuating the myth of violence as a property of maleness. The implications of such bias, and the resultant myth, are seen in a number of ways. One is a lack of sufficient attention to male victims of intimate partner violence. A second is a lack of sufficient attention to children whose mothers are violent. A third is an insufficiency of programs such as anger management and conflict resolution training being available for women who could benefit from them. Fourth, a continued discounting of female violence may be sending a message to children that it is acceptable for a woman to be violent—to her intimate partner, and to her children. Fifth, parents in lesbian or gay relationships may be unable to obtain protection and assistance in which case their children will also be denied protection. And perhaps most important in context, disregard of maternal or female partner violence likely may well increase the modeling and imitation of interpersonal violence. From a children's rights perspective, if the outcome variable of the research is the effect of partner violence on the child, then a child-centered approach would seem most objective. In the best interests of the child, the research must become de-politicized. Objective evidence is a prerequisite of effective prevention and intervention.

INTIMATE PARTNER VIOLENCE

The status of research on intimate partner violence (IPV) is in some ways similar to that of youth violence in the 1950s. During that period, most of the research on violent adolescents was done with male youth because it was assumed that females were unlikely to be violent. Although this may still hold true to some extent, the evidence, at least from the North America, shows a pattern of significant increases in all forms of violence among adolescent girls, an increase that outpaces that of males (Graves 2007). As a consequence, violence among female youth is now given much more attention, and those who study youth violence no longer understand violence to be a characteristic of maleness. Adolescent girls are quite capable of violent behaviors. We are reminded of the brutal killing of 14-year-old Reena Virk, in British Columbia, Canada. Reena Virk, an immigrant to Canada, was the victim of a beating and subsequent drowning by a gang of seven girls and one boy (Graydon 1999). Researchers and policy-makers are now well aware of the problem of violence among female adolescents, and few continue to focus their attention solely on males. The research and policy recommendations regarding intimate partner violence have not yet achieved a gender-neutral approach.

Systematic research on IPV started in the 1970s (Hines, Brown and Dunning 2007). Almost four decades later, there are still those who deny its perpetration by females and argue that IPV is essentially a reflection of inequality. Intimate partner violence is understood to be a "gendered problem of men's violence against women" (Hines *et al.* 2007, p.63). This definition seems to discount the etiology of inter-personal violence.

Females who have been victims of maltreatment in childhood are at risk of becoming violent in their interpersonal relationships. As discussed in the previous chapters, children who are subjected to poor or abusive parenting tend to show behavioral problems and deficits in emotion regulation, social information processing, and peer relation-ships. These outcomes are seen in both boys and girls. The aggression the children display early is carried across relationships through the lifespan. Being prone to rejection by their more socially skilled peers, maltreated children come together in antisocial peer groups in which their aggressive behaviors are reinforced. As older adolescents and young adults, they select their intimate partners from their deviant peer group (Feiring and Furman 2000). Expectations and standards of behavior—social, sexual, and dyadic—are regulated within this peer group. Thus young adults with a history of maltreatment, both female and male, are at elevated risk for partner violence (Moffit *et al.* 2001).

Nonetheless, much of the research examining the effects of IPV on children uses only the traditional definition of intimate partner violence as violence perpetrated by males against females (e.g. Bogat *et al.* 2006; Currie 2006; Herrera and McCloskey 2001; Levendosky *et al.* 2003, 2006; McFarlane *et al.* 2003; Wolfe *et al.* 2003; Ybarra, Wilkens and Lieberman 2007). This same definition is seen also in the collection of statistics and in justice system responses to IPV.

A recent World Health Organization study (2005) exemplifies the tendency to use only the traditional definition of violence in the collection of IPV statistics. In its multi-country study of IPV, the World Health Organization explicitly adopts the traditional definition of

IPV: "Violence against women is an extreme manifestation of gender inequality..." (p.22). As elsewhere (e.g. Herrera and McCloskey 2001) the underlying assumption appears to be that violence is a male behavior that is promoted by unequal relations between men and women. In consequence the data collected and their interpretation reflects this assumption. In fact, the first recommendation emerging from the WHO study calls for the promotion of gender equality and women's rights. This is a laudable recommendation, one that we fully support. However, it is not clear that equality between men and women will end IPV. More equal relations may well lessen the incidence of IPV or at least its severity. Much of the existing research shows that male violence has more negative consequences for females with women experiencing more injury (e.g. Archer 2000). However, IPV is unlikely to end if we fail to acknowledge the existence and seriousness of non-traditional couple violence, and the non-gendered etiology of IPV in child maltreatment.

The traditional understanding of IPV is evidenced in the way the justice system responds to its victims. Serious responding to IPV is most likely when the reported IPV is in the context of a heterosexual relationship, and the male is the identified perpetrator and the female the identified victim (Seelau and Seelau 2005). If law enforcement officials do respond to calls from males who identify themselves as victims of IPV, there often is an assumption that the male is not being truthful. Female abusers have been able to obtain restraining orders under false pretences, and able to take children away from their fathers, even when the fathers are the victims not the perpetrators of abuse (Hines *et al.* 2007). Such actions clearly are not in the best interests of the affected children.

Part of the problem here may be that there is not a common understanding of what constitues IPV. Two subtypes of IPV have been described. One is "typical couple violence" and describes minor reciprocal violence between husbands and wives. This type may be fairly common especially among non-clinical community samples of adults (Johnson 1995). The second, labeled "patriarchal terrorism," describes male to female violence and is assumed to be the more severe type (Johnson 1995; Johnson and Ferraro 2000). This second type likely is more prevalent in non-community samples, such as shelters for victims of spousal assault, and is more likely than typical couple violence to result in physical injury. But it is not helpful if it is the only type of IPV that is collected in statistics such as those of the WHO, nor if it is the only type of violence to which justice officials respond. The important consideration here is that both subtypes of IPV can and do affect children. Respect for children's protection rights requires assessing and understanding all forms of violence between the adults in their lives, not just the most severe, and not just male to female.

Article 2 of the Convention, the non-discrimination principle, states that children's rights must be respected and protections must be provided without any discrimination on the basis of parental status. Children whose witnessing of non-prototypical parental violence goes ignored are children whose rights are not being respected. Their risk status for the deleterious outcomes of witnessing IPV may be significantly elevated. A further concern is the possibility of seriously underestimating the pervasiveness and severity of the problem of IPV in children's lives. If rates reflect only male to female violence in heterosexual relationships, it is likely that many more children are being exposed to IPV than is acknowledged. Children, it seems, are continuing to be the unseen, unintended, and unassisted victims of IPV (Holden and Ritchie 1998). There is growing evidence that IPV is neither solely perpetrated by males nor found only in heterosexual relationships.

Researchers who have not limited their samples to women in battered women's shelters, crime data, or hospital reports, find that women perpetrate as much violence in relationships as do men (e.g. Archer 2000; Fergusson, Horwood and Ridder 2005; Headey, Scott and de Vauss 1999; Hines *et al.* 2007; Holtzworth-Munroe 2005; Morse 1995). Such reports, however, often have been dismissed. Women, it is argued only become violent to retaliate against or protect themselves from a violent male, and since women do not cause injury, their violence is unimportant. There is little evidence to support the argument. Hines and colleagues (2007) cite an array of studies indicating that women are more likely to be violent because they are jealous, or angry, or to gain control of a partner, than they are to retaliate against male violence. And women are capable of inflicting injury. The first ever American helpline for battered males allowed the analysis of males who were physically abused by their wives (Hines *et al.* 2007). Their findings, consistent with an earlier Australian community survey (Headey *et al.* 1999), provide compelling evidence that males not only can be victims of IPV, but also can receive serious physical injury. The men in the Hines study described being threatened, punched, and stabbed; one had physical injuries sustained after being raped with a dildo, and another had both his eardrums broken. Predictably, 92 percent of the abusive wives had a childhood history of maltreatment. As described in the previous chapter and reiterated above, there is a strong association between childhood maltreatment and adult IPV. It is true that males generally are more likely to inflict serious injury on their partners than females, but that females can and do initiate violence and injurious violence against males should not be ignored.

Intimate partner violence exists also in same-sex relationships. Prevalence rates of IPV in gay and lesbian relationships are thought to be comparable to those among heterosexual couples (Ristock 2003; Seelau and Seelau 2005; Stanley *et al.* 2006). Reported rates in the United States range from 17 to 52 percent of lesbian couples (Ristock 2003); 21 to 50 percent of gay male couples (Stanley *et al.* 2006), and approximately 33 percent of heterosexual couples (Seelau and Seelau 2005). The variations generally reflect differences in definitions of IPV. There is also a similarity in types of violence in relationships regardless of sexual orientation. For example, the 80 lesbians in Ristock's (2003) study described a range of emotional abuse (e.g. threats to kill, driving recklessly to frighten), verbal abuse (e.g. yelling, name-calling), physical abuse (e.g. punching, slapping, using weapons), and sexual abuse (forced sex, rape with an object). And most of the women reported experiencing a combination of each type of abuse. Similar findings are reported in a large study of gay and bisexual males with male intimate partners (Stanley *et al.* 2006). As recorded in IPV among heterosexual couples, physical abuse reported in same-sex partners ranged from assaults resulting in minor bruising to broken bones, knife wounds, and head trauma; emotional abuse included yelling and threats with an axe.

Overall, much of the evidence suggests that IPV often is a characteristic of a couple's relationship. Researchers in Australia and New Zealand who have asked both males and females about their experience with violence have obtained data suggesting that typical couple violence is relatively common, and is best conceived of as a property of the relationship rather than an individual (Fergusson *et al.* 2005; Headey *et al.* 1999). In a sample of women in Canada, recruited into a study on the basis of being victims of husband abuse, over two thirds admitted they also were perpetrators of violence to their husbands (Currie 2006). A United States study of at-risk mothers similarly shows that both parents take the role of perpetrator of violence within the relationship (McGuigan and Pratt 2001). Researchers of IPV with Israeli adolescents (Sternberg *et al.* 2005) and with Italian children (Baldry 2003a) also report that both mothers and fathers initiate violence. And studies of gay male relationships generally report reciprocity of violence where IPV exists (Stanley *et al.* 2006).

The consistency of findings across informants, samples, and countries supports the suggestion that IPV may be a style of disagreement among a significant proportion of parents of young children. It is a style that has a powerful educative effect on the children who witness it. Contrary to what many parents think, there is strong evidence that children are acutely aware of the violent interactions between their parents (Jaffee, Wolfe and Wilson 1990; O'Brien *et al.* 1997; Osofsky 1995; Richters and Martinez 1993). Sometimes, children are involved directly. A telephone survey of battered women revealed that more than half of their children had verbally intervened while in the same room (Edleson *et al.* 2003). And researchers report that children's descriptions of their parents' violent interactions can be more credible and accurate than are those of their mothers (e.g. Sternberg *et al.* 2006; Wolfe *et al.* 2003).

A major problem, then, is that children often are present and witnessing these acts of violence whether that violence is the less severe typical couple violence or patriarchal terrorism, and whether that violence is between same- or opposite-sex parents (Hines *et al.* 2007). Young children are disproportionately present in households with IPV largely because IPV is more prevalent among younger adults (e.g. Fantuzzo *et al.* 1997; Jellen, McCarroll and Thayer 2001; Levendosky *et al.* 2006; Ybarra *et al.* 2007). And the prevalence of IPV seems high. In one study in the United States, for example, it was determined that 10.3 percent of children live in homes where IPV involves hitting or throwing objects, and a further 31.5 percent in homes where parental disagreements are dealt with through shouting and heated arguments

(Moore *et al.* 2007). These data suggest a high number of IPV-exposed children. These children will not receive appropriate attention as long as the existence of other than traditional IPV (i.e. male to female) is discounted and its potentially serious consequences for children disregarded. There is agreement in the literature that children in families in which there is IPV are more likely than are those raised in harmonious families to have a range of psychological (lowered self-esteem, anxiety and depression) and behavioral problems. In keeping with the theme of this book, we focus here on the behavioral dimension of these problems.

From the perspective of social learning theory, it would be expected that both boys and girls who witness interparental violence will learn that IPV is an acceptable part of family relationships, a way to gain control over others, and a justified means of conflict resolution. In fact the data generally are consistent with this. When there is an association between parent and child aggressive behaviors, it appears to be largely a result of parental modeling of aggression (Loney *et al.* 2007). Exposure to IPV is one of the strongest and most consistent correlates of violence (Graves 2007). A 20-year longitudinal study of 543 children clearly showed that when parents engage in IPV, their coercive and aggressive styles of control and conflict resolution become generalized to all the child's relationships (Ehrensaft *et al.* 2003). Similarly, the findings of Koblinsky *et al.* (2006) demonstrate a strong modeling effect of family conflict among preschool children who experience exposure to even relatively mild IPV between their parents. The children were observed to model their parental aggressive behaviors in their relationships with their peers, with their parents, and with their pets and other animals (Currie 2006; Duncan, Thomas and Miller 2005).

Exposure to parental IPV has a demonstrable effect as young as infancy (Bogat *et al.* 2006). By preschool, compared with their non-exposed peers, children who have been exposed to IPV in their families are likely to show significantly more anger, peer aggression, behavior problems (Graham-Bermann and Levendosky 1998; Harden *et al.* 2000; Koblinsky *et al.* 2006; Linares *et al.* 2001), and negative interactions with their mothers (Levendosky *et al.* 2003). The indications are that the observed early aggression is life-course persistent. Researchers who have examined samples of children from preschool through adolescence find those exposed early to parental IPV are significantly more likely than others to have fewer prosocial behaviors and poorer communication skills, and to show high rates of interpersonal aggression, delinquency, and violent behaviors (Dadds *et al.* 1999; Harris, Lieberman and Marans 2007; Kernic *et al.* 2003; McFarlane *et al.* 2003; Thormaehlen and Bass-Field 1994).

Exposure to IPV in childhood also has been linked with bullying in school. In a study of 1059 elementary-aged Italian school children, exposure to parental violence was strongly associated with bullying (Baldry 2003a). It is noteworthy in this research that the link was stronger for girls than boys whether the IPV to which they were exposed was from father to mother or mother to father. The latter was the strongest association.

Those who have studied older adolescents and adults who experienced childhood exposure to IPV demonstrate an association between IPV and the perpetration of dating and marital violence, and criminal offending (Ehrensaft *et al.* 2003; Fergusson and Horwood 1998; Magdol *et al.* 1998; O'Keefe 1998). As Moss (2004) found, the effects of childhood exposure to parental IPV show clear short- and long-term effects.

In addition to elevated rates of interpersonal aggression and violence among children exposed to IPV, a link with animal cruelty has been demonstrated. There is, of course, a connection between animal abuse by children and violence in adolescence and adulthood (Merez-Perez, Heide and Silverman 2001; Slavkin 2001), including criminal violence, for both males and females (Felthous and Yudowitz 1997). Researchers have obtained evidence that exposure to IPV is a strong predictor of children's cruelty to animals (Ascione, Weber and Wood 1997; Currie 2006), that is significantly heightened if mothers are also cruel to animals (Baldry 2003b). In order to assess the correlates of those who were cruel to animals, Duncan *et al.* (2005) reviewed charts of children who were in residential treatment because of diagnosed conduct disorder. Their analysis showed that the children who had a significantly greater history of childhood abuse and exposure to IPV were those most likely to be cruel to animals. The authors concluded that these children were modeling the behavior they had experienced both directly and indirectly in their homes.

One issue that has not yet been resolved is whether the co-existence of child physical abuse has an additive effect on the severity of outcomes associated with exposure to IPV. As noted previously, children younger than five years of age are disproportionately present in families where there is IPV. Children younger than five years also are at greatest risk for child maltreatment (McGuigan and Pratt 2001). It is not surprising then to find that high rates of physical abuse are found in families where there is IPV (Harris *et al.* 2007; Osofsky 2003). In particular, the evidence suggests a strong tendency for battered women to physically abuse their children (Harris *et al.* 2007). McGuigan and Pratt (2001) undertook a longitudinal assessment of a sample of families at risk of IPV and child maltreatment. Their aim was to determine if IPV during the first six months of the child's life predicted child abuse during the child's next five years. Their data demonstrated a very strong effect: IPV tripled the likelihood of physical abuse of the child. This would seem to indicate a general problem with conflict resolution and control in the family, making it difficult to disentangle the effects of IPV from those of child physical abuse. Not all researchers of the effects of IPV have taken the co-existence of child physical abuse into account (Kernic *et al.* 2003). And consistent results are lacking among those who have. For example, in their study, Kernic *et al.* (2003) found that children exposed to IPV but not maltreatment were 1.6 times more likely than the norm to score in the borderline/clinical range of aggressive child behavior problems, whereas those exposed to both IPV and physical abuse were three times more likely to have this extreme disturbance score. But not all researchers have found an additive effect of IPV and physical abuse (Sternberg *et al.* 2006).

Three reviews of the literature suggest that child physical abuse does not add to the negative effects of IPV. Wolfe *et al.* (2003) examined 41 studies to look for commonalities in outcomes. Conclusions were difficult due to a number of methodological difficulties most notably generalizing from samples drawn from shelters and relying exclusively on maternal ratings of child behavior problems. Nonetheless, they were able to conclude unequivocally that both boys and girls across ages who are exposed to IPV are at elevated risk for behavior problems, many at clinically significant levels. In their meta-analysis, concurrent child physical abuse was found to minimally, but not significantly, increase the negative effects of exposure to IPV. Kitzmann *et al.* (2003) came to similar conclusions in their meta-analysis of 118 studies. They estimated that 63 percent of children exposed to IPV displayed difficulties with behavior and emotion regulation. They also failed to find any differences in outcome by the child's age or gender, and they did not obtain evidence of any increased negative outcomes where IPV was accompanied by child physical abuse. A third review was undertaken in an attempt to further clarify the overall findings of the existing literature.

Using the technique of a mega-analysis, Kathleen Sternberg and her colleagues (2006) examined further the effects of age, gender, and concurrent child physical abuse on the behavior problems associated with childhood exposure to interparental violence. A mega-analysis has two key differences from a meta-analysis. One is that it uses the original (raw) data that were collected by the primary researchers. The second is that it is limited in analysis to studies in which the outcome variable—in this case behavior problems—has been assessed with the same measurement tool. Mega-analysis thereby allows greater precision, reliability, and more flexible testing of hypotheses. The data were obtained for 24 studies, comprising 1870 children aged 4 to 14 years. Of these, 986 were boys and 884 girls; behavior problems (measured with the Achenbach Child Behavior Check List), and family violence histories (assessed with the Straus Conflict Tactics Scale) were available for each of these children. The children's maltreatment histories were used to categorize them into one of four groups, each group having a large enough sample size to allow reliable analyses. There were 156 children who had been physically abused by one or both parents, 338 who had witnessed parental IPV, 761 who had experienced both physical abuse and IPV, and 705 who had experienced neither abuse nor parental IPV. The findings from their analyses are as follows. Seven- to 14-year-old children who experienced any form of violence (either abuse or IPV) were more likely than the no-violence group to show clinically significant levels of aggressive and antisocial behavior problems. At ages four to six years, the children who had been both physically abused and exposed to parental violence were at significantly greater risk of aggression than those who had been exposed to one form of violence, or the no-violence group.

Thus the additive effect of being abused was seen only with the youngest children. Consistent with the findings from the reviews conducted by Wolfe *et al.* (2003) and Kitzmann *et al.* (2003), the child's gender did not influence the effects of family violence on behavior problems as a sole predictor, or in association with the child's age, or the type of violence to which the child was exposed.

The findings from the mega-analysis are illustrative, but cannot be considered conclusive until more methodologically sound and objective research studies are conducted. Nonetheless, the consistency of findings indicates that exposure to IPV, whether severe or not, increases the likelihood of aggression and later violence in the affected children. Not all children will, of course, show clinical levels of behavior problems. In Sternberg's analysis, most did not. However, as Kitzmann (Kitzmann *et al.* 2003) so astutely noted, an absence of serious problems does not mean the child is unaffected. Indeed, many children who are exposed to IPV also have parents involved in criminality or substance abuse.

PARENTAL CRIMINALITY

The idea that children learn criminal behavior from their parents has a long history. Among the earliest demonstrations of the intergenerational nature of criminal behavior is seen in the British study undertaken by Thomas Ferguson (1952). Ferguson assessed a wide range of possible predictors of criminal offending among 1359 adolescent boys. The predictors included poor housing, poor academic achievement, the boys' size, the boys' father's occupational status, whether the boys' mother was working, if the parents were divorced, and who else, if anyone, in the family had been convicted of a crime. Ferguson's findings showed a strong relation between convictions among the boys and their family members. Where no family member had a conviction, only 9 percent of the boys came into conflict with the law. If one family member had a conviction, 15 percent of the boys were convicted of a crime. The percentage rose to 30 for boys who had two family members with criminal histories, and to 44 percent where there were three or more convicted family members. Consistent with a modeling hypothesis, the probability of a conviction among the boys was highest for those who had fathers or brothers convicted of a crime, relatives the boy would be most likely to imitate. A similar pattern of intergenerational convictions was demonstrated in early studies in the United States. Indeed, not only did the early data indicate a link between parents and children, but also similarities in the rates and types of offenses that were committed by each (Robins, West and Herjanic 1975). Since these early studies, there has been consistent evidence that parental criminality is a strong predictor of child aggression and antisocial behavior, and elevates the risk of the child coming into conflict with the law during adolescence. What has been difficult to demonstrate is whether this association stems solely from the parental criminality, from the poor parenting and child abuse that tend to accompany parental criminality, or from the situational factors that are an inevitable concomitant of parental incarceration.

Much of what we know about the concentration of criminality in families comes from the work in the UK of David Farrington (Farrington 1995; Farrington, Barnes and Lambert 1996; Farrington, Gundry and West 1975; Farrington, Lambert and West 1998; Farrington et al. 2001; West and Farrington 1977). The source of extensive data has been the Cambridge Study in Delinquent Development, a prospective longitudinal study in which Farrington and his colleagues followed 411 boys in London (England) from age 8 to 46 years. Among their many findings are the following three. First, having a member of the immediate family (father, mother, brother, sister) who is convicted of a crime is a significant predictor of the likelihood that the boy will be convicted. Based on social learning theory it would be predicted that same-sex models and older siblings would more likely be imitated than others. Consistent with this, same-sex relatives and older siblings were found to be the strongest predictors of the boy's convictions. Second, having a parent convicted of a crime prior to the boy's tenth birthday predicted the boy's antisocial and criminal outcomes independently of all other possible predictors, including poor parenting and separation from parents. Third, there was a strong tendency for husbands and wives/mothers and fathers to have similar conviction rates. This is presumed to result from pairing from antisocial peer groups as described earlier to explain the reciprocal nature of IPV. Sixty-one percent of the fathers who were convicted of a crime had wives with convictions also. Where the boy's mother had no criminal conviction, only 23 percent of the fathers did so. This pattern was reflected in the boys' generation as they matured and partnered. Eighty-three percent of the boys who were convicted of a crime had wives so convicted compared with 35 percent of the boys whose wives were not convicted of a crime.

Similar findings have been obtained more recently in a comparable United States study. The Pittsburgh Youth Study (Farrington *et al.* 2001) is also a prospective longitudinal study of the development of aggression and criminal offending behavior in boys, although the period of study has been significantly shorter. Five hundred schoolboys were enrolled in the study when they were in grades 1, 4 or 7 (ages approximately 6, 9 and 12 years). The boys' behavior was assessed every six months for the ensuing three years. Information was obtained about criminality among the boy's parents, grandparents, and extended family. The pattern of findings from the United States' study reflects those of the British study. Criminality was concentrated within families and any arrested relative, including the boy's grandfather, grandmother, father, mother, uncle, aunt, brother, and sister, predicted the boy's delinquent behaviors. Again, the father's criminality was the greatest predictor of behavior problems and criminal offending in the boy.

These longitudinal studies provide very compelling evidence for an intergenerational link of criminal behavior. They do not, however, provide an explanation for that link. One of the most common findings among surveys of families in which there is parental criminality is that there are also high rates of conditions such as IPV and child maltreatment that themselves are associated with child behavior disorders and aggressive criminal offending.

Parental criminality is likely to be found in families with whom child welfare agencies are involved (Wright and Seymour 2000). Susan Phillips and colleagues (2004) used data from the American National Survey of Child and Adolescent Well-Being to provide a national (United States) estimate of arrest among parents of children who were subjects of child maltreatment investigations. They found that approximately one in eight children (boys and girls) who had child welfare system involvement for child maltreatment had parents who had been arrested within the six-month period preceding the maltreatment investigation. Over 90 percent of the parents arrested were mothers. The researchers identified the following differences between mothers who maltreated and were arrested, and those who maltreated but were not arrested. Among those arrested were higher rates of impaired parenting, neglect, economic problems, substance abuse, mental illness, and IPV. In addition those arrested were more likely than those not to have had previous contact with child welfare services. These data suggest that children whose mothers are arrested are likely to have been exposed to numerous adverse experiences and risk factors for the development of aggressive antisocial behaviors. Poor parenting and poor family functioning have been posited to account for the link between parent criminality and children's involvement in aggression and the juvenile justice system (Brendgen et al. 2002). Other researchers have documented the presence of substance abuse and other such adverse circumstances in the families of children whose mothers have been incarcerated (e.g. Myers et al. 1999; Poehlmann 2005). Many incarcerated mothers also report having abused substances through their pregnancy (Hanlon et al. 2005).

Studies of children with incarcerated parents have found up to 70 percent of the children to display aggressive antisocial behaviors, and up to 60 percent to have recorded delinquencies (Phillips et al. 2002). Clearly, children whose parents are incarcerated are having markedly more difficulties than their peers from non-criminal families. In an effort to shed more light on these data, Phillips and her colleagues analyzed data from records of 258 adolescents in a mental health setting, some of whose parents had been incarcerated. Interestingly, the researchers did not include young people in custody, thus they omitted those youth most likely to have been affected by parental criminality. What they did find was that upon entering treatment, the adolescents who had experienced parental incarceration had significantly higher rates of disruptive behavior disorders than others. The youth with parental criminality also had been exposed to a greater number of risk factors including parental substance abuse, mental illness, as well as to child abuse and neglect.

Most of the research summarized above has examined the effects of parental criminality on boys only. As described previously, only more recently has attention been paid to girls. This attention has been sparked by observations of a growing incidence of antisocial aggressive behavior among girls and of female juvenile arrests. As noted by the American Bar Association and National Bar Association (2001), delinquency cases in the United States involving females increased by 83 percent between 1988 and 1997. A question of interest that has emerged from this increase is whether the predictors of female aggression and juvenile offending really are the same as those of males. One study whose findings help shed light on that question was of 62 girls between the ages of 13 and 17 years who had histories of serious delinquency problems (Leve and Chamberlain 2004). The girls had been referred for treatment. The examination of the girls' histories suggested that biological parent criminality was a powerful predictor of early onset delinquency in girls. Early onset (prior to age 14 years) delinquency is considered more serious than later onset because it is highly predictive of chronic adult offending (Loeber and Farrington 2000). Early onset delinquency also is associated with parental criminality. Youth who offend early are more likely to have a parent (or sibling) who has been convicted of a felony (a criminal offense subject to a prison term) (Alltucker *et al.* 2006).

Criminal aggressive and antisocial behavior is of particular concern with girls for two reasons. First is because of its strong association with sexual health risk behaviors and early school-leaving (Leve and Chamberlain 2004). Early pregnancy is a common and problematic outcome. It is an outcome associated with poor parenting, and with a second generation of children with conduct problems (Wakschlag *et al.* 2000). The intergenerational transmission is evident in research findings. A direct relation has been demonstrated between adolescent mothers' antisocial behaviors and conduct problems in their sons. And an indirect relation, mediated by poor parenting, has been demonstrated between antisocial adolescent mothers and conduct problems in their daughters (Rhule, McMahon and Spieker 2004). The second concern is that many who become young mothers maintain single motherhood and criminal behavior. Their problems, and those of their children, are magnified if they are incarcerated.

There has been a growing trend toward the incarceration of females, especially young mothers (Dallaire 2007; Miller 2006; Morgan 1997). Nowhere are the statistics more dramatic than in the United States where there has been a 400 percent increase in incarcerated females since 1986 (Miller 2006). Most of these women are single mothers (Dallaire 2007; Miller 2006). In consequence, their children likely will be exposed to numerous adverse experiences. They will be separated from their parent, perhaps their siblings and friends, and may experience a number of temporary placements. Many of these children will have been exposed to violence and family dysfunction prior to their mother's arrest (Mackintosh, Myers and Kennon 2006). The majority show behavioral difficulties, especially aggression (Mackintosh *et al.* 2006). Children of incarcerated mothers become increasingly at risk for their own involvement in the justice system. About one half of youth in the juvenile justice system have a parent who is incarcerated (Mumola 2000).

It is not clear in the literature if parental incarceration has an effect on child outcomes independent of the effects of maltreatment and poor parenting and/or substance abuse through pregnancy. And for many children, a parent's incarceration is not a one-time event, but part of recurring parental involvement in the criminal justice system (Phillips *et al.* 2002). It might then be expected that parental incarceration, with its separation and stigma, poses a risk over and above that of co-existing maltreatment. Phillips' (2002) data suggest some independent effect of incarceration on behavior problems, but the findings are not strong. Johnston (2006) likewise found that parental incarceration was less important a predictor of children's daily lives than parental behavior.

The most extensive analyses of the effects of parental incarceration to date have been conducted by Murray and Farrington (2005). They note that the existing research suggests that parental incarceration may function as a risk marker for children and/or as a risk mechanism. As a risk marker, parental incarceration may reflect a genetic risk for criminality, or the existence of child maltreatment, mental health problems, and IPV. In essence the risk factors that are seen in children of incarcerated parents are the known risk factors for aggressive and antisocial behavior among children. There are a number of ways in which parental incarceration can be conceptualized as a risk mechanism. Most frequently suggested is separation of the child from the parent. As discussed in the context of attachment, parent–child relationships can be seriously disrupted by separation. Children frequently lose contact with their incarcerated parent (Miller 2006). Geographical distance is cited as one major problem, and parental reluctance as another (Miller 2006). Separation may be particularly traumatic for the child who has not been told why the parent is now absent, or who has been provided an inadequate explanation (Miller 2006; Murray and Farrington 2005). A second possible risk mechanism is through providing a role model for criminal behavior. As noted earlier, for example, there are high concordance rates between fathers and sons in patterns of criminality suggesting the possibility of modeling and imitation. In addition, Murray and Farrington (2005) describe the family changes that accompany parental incarceration as a possible risk mechanism. The most common changes observed are financial hardship, relationship breakdowns, and difficulties with childcare arrangements.

Using the data from the Cambridge Study in Delinquent Development described previously (boys only), Murray and Farrington (2005) attempted to isolate the effects of parental incarceration. They were, in large part, focussed on the issue of the separation of child from parent that is an inevitable concomitant of parental incarceration. To this end, they added a control group of children who were experiencing separation from parent with comparable changes in their daily lives, but for different reasons (for example parental hospitalization). Their analyses provided the following information. Separation from parent due to incarceration predicted worse child outcomes than did other reasons for separation, and was a strong predictor of antisocial and delinquent outcomes that were stable up to the age of 40. Boys who were separated from parents because of parental incarceration had more co-existing risk factors for antisocial and delinquent outcomes than the other groups, thus one might suggest that these risk factors accounted for the observed differences in outcomes. However, their data also indicated that the effects of incarceration were in addition to the other risk factors, including separation from parent. Unfortunately, the researchers were unable to test the modeling hypothesis. This, together with the inclusion of only male children, a relatively small sample size (40), and cohort changes in prison populations, does limit the generalizability of their findings. Nonetheless, their data provide preliminary evidence that parental incarceration is both a risk factor and a risk mechanism for children. And with or without incarceration, there is significant evidence for a relation between parental criminality and child involvement in aggression and antisocial behavior as summarized above. It seems reasonable to assume the risks are cumulative in effect.

PARENTAL SUBSTANCE ABUSE

After conducting a longitudinal study of juvenile detainees in the United States, Dembo and colleagues (1992) concluded that drug abuse and delinquent behaviors among youth were a result of their parents' substance abuse and criminality, as well as their personal histories of child maltreatment. Little has changed since these early findings.

Prevalence estimates of parental alcohol and drug abuse are very high. Comprehensive studies performed in the United States are illustrative. In a recent study of urban minority children aged six and seven years, half of them reported exposure either to illicit drugs or to drug deals in their homes, and 12 percent reported seeing both (Ondersma *et al.* 2006). General estimates are that one in four children in the United States has been exposed to substance abuse in the family, and one in six has a parent who has used illicit drugs in the year prior to data collection (VanDeMark *et al.* 2005). Based on the National Household Survey on Drug Abuse, it is estimated that approximately seven million children in the United States have at least one parent who is dependent on illicit drugs or alcohol (cited in Conners *et al.* 2004). The probability of intergenerational transmission of poor parenting and substance abuse is implied by the profile of the substance-abusing parent, and the comorbid adverse conditions for healthy child development.

Parents who abuse substances share many characteristics with parents who maltreat their children but do not abuse substances. Included among these is a shared personal history of childhood neglect. However, there are additional characteristics that increase the probability of poor parenting and negative child outcomes as well as the intergenerational transmission of substance abuse. Substance-abusing parents tend also to have substance abuse in their family of origin, select partners who are substance abusers and suffer the neuropharmacological effects of the substances they ingest (Dunn *et al.* 2002; Ravndal *et al.* 2001). Studies of substance-abusing fathers suggest that compared with alcohol abusers, drug abusers are more likely to be living in poverty and be involved in criminal activity, and less likely to have social supports (Cooke *et al.* 2004). Maternal substance abusers are usually single parents who are under-educated and have mental health difficulties, a history of child maltreatment, poor problem-solving skills, and a lack of social supports. They tend to be unemployed, have few financial resources, and reside in unstable housing situations. Substance abuse is a critical factor in families involved with child welfare systems (Semidei, Radel and Nolan 2001). In addition, a history of conduct disorder, early onset antisocial behavior and criminality are commonly found among substance-abusing women (Dunn *et al.* 2002). It is not surprising then that substance-abusing parents show impaired parenting skills. Their own histories make them poor candidates for effective parenting. Moreover, addictions change priorities.

Parenting among substance abusers generally is unresponsive and inconsistent (VanDeMark *et al.* 2005). It is characterized by faulty expectations about child development, and inappropriate discipline (Conners *et al.* 2004; Donohue, Romero and Hill 2006). Substance-abusing parents provide inadequate supervision of children, and tend to be either permissive or coercive in their socialization strategies (Locke and Newcomb 2004). With their own lives in difficulty or chaos, and with the effects of drugs, it is very difficult for parents to provide children with the safety, nurture, and love which they need and to which they have a right. Brad Donohue provides a compelling example of this (Donohue *et al.* 2006). A toddler may be left in a car alone for a period of time while her parent is using cocaine at a friend's house; the cocaine intoxication distracts the parent from attending to the needs of the child. If the parent is a chronic cocaine user, she likely will suffer from irritability which in turn increases stress and the probability of forgetting about the child in the car. Cocaine-related irritability may also decrease tolerance for child misbehaviors, thereby increasing the possibility of physically abusive behaviors.

High comorbidity of substance abuse and child maltreatment, especially neglect, is seen in substance abuse treatment and child protection settings (Donohue *et al.* 2006). Parental abuse of drugs or alcohol, or both, is found in more than 50 percent of parents who neglect their children (Dunn *et al.* 2002; Tyler *et al.* 2006). And the neglect tends to be both severe and chronic (Donohue *et al.* 2006; Semidei *et al.* 2001). Some report up to 70 percent of cases of mal-treatment have been influenced by parental substance abuse (e.g. Locke and Newcomb 2003). The substances most often associated with child maltreatment are alcohol, cocaine, opiates, and heroin; a significant minority of parents report multiple drug use (Chance and Scannapieco 2002). Many of the children of these parents come to the attention of child welfare agencies at a young age, and repeatedly (English, Marshall and Orme 1999; Semidei *et al.* 2001). Client profiles indicate that substance-abusing parents have more problems than do child-welfare-involved parents who are not substance abusers (Semidei *et al.* 2001). Intimate partner violence is one such problem.

The comorbidity of IPV and parental substance abuse consistently has been demonstrated (Cunradi, Caetano and Shafer 2002; Dube *et al.* 2002; Egeland and Sussman-Stillman 1996; Leonard 2002; Stevens and Arbiter 1995; White and Chen 2002). Even sub-clinical levels of drinking among parents in the community have been found to be associated with IPV, and child behavior problems (Keller, Cummings and Davies 2005). In this latter study (Keller *et al.* 2005), the authors conclude that parental problem drinking affects child outcomes through both the IPV, and the poor parenting with which it is associated. Whether children are affected by parental substance abuse through its correlates of impaired parenting, child maltreatment, or exposure to IPV is not clear. That parental substance abuse does increase problematic outcomes for children is very clear.

Children whose parents abuse substances, drugs or alcohol are considered to be at high risk for a range of behavioral problems, most notably aggressive antisocial behaviors and substance abuse. If the child's mother was using substances during her pregnancy, then the child's risk status is elevated as a result of neurobiological damage, as discussed in Chapter 2. In addition, maternal substance abuse during the child's first year of life is associated with insecure attachment as discussed earlier. Continued substance abuse by either the child's mother or father is associated with children's aggressive, antisocial, and criminal behaviors. There are many reports in the literature of increased behavior problems among children of drug- and alcohol-abusing parents (e.g. Fals-Stewart *et al.* 2004; Haugland

2003; VanDeMark *et al.* 2005), including clinical levels of conduct disorder (Cooke *et al.* 2004; Dunn *et al.* 2002). Compared with children whose parents do not abuse substances, these children show high levels of fighting, teasing, irritability, and anger, and of interpersonal difficulties at school. By adolescence, children of substance-abusing parents show increased aggressive and antisocial, delinquent behaviors (Cooke *et al.* 2004; Dunn *et al.* 2002; VanDeMark *et al.* 2005). Many are also abusing substances themselves (Child Welfare League of America 2001; Dunn *et al.* 2002; West and Prinz 1987; Widom 2000). There is also some evidence to suggest specificity of effects: for example, a father's alcohol abuse predicts an adolescent's alcohol use (Dunn *et al.* 2002). Overall the data are very clear that parental substance abuse is a strong risk factor for the development of behavioral disorders, and in particular for substance abuse. What is not clear is why. As with parental criminality, it is likely that parental substance abuse is both a risk mechanism and a risk marker.

It may be important here to stress that negative child outcomes are not always found among families in which one or both parents abuse substances (Dunn *et al.* 2002; Haugland 2003). For example, in Nancy VanDeMark's study of the children of women entering treatment, most of the children did not evidence behavioral problems, although a significant proportion had clinically significant behavior disorders (VanDeMark *et al.* 2005). What differentiates among child outcomes is not clear. It has been suggested that the comorbid factors of child maltreatment and exposure to IPV are what account for the observed behavior problems among children of substance abusers (Nicholas and Rasmussen 2006).

Dunn and colleagues (2002) in their review of the literature suggest that the quality of parenting the child receives may be a more important predictor of behavior problems than the fact of parental substance abuse. Consistent with this suggestion are the findings of a population health study conducted in Germany (Barnow *et al.* 2004). The focus of this study was on identifying predictors of adolescent aggression and delinquency in families with a history of alcoholism. The analysis did not demonstrate the expected association between parental drinking and adolescent antisocial behaviors. Perceived parental rejection, however, was a strong predictor of adolescent aggression and delinquency. Nonetheless, the researchers also report that in a different analysis of the same data set, they find a link between the number of relatives a child had who were alcohol abusers (the density of alcoholism in the child's life), and the rate of aggressive and antisocial behaviors in the children.

A systematic attempt to disentangle the effects of parenting, exposure to IPV, and parental alcohol use on behavior problems was undertaken by Karen Nicholas and Elizabeth Rasmussen (2006). Their analysis yielded no predictive power of parental alcohol use. Instead, their findings showed that for females, emotional abuse by a father predicted aggressive behaviors, and for males the key predictor of aggression was physical abuse by a father. Unfortunately their methodology precludes generalizing the findings to the population. Their sample comprised first-year university students in a psychology class of whom 94 percent were white and middle class. In context, this is an elite sample. The young people are in university, not in detention, and if they are abusing substances themselves, it is not at levels high enough to disrupt academic functioning. Second, the study's data rely exclusively on retrospective self-report from only the students, making its validity suspect. The question of how parental substance abuse affects children remains unclear. However, parenting style and child maltreatment clearly do play a role.

Since substance abuse accompanies the aggressive and antisocial behavior of children of substance abusers, the role of hereditary in substance abuse should be acknowledged. Twin studies indicate that concordance rates for general substance abuse are twice as high among monozygotic twins than they are among fraternal twins (Brown, Mott and Stewart 1992). And alcohol abuse is known to have a moderate genetic component (Chassin *et al.* 2003). However, genetics cannot fully account for the observations of substance abuse among the children of substance-abusing parents. It is unlikely that high rates of substance abuse among adolescents whose parents abuse substances is simply a result of hereditary. Hereditary accounts for predispositions, adverse environmental factors such as maltreatment or modeling of substance abuse interact with them. In fact, there is some evidence in the research of a modeling effect of parental substance abuse (Jung 2001; Locke and Newcomb 2004). Children who observe their parents' alcohol and drug use may adopt the same patterns of behavior.

It seems most likely that parental substance abuse has multiple influences on children's behavior disorders, through neglectful and abusive parenting, through exposure to IPV, through hereditary, and through providing a model of behavior for imitation. Which of these risk factors for childhood aggression has the strongest predictive power has not yet been identified. Perhaps it does not matter. None that is avoidable should be present in the lives of children.

MATERNAL DEPRESSION

Maternal depression is the most studied of parental psychopathologies in relation to childhood conduct disorders (Chronis et al. 2007). Depression, like other forms of mental illness, does not provide models of aggressive antisocial behavior as directly as IPV, parental criminality, and parental substance abuse. Nonetheless, a depressed parent displays behaviors that both model poor parenting, and are predictive of childhood conduct problems.

Depression can result from biological, genetic, and psychological factors, and in the general population, psychotherapeutic and pharmacological treatments can effectively reduce depressive symptoms (Highet and Drummond 2004). However, not all depression is at clinically significant levels, and in many research studies of mothers, depression is assessed as a function of depressive symptoms that impair parenting behavior, rather than as clinically diagnosed depression. One notable exception is a study of mothers with histories of child-onset depression (Forbes et al. 2006). Depressive symptoms most often appear in mothers who are experiencing adverse life events such as poverty (Koblinsky et al. 2006; Leschied et al. 2005), intimate partner violence (Bogat et al. 2006), or single-mother status (Brown and Moran 1997). Single teenaged mothers, in particular, have high rates of depression that are presumed to result from their typical living circumstances of poverty and resource constraints (Dahinten et al. 2007). Poverty and maternal depression, including sub-clinical depression, are risk factors with pervasive effects on the child's social development (McCartney et al. 2004).

There are a number of reasons why the research has focussed on the relation between depression in mothers and child outcomes. Females are much more likely than males to be diagnosed with depression. Depression tends to be disproportionately found in single-mother families. And as previously discussed mothers remain the primary caregivers of their children, particularly during the first year of life during which the attachment relationship develops (Leschied *et al.* 2005). Chronis *et al.* (2007) cite sources demonstrating a different reason for the focus on depressed mothers. They claim that fathers who are willing to participate in research studies in this context tend to be psychologically healthy. There is at least one study, however, of fathers who are not so healthy. A study was conducted in New Zealand to examine the psychological health of men whose partners had been diagnosed with postpartum depression (Roberts *et al.* 2006). The question addressed in this study of 174 couples with an infant was whether the male partners of depressed mothers would themselves show symptoms of depression. That did turn out to be the case. Unfortunately, it is, of course, quite impossible to determine the direction of effect here. It may be that having a depressed husband is a risk factor for developing postpartum depression. In support of this explanation was the finding that the men who also showed signs of depression showed increased aggression levels compared to those whose wives did not have postpartum depression. Nonetheless, their findings demonstrate the importance of including males in research examining the effect of depression on child outcomes. Their study is important also in demonstrating—at least in a preliminary way—that the male partners of depressed mothers may be unable to adequately provide the kind of social support to their wives that has been found to lessen depression (Levendosky *et al.* 2004). Moreover, these men likely are unable to buffer the negative effects of maternal depression on child outcomes.

Maternal depression is a significant risk factor for the development of disruptive behavior disorders in children. There have been consistent findings of a link between maternal depressive symptomology and behavior problems in children (Chronis *et al.* 2007; Dawson *et al.* 2003; Elgar, McGrath and Waschbuch 2004; Harden *et al.* 2000; Koblinsky *et al.* 2006; Levendosky *et al.* 2006; Romano *et al.* 2005). That maternal depression is causal is suggested by findings that the more chronic the depression across the child's development, the greater the behavior problems (Chronis *et al.* 2007). Especially compelling is that even where there is the existing conduct problem of attention deficit hyperactivity disorder (ADHD), maternal depression is predictive of the development of elevated conduct problems.

An eight-year study of children diagnosed with ADHD, aged four to seven years at initial assessment, was conducted to identify the developmental course and predictors of conduct problems (Chronis et al. 2007). Among this group of children, maternal depression predicted conduct problems two to eight years following the initial assessment. Positive parenting of the children with ADHD was a strong protective factor against the development of conduct disorders. These findings are consistent with many suggestions that depression exerts its effects by impairing parenting. The self-absorption that is a key characteristic of depression results in mothers engaging in more negative and fewer positive behaviors. Compared with mothers who are not depressed, depressed mothers are less engaged, responsive, and warm. They tend to be less attentive to, less interested in and involved with, and more critical of and punitive with their children (Bogat et al. 2006; Chronis et al. 2007; Dahinten et al. 2007; Levendosky et al. 2006; Lyons-Ruth et al. 2002). It is particularly difficult for depressed mothers to display the sensitive and contingent responding needed for secure attachment quality if they are suffering from postpartum depression through the first year of the child's life.

There has been much media and scientific attention to the problem of postpartum depression, and that is our focus here. However, we believe it important first to point out that there is evidence from Britain suggesting that maternal depression during pregnancy is at least as common as is postpartum depression (Evans et al. 2001). Depression, because it is a source of stress, poses a threat to the mother's well-being during her pregnancy, and to the healthy development of the fetus. Unfortunately, treatments may be just as problematic. The most widely prescribed treatment for maternal depression during pregnancy is selective serotonin reuptake inhibitors (SSRIs). However, there is compelling evidence that this medication crosses the placenta and exposes the infant to increased serotonin levels during early development (see Chapter 2 for a discussion on serotonin). SSRI-exposed neonates show disruptions of a wide range of neurobehavioral outcomes (Zeskind and Stephens 2004). Whether the observed disruptions reflect withdrawal or serotonin toxicity, and whether they endure and compromise subsequent neuro-development, is not clear at this time. Considerably more research is needed in the area of prenatal depression if we are to provide effective treatments that do no harm to the fetus. We are more knowledgeable about the types and effects of postpartum depression.

Postpartum psychosis, the most serious form of postpartum depression, is rare. Its consequences also are the most serious. Left untreated, postpartum psychosis can result in maternal infanticide and suicide (Nager, Johnsson and Sundquist 2005). In recognition of the problem, postpartum psychosis or depression is a legal defense for infanticide in 29 countries. Few depressed mothers do actually kill their infants. However, postpartum depression is a significant mental health issue for many new mothers, and a significant risk factor for the compromised development of their children.

Survey data suggest surprisingly similar prevalence rates and pre-dictors of postpartum depression in industrialized and developing countries. Some of the reported estimates are as follows: France and Italy, 11 percent (Romito, Saurel-Cubizolles and Lelong 1999); India 23 percent (Patel, Rodrigues and de Souza 2002); Lebanon, 21 per-cent (Chaaya *et al.* 2002); Morocco, 19 percent (Agoub, Moussaoui and Battas 2005); New Zealand, 8 to 13 percent (Roberts *et al.* 2006); Nepal, 12 percent (Regmi *et al.* 2002); North America, 10 to 30 per-cent (Crockenberg and Leerkes 2003; Swain *et al.* 2007); Pakistan, 28 percent (Rahman, Iqbal and Harrington 2003); South Africa 34 per-cent (Cooper *et al.* 1999; Tomlinson *et al.* 2006); United Arab Emirates, 18 percent (Abou-Saleh and Ghubash 1997); United King-dom, 10 to 13 percent (O'Brien *et al.* 2004). One exception to the prevalence data is seen in a recent report from Sweden (Rubertsson *et al.* 2005). In their national study, Rubertsson and colleagues identi-fied the prevalence of postpartum depression at only 3 percent. Inter-estingly, in an independent study (Fabian, Radestad and Waldenstrom 2006) researchers found that 3 percent of Swedish women did not attend Sweden's parent education classes that are a part of the Swedish child health promotion program. We do not know if these were the same 3 percent who suffered postpartum depression. It is an intriguing possibility.

Postpartum depression is influenced by the hormonal fluctua-tions and sleep disturbances that follow childbirth (Highet and

Drummond 2004). There is some evidence that it is more likely when there have been obstetric complications, complications with the pregnancy, a difficult labor, or complications during the early postpartum period (Agoub *et al.* 2005; Johnstone *et al.* 2001; Josefsson *et al.* 2002). The association between sociodemographic characteristics of the mother and postpartum depression is not clear. Agoub *et al.* (2005), among others, found no effect of mothers' age, education level, employment, or number of children. Rubertsson *et al.* (2005), in the study in Sweden, did find that unemployment was a predictor of postpartum depression. However, their data also showed a strong correlate of postpartum depression was not being a native speaker of Swedish. In essence, it may be that being an immigrant with few social supports and financial stress was what accounted for the observed relation between unemployment and postpartum depression.

What consistently has been found across countries is an association between postpartum depression and the stressful life events that frequently are related to sociodemographic characteristics, most notably a violent or abusive partner, financial difficulties, and a lack of social supports (e.g. Agoub *et al.* 2005; Patel *et al.* 2004; Romito *et al.* 1999; Tomlinson *et al.* 2006). In South Asia, the sex of the neonate is also a predictor of postpartum depression. This stems from the traditional preference for a male child and the guilt associated with giving birth to a girl child (Patel *et al.* 2004).

A lack of social supports and IPV may not be a cause of postpartum depression, but it certainly exacerbates it (Crockenberg and Leerkes 2003). Lack of social supports is a well-documented stress factor that is associated with more harsh and punitive parenting (Mapp 2006). Coping with a newborn, reduced sleep, and additional resource demands are difficult enough; having to cope also with marital difficulties and a lack of social supports must be expected to seriously impair caregiving and socialization. In fact, postpartum depression is strongly associated with parenting difficulties, and with elevated emotional and behavioral problems among children (Murray and Cooper 2003).

Swain *et al.* (2007) report the increasing research data from longitudinal studies showing that mothers suffering postpartum depression are less sensitively attuned to their infants, less psychologically available, and less able to interact with their infant in ways that lead to the development of a secure attachment relationship. When mothers are sad, irritable, and withdrawn, infants respond with fussiness and withdrawal; toddlers and preschoolers demonstrate emotion regulation difficulties, and difficulties controlling their aggressive impulses (McCartney *et al.* 2004). The children of mothers with postpartum depression tend, then, to become more difficult to care for and may in turn elicit further maternal depression. It is not surprising that maternal depression early in the child's life is a strong predictor of children's behavior problems (McCartney *et al.* 2004). Maternal depression that occurs in the context of life stresses in addition to caring for a new infant may be particularly predictive of later child problems.

The importance of postpartum depression in influencing the child's developmental path cannot be over-emphasized. The first year of life is critical to healthy brain development, emotion regulation capacity, and the development of secure quality of attachment, as previously discussed. Postpartum depression that continues through the first year of the infant's life threatens these developmental processes in ways that are predictive of later aggression and antisocial behaviors. Postpartum depression that is brief and ends within the first few weeks of the infant's life is not associated with such adverse outcomes (Morrell and Murray 2003). And the good news is that early interventions can successfully treat postpartum depression (Highet and Drummond 2004; Weissman *et al.* 2006). It is of critical importance to respecting children's rights and for healthy child development that efforts be made to prevent, detect, and treat postpartum depression.

CO-OCCURRENCE AND CLUSTERING

What is very clear in the literature that examines parent or parenting predictors of child behavior disorders is that there is significant clustering in families of problems. Children rarely experience one form of adversity. Rather, victimization tends to cluster. Neglect and abuse, for example, have high rates of comorbidity and tend to occur where there is more severe social and economic disadvantage especially among ethnocultural minority and Aboriginal families (Chaffin 2006). Parents in such families typically have low education and income levels and few personal resources: they tend to lack social supports, abuse substances, and have very limited parenting skills (Chaffin 2006). In a study of a New Zealand birth cohort, David Fergusson and his colleagues (Fergusson *et al.* 2005) found that levels of intimate partner violence occurred most with younger maternal age, less maternal education, low socioeconomic and single-parent status, greater abuse of substances, and a history of abuse, poor quality attachment, and mental health problems. Those who reported the higher levels of IPV were likely to have a partner lacking in educational qualifications, and one who had drug use and or other antisocial behaviors. They also had dependent children. Many studies have identified single parenting, especially single teen mothering, to be particularly problematic. Early childbearing is associated with a history of antisocial and aggressive behavior, poverty, limited education, and impaired parenting (Dahinten *et al.* 2007; Rhule *et al.* 2004). Children of teen mothers are at significantly elevated risk of developing conduct problems compared with children of older mothers and children with two parents (Brannigan *et al.* 2002; Rhule *et al.* 2004). The risk is magnified when the teen mother is a minority single mother living in poverty (e.g. Finkelhor, Ormord and Turner 2007). In fact there is strong evidence that violence rates disproportionately involve minorities living in poverty, and that violent adolescents are most often reared in single-parent homes (Graves 2007).

In essence, disadvantage, adversity, and stress tend to cluster in families such that parents and children are seriously affected. Stress that is chronic and present early in the child's life is highly detrimental to parenting, to parent–child relationships, and child development (Crnic, Gaze and Hoffman 2005). And cumulative stress leads to more deleterious and less reversible outcomes (Finkelhor *et al.* 2007). It was the multiple adversities in Adam's life that resulted in him being a young single father with low educational attainment and a history of incarceration. The probability of intergenerational transmission of aggressive and antisocial behaviors to Adam's son and all such disadvantaged families, are high in the absence of interventions.

RIGHTS AND RESILIENCE

As has been described through this and the previous two chapters, it is primarily risk factors in the family that are associated with the development of early onset life-course persistent aggressive and violent behaviors. But not all children who experience the risk factors of adverse parenting and family circumstances will develop behavior problems. Some children appear able to develop positively despite considerable risk exposure. These children are said to be resilient. The factors that promote "resilience" have been the subject of much discussion and research.

In the earlier literature, it was believed that a resilient child possessed some sort of innate hardiness or invulnerability that enabled the child to withstand or overcome the effects of adversity. However, as Margaret Waller (2001) noted, there are two major problems with attributing resilience to the personality of the child. First is that this attribution lends itself to a "blame the victim" stance. The child who fails to show resilience in the face of adversity simply is a weak child. Second, and following from the first, a focus on personality as an exclusive source of resilience is not consistent with the ecological model of child development. It disregards the importance of the contexts of development. Families do not function in a vacuum but in a society. Resilience, then, depends not simply on the child, but largely on the nature of the family's social context. In his early writings on the ecology of development, Bronfenbrenner (1986) described the importance of families being assisted by their communities to provide effective parenting. Subsequent research has identified the factors in the community, as well as in the child, that can promote resilience.

Researchers examining the factors that are associated with resilience have identified the following to be critical. Within the child the primary sources of resilience are those associated with healthy prenatal development and secure attachment—problem-solving ability and social competence (Graves 2007). Within the family, positive and democratic parents and positive relationships among family members are the most important characteristics (Carlton *et al.* 2006; Chronis *et al.* 2007; Graves 2007; Koblinsky *et al.* 2006). Within the school system resilience is predicted by positive school climate and participation opportunities (Edwards, Mumford and Serra-Roldan 2007), and peer acceptance and friendship (Criss *et al.* 2002). In the neighborhood and broader community, resilience factors include social supports and resources (Luthar, Cicchetti and Becker 2000; Wolfe 1998; Zielinski and Bradshaw 2006).

These are the protective factors. They are factors that are defined by their potential to exert a positive effect in adverse or high-risk conditions, and to protect the child by shifting the balance between risk and protection in the child's life. And of course, the influence among them is bi-directional. For example, the more available childcare and professional help is in a neighbourhood, the lower the rates of child maltreatment (Zielinski and Bradshaw 2006). The lower the rates of child maltreatment, the greater the likelihood the child will develop positive social skills and be able to experience peer acceptance and friendship in school. Successful peer relationships are protective factors that are associated with the reduction of aggressive and anti-social behaviors among children being reared in families where there are adverse conditions such as intimate partner violence and harsh physical punishment (Criss *et al.* 2002). The identification and acknowledgement of the protective factors has important implications for policies and programs.

The Convention on the Rights of the Child requires that the best interests of the child be a primary consideration in all actions affecting the child and requires that signatories assist parents with their child-rearing responsibilities. Governments can assist families in a reactive or proactive way, responding to problems after they occur or preventing them from occurring. And governments can assist in a targeted or universal way focussing either on children and families at risk, or on all children and families. Proactive and universal approaches are most consistent with the Convention and more likely to promote resilience.

Targeted programs may be necessary in extreme circumstances, but there should also be universal programs. As discussed elsewhere (Covell and Howe 2001a), universal programs have three benefits over targeted programs. One benefit is that universal programs can assist with adaptive coping across a wide variety of possible adversities in the child's life. We cannot predict what adversities a child may face during development. A second is that the potential for stigmatization of the family is eliminated and therefore the program is more likely to be accepted and supported by the general population. A third is that universal programs do not require *a priori* risk identification; not all adverse parental behaviors or family circumstances are identifiable by the traditional risk indicators of family structure, income, or ethno-cultural status. Reactive programs tend to come too late in the history of parental failure and too late to prevent long-term negative outcomes to the child. As Richard Gelles described foster care, reactive interventions are like "an expensive ambulance at the bottom of the cliff" (Gelles 1996, p.131). They do little to promote resilience.

As discussed in the first chapter of this book, the Convention obligates programs and policies that are evidence-based and pro-active, and respect the rights of every child to conditions for optimum development. We need to acknowledge that even if a child reared in adverse circumstances does not display conduct disorder, and does not become involved in violence or criminal offending, it does not mean that the child's development has not been compromised in some way. At the very least, we must expect that such a child will not reach her potential. The Convention requires that no child be dis-criminated against in any way because of family circumstances, it does not restrict its relevance to children with obvious problems.

A child rights approach to the promotion of resilience, then, would focus not only on the identified protective factors for children known to be in adverse family environments, but also on proactive and universal policies and programs that have the capacity to promote optimum development for all children. Danielle Dallaire (2007) has labeled these as "promotive factors"; they promote positive outcomes for all children regardless of the child's or the family's risk status. Con-sistency with the Convention would see governments, supported by their citizens, put into place the programs and policies that are known to promote healthy development for all children, and the reduction of violence among those in adverse rearing conditions. These are described in the following chapters.

CHAPTER 5

Policy Interventions

The environment helps to shape who you turn out to be.

It is not simply families that raise children to become violent. It is also the unfriendliness of child and family policies that fail to provide families and children with the support needed for healthy child development and the enjoyment of children's rights, as noted in the previous chapter. Children and families like Adam and his son do not live in a vacuum. They live in the context of social and political environments, government actions, and public policies that have a major impact on their health and well-being. When governments fail to provide children and families with supports, and when they maintain weak child and family policies that run contrary to the rights and best interests of children, they are putting children at risk of entering into a pathway of childhood aggression and violence. The situation for Adam might have turned out very differently had there been strong policies in place to assist his mother.

Under the Convention on the Rights of the Child, governments have the obligation to ensure the progressive implementation of children's protection, provision, and participation rights. And as part of this obligation, governments have the responsibility to help parents and caregivers in looking after the needs and best interests of children. Families that live under difficult conditions may require the help and support of governments. They may require supportive policies and programs in dealing with the problem of poverty or lack of childcare or inadequate health care or family breakdown. But when governments are delinquent or negligent in providing for this support, and when the rights and best interests of children are compromised as a result, children are put at risk of antisocial and violent behavior. So the risk factors are not simply ones of negative parenting, family conflict, and child maltreatment in the home. They are also found in the failure of governments to secure the rights of children and provide for strong child and family policies. In short, child-unfriendly policies are a risk factor for the raising of violent children.

We now examine the characteristics of child-friendly and -unfriendly policies. We do so in reference to a comparison of policies in economically developed countries and, in particular, because the contrast is so great, to a comparison of policies in the Nordic countries and North America. The purpose is to illustrate the linkage between the unfriendliness of policies and the raising of violent children. But before we make the comparison, it is useful to clarify the meaning and features of child and family policy.

CHILD AND FAMILY POLICY

Thomas Dye defines public policy as "whatever governments choose to do or not do" (Dye 1995, p.2). Within public policy is child and family policy, which is a branch of wider social policy and family policy. "Social policy" refers to whatever governments choose to do or not do in broad social matters such as health care, income security, and education. Its focus not only is on families but also on individuals who are not part of families. Family policy is narrower. It is a part of social policy that covers whatever governments choose to do or not do in matters of family such as social services for families, family income support, and the structure of the family. It gives attention to issues affecting all members of families, not only children. Child and family policy is narrower. It is a part of family policy that deals with matters of particular concern to children. Attention here may be given to parents and other adult members of families but in relation to outcomes for children.

The subject matters of child and family policy are many. Major ones include childcare and early childhood education, family income support and family or child benefits (or allowances), child welfare or child protection (the protection of children from parental maltreatment), child health care, and programs of early childhood intervention. But it is important to note that matters affecting children do not always fit neatly under a category called "child and family policy". Policies that deal with broad topics such as the environment, taxation, and criminal justice have obvious implications and importance for children. But this said, the subject matter under the umbrella of child and family policy captures much of what governments choose to do or not do for children.

What is striking about child and family policies is the variation from one country to another. This is a matter not simply of economic development where wealthy countries have strong and comprehensive policies for children and poor countries have weak ones. When we compare countries at similar levels of economic development, we see quite significant differences in policy directions and approaches. In Western economically advanced countries, for example, there are very important differences in child and family policies, which are part of a pattern of differences in overall social policies and types of welfare states. To understand these more general differences, it is helpful to look at the influential work of Gosta Esping-Andersen (1990, 1999). Esping-Andersen identifies three general types of welfare states or welfare regimes in Western industrialized countries, which he calls the "three worlds of welfare capitalism." These are the welfare states of the mainly Anglophone nations (the United Kingdom, the United States, Canada, Australia, and New Zealand), the Nordic nations (Sweden, Norway, Finland, Denmark, and Iceland), and the rest of continental Europe (distinctions later have been made in the literature between the welfare states of northern and southern continental Europe).

According to Esping-Andersen, what distinguishes these three welfare state types is the relative strength and delivery of social programs, the degree to which citizens are "decommodified" (that is, their well-being is made less dependent on market forces and employers), and the extent to which economic inequality is reduced through social policies and programs. In general terms, with their greater reliance on free markets, it is the Anglophone nations that have the weakest and least comprehensive social policies and programs, the least amount of decommodification, and the greatest amount of inequality. The Nordic countries, with their greater willingness to use the state for social purposes, have the most muscular policies, the most decommodification, and the least inequality. In the middle are continental European countries such as Germany and France. Although Esping-Andersen is quite aware of the major differences among countries within the three worlds, he also points to their overall policy similarities relative to the other worlds.

Particularly striking from Esping-Andersen's analysis is the contrast between Anglophone nations such as the United States and Nordic countries such as Sweden. In the United States, despite the considerable expansion of social welfare programs since the Second World War (with a certain degree of contraction since the 1980s), the welfare state provides a relatively basic and modest social safety net (Noble 1997; Olsen 2002). In comparison to most other developed countries, social programs are limited in scope, targeted towards particular groups (rather than being universal), and having strict eligibility criteria and modest benefit levels. The range of social services is comparatively small, the level of overall social spending is relatively low, and the level of taxation—which would provide funding for the welfare state—is low. More than in most other industrialized countries, the provision of social welfare in the United States is left to voluntary organizations, employers, and the private sector. As a result of all this, although the welfare state does accomplish a certain redistribution of income from higher to lower income groups, the impact is very modest. The outcome is a relatively high level of income inequality. Other Anglophone nations have similar characteristics although not to the same degree.

The Nordic welfare state, as perhaps best represented by Sweden, is quite different. Where the goal of the welfare state in the Anglo-American world is simply to alleviate poverty and other social ills, the aim of the Swedish welfare state is to try to abolish poverty entirely, promote full employment, and achieve a more egalitarian distribution of income (Olsen 2002). Social programs and services are relatively comprehensive in scope and involve high levels of standards and benefits. Although some programs are targeted to those in need and involve means tests, they are a relatively minor part of the overall welfare state. More central are universal or near-universal programs based on the rights of citizenship, which provide services or benefits for particular demographic categories of people such as health care for the ill and family benefits for parents with children. These programs are supplemented by social insurance programs that provide generous benefits in areas such as pensions and sickness insurance on the basis of contributions levied on earned income. In the Swedish welfare state, the range of social services is comprehensive, the level of social spending is relatively high, and the level of taxation is high. In contrast to other countries, the provision of social welfare is done much more through the state rather than through employers and voluntary organizations. As a result, there is a much greater redistribution of income and much less economic inequality in Sweden. There is a similar pattern in the other Nordic nations.

As pointed out by Clem Brooks and Jeff Manza (2006), welfare states in virtually all economically advanced countries have been resilient, despite economic difficulties and a more competitive global environment since the 1980s and despite the widespread introduction of programs of fiscal restraint and cuts in social spending. Contrary to predictions of universal retrenchment and a major decline of welfare states everywhere, welfare states have endured in the Anglophone world just as they have in the Nordic world and continental Europe. In some countries such as Germany, as can be seen in the data presented by Brooks and Manza, social welfare spending actually has increased since the 1980s. However, although there have been economic problems, challenges, and resilience, the differences in social programs and in the level of social spending between the Nordic countries and Anglo-American democracies have remained sharp. Although levels in social spending (as a percentage of GDP) in Sweden did decline in the mid-1990s due to economic difficulties, spending was over 30 percent of GDP by the turn of the century, compared with about 15 percent in the United States. And by the end of the 1990s, where spending was about 30 percent of GDP in the Nordic countries overall, it was at about 18 percent in the Anglo-American world as a whole.

As part of the pattern of differences in social policy, there also have been major differences in family policy. Walter Korpi (2000), in reference to comparative family policy data and with a focus on gender roles and gender equality, divides family policies into three basic types. They differ in terms of policy efforts to bring about gender equality and institutional support for women and families. First, as evident in the Anglo-American world, there is the market-oriented family policy model, where there is a general preference to leave issues of gender equality and family support to market solutions. The practice is that governments will intervene to provide support for women and families but at relatively modest levels. Second, there is the dual-earner support model, as found in the Nordic countries, where support for the family is very strong and in particular, for dual-earner families. This is in the context of the policy goal of facilitating the entry of women into the labor force and promoting gender equality in families and in society. And, third, there is the general family support model, as found in much of continental Europe, where support to the family is relatively generous but geared to the maintenance of the traditional family type where the father is the main earner and the mother the main provider of care for children and the household. As with social policy, what is particularly striking from Korpi's analysis and from the comparative data is the contrast between family policies in the Nordic and Anglo-American world. In the former are relatively vigorous and comprehensive policy efforts on behalf of women and families and in the latter, relatively weak policies.

When we focus specifically on children and on child and family policies, we see a pattern of similarly striking differences. In the Nordic countries, as will shortly be discussed in more detail, child and family policies are relatively comprehensive and muscular. Sweden, for example, has established a universal and high-quality system of childcare, financed and delivered by the state (Moss and Petrie 2002; Olsen 2002). Sweden also provides for a strong program of family income support and a proactive system of child welfare. In contrast, in the Anglo-American world, policies and programs are comparatively weak (Olsen 2002; Peters *et al.* 2001). In the area of childcare, for example, the United States and Canada rely primarily on informal and unregulated care that is privately funded and privately delivered by relatives, neighbors, and sitters. Family income support is at a relatively low level in both countries and child welfare systems tend to react to problems after they occur rather than working at prevention. Again, this will be discussed in more depth shortly.

Finally, there is significant variation in child and family policy not only across countries but also within countries. This is particularly evident in countries with federal states. In the federal states of both

Canada and the United States, although the federal government makes a major financial contribution to social and family programs, the provinces and states have major responsibility for child and family policy. And in both countries, given the different priorities of different provinces and states, there is significant variation in policies across provincial and state jurisdictions. In Canada, the province of Quebec has a much stronger and more comprehensive system of childcare and parental leave than the other provinces (Le Bordais and Marcil-Gratton 1994; O'Hara 1998; Turner and Turner 2005). In the United States, to the extent that there are policies and programs of income and childcare support for low-income families with children, policy efforts have been much more robust in northern and north-eastern states such as Minnesota and Vermont, than in southern and south-western states such as Alabama, Texas, and South Carolina (Meyers, Gornick and Peck 2001).

Also noteworthy is the stability in policy variations over time. As pointed out by Gregg Olsen (2002) in his comparative study of Sweden, the United States, and Canada, major differences in social, family, and child-related policies have persisted despite the powerful forces of globalization and major international economic change. It is true, says Olsen, that over the past few decades, these forces have had the effect of creating more uniform and austere policies. In Sweden, as well as in Canada and the United States, fiscal restraint and cost-cutting measures have been introduced and, in virtually all welfare states, programs have become less generous than they were in the past. Levels of inequality and poverty have risen in Sweden just as they have in North America. However, despite the impact of these forces and despite the recent contraction of the welfare state, the variations in policies remains pronounced. Policies continue to be significantly friendlier to children and families in Sweden and the other Nordic nations than they do in the United States and Canada.

We now examine in more detail the differences in child and family policies between the Nordic world and North America. We focus on these particular countries because they are at similar levels of economic development, the policy variations are great, and the variations illustrate well the linkage between child-friendly or -unfriendly policies and childhood violence. The United States and Canada have the added advantage of being federal states. This allows for an analysis of linkages between policy variations by state and province and childhood violence. But before we make our comparisons, it may be helpful first to describe the meaning of child-friendly policies.

CHARACTERISTICS OF CHILD-FRIENDLY POLICIES

Child and family policies may be described as child-friendly if they have the following basic characteristics. First, they are child-friendly if they reflect a commitment to the fundamental rights of children, including the child's right to healthy development and protection from violence and maltreatment. Child-friendliness is not necessarily the same thing as family-friendliness. Where family-friendly policies may be designed to give support to parents, child-friendly polices are ones that are focussed on the rights and best interests of children. Programs of childcare, for example, are aimed at providing for the best interests of children, not simply at looking after the daycare needs of parents or helping women enter the labor force.

A country with child-friendly policies would have signed and ratified the UN Convention on the Rights of the Child, committing itself to implementing the basic rights of children. It also would have established a special independent agency such as a children's ombudsman or children's commissioner to give focus to the rights of the child and help put the Convention into effect. Because children have so little power and resources themselves, they require institutional support and advocacy to help with the implementation of their rights. Furthermore, as an expression of a country's commitment, the Convention would have been incorporated into child-related laws and policies, and child impact assessments would be a standard procedure when policies are formulated affecting children. Child-friendliness means implementing the Convention and working against conditions that deny or compromise the rights of children and that steer children into pathways toward unhealthy development and violence.

Second, policies are child-friendly if they are based on the best available research on healthy child development and the best interests of the child. As an important part of this, they would reflect research findings on risk factors and protective factors against aggressive and violent behavior. Thanks to the results of research and especially prospective longitudinal studies done in several countries over the past few decades, an impressive body of knowledge has been accumulated about risk factors and protective factors for childhood violence (Farrington and Welsh 2007). As discussed in the first part of this book, much is now known about the sources of aggressive and anti-social behavior and about what can be done to protect children against it. Lack of knowledge is not a credible excuse for policy inaction. Child-friendly policies are ones that would pay serious attention to this body of knowledge and work to build strategies and programs in the best interests of children based on the research. Research would be used to inform best practices about achieving the goal of promoting healthy child development through reducing the risks, enhancing the protective factors, and implementing prevention programs.

Third, policies are child-friendly if their goals actually are implemented. It is one thing to know the research and be committed to the rights of the child. It is quite another to put the policies into effect. Known from the research into protective factors and into effective programs is the following. At a general level, as summarized by the World Health Organization (2002b, 2007), and the United Nations *World Report on Violence Against Children* (2006), child and family policies serve as protective factors when they provide families and children with supports in the areas of health care, appropriate parenting, childcare, adequate family income, and relief from poverty and deprivation. Policies are beneficial and protective of children to the extent that they reduce economic and psychological stress in the family, provide for the basic needs and health of parents and children, and promote positive parenting and family wellness. This requires strong, comprehensive, and effective policies on child and family health care, childcare, child welfare, parenting support, and income security. It also requires that these policies be proactive rather than reactive, foreseeing problems such as the accumulation of risk factors for childhood violence and preventing these problems with supports, rather than dealing with the problems after they occur.

Implementing such general policies of support is an important expression of child-friendliness. So too is implementing policies based on research showing the critical importance of the early years and identifying early prevention programs that work, or to show promise in working, in preventing childhood violence. Over the past few decades, a solid body of research has developed identifying not only risk and protective factors but also evidence-based programs of early childhood prevention. These programs are found in literature on public health, crime prevention, and developmental psychology and are summarized by Farrington and Welsh (2003, 2007), Karoly (2005), Kellermann and his associates (1998), Shonkoff and Phillips (2000), Welsh and Farrington (2006), the United Nations (2006) and the World Health Organization (2002b). A key message in the literature is that, for programs to be effective, they need to start early and in the home. Intervention in the first few years of a child's life is more effective than later, and family-based programs are more effective than school or community-based programs (Farrington and Welsh 2003; Kellermann *et al.* 1998). The major evidence-based programs identified in the research are as follows.

First are programs of home visitation (Farrington and Welsh 2007; Kellermann *et al.* 1998; Olds *et al.* 1998, 1999; Raikes *et al.* 2006; Williams and Van Dorn 1999; World Health Organization 2002b). These are programs in which nurses or public health professionals or paraprofessionals visit mothers and parents on a weekly or monthly basis beginning at birth (and sometimes during the prenatal period) and up to one, two, or three years after the birth. The objective is to provide information and counseling on healthy pregnancies, infant and childhood health, and positive parenting practices. It also is to provide mothers and parents with emotional and social support, to listen to problems and concerns and to convey to the mother a sense of care. Evaluations and long-term follow-up have shown that children who have received home visitation have a lower incidence of antisocial and criminal behavior than those who have not been involved in the program. Overall, home visiting has been shown to be effective in preventing child abuse and to be promising in reducing later childhood violence.

Second are programs of parent education or parent management training (Bernazzani and Tremblay 2006; Farrington and Welsh 2007; Kellermann *et al.* 1998; United Nations 2006; World Health Organization 2002b). These refer to training in which parents are educated to alter their child's behavior in the home. They build on the knowledge that parenting skills are not instinctive, that there is an important linkage between inappropriate parenting and later childhood violence, and that parenting skills can be improved through education. The programs come in a variety of forms in terms of the timing of sessions, the mode of delivery, and specific content and approach. But the general goals are to provide information about appropriate care and discipline, to prevent parental rejection or maltreatment, to encourage parents to read to and listen to their children, and to promote healthy child–parent relations. Evaluations have shown these particular programs to be quite promising in decreasing aggressive and violent behavior.

Third are programs of parent education in combination with childcare (Farrington and Welsh 2007; Welsh and Farrington 2004). These refer to parent education programs that include childcare or daycare services for the parents' children. Through this combination, as parents benefit from gaining knowledge in positive parenting, children benefit from social interaction from other children and from the stimulation of their cognitive skills. Evaluations have shown the combination to be effective in preventing child antisocial and aggressive behavior. The effect is independent from parent education programs alone or childcare services alone.

Fourth are programs of high-quality childcare and early childhood education (Farrington and Welsh 2007; Kellermann *et al.* 1998; Shonkoff and Phillips 2000; World Health Organization 2002b). These come in a variety of forms and involve education in the form of intellectual enrichment and social skills training. Settings include preschools, nursery schools, and high-quality professional childcare where childcare is regarded as an educational rather than a custodial undertaking. The programs also include early intervention and head start programs for at-risk children. Primary examples include the famous Perry Preschool Program and Abecedarian Program in the United States and the Sure Start program in England. The overall aims of the programs are to improve the social and intellectual development of the child, build resilience by providing for enriched early education, and strengthen the child's bond to school or to the educational process. Evaluations have shown such programs to be very promising in reducing the risk of later childhood and youth violence.

Fifth are legal measures and public education programs against the use of corporal punishment against children (Durrant 1999,

2000; Gershoff 2002; Grogan-Kaylor 2004; Herrenkohl *et al.* 1997; Straus, Sugarman and Giles-Sims 1997; United Nations 2006). Programs and measures against the use of corporal punishment build on the body of research discussed in Chapter 3 that shows linkages between the parental use of corporal punishment—especially harsh and frequent corporal punishment—child abuse, and later antisocial and aggressive behaviors among children experiencing the punishment. As shown in the research done by Joan Durrant (1999, 2000), where corporal punishment has been legally banned and where the ban has been accompanied by a public education campaign showing the value of alternative forms of discipline, child abuse and later childhood violence are less likely to occur.

Finally, sixth are programs to prevent teen pregnancies (Kellermann *et al.* 1998; World Health Organization 2002b). As noted by Arthur Kellermann and his colleagues (1998, p.274), children who are "born to unprepared parents are more likely to be abused, and as a result, are more likely to victimize others later in life." When young parenthood is combined with factors such as poverty and lack of consistent supervision by a single parent, children are put at increased risk of future violent behavior. Thus it is important that there be in place strong programs such as ones of sexual health education to reduce unintended teen pregnancies. Assessments have shown that well-designed programs of sexual health education are effective in increasing the use of contraceptives or delaying sexual intercourse.

Child-friendly policies are ones that listen to the research, support further research as needed, and implement programs based on the evidence. Policies are also child-friendly when they provide for universal programs to the greatest extent possible. Two general types of prevention programs are possible: universal and selective programs (Farrington and Welsh 2007). Universal programs target an entire population or segment of a population and, as described in the previous chapter, are more beneficial and rights-consistent than are targeted programs. No child is left behind. But failing universal programs, should selective or targeted programs be used for reasons of costs or other considerations, child-friendly policies are ones that would assure wide coverage for all children and families who are at risk.

POLICIES IN THE NORDIC COUNTRIES

No country or jurisdiction has fully fledged child-friendly policies. But in relative terms, some countries are much closer to this than others. With their relatively comprehensive welfare states and robust social and family policies, the Nordic countries are closer than most other economically advanced countries and much closer than North America. Although policies are far from perfect in the Nordic countries, there is a mountain of evidence to suggest that their child and family policies are the closest approximations to ones that can be characterized as child-friendly. The indications are as follows.

First, the Nordic countries have demonstrated a clear commitment to the rights and well-being of children. They were at the forefront of international efforts to establish the Convention on the Rights of the Child in 1989 and they were among the first to ratify the Convention, which they did with no or few reservations (United Nations Treaty Body Database 2007). Sweden ratified the Convention in 1990, Norway, Denmark, and Finland in 1991, and Iceland in 1992. The Nordic nations also have been world leaders in creating special agencies and institutions in support of the rights of children and of the implementation of the Convention. Norway was the first country in the world to establish an independent children's ombudsman, with the appointment of Malfrid Flekkoy (1981–9). She was given the task of monitoring and improving the situation of children, monitoring Norway's implementation of the Convention and advising the Norwegian government on developing child-friendly policies and Convention-consistent legislation (Flekkoy 1991; UNICEF 2004). Norway established the office of the children's ombudsman in 1981 (well before the country ratified the Convention), serving as a role model for other countries. Similar offices or structures were established by Sweden in 1993, Denmark and Iceland in 1994, and Finland in 2005.

Moreover, the Nordic countries have been among the most serious and conscientious implementers of the Convention, as evident in the reviews by the UN Committee on the Rights of the Child on the progress by countries in implementing the Convention (see the Committee's Concluding Observations in the United Nations Treaty Database 2007). Sweden, for example, was the first country in 1999 to require that all national government decisions affecting children are subject to child impact assessments, as recommended by the UN Committee. This means that decisions are assessed from the point of view of the rights and best interests of the child with the burden of proof on those who propose policies that are potentially at odds with the child's best interests (Durrant 2007; Sylwander 2001). Another example is Norway, which amended its Human Rights Act in 2003, incorporating the Convention into human rights law. The effect among other things is that if there is a conflict between the Convention and other Norwegian legislation, the Convention takes precedence. This is a major step forward.

But the most important reflection of the commitment of Nordic states has been in the substance of their child and family policies. The Nordic nations have been world leaders in developing and implementing strong and comprehensive policies supportive of children. Although the policies are family-friendly and designed to be supportive of parents, they are also child-friendly, in that they have as a primary aim the rights and best interests of children. To be sure, there are many shortcomings, as pointed out by the UN Committee on the Rights of the Child. Risk factors such as child maltreatment, family poverty, and family instability are still in ample supply and policies fall short in many areas in providing for the rights and best interests of children (Satka and Eydal 2004). But relative to policy developments in most other countries, policies in the Nordic world show a high level of respect for the rights of the child. Policies have been put into place that work aggressively at reducing the risk factors and building the protective factors. Although far from perfect, they do much to steer children away from a pathway into antisocial behavior and violence and into a pathway of healthy development and productive citizenship. This may be seen when we review general policies and outcomes in the areas of childcare and early childhood education, income support for families, child welfare, corporal punishment, child health, and early prevention programs such as parent education, home visitation, and sexual health education.

Childcare

First, the Nordic countries have developed among the most advanced systems of childcare in the world. Their level of public spending on childcare and early childhood education is at the top end of spending among industrialized countries, as noted by the Organization of Economic Cooperation and Development (OECD). According to data from the OECD *Family Database* (2007), in a comparison of 28 countries in spending on childcare and early childhood education services in 2003 (as a percentage of GDP), the Nordic countries all ranked in the top seven. The top two countries were Denmark and Iceland, with a level of spending over twice the OECD average. But spending levels in Sweden, Norway, and Finland were also quite high. Such spending serves as a protective factor, helping to relieve families from financial pressures and from the stress associated with shortages of childcare.

What is significant is not only the spending but the coverage and quality of care. Sweden in particular has put great effort into the building of a strong system of public, universal, and high-quality childcare through a network of preschools (for children between ages one and six), family daycares, and leisure-time centers (for school-age children) (Moss and Petrie 2002; O'Hara 1998; Olsen 2002). It is a system funded through payroll taxes paid by employers, general government revenues, and nominal parental fees that cover 15 percent of the cost. It is comprehensive in its coverage. Municipal authorities have responsibility for the delivery of childcare services and, since 1996, are required by law to provide childcare spaces for all children between the ages of one-and-a-half and six. The system is largely financed and delivered by the state and is now part of the education system. This is reflected in the fact that the service is under the responsibility of the Ministry of Education rather than, as before, the Ministry of Social Affairs. Childcare in Sweden is no longer regarded simply as "sitting" or as custodial exercise but as early education—hence the increasing use of the terms "early childhood education" and "early learning." Furthermore, the system is one that is very much concerned with quality. Municipal authorities are required by the central government to maintain high standards in terms of staff–child ratios, health and safety, and the qualifications of staff.

To complement the system of public childcare, the Nordic countries have also developed very strong programs of parental leave (Moss and Petrie 2002; Olsen 2002). Since 1974, Sweden, for instance, has provided for a generous system of parental insurance benefits, funded by a combination of employer payroll taxes and general revenues, in order to allow a parent or parents paid leave to take care of their young children at home, should they wish. All parents are able to take a paid leave of absence from work for a total of 15 months, provided that they had been in the labor force for the previous eight months. The benefit level is high. For the first 12 months, the benefit is 80 percent of prior earnings and, for the last three months, it is a flat-rate benefit. The benefit period is quite generous in comparison to other countries. It is divided equally between mothers and fathers, but either can transfer their portion to the other parent except for two months, which are reserved for fathers. This two-month exception rule, which was instituted in 2002 (to replace a one-month exception rule that had been established in 1995), is to encourage fathers to become more involved in parenting—although there had been a growing trend in this direction before the rule. One other remarkable thing about the system is that even prior to birth, pregnant women who have to stop working are eligible for a benefit of 80 percent of their prior earnings for up to 50 days during the last two months of pregnancy. Such a strong system of leave does much both to provide parents with financial help and to allow them to spend more time with their children. And it also helps to elevate the status and importance of parenting.

Income support

The Nordic countries also provide for a strong system of family income support that few other countries can match. According to OECD data, in comparing 30 countries on their level of family spending in terms of cash transfers to families, services, and tax measures in 2003 (as a percentage of GDP), Denmark, Norway, and Sweden were in the top five countries while Iceland and Finland were in the top 11 (OECD 2007). This is consistent with trends since the Second World War, and especially since the 1980s, showing an increasing level of generosity in the family income support programs of the Nordic countries (Ferrarini 2006; Olsen 2002; Ozawa 2004). These programs involve a vast array of supports, including family benefits to assist parents with the costs of raising children (variously called family allowances or child benefits), housing benefits for low-income families, special allowances for children with disabilities, sickness benefits for parents in order for them to stay home to care for their sick children, pensions for children with a deceased parent, and assistance to custodial parents with child support payments. The generosity of family cash benefits is particularly noteworthy. Sweden, for example, has developed a universal system where all parents who have children under age 16 receive a very sizable allowance that can be extended if the child remains in school.

Such strong programs of income support have made a major contribution to the relatively low levels of family poverty and child poverty in the Nordic world. In a study of the well-being of children in 24 economically advanced OECD countries, UNICEF (2007) found the level of child poverty to be lowest respectively in Denmark, Finland, Norway, and Sweden. Child poverty was measured as the percentage of children growing up in relative poverty, defined as living in a household where family income is less than 50 percent of national median family income. According to the data, which were gathered from 1999 to 2001, the percentage of poor children in Denmark was 2.4, Finland 3.4, Norway 3.6, and Sweden 3.6. These levels are remarkably low when considering the OECD average of 11.2 percent. Such levels are consistent with historical trends in child and family poverty among industrialized nations since the 1980s, showing the rates of poverty to be significantly less in the Nordic world than in other countries (Cornia and Danziger 1997; Ferrarini 2006). This reflects in large part low levels of income inequality and the relatively strong policy efforts of Nordic governments in support of families and children. In face of economic difficulties during the 1980s and especially the 1990s, these governments did cut back on certain programs. But the cuts were modest with the result that overall levels of child poverty have remained remarkably low.

Child welfare

Another area of strength is in child welfare policies. The Nordic countries have developed child welfare policies and systems that are relatively effective in dealing with problems of child maltreatment. As discussed by Neil Gilbert (1997), from a comparative perspective, child welfare systems in economically advanced countries may be divided into two basic models. One is the legalistic child protection model, as found in the Anglo-American world. Its primary focus in on reacting to suspected cases of child abuse or neglect after they occur, with a highly legalistic procedure involving child protection agencies and sometimes the police, lawyers, and family court judges. An incident of child maltreatment is seen largely to be the fault of individual parents or caregivers who abuse or neglect their children. The best approach is thought to be one of responding to the maltreatment in a legalistic way, apprehending children from their homes if necessary, having a protection hearing, and placing the children in foster care or institutional care. The other model, as found in much of continental Europe, is the family service model. Its focus is on being proactive. Here, the problem of child maltreatment is assumed to be one largely of social and economic conditions creating stress and pressures on parents such that abuse or neglect is an outcome. To protect against such an outcome, the best approach is assumed to be a proactive policy of providing families with support. This support would include programs of parent education, home visitation, information and referral services, counseling and family therapy services, parent and children support groups, and respite care. Children ultimately may have to be removed from the home through a legalistic procedure, but the main focus of the system is on prevention and early intervention.

Child welfare systems in the Nordic countries follow the family service model. In Sweden, for example, the main focus is on early prevention and family supports (Andersson 2006; Khoo, Hyvonen and Nygren 2002). The system essentially works this way. As with childcare, Sweden's child welfare system is decentralized, with responsibility for administration given to the municipalities. The reporting of child abuse is mandatory and under the Social Services Act, social welfare committees in each municipality have the obligation to ensure that children grow up in safe and secure conditions. The guiding principle is the best interests of the child. Responsibility for protection is not solely in the hands of a particular child protection agency, as in North America, but across the many agencies and sectors in the field of social welfare and health. Programs of support—home visitation, parent education, substance abuse programs, psychiatric treatment—are made available not simply to families where there has been demonstrated abuse, but to all families in need. Moreover, all children and parents in Sweden have the right to ask for assistance through a "contact person" or "contact family," who is officially approved and paid by the state and who provide a support service for children.

The system in Sweden is very much geared to monitoring the health and welfare of children and providing multiple access points for children and families in need. The system requires a high level of collaboration among agencies (Wiklund 2007). The objective is to identify children at risk and prevent child maltreatment or to stop it early. But if there is a case of abuse or neglect, authorities in the social welfare and health field have the obligation to report this to the social welfare committee of each municipality. The committee in turn has the responsibility to investigate the report and make an assessment. Should it be necessary, the committee will refer families to any one of a number of in-home support programs and services. Should it be absolutely necessary, as a last resort and authorized by a court, a decision will be made to intervene and place the child in short-term or long-term foster care or residential care, where there is a strict system of monitoring and where children are able to keep contact with their biological parents. With certain variations, comparable child welfare systems exist in the other Nordic countries.

The child welfare systems in the Nordic countries are not without their problems. As in other countries, there are problems with bureaucracy, the shortage and turnover of professionals, and the continuing incidence of child abuse and neglect. In Sweden, there is sometimes the problem of ineffective collaboration in identifying risk (Wiklund 2007). But in relative terms, the systems perform well. It obviously is difficult to compare systems in how well they do, given the different ways in different countries of defining and recording child abuse and in different rates of reporting it. But one revealing indicator is in the comparison of child maltreatment deaths resulting from abuse and neglect in different countries. The comparison is not perfect, given the different medical and technical capabilities in different countries for the precise identification of child maltreatment deaths. But the numbers are highly suggestive. The UNICEF Innocenti Research Centre in Florence, Italy, has done a study of child maltreatment deaths in 27 economically developed countries, showing the annual number of deaths among children under age 15 averaged over a five-year period during the 1990s and calculated as deaths per 100,000 children to control for population (UNICEF 2003). The study showed that while the numbers of actual and suspected maltreatment deaths in the Nordic countries were not the lowest—Spain, Greece, and Italy were the lowest—they were relatively low, well under the average of 1.1 deaths per 100,000. Norway and Sweden were in the lowest third of countries, with 0.3 and 0.6 deaths respectively. The numbers for both Denmark and Finland were 0.8 child deaths per 100,000, again well under the average.

Corporal punishment

Another area in which the Nordic countries have been child-friendly is in policy and law dealing with corporal punishment. In 1979, with knowledge that the physical punishment of children is contrary to the rights and best interests of the child, Sweden became the first nation in the world to prohibit all forms of the corporal punishment of children, not only by teachers but also by all parents and caregivers (Durrant 1999, 2003; Durrant and Janson 2005; United Nations 2006). Finland followed suit in 1984, Denmark in 1986 (with a more explicit law in 1997), Norway in 1987, and Iceland in 2003. With the Nordic countries as leaders, other countries decided to do the same, including Austria, Croatia, Cyprus, Romania, Germany, Israel, Bulgaria, Greece, Latvia, Ukraine, Hungary, and, most recently, the Netherlands, New Zealand, and Portugal in 2007.

Sweden has served as a model for how best to proceed. Its approach was not simply to institute a legal ban all at once but also to accompany the ban with a major public education campaign, informing parents on problems associated with physical punishment and on the advantages of using alternative forms of discipline. As noted by Joan Durrant (1999, 2003), Sweden's policy and law had three main objectives. One was to alter public attitudes, producing "a shift in social pressure such that a 'good' parent would be seen as one who does not use corporal punishment" (Durrant 1999, p.436). The second was to increase the early identification of children at risk for abuse. The intention was that through the creation of clear guidelines for parents and professionals as to what was permissible and not permissible in the discipline of children, and through public reports of parents continuing to use physical force, professionals would be better positioned to identify parents—early in the abuse cycle—who were at risk of seriously abusing their children. Finally, the third, as a result of the earlier identification, was to allow for earlier intervention and support for parents still using physical force. As with the child welfare system, the focus was to be on prevention and early intervention, rather than reacting to problems after they occur.

Durrant (1999) has assessed the degree to which these objectives have been realized. As to the first objective, public attitudes have shifted in a major way. Public opinion polls in Sweden have shown a marked decline over time in public support for corporal punishment. By 1994, for example, 15 years after the ban, only 11 percent of those surveyed approved of the practice, even in its mildest forms. And with this decline has been a decline in the reported use of physical punishment. Where the parental striking of children was common 40 years ago, it has now become rare. Second, over time, the identification of children at risk of more serious abuse has increased. After the ban went into effect, public reporting of assaults against children increased. However, the seriousness of assaults did not increase over time, indicating success in identifying children at risk. The rate of criminal prosecution against abusive parents has remained steady and the numbers of child maltreatment deaths has remained very low. And third, says Durrant, through earlier identification of children at risk, the ban has contributed to a stronger emphasis on the prevention of child abuse. Less legalistic and coercive measures have been employed against parents. In line with the objectives of the ban, more focus has been given to support programs for parents—parent education, substance abuse programs—in order that problems can be dealt with before they escalate. As reported by Durrant and Janson (2005), this has contributed in a major way to a dramatic decline in parental acts of physical abuse and violence against children in recent decades.

Child health

Policies in the Nordic countries also have been child-friendly in the area of child health. This is particularly important in considering risk factors for children such as unhealthy pregnancies, fetal alcohol exposure, and maternal depression. To begin with, the Nordic countries have developed among the best health care systems in the world. In the rankings of the World Health Organization (2000), although they were not ranked at the very top—France was given this honor—they ranked very high with Norway, Iceland, and Sweden in the top 12 percent of countries (Norway was in the top 6 percent). The Nordic systems are public and universal, with very high levels of public expenditures on health care services and high numbers of doctors and hospital beds per capita (OECD 2006a). For example, among 30 OECD countries in 2004, Denmark, Norway, Sweden, and Iceland ranked in the top seven in public expenditure, spending in the range of 83 percent to 85 percent of total spending on health care. This makes an important contribution to the quality of health for children as well as adults.

As part of their health care efforts, the Nordic countries provide high-quality service and programs for pregnant mothers and infants. Two standard and key indicators of healthy pregnancies and healthy newborns are low rates of infant mortality and low birth weight rates. In UNICEF's child well-being study, the Nordic countries did extremely well on both indicators (UNICEF 2007). In rates of infant mortality (deaths before the age of 12 months per 1000 live births), Iceland, Finland, Sweden, and Norway respectively scored in the top five among 25 OECD countries (the other country was Japan). Denmark ranked in the middle. In low birth weight rates (percentage births less than 2500g), the same four Nordic countries scored in the top five (the other country was Ireland). Denmark ranked 7th. Low birth weight is associated with a number of risk factors including maternal smoking during pregnancy and similar neurodevelopmental toxins, as discussed in Chapter 2. These positive rankings among the Nordic countries are indicative of not only the well-being of mothers and infants, but also the later health of children.

Early prevention

The Nordic countries also have developed an extensive network of early child development, intervention, and prevention programs as part of their wider systems of health care, childcare, education, and child welfare. In Sweden, for example, a wide range of parent education, home visitation, and other family support programs are delivered free of charge to all young children who are in need of special support (European Agency for Development in Special Needs Education 2005). These are delivered at the local level under the authority of county councils and in keeping with Sweden's official policy of working to decrease harmful influences on children and to support parents in their parenting, as expressed in the goals of the Sweden's National Board of Health and Welfare. And of particular importance, across Sweden and the Nordic world, quality childcare—a highly important protective factor and prevention measure for children at risk—is part of the universal and comprehensive system of early childhood education. The efforts of the Nordic countries in providing for early childhood programs are evident in their public expenditures. According to the OECD (2006b), the Nordic nations spend more on early childhood services (for nought-to six-year-olds) than virtually all other countries, as a percentage of GDP. Denmark spends the most (2%), followed by Norway (1.7%), Sweden (1.7%), and Finland (1.3%).

The Nordic countries also have developed strong programs to prevent teenage pregnancies. Aggressive programs of sexual health education have been incorporated into schools and public health messages. In Sweden, for example, comprehensive and mandatory programs of sexual health education have been incorporated into the school curricula, beginning in kindergarten (Luker 2006). Children learn early and they learn much throughout their student careers in open and frank discussions about sexual activity, contraception, and sexually transmitted diseases. The result has been a relatively low rate of teenage births in Sweden and other Nordic nations. In UNICEF's child well-being study, in a comparison of 24 OECD countries, the countries of Denmark, Sweden, and Finland ranked in the top one third for low numbers of births per 1000 for women aged 15 to 19 (UNICEF 2007). Norway ranked tenth. It is not that teens in these countries do not engage in sexual intercourse. As noted in the UNICEF study, the percentage of 15-year-old teens that report having had sexual intercourse is among the highest in Finland and Sweden. The relatively low levels of teen births reflect the use of birth control and strong programs of sexual health education.

Finally, in the Nordic countries, strong crime prevention policies and strategies have been established, involving early intervention and prevention programs as a component. Since the 1970s and 1980s, in recognition of the fact that traditional law enforcement has only a modest impact on preventing youth and adult crime, national crime prevention strategies have been developed in many Western countries that incorporate two approaches to crime prevention beyond law enforcement (Crawford 1998; International Centre for Crime Prevention 1999). One is "situational crime prevention," which focusses on reducing the opportunities for crime (e.g. use of locks and surveillance) (Clarke 1995; Farrington and Welsh 2006; Rosenbaum, Lurigio and Davis 1998). The other is "social crime prevention" or "developmental crime prevention" or "crime prevention through social development," which focusses on building protective factors in families and communities against criminal involvement, especially among youth (Farrington and Welsh 2007). As part of social crime prevention and as part of national crime prevention strategies, permanent structures—usually called national crime prevention councils or agencies—have been put into operation with the task of conducting research, providing resources, and mobilizing efforts at the local level and across different levels of governments to build prevention programs, including parent education, head start, and healthy pregnancy programs.

The Nordic nations have been at the forefront of establishing strategies and councils, with a focus on using a balanced approach between social and situational crime prevention (Swedish National Council for Crime Prevention 2001; Takala 2004). Denmark was among the first Western countries to establish a strategy in 1971, followed by Sweden in 1974, Norway in 1980, and Finland in 1989. The "Nordic model" of crime prevention has been one of recognizing the importance of research in preventing crime, tackling risk factors in the family and social environment, and developing evidence-based programs of prevention. While the model acknowledges the crime prevention role of strong welfare states and child policies already in place across the Nordic world, it seeks to undertake measures and build programs that complement and reinforce this role. In surveying the strategies and councils that have been put into place worldwide, Farrington and Welsh (2007) point to the strategy in Sweden as a model for other countries. It is a model because a permanent structure—the National Council for Crime Prevention—has been successfully put into place with a large staff and budget, with influence within the structure of government, and with a capacity to mobilize partners and deliver important programs of crime prevention. Although the bulk of early prevention programs in the Nordic countries are delivered as part of ongoing and wider programs of childcare, health care, and child welfare, national crime prevention strategies make a further contribution.

Linkage to violence

All of these various child-friendly policies and programs show the seriousness of the Nordic countries in providing for not only the general welfare of children but also their rights under the UN Convention. Policy efforts to provide for child health and healthy pregnancies reflect the implementation of Article 24 of the Convention, requiring that countries ensure the child's enjoyment of the highest attainable standard of health. Measures against child maltreatment and corporal punishment reflect efforts at implementing Article 19, calling on countries to protect the child from all forms of violence, abuse, and neglect. Programs to provide children with material support and economic security show a serious implementation of Article 27, directing countries to provide for the right of every child to a standard of living adequate for the child's healthy development. Policies to provide for childcare show a serious effort to put Article 18 into effect, requiring countries to assist parents with childcare and the upbringing of children. Finally, taken together, the friendliness of these policies reflect a commitment to Article 3, calling on countries to make the best interests of the child a primary consideration in all actions concerning children.

All of these efforts are desirable in themselves. But they have an added benefit of being associated with relatively low levels of childhood aggression and violence. As we would expect, with universal systems of health care and childcare, proactive systems of child welfare, comprehensive programs of income support, and comparatively strong programs of early prevention, protective factors have been elevated such that the risk factors associated with the raising of violent children have been lessened. Although the problem of childhood violence certainly has not been eliminated in the Nordic world, it has been reduced thanks to the child-friendliness of the policies. Among the indicators of lower levels of childhood violence are parents' reports on the behavior of their children, children's reports of experience with violence, and rates of violent crime.

We would anticipate, first of all, that parents in the Nordic countries would report conduct problems and aggressive behavior in their children less frequently than in other countries. Indeed there is evidence of this to be the case. Several studies have shown that Nordic parents report fewer conduct problems among their children—including aggressive behavior—than parents in other European countries and North America (Crijnen, Achenbach and Verhulst 1999; Haugland 2003; Larsson and Frisk 1999). The reports are based on studies of how parents rate their children on the Achenbach Child Behavior Checklist. Studies in Norway, for example, have shown that only 1 to 2 percent of school-age children exhibit serious conduct problems (Sorlie 2000, cited in Drugli 2006).

We also would expect the experience of violence among children to be less in the Nordic countries, given the child-friendly policies. It would be anticipated, for example, that children would report less of a problem with bullying. There is evidence to this effect. As reported in UNICEF's child well-being study (2007), among 21 OECD countries, the percentage of young people (aged 11, 13, and 15) in Nordic countries who reported being bullied was less, overall, than the OECD average. Where the OECD mean was 31 percent, it was 15 percent in Sweden, 24 percent in Finland, 31 percent in Denmark, and 32 percent in Norway. Similarly, as found in a cross-national study by Eleanor Smith-Khuri and her associates (2004), adolescents in Sweden experienced bullying to a considerably less degree than their counterparts in Portugal, Ireland, Israel, and the United States. In her study, where 15 percent of Swedish adolescents reported being bullied during the school term, the average among the countries studied was 34 percent. Finally, as reported by the World Health Organization (2002b) during the same time period, there was a similarly lower level of bullying behavior among 13-year-olds in Sweden, Norway, and Finland (Denmark was an exception). Among those who reported not being engaged in bullying during the school term, where the average was 58 percent in 27 countries, it was 87 percent in Sweden (the highest percentage), 71 percent in Norway, and 63 percent in Finland.

Finally, we would anticipate that the rates of violent youth crime would be lower in the Nordic countries than in other economically developed countries. It would be expected that children raised in a child-friendly environment would be better protected against the risk factors and less likely to grow up to become young offenders—and later, adult offenders—engaged in violent criminal activity. According to researchers working under what is called the General Evolutionary Ecological Paradigm, in 10 to 15 years after infancy and early childhood, higher or lower degrees of child well-being and nurturance should be followed by higher or lower rates of crime and violent crime (Savage and Vila 2002). Referred to sometimes as the "lagged nurturance hypothesis," the thinking is that if children are raised in a negative or hostile environment, they are more likely to act out and eventually come into conflict with the law. This hypothesis is consistent with the life-course persistent path from early aggression and violence to later involvement in criminal violence noted in Chapter 1. The hypothesis does not mean that there is no violence between early childhood and later childhood. There indeed is a greater likelihood of early aggressive and antisocial behavior. Rather, it means that in later childhood, after the age of criminal responsibility, the aggressive behavior is more likely to show up in criminal violence and official crime statistics.

In line with the lagged nurturance hypothesis, we would expect lower rates of youth violent crime in the Nordic nations, given their child-friendliness. There is evidence to this effect. To be sure, comparing rates of crime in different countries and determining the linkage between levels of crime and levels of child-friendly policies is a complicated and difficult task. First, there is the problem of alternative explanations. Although rates of crime may be associated with stronger or weaker child policies, they also could be related to other factors including changes in the economy, different levels of income inequality, and different opportunities for crime. There is a large body of literature showing the importance of all of these factors in levels of crime (Savage and Vila 2002). And second, there is the problem of the comparability of crime rates in different countries (Shaw, van Dijk and Rhomberg 2003). Crime is often defined and recorded differently; there are different degrees in the willingness of the public to report crime; and there are different policies and practices in the use of discretion by police and criminal justice officials in laying charges and prosecuting suspects. So comparing countries on the basis of official crime statistics is a risky undertaking.

However, these problems can be addressed through careful research. In a comprehensive study of the factors involved in explaining changing levels of crime, Joanne Savage and Bryan Vila (2002) have addressed the issue of alternative explanations. This study tests the lagged nurturance hypothesis by examining the relationship between changes in the levels of child well-being and changes in rates of crime and violent crime in over 200 countries—including the Nordic countries—from 1960 to 1992. Measures of child well-being include improvements in infant mortality, average life expectancy, enrollment in school, and population per doctor, per nurse, and per hospital bed. The results show not only support for the lagged nurturance hypothesis but also evidence that improvements in child well-being have a stronger statistical relationship with lower crime and violent crime than do alternative factors such as levels of economic development, income inequality, and criminal opportunity. Although these other factors do come into play, there is a stronger relationship between the degree to which children are nurtured through child-friendly policies and programs and the degree to which there is crime, including violent crime. According to Savage and Vila, a major policy implication is that if a country wants to get serious about preventing or reducing violent crime, it should ensure that child-friendly policies and early childhood programs are in place.

The problem of the comparability of crime rates can be addressed through narrowing the type of crime to be measured. For good reason, in much of the literature, there is a focus on homicide. Because homicide is so serious and so widely regarded as such by the public and by criminal justice authorities, it is less subject to cross-national variation in terms of definition, reporting, and the use of discretion in charging and prosecution. So for comparing levels of violent crime in different countries, there are sound reasons for concentrating on homicide, the most extreme form of violence. There are two principal sources of international homicide data (World Health

Organization 2002b). One is the official rate of homicides in different countries, as based on police statistics and as reported by governments to the United Nations Office on Drugs and Crime. This provides the number of total recorded intentional homicides per 100,000 for each country per year. The other source is mortality tables. These are based on data that are provided by hospitals and medical authorities on causes of death, including death by homicide. The data are gathered from each country for each year by the World Health Organization and made available through the WHO Mortality Database. Each of these two sources of homicide data has certain drawbacks; mortality tables because of somewhat different medical capabilities in different countries for determining death, and official homicide statistics because of slightly different ways of recording homicide in some countries. But when we put the results together, it is highly suggestive of different levels of homicide in different countries.

Despite fluctuations in homicide rates over time, both kinds of data show the Nordic countries to have relatively low rates of homicides. From the WHO Mortality Database, in global terms, mortality by homicide in Europe and especially in the Nordic nations has been low (World Health Organization 2002b). According to the most recent data (1996–8), the mortality rate by homicide per 100,000 for Sweden was 1.2, Norway 0.9, Denmark 1.1, and Finland 2.2. With the exception of Finland, these rates have been much lower than ones in most other developed countries. And from police-reported homicides gathered by the United Nations Office on Drugs and Crime (2007), homicide rates in the Nordic countries also have been relatively low. According to data from 2004, the rates ranged from a low in Norway and Denmark of 0.8 per 100,000, to a high in Finland of 2.8. Over a 20-year period from 1980 to 2000, average rates ranged from 1.0 in Norway, 1.3 in Denmark, 2.0 in Sweden and 2.6 in Finland (Shaw *et al.* 2003). Compared to other regions of the world, these rates are quite low. An exception is Finland, which has had a fairly high rate among developed countries. The tragic shooting by a teenager of eight people in a Tuusula high school in 2007 is a reminder of the problem. Although there has been little analysis of the issue, the Finnish exception in homicide rates appears to be related to a high level of alcohol consumption and a drinking culture (Rossow 2001).

But overall, the Nordic rates have been relatively low. Norway, for example, has the third lowest average homicide rate in Europe for 1980–2000, after Spain and Ireland. It is important to note here that Sweden's rate is higher than it should be due to its generosity in gathering homicide statistics (Farrington, Langan and Tonry 2004). Sweden counts as homicides all homicides reported to the police, even those that upon investigation turn out to be accidents or suicides. If these latter were deducted from the statistics, Sweden's rate would be closer to that of Denmark. Moreover, in Sweden, first- and second-generation immigrants have higher rates of crime and violent crime than indigenous Swedes, and first-generation immigrants have higher rates than second-generation (Martens 1997). According to Martens, these differences provide evidence of the impact of the Swedish welfare state and child-friendly policies in reducing criminal behavior. The greater the exposure of children and families to early prevention programs and family supports, the less likelihood that criminal activity will be an outcome.

Finally, according to analyses provided by Felipe Estrada (1999), crime trends in the Nordic countries generally show that the previously upward trends in youth crime since the Second World War have leveled off since the 1980s. Although youth violent crime remains a matter of concern, the rates have been relatively low and stable. To the extent that there is violent youth crime, says Estrada, it is typically violence of a less serious nature. Joan Durrant (2000) makes a persuasive case that the relatively low rates of youth violent crime in Sweden have been due in part to the Swedish ban on corporal punishment. But as she probably would agree, behind the lower rates of violent crime not only in Sweden but also across the Nordic world have been the array of child-friendly policies put into place for the raising of healthy children. It comes as no surprise that the Nordic countries rank at the very top of the Global Peace Index (2007) for their low levels of violence. So if we want to find examples of countries with policies that increase the prospects for the raising of violent children, we have to search elsewhere.

CHARACTERISTICS OF CHILD-UNFRIENDLY POLICIES

Child and family policies may be characterized as child-unfriendly if they have features opposite to those described in the previous section. First, the policies would not reflect a commitment to the rights of the child. The country responsible for the policies would not have signed and ratified the Convention on the Rights of the Child or, if it did, it would have given the Convention only symbolic treatment. It would not have established independent national agencies such as a children's ombudsman or commissioner to advocate for children and the implementation of the Convention. Again, if it did, it would have done so only in a symbolic way. The Convention also would not have been incorporated into domestic laws and the policy goals related to children.

Furthermore, there would have been little support for research into healthy child development and into risk factors for aggressive and violent behavior or, if there was support for research, there would have been no or little attempt to connect the research to policies, laws, and programs affecting children. If there was the creation of knowledge about the importance of the early years, and about best practices on steering children into a pathway of healthy development rather than violence, this knowledge would not have been used or not used in a serious way. And if there were awareness of risk factors and evidence-based prevention programs through the results of longitudinal studies and other research in other countries, this too would not have been acted upon.

Finally, apart from the issue of listening to research, policies friendly to children and families would not have been implemented or not implemented in a serious way. At worst, policies would have been damaging to children and in violation of their rights. At best, they would have been neglectful of children, failing to provide for their well-being and basic rights. Programs of childcare and health care might exist but on a limited basis. Policies of providing for family income support might be in place but on a modest scale. Systems of child welfare and child protection might be established but geared mainly to reacting to problems rather than preventing them. And programs of early prevention such as parent education and home visitation might exist but in the form of being targeted, scattered, and underfunded. Measures might be in place for particular children in particular parts of a country but not for all children, contrary to the principles of non-discrimination and the best interests of the child in the Convention. In short, in countries with child-unfriendly policies, the environment would be fertile for the raising of violent children.

POLICIES IN NORTH AMERICA

As in the case of child-friendly policies, no country or jurisdiction has fully fledged child-unfriendly policies. Virtually all countries have measures in place to provide for the welfare of children, especially in the developed world. But in comparative terms, some countries and jurisdictions are much closer to child-unfriendliness than others. With their relatively weak welfare states and child policies, the North American countries of the United States and Canada come much closer to child-unfriendliness than the countries of northern and western Europe. Although policies in North America are far from exhibiting all of the characteristics of child-unfriendly policies as described above, the evidence does suggest that in many ways, among economically advanced countries, they are the closest approximations. The evidence is as follows.

First, the United States and Canada have failed to demonstrate a clear and full commitment to the rights of children. Although the United States did sign the Convention on the Rights of the Child in 1995, it is only one of two countries in the world that has yet to ratify the document (the other country is Somalia). Among the reasons for US failure is the fear that the Convention would override US sovereignty over family policy and that children's rights might override parental rights (Price 1996). Without the Convention being ratified, the United States has no special agency such as a national children's ombudsman to advocate for children and the implementation of the Convention. The principles and standards of the Convention have not been incorporated into US law although authorities at local and state levels have used the Convention as a framework for developing some policies related to children. Canada has done much better. A supporter of the Convention, Canada ratified the document in 1991. But since then, its level of commitment has wavered as reflected in the lack of a national children's ombudsperson or commissioner to advance the implementation of the Convention and in the failure to incorporate the Convention into Canadian law (Howe and Covell 2007). Without incorporation, while the Convention does have persuasive force in Canadian courts and in the interpretation of law, it does not have obligatory force.

But the most important indication of the relative lack of US and Canadian commitment to children and their rights is in the substance of their child and family policies. Compared to policies in much of Europe and especially in the Nordic nations, policies and programs in North America lack comprehensiveness and muscle. It is not that the policies have been purposively hostile to children, seeking to provoke antisocial and violent behavior, although historically certain policies have had this effect. For example, in large North American cities, policies that had clustered public housing in large projects had the effect of concentrating poverty, drug dealing, and gangs in particular areas and magnifying the risk factors for childhood violence (Garbarino 2000). In Canada, policies that had established residential schools for Aboriginal children in order to "civilize" them and assimilate them into white mainstream society had the effect of damaging child–parent bonds and preventing young people from learning parenting skills, which increased the risk factors for later violent behavior among both the children affected and their children (McGillivray 1997). Fortunately, these kinds of policies are in the past. The problem now is not so much hostility or gross negligence as the unfriendliness and delinquency of policies.

The problem also is not lack of research and knowledge. Through funding and support for universities and research institutions, Canadian and US governments have contributed to the development of an impressive body of knowledge on risk factors, protective factors, and prevention programs. And with this knowledge, a wide number of early prevention programs have been put into place across North America to improve the well-being of children and prevent antisocial behavior, including head start and parent education (Shonkoff and Phillips 2000). Policy-makers are aware of the research and of the benefits of strong family policies and early prevention programs. To a degree, they have acted. But for the most part, policy efforts in North America have been comparatively weak and programs scattered and limited in scope. The result has been relatively poor outcomes for children. The evidence is as follows.

Childcare

First, the United States and Canada have among the weakest programs of childcare among economically advanced countries. Their level of public expenditure on childcare and early education is at the lower end of spending among OECD countries and far behind all of the Nordic nations (Heymann, Penrose and Earle 2006; OECD 2007). In 2003, for example, public spending in the United States (as a percentage of GDP) was one quarter that of Denmark and one half that of Iceland (OECD 2006b). Expenditure in Canada was even less than in the United States (McCain, Mustard and Shanker 2007). But apart from spending, the programs in North America suffer in terms of coverage and quality. Both countries are similar in that there is no universal and public program of childcare and early childhood education (Olsen 2002). Instead, most childcare is provided for in the private sector through informal care by relatives or sitters, or in unregulated daycare homes. And there is no national legislation and few national standards. Instead, because childcare is the responsibility of the states and provinces/territories, each with different resources and priorities, there is major variation and hodgepodge of programs (Friendly 2007; McCain *et al.* 2007). Finally, in both countries, there is a similarly modest degree of financial assistance provided to parents and centers by governments through subsidies and tax deductions.

But there are also certain differences (Olsen 2002). Government financing is somewhat different. In Canada, the federal government provides financial assistance to the provinces and territories for childcare through the Canada Social Transfer, subject to negotiations. And since 2006, the federal government also provides a modest amount of money directly to parents for childcare. In the United States, the federal government funds childcare directly through the Social Security Act, where aid is given to states to assist low-income families with childcare, and through the Child Care Food Program, where meals are given to children from low-income families who are in childcare programs. There are also differences between the countries in delivery and regulation of childcare. In Canada, there is greater variation in types of programs across the country, although Canada has more licensed daycare facilities than does the United States. In the United States, there is more variation in regulations from state to state, less effort at enforcing regulations, and more employer-funded and commercial forms of childcare. But the essential similarity between the two countries is that there is a major shortage of childcare for most families and a lack of national standards and quality in the system. What this means for many children in Canada and the United States, relative to children in northern Europe, is a compromising of their best interests and rights to quality care, as called for in the UN Convention (Friendly 2007; Heymann *et al.* 2006).

However, just as there are important childcare differences between North America and northern Europe, there are important differences within the United States and Canada. Some states and some provinces provide for more childcare and higher quality care than others. American researcher Marcia Meyers and her associates divide American states into five clusters, in terms of the level of childcare support (as well as income support) for low-income families with young children (Meyers *et al.* 2001). At one extreme, in cluster one, are the southern and south-western states of Alabama, Texas, Kentucky, Arkansas, Mississippi, South Carolina, and West Virginia, which provide very meager support. At the other extreme, in cluster five, are the northern and north-eastern states of Minnesota, Wisconsin, Vermont, Maryland, New Jersey, and New Hampshire, which provide relatively generous support. This division by clusters corresponds to the divide between the northern and eastern "blue states" (or liberal states) and the southern and western "red states" (or conservative states). In Canada, there are also differences, especially ones between Quebec and other provinces. Quebec has established the most ambitious and progressive childcare system in the country (Friendly 2007; Peters *et al.* 2001). In 1997, building on previous developments, it created a public program with a flat fee of five dollars per day (it is now seven dollars per day), and expanded the number of childcare spaces in a major way. And childcare was made available not only to working parents, as in most of Canada, but also to parents who are students or who have children at risk. The Quebec system is widely regarded among child advocates as a model for the other jurisdictions.

There are similar patterns in North America in regard to policies on parental leave. The United States is the only economically developed country that does not provide for paid parental or even maternity leave (Heymann *et al.* 2006). The federal Family and Medical Leave Act, established in 1993, guarantees only 12 weeks of unpaid leave and applies only to about 60 percent of mothers. This leaves American families subject to the generosity of employers. Canada's system is much more advanced, but also much less generous than in the Nordic countries (Olsen 2002; Peters *et al.* 2001). Beginning in 1971, paid leave was made available for biological mothers—who had been in the workforce—through the federal unemployment insurance system. Coverage and the benefit period were expanded over time. By 1991, benefits were given not only to biological mothers but also to fathers and adoptive parents. The benefit period—initially ten weeks—was extended after 2001 to 12 months (McCain *et al.* 2007). Mothers now can collect benefits of 55 percent of prior earnings for the first four months and either parent can collect the same for the last eight months. In addition, a period of unpaid maternity and parental leave has been provided, which varies by jurisdiction. In Saskatchewan and Quebec, for example, the period for maternity leave is 18 weeks while in Alberta it is 15 weeks. But overall, the time periods, benefit amounts, and rules regarding waiting periods and contributions are less generous than in the Nordic nations and in much of Europe.

But again, there is variation in North America. Quebec has developed the most progressive system of leave on the continent. In 1997, it reformed its system of parental leave, topping up benefits from the federal unemployment insurance program and extending coverage (McCain *et al.* 2007). Where benefits in other parts of Canada remained at 55 percent of prior earnings, they became 75 percent in Quebec. And where coverage was limited to parents as employees in workplaces in the rest of Canada, coverage was extended to self-employed parents in Quebec. Quebec also extended its period of unpaid leave to 34 weeks, the most generous in Canada. In the United States, in 2002, California—generally considered to be a "blue state"—became the first and only state to establish paid parental leave (Wisensale 2006). It enacted a modest law providing paid leave of six weeks at 55 percent of prior earnings. Other blue states such as Massachusetts and New Jersey are now considering the same. In addition, states such as California, Washington, and Wisconsin provide for unpaid leave, ranging from 12 months in California to six months in the other two states. But overall, US policies on leave are very weak in comparison to Canada and certainly to northern Europe. They are also very weak, in relative terms, in assuring women the right to breastfeed their children during the work day and in assuring parents the flexibility during the work week to attend to the health and educational needs of their children (Heymann *et al.* 2006).

Income support

North America also lags far behind in providing for policies and programs of family income support. According to OECD data that compared 30 developed countries on their level of family spending in 2003 (as a percentage of GDP), the United States and Canada ranked low, in the bottom third (OECD 2007). In overall spending on cash transfers, services, and tax measures in support of families, spending in the two North American countries was almost one half that of the OECD average and almost one third of Denmark. This is in line with spending trends since the Second World War, showing a major gap in the level of generosity between North America and northern Europe (Ferrarini 2006; Olsen 2002). The United States provides for no universal system of family or child benefits and for only meager allowances to low-income families, thanks to small amounts of federal funding for states—which has been reduced significantly since the 1990s—and to highly restrictive state social assistance programs. In Canada, in conjunction with the provinces, the federal government has developed a system called the National Child Benefit, which provides monthly child benefits to low-income and middle-income families on a graduating scale (Battle 2007). The benefits have steadily increased over time, providing by the mid-2000s significant monthly payments to low-income families for each child. But with cuts to provincial social assistance and other programs, and with the tightening of the federal employment insurance program, the

National Child Benefit system has made little headway in dealing with the problem of family and child poverty. Furthermore, in both countries and in contrast to a country like Sweden, the systems of providing for child support are ones in which payments are relatively low and the enforcement of child support weak or varied (Olsen 2002).

Again, as with childcare, there is considerable variation in income support programs across both countries. In the United States, state efforts in providing support for low-income families are much stronger in the northern and eastern blue states and weaker in the conservative red states of the south and south-west (Meyers *et al.* 2001). In Canada, the variations are not as great due to a stronger role of the federal government in providing fiscal transfers and equalization payments to the provinces. Nevertheless, there is a certain degree of variation because different provinces have made different policy efforts in assisting families. For example, Quebec has done much to relieve poverty through its strong system of low-cost childcare, in combination with relatively generous social assistance. In contrast, in provinces such as Alberta and British Columbia, childcare has remained costly and aggressive action has been taken over the past decade to scale back social assistance. And in the area of enforcing child support, unlike other provinces, Ontario, Nova Scotia, and Manitoba have legislated tough measures—such as the garnishment of wages—to ensure payments for custodial parents (Covell and Howe 2001a; Peters *et al.* 2001).

Overall, policy efforts at family income support in North America have been weak. This is reflected in high levels of income inequality compared to other developed countries and in relatively high rates of child poverty. In UNICEF's child well-being study, in a comparison of 24 economically advanced countries, the United States had the highest rate of child poverty (by a large margin) and Canada had the tenth highest rate (UNICEF 2007). According to the data, 22 percent of children live in poverty in the United States and 14 percent do so in Canada. This is well above the OECD average of 11 percent and in startling contrast to the 2 percent in Denmark and 3 percent in Finland. And these differences are in line with trends in poverty since the 1980s. As noted by Tommy Ferrarini (2006), between 1980 and 2000, the level of child poverty in countries with market-oriented family policies—the United States and to a lesser extent Canada—has been consistently high while the level in Nordic countries has been consistently low, the former over three times the level of the latter.

There also are startling variations in rates of child poverty within the United States and Canada, due in part to variations in policy efforts at income support. As reported by the Annie Casey Foundation (Kids Count Database 2007), by a significant margin, American rates of child poverty—as measured by income levels of less than 150 per cent of the federal poverty line—are highest in the southern and south-western states of Mississippi, New Mexico, Louisiana, Arkansas, Texas, and West Virginia (Kids Count Database 2007). These rates are over double the rates in states with the lowest child poverty—the northern and eastern states of New Hampshire, Maryland, New Jersey, and Connecticut. It is interesting to note that the rates vary by ethnicity and skin color. Again, by a significant margin, the poverty rates are highest among black American children, followed by American Indian and Hispanic or Latino children. The rate is over three times higher for black children than for non-Hispanic white children. There also is considerable variation in Canada. In the 2006 report card issued by Campaign 2000, among provinces, rates are highest in British Columbia, Newfoundland and Labrador, and Saskatchewan, and lowest in Prince Edward Island, Alberta, and Quebec (Campaign 2000 2007). The child poverty rate in British Columbia is over double the rate in Prince Edward Island. But it is in the three northern territories of Nunavut, the Northwest Territories, and the Yukon that rates are highest. Part of the reason is that they have the highest portion of Aboriginal children and families. The rate of Aboriginal child poverty is over double the overall rate of child poverty in Canada, with over 40 percent of Aboriginal children living in poverty.

Child welfare

Another area of relative policy weakness in North America is the operation of child welfare systems. In contrast to the family service model used in much of Europe, the reactive and legalistic child protection model is the one primarily used in United States and Canada (Cameron and Freymond 2006; Gilbert 1997; Peters *et al.* 2001).

Although there are some variations in the model among the states and provinces—which have jurisdiction over child welfare in both countries—the primary focus is given to the process of responding to suspected cases of child abuse or neglect after they occur. Central in the process is the work of stand-alone child protection agencies, which react to reports of abuse or neglect in a legalistic way, apprehending children from their homes if necessary and placing them in care after a child protection hearing in family court. In the system, family supports and programs such as parent education are given relatively little attention.

There has been a recent movement to incorporate some elements of the family service model in both countries. In the United States, there has been growing recognition among child welfare practitioners and community leaders that partnerships need to be developed between child protection services and communities in order to deal proactively with the problem of maltreatment (Schene 2006). The thinking is that stand-alone child protection agencies cannot deal with the problem by themselves. They need to partner with community groups and jointly identify problems and establish supports and prevention programs for families so that child abuse and neglect can be prevented. And with this new thinking, some degree of reform has occurred in every state with federal funding (through the 1993 Family Preservation and Support Initiative) providing support for community partnerships and family services and programs. In Canada, there also has been a degree of change (Swift and Callahan 2006). In Quebec, for example, the child protection system was overhauled during the 1990s to allow for a greater focus on prevention through the coordinated efforts of social service agencies and local communities. And in many parts of Canada, Aboriginal communities have gained greater control over the delivery of child welfare programs, using a traditional community care approach. There also have been growing calls and some degree of movement in Canada for a new community approach to child welfare, agency–community partnerships, and an expanded use of the family resource programs and centers funded by the federal government.

However, in both countries, to the degree that these elements have been incorporated into child protection systems, they have been minor add-ons at best. The reality is that the systems in both countries are under enormous stress as it is, given the increased reporting of abuse and neglect, the growing number of caseloads and the limited financial resources in relation to the caseloads. In the United States, despite the recent appreciation for prevention work, the bulk of federal funds to the states for child welfare is spent on protection services and foster care (Schene 2006). Little is left for prevention programs such as parent education, home visitation, and head start. These programs remain few in number and are scattered across the country, suffering from a serious lack of funding (Leventhal 2005; Olsen 2002). Most American families do not have access to programs or family supports that could enhance their parenting. Similarly, in Canada, with major federal cuts to the Canada Social Transfer and with fewer financial resources to deal with growing caseloads, most attention is given to protection services rather than to prevention programs and systemic problems (Swift and Callahan 2006). Despite greater recognition of the importance of prevention, as in the United States, programs like home visitation and parent education remain in very short supply (McCain *et al.* 2007).

A revealing indicator of the degree of child-friendliness in child welfare systems is the number of child maltreatment deaths resulting from abuse and neglect. In the study of child maltreatment deaths by the UNICEF Innocenti Research Centre, the United States and Canada compared quite unfavorably to most of the 27 economically advanced countries studied (UNICEF 2003). The study showed that for children under the age of 15, the annual number of actual and suspected maltreatment deaths—averaged over a five-year period—in the United States was 2.4 per 100,000, the third worst ranking. Only Mexico and Portugal had worse records. This was in marked contrast to the low numbers of maltreatment deaths in such countries as Norway (0.3) and Sweden (0.6), with their family services models. Canada's ranking was not as poor as the United States, but it was at the lower end at 1.0 child deaths per 100,000. It is noteworthy that in the United States, black children and American Indian children—facing a greater accumulation of risk factors—are much more likely to suffer child maltreatment and child maltreatment deaths, as are Aboriginal children in Canada.

Corporal punishment

Another area of policy unfriendliness is in regard to the use of corporal punishment. In the United States, it is legally permissible not only for all parents to use corporal punishment against their children but also for many teachers in public schools and many foster parents and alternative caregivers. Approximately half of the US states allow their elementary and secondary schools to use physical punishment in the disciplining of students (Imbrogno 2000). And over one third of states permit its use for foster care and alternative care providers. The states most likely to allow corporal punishment in their education and alternative care systems are in the south and south-west. These are also the states where corporal punishment is most used. But with respect to parents, the practice is legally permissible in all states. The one state where there has been a major move to ban the parental use of corporal punishment is Minnesota (Bitensky 1998). This has been done not through new law but through interpreting the law such that the physical punishment of children is equivalent to assault. But with conflicting legal opinions, it is unclear if there actually is a legal ban in Minnesota.

In Canada, the use of corporal punishment is more restricted (Durrant *et al.* 2004). Up to 2004, the practice was banned in schools under education legislation in nine jurisdictions as well as in foster care homes and institutional care facilities. But it was not prohibited for parents. Section 43 of the federal Criminal Code allowed parents to use reasonable force for the purpose of correcting children. However, in *Canadian Foundation for Children, Youth and the Law* v. *Canada* (2004), the Canadian Supreme Court ruled that the parental use of corporal punishment was restricted to children between the ages of 2 and 12 and that it could not be done with objects or strikes to the head (Durrant 2007). But apart from these restrictions, the parental use of physical punishment remains legally permissible in Canada. This is unfortunate because, as discussed in Chapter 2, the practice is a risk factor for child maltreatment and the raising of violent children.

It is noteworthy that in North America, measures other than the law have been attempted to reduce the incidence of corporal punishment. Through programs of parent education and information campaigns, attempts periodically have been made to teach parents about problems with the practice and encourage them to use disciplinary methods other than physical punishment (Covell 2005). Efforts have been strongest in Canada and in the province of Quebec. Against much stronger resistance, efforts also have been made in the United States, particularly in northern states such as Wisconsin and Minnesota. These efforts appear to have had some impact on lessening parental usage of and support for physical punishment. As discussed in Chapter 3, although a slim majority of parents report that they continue to use physical punishment as a means of child discipline in Canada (51%), and a wider majority in the United States (60% to 90%, depending on the age of the child), the prevalence rates are lower than they were in previous decades, when the practice was routine. Again, the regional variation is noteworthy in both countries. In Canada, usage is lowest in Quebec and highest in the western provinces. In the United States, it is lowest in the northern states and highest in the south and south-west. But even when we consider jurisdictions in North America with the lowest reported usage, rates are much higher than they are in a country like Sweden.

Child health

Finally, policies in North America compare unfavorably in the area of child health. To begin with, in the rankings of the World Health Organization (2000), the health care systems of the United States and Canada are assessed at the low end of developed countries. With its private system of health care and with nine million children—one in nine—without health care insurance, the United States ranks 37th at the very bottom. Canada does much better with its public and universal system. Nevertheless, it has a mediocre ranking of 30th among 37 industrialized countries, far behind countries like France and Norway. Connected to their poor ratings, the United States and Canada rank at the lower end of OECD countries in terms of public expenditures on health care and health outcomes. According to OECD health data for 2004, in comparison to the Nordic countries, both countries had much lower levels of public expenditure on health care (as a percentage of GDP) and lower numbers of doctors and hospital beds per capita (OECD 2006a). This was the case especially for the United States, the only developed country without some type of national and universal system of health care. For instance, among

30 OECD countries for 2004, public expenditure on health care in the United States was 45 percent of total expenditure (Sweden's was 85%). Public expenditure on health care in Canada was higher at 70 percent, but behind all of the Nordic nations.

Together with other indicators, this has an obvious impact on health outcomes for children as well as adults. For example, as found in UNICEF's child well-being study, the United States and Canada did not compare well on the two standard and key indicators of healthy pregnancies and healthy newborns, rates of infant mortality and low birth weights (UNICEF 2007). On rates of infant mortality, among 25 OECD countries, the United States had the second worst record with 7.0 deaths per 1000 live births, compared to the average of 4.6 deaths (the worst record was Hungary). Canada had the fifth worst record with 5.4 deaths, over double the rate of Iceland. In regard to low birth weight rates (percent birth weight less than 2500 grams), among the same 25 countries, the United States had the fourth worst record with 7.9 percent low birth weights. Canada's record was better at 5.8 percent, but behind all the Nordic countries. Moreover, more recent data for Canada show that low birth weights have increased to 6.1 percent (Canadian Institute for Health Information 2007).

Once again, across North America, there are important regional variations. In the United States, according to data from the Annie E. Casey Foundation, rates of infant mortality for 2003 were significantly higher in the southern and western states than in the north and east (Kids Count Database 2007). The rate ranged from a high of 10.7 deaths per 1000 in Mississippi to a low of 4.0 in New Hampshire. Black children had the highest rate (14.0), more than double the rate for non-Hispanic white children and more than triple the rate for Asian and Pacific Islanders. The rates of low birth weight infants followed a similar regional pattern, with a high of 11.4 percent per 1000 in Mississippi to a low of 6.0 percent in Washington and Alaska. Again, black children had the highest rate at 13 percent compared to 7 percent for both Hispanic and non-Hispanic white children.

In Canada, variation also has been pronounced. According to Statistics Canada (2007a), the rates of infant mortality for 2004 were highest in the northern territories and lowest in the Atlantic provinces and Quebec. The territory of Nunavut had the highest rate at 16.1

deaths per 1000 and Prince Edward Island had the lowest at 4.3 deaths. There was a similar pattern in regard to low birth weight infants. According to the Canadian Institute for Health Information (2007), for 2005–6, Nunavut had the highest rate at 7.3 percent and Prince Edward Island had the lowest at 5 percent. Particularly striking in Canada are the differences in health status between Aboriginal children and non-Aboriginal children, which helps to explain the regional variations described above. It is not accidental that rates of infant mortality and low birth weights are highest in Nunavut, the jurisdiction with the highest proportion of Aboriginal people. Despite recent improvements, health problems for Aboriginal children remain significantly higher than for other children in Canada.

Early prevention

With the growth of research on the importance of the early years in both Canada and the United States, there has been a growth of early child development and prevention programs, including parent education, home visitation, head start, and healthy pregnancy programs. Some of these programs are separate and stand-alone programs and others are part of wider child welfare, childcare, and health care systems. In the United States, all kinds of programs have been established, ranging from the home-visiting programs pioneered by David Olds in Elmira, New York, to head start programs such as the famous Perry Preschools and the Abecedarian Project, to various kinds of parent education and quality early childhood education programs (Farrington and Welsh 2007; Shonkoff and Phillips 2000). In Canada, a wide number of programs also have been developed, including the federal program of Aboriginal Head Start, the Ontario program of Healthy Babies Healthy Children, and the various early learning initiatives and parenting programs in provinces such as Ontario, Manitoba, and Saskatchewan (McCain et al. 2007).

However, in both countries, programs have suffered from a serious lack of government funding and support. In the United States, for example, despite the recent appreciation for prevention work in the field of child welfare, most funds in the system continue to be spent on protection services and foster care (Schene 2006). With growing caseloads and financial restraint at federal and state levels, little is left for prevention programs such as parent education. Overall, whether programs such as parent education, home visitation, and head start are part of child welfare or childcare systems or separate programs, they remain inadequate in number in proportion to the need and scattered across the country, starved from a lack of funding (Leventhal 2005; Olsen 2002). Most US families and children do not have access to early child development programs or family supports that could enhance parenting. When US spending for early childhood programs is calculated as a whole, the spending is 0.5 percent of GDP, one of the lowest levels among developed countries (OECD 2006b). Denmark, by contrast, spends 2 percent.

Similarly, in Canada, despite similar and growing appreciation for the importance of early prevention, government support has been lacking. In child welfare systems, for example, with major federal cuts to the Canada Social Transfer and with limited provincial financial resources available to deal with growing caseloads, most attention has been given to protection services (Swift and Callahan 2006). Overall, according to the OECD (2006b) and McCain *et al.* (2007), a major problem with Canada's early child development programs is that they are an uncoordinated and fragile patchwork of programs that fail to respond adequately to the needs of children and families. They involve a tangle of roles and responsibilities, there are too few programs to meet the demand, and there is too little funding to make them effective on a large-scale basis as protective factors for children. Canadian spending on programs is even lower than that of the United States. According to the OECD (2006b), when early child development programs for children aged between nought and six years are put together, Canada spends 0.3 percent of GDP on programs, compared to 0.5 percent by the United States and 2 percent for Denmark. Canadian spending is behind almost all other OECD countries.

Canada and the United States also lag behind in efforts to prevent or reduce teen pregnancies. Since the 1970s, in response to the problem of teen pregnancies, programs of sexual health education have been put into schools in both countries. But efforts have been weak in comparison to much of Europe and the strength of programs has varied by province and state and by school district. In the United

States, progress toward Swedish-style comprehensive sexual health education has been undermined by a conservative movement for abstinence-only education, which has been bolstered by federal funding for schools that provide sex education in the form of abstinence-only education (Luker 2006). Because the abstinence approach has not been effective, an outcome has been a relatively high rate of teenage births in the United States. In UNICEF's child well-being study, among 24 OECD countries, the United States had the highest rate by far of births per 1000 women aged 15 to 19 (UNICEF 2007). Where the OECD average was 16.0 births, the rate in the United States was an astounding 46.0. As we might suspect, the rates of teen births (for mothers aged 15 to 19) are highest in the south and west, with a high of 63 births per 1000 in Texas, New Mexico, and Mississippi, compared to a low of 18 and 19 in New Hampshire and Vermont respectively (Kids Count Database 2007). Rates are also highest among Latino populations, followed by African-Americans.

Canadian efforts at sexual health education have been stronger, although not at the level of the Nordic countries. Due in part to resistance from conservative and family values groups, attempts to put Swedish-style programs into schools have met with mixed results. An outcome has been that the rate of teenage births has remained higher than most other Western countries, although it has been declining in recent years. As indicated in the UNICEF study, where the rate of teen births in the United States was 46.0, compared to 8.0 in Denmark and 9.0 in Sweden, Canada's rate was 20.0 births, above the OECD average of 16.0 (UNICEF 2007). And as in the United States, there have been important regional variations. Rates have been highest in the northern territories and Prairie provinces and lowest in Quebec and the Atlantic provinces. For example, for the 2001–3 period, the highest rate in Canada was in Nunavut at 31.9, and the lowest in Quebec at 1.6 births per 1000 (Statistics Canada 2007b). And as we might expect, rates have been significantly higher among Aboriginal communities.

Finally, in the area of crime prevention, policy efforts in North America have also lagged behind much of Europe. On the positive side, as in Europe, there has been a rising interest among governments in social crime prevention as part of crime prevention strategies, and in early prevention and intervention programs as part of social crime prevention. Policy-makers in the field of criminal justice in both Canada and the United States have come to appreciate the need for prevention programs such as parent education and home visitation as part of new crime prevention strategies (Public Safety Canada 2007; US Department of Justice 2000). Based on this appreciation, since the 1990s, new crime prevention initiatives have developed in both countries where governments have funded numerous projects featuring social as well as situational crime prevention. In the United States, this has been done mainly in cities and municipalities. In Canada, it has been done at the national level under the National Crime Prevention Strategy launched in 1994, where funding has been provided by the federal government—about $32 million per year since 1998—to local communities for various crime prevention projects (Hastings 2005). Among these projects have been early child development and family support programs.

But on the negative side, to date, there has not been comprehensive and effective implementation of crime prevention policy, particularly in the area of social crime prevention. In the United States, although there has been a measure of success of some crime prevention projects in some cities, there remains no national crime prevention strategy (Farrington and Welsh 2007). As noted by Farrington and Welsh (2007), a national strategy is needed to coordinate efforts, mobilize community partners, provide expertise, and provide funding for local governments and communities. This has yet to be done in the United States. In Canada, although a strategy has been put into place, it has yet to be seriously implemented. There have been a number of challenges and problems in the way of progress (Hastings 2005). One is that there has been a general failure to formally evaluate programs, and thus to learn lessons for their improvement. Another is that there has been a tendency to overly rely on local communities to identify and solve problems, without appreciating the fact that many communities lack the capacity and resources to do this. Finally, another is that there is a division within government and the public about how best to respond to crime and violent youth crime. Those in government who champion social crime prevention and early child development programs are only one part—and not the dominant part—of the policy community. Others favor situational crime prevention or punitive responses to offenders. Because others have had considerable influence in political decisions about priorities and the allocation of resources, efforts at implementing early prevention programs have been stalled or weakened.

In summary, despite positive developments in certain areas, child and family policies in North America have been much less child-friendly than are those in the Nordic countries. And with this unfriendliness has been unfriendliness toward the Convention on the Rights of the Child, which calls for the progressive implementation of children's rights. Policy efforts to provide for early child health care reflect an inconsistency with Article 24 of the Convention, directing countries to ensure the child's enjoyment of the highest attainable standard of health. Efforts against child maltreatment and corporal punishment fall short on Article 19, requiring countries to protect children against abuse, neglect, and violence. Measures to provide children and families with economic support are inconsistent with Article 27, directing countries to provide for the right of every child to an adequate standard of living. Policies to provide for childcare show a lack of attention to Article 18, requiring countries to assist parents with childcare and the upbringing of children. Finally, taken together, the unfriendliness of the policies show a disregard for Article 3, calling on countries to make the best interests of the child a primary consideration in all actions concerning children. The United States perhaps may be excused on legal grounds because it did not ratify the Convention. But it cannot be argued—as it has been done—that US children are better off than in other countries. Neither can this be argued in Canada.

Linkage to violence

We would expect that in North America, given the relative unfriendliness of policies in support of positive child development, there would be a relatively higher incidence of early onset life-course persistent aggression among children and higher levels of childhood and youth violence. Indeed there is much evidence to this effect. With weaker systems of childcare and health care, largely reactive child welfare systems, limited programs of income support, and limited efforts in providing for programs of early childhood development, policies have failed to build protective factors that work against the raising of violent children, as has been done in the Nordic nations. We also would expect that due to the variations in policy efforts across the different jurisdictions in North America, there would be variations in levels of violence. This too is the case.

First, there is evidence that parents in North America report conduct problems and aggressive behavior in their children more frequently than do parents in Europe and the Nordic countries. As previously discussed, prevalence rates of conduct problems in children have been found to be lower in the Nordic countries than in other European countries and the United States (Crijnen *et al.* 1999; Haugland 2003; Larsson and Frisk 1999). Based on studies of how parents rate their children on the Achenbach Child Behavior Checklist, North American parents report more problems. This is consistent with general reviews of literature on antisocial behavior and conduct disorder showing cross-cultural variation in aggressive behavior and relatively high levels of antisocial behavior among children in the United States (Dishion, French and Patterson 1995). Where studies show one to two percent of children in Norway to exhibit serious conduct problems (Sorlie 2000, cited in Drugli 2006) studies show the range in the United States is up to 13 percent for boys and five percent for girls, and in Canada, six percent for boys and three percent for girls (Maughan *et al.* 2004).

Second, there is evidence that children experience violence in the form of bullying to a greater degree in North America. We learn from UNICEF's child well-being study that among 21 OECD countries, the percentage of young people (aged 11, 13, and 15) who reported being bullied (at least once in the last two months) was greater in North America than the OECD average (UNICEF 2007). Where the OECD average was 31 percent, it was 37 percent in Canada and 34 percent in the United States. These percentages were higher than all the Nordic countries and over twice as high as Sweden. And from a cross-national study of adolescents by Eleanor Smith-Khuri and her associates (2004), we learn that there was significantly more bullying behavior among US youth than among their Swedish counterparts. Where 15 percent of Swedish adolescents reported being bullied in her study, 40 percent of US youth reported the same. Finally, we learn from a report by the World Health Organization (2002a) that there is a higher level of bullying among 13-year-olds in Canada and the

United States than in Sweden, Finland, and Norway (Denmark was an exception). Where 45 percent of Canadian adolescents and 43 percent of American adolescents reported being engaged in bullying (sometimes or once a week), the percentages in Sweden, Norway, and Finland were 13, 29, and 37 respectively. Of particular note here was the frequency of bullying. Where 8 percent of American adolescents and 7 percent of Canadian adolescents reported being engaged in bullying once a week, the number in Finland was 4 percent, Norway 2 percent, and Sweden 1 percent.

Third, there is evidence of relatively higher levels of criminal violence. As discussed previously, according to the "lagged nurturance hypothesis," lower or higher levels of crime and violent crime should follow from relatively friendly or unfriendly policies on the welfare of children (Savage and Vila 2002). In North America, with its relatively weak child and family policies, we should expect higher rates of violent crime committed by youth (10 to 15 years after infancy and early childhood) and later by adults. This expectation indeed is borne out in homicide statistics, which again is a reasonably good way of comparing violent crime across countries. From both mortality data and official crime statistics, the level of overall homicide is higher in North America, and especially the United States, than in Europe and the Nordic countries.

To begin with, from the World Health Organization's Mortality Database, mortality by homicide in North America has been comparatively high among economically advanced countries (World Health Organization 2002a). According to the most recent data (1996–8), where the mortality rate (per 100,000) by homicide was under 1.2 in Sweden, Norway, and Denmark, it was 1.4 in Canada and an amazing 6.9 in the United States. The one Nordic country with a rate higher than Canada was Finland at 2.2. Similar differences were in evidence when comparing youth homicide rates, again based on mortality tables. Where the homicide rate for youths aged 10 to 29 years in Sweden, Norway, and Finland was a small fraction of 1 per 100,000, and in Denmark 1.5, it was 1.7 in Canada and an astounding 11 per 100,000 in the United States. It perhaps is not surprising that the US rate has been so high, given the weak gun laws in the United States and the greater access to and availability of firearms. Firearm-related homicide in the United States was 4.4 per 100,000, compared to a tiny fraction of one percent in the Nordic nations. However, although weak gun laws explain part of the variation in homicides, they do not explain all of the variation. Even when gun-related homicides are subtracted from the US statistics, the homicide rate in the United States is still more than double the rates in the Nordic world.

There was a similar pattern of differences in homicide rates when calculated on the basis of police-reported homicides, as gathered by the United Nations Office on Drugs and Crime (2007). According to data from 2004, where homicide rates ranged from a low in Norway and Denmark of 0.8 per 100,000 to a high in Finland of 2.8, the rate in Canada was 2.0 and in the United States 5.6 (the US rate is for 2005 as the rate for 2004 was not available). These differences are in accord with a general historical pattern of differences. Between 1980 and 2000, based on data from the UN Office on Drugs and Crime, where the average homicide rate in Norway, Denmark, and Iceland was under 1.3 per 100,000, and in Sweden 2.0, it was over 2.0 in Canada and approximately 7.0 in the United States (Shaw *et al.* 2003). Only Finland had a higher average rate than Canada.

Although a focus on homicide may be the most objective way to compare rates of violent crime, if we do consider violent crimes such as assault and rape, the same pattern of differences is evident. According to data from the United Nations Office on Drugs and Crime (2007), rates of assault and rape have been much higher in North America than in the Nordic nations. In 1998–2000, for example, average rates for assault per 100,000 were 742 in Canada and 822 in the United States, compared to 171 in Denmark, 514 in Finland, 513 in Iceland, 306 in Norway, and 122 in Sweden. Average rates for rape were 80 in Canada and 33 in the United States, compared to nine in Denmark, ten in Finland, 26 in Iceland, 11 in Norway, and three in Sweden. Here, Finland was not an exception. All Nordic countries had lower rates than Canada and the United States and most had much lower rates. Again, it is important to keep in mind that problems of comparability are greater for assault and rape than homicide. Nevertheless, the results are suggestive and, when taken together with homicide statistics, present evidence of major differences in violent crime between North America and the Nordic world. It comes as no surprise that among 121 countries, the

United States ranks 96th in the Global Peace Index (2007) for levels of violence, compared to the very low levels in the Nordic world.

There is also variation in patterns of violent crime within North America. These differences vary with the relative strength of child and family policies. In the United States, according to the most recent data from the Federal Bureau of Investigation (2007), the rate of police-reported homicides and other types of violent crime were the highest respectively in the southern and western states—the states with the least policy efforts on behalf of children and families. In 2005, the average rate of violent crime in the southern states was 543 incidents per 100,000 and in the western states 469. And the average homicide rate in the southern states was 6.6 per 100,000 and in the west 5.8. The very highest homicide rates were in Louisiana and Maryland, both with a rate of 9.9 per 100,000. Meanwhile, the northern and eastern states had the lowest rates of violent crime and homicides. In 2005, according to the FBI, the average rate of violent crime in the north-eastern states was 393.6 per 100,000 and the average homicide rate was 4.4. The state with the lowest homicide rate was North Dakota at 1.1 per 100,000, followed by Vermont and Iowa both at 1.3. Furthermore, according to FBI data, African-Americans were disproportionately involved in homicide and violent crime. Where the black proportion of the American population was about 12 percent in 2005, African-Americans made up an astounding 37 percent of homicide offenders. All of these differences are consistent with historical patterns of variations in violent crime.

There also has been significant variation within Canada, which corresponds in part to the friendliness of child and family policies. Rates of police-reported homicides and violent crime historically have been the highest in the northern territories and Prairie provinces—especially Saskatchewan and Manitoba—and lowest in Quebec, the Atlantic provinces and Ontario. According to Statistics Canada (2007c) for 2006, the rate of homicides was highest in the territory of Nunavut with 6.5 per 100,000. Nunavut also had the highest rate of overall crimes of violence. At the other extreme, rates of homicide were lowest in Quebec (1.2), New Brunswick (0.9), and Prince Edward Island (0.7). Moreover, the rates of overall crimes of violence were lowest in Quebec, Ontario, and Prince Edward Island. There was a similar pattern of regional variation in regard to homicides and violent crime committed by youth (ages 12 to 18). In the period from 1977 to 2005, the rates of violent youth crime were consistently the highest in the northern territories, followed by the Prairie provinces (Howe 2007). The lowest rates were in Quebec and the Atlantic provinces. In 2005, for example, the rate of youths charged with violent crimes was 1674 per 100,000 in the northern territories and 1250 in the Prairie provinces, in contrast to 522 in Quebec. Although a number of factors account for the differences, important among them is the strength of child and family policies in Quebec and the weakness of policies in the northern territories (Howe 2008). Finally, it is important to note that just as African-American youth have been disproportionately involved in violent crime in the United States, Aboriginal youth have been disproportionately involved in Canada.

In summary, the differences in levels of childhood aggression and violence between North America and the Nordic countries and within North America are no accident. They are linked to the friendliness of policies toward children and to the seriousness of the implementation of children's rights. The comparisons show that when the rights of the child are taken less seriously, and when policies are less friendly to children, the raising of violent children is a more likely outcome. Together with child-unfriendly parents and families, child-unfriendly policies are a risk factor for the raising of violent children. Why this is so is the subject of the next chapter.

CHAPTER 6

CULTURAL CONTEXTS

You need to step back and think about what is important.

Just as child and family policies are an important context in the lives of children and families, cultures are an important context in the making of child and family policies. Of particular importance is the influence of political values, beliefs, and attitudes, which are a central part of what is called "political culture" in the field of political science. By contributing to the building of policies friendly to children and families, political values and beliefs act as a protective and promotive factor for healthy child development. But by thwarting or inhibiting such policies and by sustaining weak ones, they serve as a risk factor for putting children like Adam and his son on track for aggressive and violent behavior.

When political cultures contain widely held attitudes, values, and beliefs that ignore or denigrate children, deny children the status of persons with rights, and refuse children strong policies in support of their rights, they make an important contribution to the raising of violent children. They do so because of their failure to provide for a cultural context favorable to the building of policies for healthy child development. Without child-friendly cultures and policies in place, children are left exposed to the risks of being raised for violence. We now examine the linkage between political cultures and child-friendly or unfriendly policies. We begin by examining the meaning of political culture in relation to children. We then illustrate the importance of political culture as a context for policies by looking at political cultures in the Nordic world and North America and examining their influence on child and family policies.

But in introducing the subject, it may be helpful first to examine the question of why there has not been a closer connection in North America between research evidence that points to the need for strong policies on behalf of children, and policy decisions that fail to listen to the evidence. We return to this question at the end of the chapter.

RESEARCH AND POLICY

It is natural to ask the following question: Why has a greater policy effort not been made in North America on behalf of children and their families? The risk factors for children who become involved in antisocial and violent behavior are well known in the research on child development. The protective factors are also well known. And so are evidence-based prevention and early intervention programs. Yet the research that has accumulated through longitudinal studies and findings in the various fields of public health, developmental psychology, and crime prevention has not been seriously used in the United States or Canada to inform strong and comprehensive policies for children (Meyers and Wilcox 1998; Pettit and Dodge 2003; Waddell *et al.* 2001, 2005). What accounts for the disconnection between the research and public policy?

Canadian policy researchers Charlotte Waddell and her colleagues (2001, 2005) and their American counterparts Judith Meyers and Brian Wilcox (1998) have shed considerable light on this issue. In reflecting on the disconnection between an impressive body of research and relatively weak policy efforts in the United States, Meyers and Wilcox identify the essential problem. Policy-makers in the United States, they point out, could work to prevent childhood violence and promote healthier child development on a wide number of fronts. At federal and state levels, they could expand early prevention and intervention programs, build stronger family supports, reform child welfare systems, and improve programs of family income assistance. But they generally have failed to do this. The key reason, according to Meyers and Wilcox, is this: "What may represent good policy may not be good politics, and the reverse may be true as well: What is good for political gain may not reflect sound policy" (Meyers and Wilcox 1998, p.469). In other words, despite scientific knowledge and solid research findings on risk and protective factors, and despite the availability of evidence-based programs to prevent or reduce childhood violence, policy is based to a large extent on pragmatic political considerations. Instead of policy grounded on rationality, the best available research, and best practices, it reflects the intrusion of politics.

Waddell and her associates (2001, 2005) reflect on a similar research–policy disconnection in Canada. They take the analysis a step further with a research study on policy-makers in Canada. Their study was based on interviews with Canadian politicians and senior civil servants who had been involved in making policy regarding conduct disorder and children's mental health and antisocial behavior. The study was wide ranging, including policy-makers from three levels of government (federal, provincial, local), four sectors of government (health, education, social services, justice) and four regions of Canada (eastern, central, prairie, western). In presenting their research results, they linked their findings to political science literature on the policy process (e.g. Lavis 2004) and to studies on the utilization of knowledge (e.g. Denis, Lehoux and Champagne 2004; Lomas 1990). In reference to these bodies of literature, they drew the following conclusions as to why there is not a stronger connection between research and policy.

First, as reported in the interviews, policy-makers have to contend with what they see as an "inherent ambiguity" in the policy process, meaning that there are many different ways of perceiving problems and responding to them. Logic and rationality are not the decisive factors. Rather, from the point of view of the policy-makers, the policy process is a non-rational and complicated process where relations among policy actors are often difficult, where the actors are flooded with all kinds of information (often competing information), and where decisions have to be made amidst this ambiguity, sometimes quickly and often without consensus. Second, while contending with the ambiguity, policy-makers have to deal with institutional constraints, competing interests, and competing ideas. They are faced with a number of institutional constraints that limit their ability to act, including federalism, the division of powers, and a fragmentation of responsibility for policy across different sectors and levels of government. They are also faced with competing interests that they have to try to reconcile, including pressures from special interest groups and public opinion. And they are faced with competing ideas that they have to respond to, including ones from research findings but from other sources as well. From the perspective of policy-makers, although research findings are important, they are only one factor in a mix of considerations and generally not the factor with the most weight.

As pointed out by Waddell, many obstacles stand in the way of research findings having decisive influence on child and family policies. It is not that policy-makers are insensitive to children. On the contrary, as they express in the interviews, they are quite sympathetic to children and often appreciative of the problem of childhood violence. In the words of one civil servant: "There are no bad kids. There are kids who are in bad circumstances, who have made bad choices. If you help their circumstances and show them better choices, you can do good things with these kids" (Waddell *et al.* 2005, p.1654). Put into the language of researchers, most policy-makers would agree that if risk factors can be diminished and protective factors expanded through strong child policies, the prospects for healthy child development can be enhanced and the pathways into violence narrowed. The problem is not the unwillingness of policy-makers to act for the best interests of children. Rather, it is the external forces that constrain what they can do.

The constraints are these. Among institutional constraints, there are the difficulties presented by federalism and by the conflict or lack of cooperation among policy actors across the different levels and sectors of government, which limit or prevent coordinated action and significant policy efforts. There are also the financial constraints on action due to past policies of fiscal restraint. In the area of competing interests, there are pressures not only from child advocacy groups but also from interest groups and from public opinion with demands on policy-makers different from those of child advocates. There are also pressures from the media, which have major influence on public opinion through sensational coverage of extraordinary or negative events concerning children and violence. Finally, in the area of competing ideas, although research findings may have some influence, there is the considerable influence of ideas about children that are quite contrary to those expressed in research studies. These include the widely held belief among the public that children and youth who commit violent crime should be held more accountable for their actions. According to this belief, because youth crime is the product of the leniency of the law, the focus of policy should be more on punishing young offenders. A major problem here is that researchers and policy-makers typically live in two different worlds. Many researchers tend to stay in their own academic world, seldom getting involved in policy debate, countering opposing positions, and trying to influence the direction of policy. This obviously adds to the difficulty of getting research linked to policy.

What Waddell and her associates identify as obstacles to the influence of research in Canadian policy-making can also be seen to apply to the United States and to a greater degree. In the United States, there are the similar institutional constraints of federalism, the fragmentation of responsibility for child and family policy, and fiscal constraint. There are also similar competing interests and competing ideas. As pointed out by Meyers and Wilcox (1998), these obstacles have been compounded by a surge of conservative ideology since the 1980s that seeks to roll back social welfare spending and to take a tougher and more punitive policy approach to dealing with violent youth crime. Difficulties are also compounded by recurring problems with public debt, pressures from an aging society for a greater portion of government revenues to fund entitlements for seniors, and the major devolution of policy responsibility, where local and state officials have been given more responsibility for child and family policy but without commensurate funding.

This does not mean that research evidence can have no influence. According to Waddell and her colleagues (2005), research findings can have influence but only if certain conditions are in place. One is that researchers become heavily involved in policy debate and do not allow opposing ideas to dominate discussions. For this to happen, researchers would have to present compelling evidence—in user-friendly language—of the need for a strengthening of protective factors through strong policies and programs of violence prevention. Another condition is that strong research–policy partnerships are developed where sympathetic policy advisors and senior officials bring research findings to the attention of key politicians who make the final decisions. This could work in a number of ways. The advisors themselves could use the research evidence to convince politicians of the need for policy change. Or they could arrange meetings between key researchers and key politicians. Or they could cultivate long-term relationships between government officials and trusted experts who are able to synthesize the research evidence on healthy child development and effectively communicate advice to those in the policy community.

But of particular importance for research to have influence is that it has resonance with the public. As pointed out by the policy-makers in the Waddell interviews, this is crucial. Even if strong research–policy partnerships are formed and even if researchers become heavily involved in policy debate, difficulties are likely to arise if the conclusions and policy recommendations from the research are out of step with prevailing public attitudes, values, and beliefs. Politicians are unlikely to act if they know there may be political costs from an angry or wary public or from interests that oppose the policies. Politicians may be sympathetic to the research findings and they may still act despite the opposition from particular interests or from a particular segment of public opinion. But they are unlikely to do so unless they have a strong core of public support behind them. If politicians are sympathetic to the research findings, and if there is a fit between the findings and public opinion, and if public opinion is solid, politicians are likely to act because it is in their political and electoral interests to do so. With the wind of solid public opinion behind them, they are unlikely to be deterred by opposing interests, the difficulties of federalism, or institutional obstacles.

Public opinion often is not a decisive factor in the making of policies. Policy-makers often make policies that are contrary to public attitudes. But in democratic political systems, public opinion can be and frequently is a significant force in the making of public policy if an issue is salient to the public and if public opinion is solidly on one side of the issue (Bernstein 2003; Glynn *et al.* 1999). In such a situation, it is in the political interests of politicians and policy-makers to develop or maintain policies that are in harmony with prevailing public attitudes, values, and beliefs. Research evidence can have influence if the aims of policies based on the research are consistent with public attitudes on a subject and have public resonance. But this begs the question of why it is that research findings on risk factors and protective factors have greater public resonance in some countries than in others.

Why is it that public opinion is less supportive of child-friendly policies in some countries than in others? To address this question, we need to understand the values and beliefs in a country's political culture that helps to shape public opinion. Public opinion about the proper direction of policies does not arise out of thin air. Although many factors are involved in shaping public opinion, key among them is a country's political culture. The values that people hold and the beliefs that they share are an important factor in determining their attitudes on particular issues. Public attitudes, in turn, are an important contextual factor in the making of policies. We do suggest that cultural and attitudinal factors determine the course of policies. There are also the factors of competing interests and political structure. It matters, for example, whether a country is a federal or unitary state and whether the interests of organized labor or the business community are weak or strong. But we do suggest that public attitudes, values, and beliefs are an important influence on policy and that they are a risk factor for the raising of violent children.

POLITICAL CULTURE AND CHILDREN

Political culture refers to the particular mixture of values, beliefs, attitudes, and ideologies in a country that are relevant to politics, government, and public policy. There are many different aspects of political culture, including beliefs about the proper structure and role of government, the nature of rights and responsibilities, the proper direction of public policies, and proper forms of political participation (e.g. Almond and Verba 1963; Inglehart 1988; McClosky and Zaller 1984). We focus here on those aspects of political culture that are most relevant to children, families, and child and family policies.

Political culture is a significant force in the lives of people not because it directly determines the course of government action and public policies but because it is an important contextual factor in influencing public attitudes, the views of policy-makers, and the direction of policies. Although political culture may not be the cause of all policy outcomes—the relative strength of competing interests and institutional factors are also in the mix—it is a major contributing force in shaping and constraining what happens. To a significant degree, in a democracy, policies are what they are because people think they should be what they are. In other words, values and beliefs matter. And they matter for child policies and for children.

As with the features of welfare states, what is noteworthy about political culture is its variation from one country to another. To be sure, in all Western countries, there are core values and beliefs that are held in common. In international comparisons, Western countries typically are described as "liberal democracies" with political cultures that prize the values of individual freedom, equality, and human rights, and that support democratic political systems, the rule of law, and capitalist economies modified by the welfare state and government regulation. But that said, among different Western countries, there are different degrees of emphasis on these values and beliefs, a different balancing of values, and different interpretations of their meanings. Of particular importance, depending on the strength of the different political ideas and ideologies—liberalism, conservatism, social democracy—there are differing perspectives on the meaning of individualism, freedom, equality, rights and responsibilities, and the role of government. And related to this, there are differing views on the family, children, and the proper direction of child and family policy. The differences may be summarized as follows.

Individualism and the role of government

To begin with, there are two quite different perspectives on the meaning of individualism (Lukes 1973). In one version of individualism, associated with the ideas of classical liberalism, the values of individual freedom, equality of opportunity, individual rights, and individual responsibility are all held to be important, but understood in a particular way. Individual freedom is understood in the sense of what Isaiah Berlin (1969) famously called negative liberty or "freedom from": we are free when we can do whatever we want in the absence of constraints. Equality of opportunity is understood in the narrow sense of an equal starting point in a race, ensured by fair rules: we have equality of opportunity when legal impediments and discrimination in the law are removed. Individual rights are seen narrowly as traditional political and civil rights: freedom of speech, freedom of religion, voting rights, due process of law, and equality under the law. Finally, individual responsibility is understood in the limited sense of personal responsibility: we should assume responsibility for ourselves (and our families) and not be a burden on others or the government.

Related to these understandings, the proper role of government is conceived to mean only providing a protective framework for the values of individual freedom, basic rights, and equality of opportunity in a free society and in a free market economy (Conway 1995; Friedman 1962). To the greatest extent possible, individuals should be responsible for themselves. Although they may require assistance from time to time, this should be done largely on the basis of charity, not through comprehensive government programs and a high level of taxation. Government is to be feared because it threatens or takes away from freedom and from a well-functioning market economy. It also is suspect because it undermines individual initiative and creates a sense of dependency and entitlement. So its power needs to be carefully held in check and its role limited to providing only a protective framework for the exercise of individual freedom and rights. And by assuring that people have equal rights in the law and that legal impediments to their freedom are removed, equality of opportunity is provided for. In short, the scope of individual freedom and a free market economy is to be maximized and the role of government and public policy is to be minimized.

In another version of individualism, associated with the ideas of social democracy and social liberalism (or modern liberalism or welfare state liberalism), the values of freedom, equality, rights, and responsibility again are held to be important, but in a broader sense (Gould 1988; Gray 1991). Individual freedom is understood to mean positive liberty or "freedom to": we are free when we have the capacity to realize our human potential through a positive social environment (Berlin 1969; Taylor 1979). Equality is seen to include wider equality of condition and equality of opportunity in the sense of equality of access to opportunities through the breaking down of social and economic barriers to equality. Rights are thought to include not only traditional political and civil rights but also social rights such as rights to health care and basic economic security. And finally, individual responsibility is seen not only as personal responsibility and self-reliance, but also as social responsibility or responsibility for participating in the wider society and contributing to its welfare.

Following from these wider understandings, although the power of government is to be held in check, its role is to be expanded (Conway 1995). A larger role for government is required in order to promote positive freedom and to advance greater equality of condition and equality of opportunity. To provide for greater equality, it is not enough that legal barriers to equality be removed. Government must also become involved through social policies and programs to overcome barriers to equality. A larger role for government also is required to regulate and stabilize the economy and to provide for social rights that are considered to be part of citizenship. Health care, for example, is thought to be a basic right, not simply a privilege or charitable measure. And finally, government is needed to provide a broad array of social programs because it is to be an agent of social responsibility. Although individuals are to exercise personal responsibility to the extent that they can, conditions in the social environment—unemployment, illness, poverty, racism—put their well-being in jeopardy. Government, therefore, has to exercise social responsibility and promote positive social conditions so that a higher form of individualism—social individualism—can flourish (Gould 1988). Individuals flourish not as egotistic selves but through solidarity with others, the support of the community, and the support of government as an agent of social responsibility.

Family and family policy

Related to these contending perspectives are differing views on the family and family policy. Margrit Eichler (1997) provides a helpful analysis through describing three models (or ideal types) of the family, each containing different assumptions on the proper direction of family policies. These models arise in Western countries in historical sequence. The earliest is the patriarchal model, dominant until the Second World War, though retaining influence among social conservatives and family values groups to the present day. Here, the family is regarded essentially as a private institution that should be free from government intrusion. Men and women operate in separate spheres, with husbands as heads of households and wives as subordinates.

Legal marriage between one man and one woman is the sole foundation of the family. Husband-fathers have responsibility for the economic well-being of the family and wife-mothers for providing care and services. Government has no or little responsibility for the economic or care function, especially when parents are present, other than to provide for basic security. This model resembles the individualism of classical liberalism with its emphasis on a limited role for government and the autonomy of the family. But it is highly illiberal in regard to equality between men and women.

The individual responsibility model, emerging after the Second World War, is very different. Here, says Eichler, there is a strong belief in gender equality. Legal marriages are no longer the sole foundation of the family unit as common-law relations are recognized. Men and women are equally responsible for the economic and care functions. Division of parental and household responsibilities is based on choice rather than on patriarchal culture and expectations. Finally, as in the patriarchal model, government has little responsibility for the economic or care function if the parents are present except that temporary and limited support will be provided when needed. Government programs for families are to be kept at a very modest level. This model is quite in keeping with the individualism of classical liberalism. The family is largely responsible for itself, parents have fundamental rights in the raising of children, and the role of government and social policy is limited to providing only a protective framework for family members. Government intrusion is to be avoided.

The other model is the social responsibility model. It also emerges after the Second War, and especially after the 1960s, but more so in some countries than others. Here, the family is regarded as a public institution that should be subject to regulation because of its importance and extensive impact on family members and on society as a whole. This model is consistent with the social individualism of social democracy and social liberalism. To begin with, says Eichler, there is a very strong commitment to minimizing gender inequality. Like the individual responsibility model, legal marriage is not privileged as the foundation of the family and both parents are responsible for the economic and care functions. But unlike the individual responsibility model, government shares responsibility with both parents for the care of children and for the well-being of all family members. Parents have parenting responsibilities, but these are not tied to parental rights. And governments have a major obligation to assist parents, especially when a parent is absent or unable to provide care for dependent children. According to Eichler, although both the social and individual responsibility models now contend for attention in the making of family policies, it is the social responsibility model that is most in accord with the needs of most contemporary families.

The status of children

Finally, there are very different perspectives on the status of children and on policies specifically related to children. Three major ones may be identified, in order of their historical emergence in Western countries. First is the traditional view of children as the property of their parents, which corresponds in part to the patriarchal model of the family (Covell and Howe 2001a; Hart 1991). According to this view, although children should not be regarded as the absolute property of their parents (as they were under the old Roman principle of *patria potestas*), they ultimately are the responsibility if not the property (subject to minimal restrictions) of their parents. Parents have fundamental rights over their children, although they also have certain moral and legal obligations and responsibilities to provide for the care and protection of their children. To a limited extent, if parents are failing to provide care and protection, governments may intervene through protective laws for children such as child welfare, health care, and education legislation. But the intervention should be at a minimal level, with the least amount of state intrusion and with a maximum allowance for parental rights. Parents have the natural right to have children and to raise children as they see fit.

Second is the view of children as a special and vulnerable class of not-yets in need of paternalistic state protection (Covell and Howe 2001a; Verhellen 1994). Emerging in the late nineteenth and early twentieth century, this view corresponds in part to the individual responsibility model and in part to the social responsibility model. Here, it is assumed that while parents still have fundamental rights over their children, these rights are much more circumscribed. When children are in need or when they are maltreated, government has a responsibility to step in and provide for the protection and nurturing of children. Children's needs and child welfare come before parental rights. However, in this perspective, children are not viewed as full persons. Rather, they are seen as not-yets or as potential persons in need of nurturance and care. Governments do have a responsibility to intervene in the affairs of the family when parents are failing or unable to fulfill their responsibilities. But governments intervene not on the ground that children are persons with basic rights but because parents have been unable to do their duty. Children are vulnerable not-yets who require the protection and care of the state and state authorities have a duty to assist.

Finally, third is the view of children as persons with inherent rights (Flekkoy and Kaufman 1997; Hart 1991; Howe 2001). Emerging in a serious way after the Second World War, this view is consistent with the social responsibility model and with the famous African proverb that "it takes a village to raise a child." Here, children are entitled to have their needs provided for not only because parents have obligations or because government has a paternalistic responsibility for children, but also because children have basic rights. And because children have rights, parents and the state share the responsibility to provide for these rights. Children have claims based not on adult sentiment or benevolence or a sense of duty, but on their status as independent persons with rights. These rights are the protection, provision, and participation rights described in the Convention on the Rights of the Child. When governments ratify the Convention, they are agreeing not only to officially recognize these rights, but also to implement them and to advance child-friendly policies and programs. They are agreeing with the assumptions of the social responsibility model of the family and with the principle "it takes a village to raise a child."

These various perspectives on children, the family, individualism, and the role of government may be condensed into two basic ones in describing political cultures in relation to children. In child-friendly political cultures, there are widely held values and beliefs that embrace a positive role for government, a social responsibility model of the family, and children as bearers of rights. Value is given to implementing the Convention on the Rights of the Child and to building strong policies on behalf of children. As part of this, value is given to child-friendly policies that work to ensure healthy child development, give support to families, and steer children away from antisocial and violent behavior. Conversely, in child-unfriendly political cultures, there are widespread beliefs in individualism, a limited role for government, a patriarchal or individual responsibility model of the family, and the status of children as parental property or not-yets. Here, there is disregard for the Convention and for policies in support of children and families. Where child-friendly cultures act as protective factors for children, child-unfriendly cultures serve as risk factors for the raising of violent children. This may be illustrated once again through a comparison of the Nordic countries and North America.

POLITICAL CULTURES IN THE NORDIC COUNTRIES

There are no pure child-friendly political cultures. To greater or lesser degrees, there is value pluralism in all political cultures, which includes values and beliefs contrary to those that embrace children's rights and strong child and family policies. But there is much evidence to show that among the closest approximations to child-friendly cultures are ones in the Nordic countries. This is reflected in Nordic values and beliefs in support of a positive role for government, the social responsibility model of the family, children as bearers of rights, and strong child and family policies. To be sure, there are important variations in values and beliefs among Nordic countries. But relative to other countries and regions of the world, there is a general commonality in outlook and approach, as reflected in the use of the terms "Nordicness" and "the Nordic model" (Kautto *et al.* 1999). Among the common characteristics of political cultures in the Nordic countries is a relatively high degree of child-friendliness.

Role of government

A first indication of child-friendliness in the Nordic world is public support for a positive role for government. Gosta Esping-Andersen (1990) describes the prevailing political philosophy or ideology that underpins Nordic welfare states as "social democratic." This is in contrast to "liberal" welfare states in the Anglo-American world and to paternalistic "conservative" welfare states in much of continental Europe. More so than in these other ideologies, social democratic values and beliefs are ones that are in support of a strong and active role for government in providing for positive freedom, equality of opportunity and condition, and social rights, considered to be part of citizenship. For Esping-Andersen, these values and beliefs in the Nordic nations have been an important driving force for the building of the most comprehensive welfare states in the world.

Why social democratic beliefs have become such a dominant cultural force in the Nordic countries is not entirely clear. But it appears to be related to the particular characteristics of feudalism in medieval Scandinavia and to the nature of the transition from feudalism to the modern state. Historians point to such factors as the presence of a largely egalitarian peasant society before industrialization, resistance to hierarchical forms of feudalism that were dominant in other parts of Europe, the early centralization of power in the hands of monarchs who were often supportive of the peasantry, the relative weakness of the aristocracy, cultural homogeneity, and the early enfranchisement of peasants and their representation in parliament (Kildal and Kuhnle 2005; Olsen 2002; Satka and Eydal 2004). These factors helped to prepare the ground for the emergence and ascendancy of social democratic values in the twentieth century and for the dominance of social democratic parties and center-left parties since the 1930s. In Sweden, since 1932, the Social Democratic Party has been in power or in a governing coalition except for two brief periods. Similarly, in Norway, since 1935, the Labour Party has been in office or in a governing coalition for most of the time. And in Finland, Denmark, and Iceland, although the Social Democratic Party has not been as dominant, it and other center-left parties have been in power or have exerted influence in coalition governments for much of the time since the Second World War.

The influence of social democratic culture has been reflected not simply in the electoral success of social democratic and center-left parties but in what they have done while in power. What they have done has been to oversee the expansion of the welfare state, especially in the period after the Second World War. Not only this but they have also been responsible for the growth of universal social programs as part of the welfare state (Kildal and Kuhnle 2005). After a long process of arguing for universalism on the basis of promoting greater equality and social cohesion—while being non-stigmatizing and administratively simple—social democratic parties succeeded in establishing universal programs in fields such as childcare and health care. However, faced with economic problems during the 1980s and 1990s—at somewhat different times in different Nordic nations—programs and services were rolled back as they were in other countries (Andersen *et al.* 1999; Kautto *et al.* 1999). But public support and the legitimacy of the welfare state were not in serious question (Andersen *et al.* 1999). And as discussed previously, by the end of the 1990s, the levels of social spending remained higher than anywhere else and much higher than in North America (Brooks and Manza 2006). Social spending in Sweden, for example, remained at over twice the level in the United States. That the welfare state has remained strong is closely connected to the fact that most citizens in the Nordic countries remain supportive of a positive role for government and are quite willing to pay high taxes—among the highest levels in economically advanced countries—to fund social programs. While taxes may be seen somewhat as a burden to individuals, and especially to middle- and upper-income individuals due to the highly progressive income tax system, they also are seen as a valuable way to provide for social welfare and social rights (Olsen 2002).

That there has been wider public support for the welfare state in the Nordic world than in most other Western countries has been reflected in public opinion surveys. Included among these surveys have been ones conducted through the International Social Survey Program, which has been a valuable source of comparative public attitudes on questions about government, public policy, and social issues. For example, data from the International Program in the 1990s has shown citizens in Sweden to have greater overall support than their counterparts in countries such as Germany, Britain, Canada, and the United States for an active role by government in dealing with such matters as reducing income inequalities, providing a decent standard of living for the unemployed, promoting jobs, and providing health care for the sick (Olsen 2002; Svallfors 2004). Over 90 percent of Swedes, for instance, expressed approval for a role by government in providing a decent standard of living for the unemployed and providing health care for the sick, which was higher than in other countries. At the same time, considerably fewer Swedes (27%) than elsewhere believed that government has too much power in society. Overall, more than in most other developed countries, people in Sweden and other Nordic countries believe that government should play a strong role in society.

This does not mean that there is uniform and overwhelming support for all aspects of government and social programs in the Nordic world. In Norway, for example, as found in research by Per Arnt Pettersen (2001), support for programs is greatest among those who personally benefit from the programs. Interested parties are more supportive of programs that they are or soon will be using. And in Sweden, as noted in research by Svallfors (1995, 2004), there is variation in public support in terms of targets of welfare spending, types of delivery, types of financing, suspicion of welfare fraud and abuse, and support according to social class. Svallfors' research shows that although there is consistent and strong support for welfare spending in Sweden, there is low support for spending on bureaucracy. And although there is wide support for the delivery of programs through the public sector, financed through a combination of taxes and employer contributions, there is considerable suspicion of welfare abuse and criticism of bureaucracy, just as there is in other countries. Moreover, there is variation in support for the welfare state in terms of social class, with higher-income groups less supportive. But overall, public support for the welfare state is very strong, in comparison to other countries.

It is important to point out that child-friendly cultures do not necessarily require Nordic-style social democratic beliefs. Welfare-state liberalism and progressive or paternalistic conservatism may also give support to the principle of a positive role of government in providing for social welfare. Nonetheless, it is true that the social democratic cultures in the Nordic world do provide a strong impetus for positive government action.

Family policy

Another indication of Nordic child-friendliness—and one associated with a positive view of government—is wide public support for the social responsibility model of the family and strong family policies. The Nordic countries share with much of Europe the common belief that the well-being of the family is a public responsibility. This stands in contrast to the belief in family matters being a private responsibility, as held in much of the Anglo-American world (Baker 1995; O'Hara 1998). Where there is great deal of apprehension about what is seen as government intrusion in family life in the Anglo-American world, especially the United States, government involvement is seen to be a welcome event among citizens in western and northern Europe.

But as pointed out by Linda Hantrais (2004), in examining surveys of public opinion in Europe, considerable variation in public opinion on the legitimacy of government intervention accounts for different approaches to family policy. In countries such as Germany, Ireland, and the United Kingdom, for example, although the traditional patriarchal model and individual responsibility model of the family are no longer accepted, there are limits on the legitimacy of government intervention in the family. Here, under the principle of subsidiarity, it is expected that governments will help to provide support for families but in partnership with local and intermediary groups such as churches and non-profit organizations. Governments are to subcontract much of the responsibility for family policy. And in southern European countries such as Italy and Greece, there is even more caution about direct government intervention. Again, governments are expected to provide assistance to families but only through networks of local and voluntary organizations such as church groups.

But in the Nordic countries, as well as in France, the situation is very different. Here, says Hantrais, direct government support for families is very strongly endorsed by the public. "In the Nordic countries, where public policy provision is taken for granted, the right of the state to intervene in the private lives of individuals to implement permissive and supportive policy measures is undisputed" (Hantrais 2004, p.149). For most citizens in the Nordic world, it is unquestioningly recognized as legitimate for government to become directly involved in providing families with programs and services. A key reason is to promote equality among men and women in the family and society, remove barriers to women's employment, equalize responsibilities for childcare and the household, and create conditions to enable parents to achieve a satisfactory work–life balance. Although there continues to be some element of support for the patriarchal and

individual responsibility models of the family, just as there is elsewhere, these views have been relegated to the margins of public
opinion.

Such broad support for the social responsibility model has been
reflected in public opinion surveys. For example, survey results conducted through the International Social Survey Program show that
citizens in Norway and Sweden are more committed overall to principles of gender equality and public responsibility for the family than
people in the Anglo-American world and much of Europe (Antecol
2003; Geist 2005; Kangas and Rostgaard 2007; O'Hara 1998). In response to the statement "A man's job is to earn money; a woman's job
is to look after the home and family," where almost half of people in
the United States agree or strongly agree, a solid majority disagrees in
Sweden (70%) and Norway (67%) (Antecol 2003). And in response
to the statement "It is not good if the man stays home to care for the
family and the woman goes out to work," where a slight majority
(52%) disagrees in the United States, a wider majority disagrees in
Norway (65%) and Sweden (61%). With such beliefs, it is not surprising that there is more gender equality and stronger family policy in the
Nordic countries than most other countries.

Beliefs about children

Another and crucial indication of child-friendliness in the Nordic
world is public support for the concept of children as bearers of rights
and for strong policies in support of children. Strong family policies
are desired not simply as a means of advancing gender equality. They
are also endorsed as a means of providing for the well-being and rights
of children.

There is a lack of data on comparative public attitudes and beliefs
about the rights of children. But the relative strength of public support for children's rights in the Nordic countries can be inferred from
a number of key legal and policy developments. As previously discussed, the Nordic countries were among the first to sign and ratify
the Convention on the Rights of the Child. Such early endorsement of
the Convention, with relatively little public opposition or hesitation,
reflected early public approval of the concept of children as independent persons with rights of their own. But well before the signing of the

Convention, there was a growing and increasingly strong belief that children had interests and rights of their own separate from their parents and from adult authorities (Satka and Eydal 2004; Therborn 1993). In discussions and debates surrounding two key events, the 1979 enactment of a ban on corporal punishment in Sweden and the 1981 establishment of the Children's Ombudsman in Norway, the principle of children's rights showed itself to have a relatively strong standing in public consciousness. Since those events, and since the ratification of the Convention, support for children's rights has grown ever stronger. And with this support has grown a widening public commitment to strong policies and laws on behalf of children and their rights.

Concerns about child welfare, which gained momentum during the early 1900s, were translated increasingly into the language of rights, especially after the Second World War. An important indication of gathering public support for children's rights was the movement in Sweden during the 1970s toward a ban on the parental use of corporal punishment against children. The practice previously had been prohibited in schools. In 1979, after successful pressure, it was legally banned by all parents and caregivers, making Sweden the first country in the world to undertake such a step (Durrant 1999, 2003; Durrant and Janson 2005; Roberts 2000). The law stated that a child is not to be subjected to physical punishment or other injurious or humiliating treatment. In 1983, the law was extended and framed in terms of children's rights in which reference was made to the child's right to care, security, and a good upbringing (Durrant and Janson 2005).

But had it not been for a growing tide of public opinion against corporal punishment, and growing public appreciation for children's rights, it is unlikely that the law would have been enacted. Surveys of opinion from the Swedish Opinion Research Institute from 1965 to 1979 showed a steady decline in the percentage of Swedes agreeing with the statement: "A child has to be given corporal punishment from time to time" (Roberts 2000). In 1965, the percentage was 53, in 1968 it was 42, in 1971 it was 35, and in 1979, the year of the ban, it was 26. Although there has been debate in the literature as to the impact of the ban on subsequent public attitudes about physical punishment in Sweden, there is little question about the important role of public opinion in bringing about the ban. It is important to note that in the debate leading to the ban in 1979 and the amendment in 1983, the ban was justified on the basis not only of the welfare and best interests of children, but also their rights. Children had the right, it was argued, to be free from all forms of violence. The argument was persuasive.

Another sign of gathering public support was the movement in Norway toward the creation of the office of the children's ombudsman, which was instituted in 1981 (Flekkoy 1991). Just as in the case of Sweden's legislation on corporal punishment, Norway's Ombudsman for Children Act would not have been passed had it not been for public support for the legislation and the rights of children. One reason for the support was the previous popularity of the office of Norway's ombudsman, created in 1962, to safeguard the rights of citizens in relation to government. But another reason was the growing recognition of children as a vulnerable group in society requiring a special office to protect their interests and rights. With public support and the unanimous recommendation of an advisory committee in the Ministry of Justice, the office was established in 1981, under the leadership of Malfrid Flekkoy, making Norway the first country in the world to do this.

The role of the children's ombudsman—an office independent from government and variously referred to as a "commissioner for children"—was to promote the rights and interests of children. Through its annual reports and its power to investigate complaints, its mandate was to ensure that all bodies of government respect the rights of children and fulfill their duties to children under Norwegian law (its mandate later would be expanded to advance children's rights under the Convention). Public support for such an institution showed that Norwegians—like Swedes—were well on the path to embracing the principle of children's rights, before the Convention was ratified. And similar support was growing in the other Nordic nations, as reflected in the subsequent creation of similar offices and similar bans on corporal punishment.

During the 1990s, the Convention was easily signed and ratified in the Nordic countries. This occurred because public support previously had been gathering for children's rights and because the principles of the Convention had considerable resonance in the political cultures. The Convention had resonance because of a number of previously evolving beliefs. One was the social democratic belief that governments have the obligation to provide for the welfare of vulnerable groups, to assist families and children in need, and to be agents of social responsibility and positive freedom. It was not much of a leap to apply this belief to children. Another was the belief in social rights. Where the idea of extensive social rights for children—the Convention's provision rights to health care, childcare, education, and basic economic security—would be a problem for some countries (e.g. the United States), it was not a problem for the Nordic countries because of the tradition of support for social rights as a part of citizenship (Eydal and Satka 2006). Citizens already were comfortable with the idea that basic needs should be provided for not on the grounds of pity or compassion but as a matter of rights. It was not much of a leap to believe that the needs of children should be provided for on a similar basis—their rights. So the Nordic political cultures made it relatively easy for the Convention to become embraced. And after ratification, with the role of children's ombudsmen in spreading public awareness about children's rights, the principle of children's rights became more deeply embedded in the cultures.

Apart from public endorsement of the Convention, an important indication of child-friendliness has been public approval of strong child and family policies in support of the implementation of the Convention. Compared to most other countries, there is much evidence to show that the Nordic countries have adhered more closely to the provisions of the Convention and to the recommendations of the UN Committee on the Rights of the Child (Eydal and Satka 2006; Moss and Petrie 2002). We need only to recall the very high ratings on child outcomes that were found in the UNICEF child well-being report (2007), as previously discussed. Nordic governments have done this because not only do they operate in political cultures where there is a greater commitment to international treaty obligations but they also are under pressure to do so in political cultures that value supports for children and families. This is evident in public attitudes on matters of corporal punishment, child maltreatment, child sexual health, childcare, and child poverty.

On the issue of the parental use of corporal punishment, there has been a steady growth of public opposition against the practice in the

Nordic nations since the Second World War. This is clearest in Sweden. As previously discussed, where a majority in Sweden supported the practice in 1965, only a minority did so by 1979, the year of the ban. By 1995 (the year of the most recent study of the issue by Statistics Sweden), only 11 percent were positively inclined to the use of milder forms of physical punishment (Durrant 1999) and only 34 percent agreed with the statement: "Mild or moderate physical punishment is sometimes necessary as a child rearing method, but should be carefully considered and not the result of anger" (Roberts 2000, p.1030). Regardless of the exact wording of survey questions, only a minority of Swedes expressed approval of even the mild use of corporal punishment, and a very small minority, of its regular use. A key reason for Swedish support of the ban is that corporal punishment puts individual children at risk of harm and it is contrary to their basic rights and best interests (Hindberg 2001). The Office of Sweden's Children's Ombudsman (2007) now estimates that public approval for the use of physical punishment in Sweden is less than 10 percent and notes that approval is much less with the younger generation than with older generations. Given such opinion in Sweden and similar opinion in the other Nordic countries, it not surprising that law and policy are now firmly against the practice.

On the matter of child maltreatment, in the Nordic countries as elsewhere, there has been strong public condemnation of the abuse and neglect of children and strong support for child welfare legislation. Nordic attitudes are somewhat different, however, in that strong value is placed not only on protective legislation—common in the Anglo-American world—but also in creating conditions that prevent or reduce the likelihood of abuse or neglect (Eydal and Satka 2006). In line with a belief in social responsibility, there is public support for a collaborative approach or for the family service model of child welfare where both the family and state are viewed as partners with joint responsibilities for protecting children and preventing maltreatment (Furstenberg 1997; Gilbert 1997; Hetherington 2006). It is widely believed in the Nordic world that a chief source of abuse or neglect is a negative social environment for parents—stress, poverty, lack of parenting skills, substance abuse—that increases the likelihood of maltreatment. To deal with the problem, it is thought that major attention needs to be given by child welfare authorities to early prevention programs and supports for families. Protection and prevention are not separate matters. They go together. From the public's point of view, the best interests of the child and the rights of children to be protected from abuse require a comprehensive network of supports for families in such forms as parent education and home visitation programs. That it takes a whole village to protect children from abuse is the view not only of child welfare professionals but also the public.

Similarly, it is widely believed that it takes a village to promote children's sexual health and discourage teen pregnancies. Unlike in North America, there has been little public opposition in the Nordic countries to sexual health programs in schools that aim to educate children about the use of contraception, the dangers of sexual diseases, and the problems associated with teen pregnancies. In Sweden, for example, there are relatively few sexual conservatives and relatively little support for the view that sexual education is the responsibility of parents rather than schools, or for the view that if there is to be such education in schools, it should be in the form of teaching abstinence (Luker 2006). From the perspective of most citizens in the Nordic world, as well as in much of Europe, it is in the best interests of children and the best interests of society that there are mandatory and comprehensive programs in schools. This view is consistent with the rights of the child to access to information and to health care. And it does much to account for why programs in the Nordic countries are so strong.

On the issue of childcare, there has been very strong public support in the Nordic world for a comprehensive, universal, and public system of childcare (Moss and Petrie 2002; Satka and Eydal 2004). This is associated in part with the belief in the social responsibility model of the family and the need to promote gender equality and provide support for dual-earner parents and single parents. But as Moss and Petrie point out (2002), it also is associated with the belief in the rights and best interests of children. From the perspective of Nordic public opinion, not only should there be accessible and comprehensive childcare in support of parents but there also should be high-quality childcare in support of children and their rights. It is in the best interests of children that there is quality care in terms of low child–staff ratios, high standards for health and safety, professional qualifications of staff, and programming that promotes social and intellectual development. And not only this but childcare should be seen as early childhood education and part of the education system. Care also should be consistent with the Convention on the Rights of the Child in terms of the best interests principle, participation rights of the child, the rights of the children with disabilities, and the cultural rights of minority children. With such opinion in mind, Nordic governments have developed among the most advanced childcare systems in the world.

Finally, on the issue of child poverty, there has been wide public support in Nordic countries for programs of social welfare and income assistance to minimize family and child poverty. Studies of public opinion using data from the International Social Survey Program have shown that welfare programs are highly valued and more widely supported in the Nordic world than in North America, Australia, and much of Europe, though differences between Nordic and many European countries are not so great (Bean and Papadakis 1998; Svallfors 1997). What is noteworthy in the Nordic world is that public support has remained strong, despite the challenges and more difficult economic times of the 1980s and especially 1990s. In Sweden, for example, although there was a certain softening of support for welfare programs during the early 1990s and growing concern about taxes, there has been no long-term trend of discontent about taxes and no withering of support for programs of social and family welfare (Bergmark 2000; Edlund 2000). The continuing strength of public support has been the result of enduring cultural beliefs in social responsibility, a positive role for government, and social rights, including the social rights of children to be free from poverty. That this is so has been reflected in continuing high levels of social spending on welfare programs and on very low rates of child poverty—the lowest of economically developed countries (UNICEF 2007).

From a Nordic point of view, because children are a particularly vulnerable class of persons, it is important that they are given protection and support, consistent with their rights under the Convention. This will enhance their prospects for healthy development and help to steer them away from a pathway into antisocial and aggressive behavior. But should this not occur, and should they enter into a pathway of antisocial behavior leading to crime, the main focus ought to be on the welfare and rehabilitation of the child rather than on punishment. This explains why there is so much emphasis on rehabilitation in Nordic youth justice systems, as opposed to accountability and just deserts in the Anglo-American world (Junger-Tas and Decker 2006). It also explains why it is in the Nordic countries that the age of criminal responsibility is 15 years rather than eight to 12 years, as in North America. But what is most important, from a Nordic perspective, is that early prevention programs and family supports are in place so that the risk of children becoming involved in antisocial and criminal behavior is significantly reduced. The thinking is that with strong supports for families, a proactive child welfare system, and programs such as parent education, children like Adam and his son will be less likely to enter a pathway into serious crime.

POLITICAL CULTURES IN NORTH AMERICA

Just as there are no pure child-friendly political cultures, there are no pure child-unfriendly cultures. Even in the unfriendliest of cultures, there is a great deal of public sympathy for children and public condemnation of those who abuse or exploit children. But support for children means more than sympathy. It means political cultures in which children are recognized and valued as bearers of rights, deserving of strong child and family policies to provide for their rights. Relative to political cultures in the Nordic countries and much of Europe, political cultures in North America may be described as child-unfriendly. Such unfriendliness is reflected in values and beliefs that are in support of a relatively weak role for government, the individual responsibility model of the family, children as parental property or not-yets, and relatively weak child and family policies. Although there are major differences between the United States and Canada and among the various regions of both Canada and the United States, such unfriendliness toward children can be seen as a general characteristic of political cultures in North America.

Role of government

One indication of unfriendliness is support for a relatively restrained and weak role for government. Esping-Andersen (1990) describes the prevailing political philosophy or ideology that underlies the welfare state in both the United States and Canada—as well as in the United Kingdom, Australia, and New Zealand—as "liberal," in the sense of classical liberalism or what many in North America would call economic conservatism. This refers to the view that although the welfare state is accepted as a necessary part of modern political and economic arrangements, its range is to be limited in the interests of market efficiency, individual responsibility and freedom, and individual initiative and self-reliance. Too strong of a welfare state is undesirable because it creates bureaucracy and undermines initiative and motivation. It is denigrated as the "nanny state" or an intrusive "therapeutic state," trying to correct social problems that are better left to private and market solutions (Nolan 1998). Such beliefs are particularly strong in the United States. They are also strong in Canada although to a lesser extent.

The roots of the liberal character of North American political cultures are not fully known. One of the most persuasive explanations is the one provided by Louis Hartz (1964) in his famous fragment theory. According to Hartz, the United States and Canada adopted classical liberalism in their cultures because of the values and beliefs of the early settlers from Britain and Europe, which emphasized individualism, economic and religious freedom, equality of opportunity, and small government. The political cultures of the settlers constituted liberal fragments from Europe because the settlers held largely classical liberal values, with little support for traditional conservative beliefs such as hierarchy and inequality. According to Hartz, liberalism was strongest in the United States, becoming almost a religion after the American Revolution, expressing itself clearly in the Declaration of Independence and the American Constitution. In Canada, liberalism was somewhat weaker because of closer Canadian cultural ties to Britain, the settlement of Canada by conservative United Empire Loyalists, and a conservative, collectivist, and Catholic culture in Quebec. Nevertheless, liberalism was a dominant element of Canada's overall political culture.

In the twentieth century, classical liberal beliefs in individual freedom, individual responsibility, and small government had a major influence across North America in restraining the development of the welfare state. Certainly, there were variations in the restraint, depending on region and which political party and politicians were in office. In the United States, where a new brand of liberalism—variously called welfare state liberalism, reform liberalism, or social liberalism—rose to prominence, the building of the welfare state was more advanced (McClosky and Zaller 1984). We see this with the New Deal of the 1930s and 1940s, the Great Society programs of the 1960s, and progressive policy developments in the northern blue states. Similarly, in Canada, where welfare state liberalism and social democracy became influential forces, social welfare programs became more developed (Manzer 1985). We see this with the growth of federally funded social programs during the 1960s and 1970s and with policy developments in social democratic Quebec after the 1960s, building on its collectivist past. But overall, despite these variations and in contrast to Europe, North America very much fits what Esping-Andersen calls the liberal or classical liberal welfare state.

The influence of classical liberal values in North America very much has been evident in the electoral success of centrist or center-right and pro-business political parties. Where the history of social democratic and center-left parties in the Nordic countries has been one of campaigning to expand social programs and services, the history of the Republicans and Democrats in the United States and the Conservatives and Liberals in Canada has been one of pledging to keep taxes relatively low and maintain a wide role for market forces. When parties in North America have campaigned to expand social programs, this has tended to be rhetorical, as reflected in the relatively low levels of social spending in the United States and Canada among OECD countries, as previously discussed. Seymour Martin Lipset (1990, 1996) accounts for such party behavior and policy developments in the United States in terms of four basic values, all colored by classical liberalism: individualism, egalitarianism, populism, and anti-statism. What is most prized in these values are individual freedom and equality of opportunity; what is most feared is intrusion by government. According to Lipset, these same values are prized in Canada though to a lesser degree. Canadians are somewhat more accepting of government intervention and higher taxes and somewhat more supportive of improving social welfare and equality of condition through government action (see also Adams 2003). But by international standards, the differences between American and Canadian values are slight.

Surveys of public opinion have shown that, overall, Americans and Canadians are less supportive of the welfare state and of a government role in providing for social programs than are citizens in the Nordic countries. For example, data from the International Social Survey Program has shown that Americans and, to a lesser extent, Canadians have a less favorable view than Swedes of government involvement to reduce income inequality, provide income support for the unemployed, promote jobs, and provide health care for the sick (Olsen 2002; Svallfors 2004). In all of these issue areas, Americans are significantly less supportive of a role for government than are Swedes. For instance, where over 90 percent of Swedes believed that government has a definite or probable responsibility to provide a decent standard of living for the unemployed, less than 50 percent of Americans believed this to be so. In most of the areas, Canadians were also less supportive of government than were Swedes, although not to the same extent as Americans. But in one area, the issue of government responsibility for health care, Swedes were only slightly more supportive of a role for government than were Canadians (96% to 94%). Also revealing in the same survey were differing views on whether government has too much or too little power. Where 66 percent of Americans and 51 percent of Canadians said that government has too much power, only 27 percent of Swedes held this view. And again, as shown in the cross-national study done by Brooks and Manza (2006), the views of citizens in different countries are closely connected to different levels in social welfare spending and different degrees of policy effort in sustaining the welfare state.

Family policy

Just as Americans and Canadians have less favorable views of the role of government and the welfare state, they have less favorable views of the social responsibility model of the family. In reviewing data from public opinion surveys, including data from the International Social Survey Program and the World Values Survey, Kathy O'Hara (1998) finds Americans and Canadians to have a relatively low degree of support for government programs in support of families, as compared to citizens in Europe and especially in Sweden and Norway. According to her analysis, where Swedes and Norwegians have strong and unambiguous support for the social responsibility model—especially for policies promoting gender equality, the entry of women into the workforce, public childcare, the equalization of male and female responsibilities in the family, and the balancing of work and family responsibilities—Americans and, to a lesser extent, Canadians have ambivalent or divided attitudes. Such attitudes allow policy-makers room to maintain relatively weak family policies. O'Hara concludes that behind these attitudes is the continuing belief that parents should be largely responsible for family affairs rather than society or the government. This is a reflection of the influence not just of classical liberalism but also of social conservatism that has become a more prominent force since the 1960s, especially in the United States.

Against the social responsibility model, there has been more support in North America for the individual responsibility model of the family and even the patriarchal model. Canadian researcher Michael Adams provides surprising data showing the strength and even growing strength of the patriarchal model in the United States (Adams 2005; Environics Research Group 2006a). As noted by Adams, in response to the statement "The father of the family must be master in his own house," 42 percent of Americans agreed in 1992, 44 percent in 1996, 49 percent in 2000, and 52 percent in 2004. The influence of social conservatism and religious fundamentalism would seem to be behind these high and rising numbers. In Canada, in the same years respectively, the numbers in agreement with the statement were 26 percent, 20 percent, 18 percent, and 21 percent, showing the relative strength of the belief in gender and the individual responsibility model. In Sweden, in stark contrast, agreement with the statement was only 10 percent in 2004, half that of Canada and less than a fifth that of the United States.

To be sure, there has been variation in public opinion by region across North America. In Canada, for example, public opinion in Quebec has become much more supportive of gender equality and the social responsibility model of the family than in other parts of the country. Adams found, for example, only 15 percent of people in Quebec in 2004 agreed with the statement "The father of the family must be master in his own house," the lowest in North America. This is not surprising, given the growing public support in Quebec for gender equality and family-friendly policies, similar to those in northern Europe. Quebec has developed among the most family-friendly policies and programs in North America on the basis of social democratic and family values and concern about the need to boost Quebec's population in face of a declining birth rate (Howe 2008; Le Bordais and Marcil-Gratton 1994; O'Hara 1998).

There also has been variation by region in the United States. In the northern and north-eastern blue states, as would be expected, there has been stronger public support for government spending on families and childcare than in the red southern and western states (Henderson *et al.* 1995). And as shown by Shirley Zimmerman (1992) in case studies of political culture at the state level, variations in political culture are closely connected with variations in the strength of family policies. In the northern state of Minnesota, for example, where there is a socially liberal or "moralistic" political culture supportive of children, family policy is stronger, as measured by the extent of family legislation and government spending on families. The reverse is true in individualistic western cultures such as Nevada and conservative southern cultures such as South Carolina. But in the overall American political culture, regardless of differences by region, public support for government spending on families and social welfare has never been great (Feldman and Zaller 1992). And regardless of time period, support has never been substantial (Schneider and Jacoby 2005).

In short, despite the variations across time and space, in comparison to citizens in northern Europe, Americans—and, to a lesser extent, Canadians—remain hesitant about endorsing the social responsibility model. If this were not the case, Americans and Canadians would have among the strongest systems of family supports in the developed world, not among the weakest.

Beliefs about children

Just as Americans and Canadians are less supportive of the social responsibility model, they are less supportive of the principle of children's rights and strong child and family policies. Particularly telling in the United States has been opposition to ratification of the

Convention on the Rights of the Child, which would have made the treaty legally binding on the United States. Although the United States did sign the Convention in 1995, it failed to ratify it because of the lack of public and political support. Ratification requires the approval of the Senate Foreign Relations Committee and a two thirds majority vote in the Senate. The Senate has been reluctant to proceed for a number of reasons, including concern that the Convention (like other conventions) would override American sovereignty, that implementation would involve costly and undesirable social and economic rights for children, and that the rights of children might override the rights of parents (Price 1996). This does not mean that the Convention is unimportant in the United States. To some extent, it remains a guide for child advocacy and professional practice and states such as Vermont have passed resolutions in support of the Convention, giving the Convention a certain degree of influence in child policy development (Melton 2002; Small and Limber 2002). But the lack of ratification does signify an overall political culture unfriendly to children's rights and thus to children.

In Canada, there was not the same strength of opposition. After consultations with the provinces, the federal government ratified the Convention in 1991. But there was resistance, especially in Western Canada and among groups promoting traditional family values (Howe and Covell 2005). Public opposition was strongest in Alberta—arguably Canada's most conservative province—with the result that the Alberta government refused to endorse the Convention. Finally, in 1999, the Alberta premier did agree to approve the Convention, in a letter to the Canadian prime minister. But it was on the stipulation that the rights of children would not be interpreted in such a way as to undermine parental rights (Howe 2007). Even after the approval of the Convention, there was considerable public resistance to children learning about the Convention in Canadian schools. In response to an initiative in 1999 by UNICEF Canada and Elections Canada to hold elections in over 1900 schools where three quarters of a million students would vote on which Convention rights were most important—an exercise in raising awareness—opposition developed among family values and conservative groups with the result that the elections were cancelled in a great number of schools (Howe and Covell 2005). The main argument made against the initiative was that knowledge about children's rights and the Convention undermines the integrity of the family and challenges parental authority.

Where political cultures in the Nordic countries have been a major push factor in the implementing the Convention and building strong child and family policies, political cultures in North America have served as a brake on these developments. Behind the relatively weak child and family policies in North America has been relatively weak support for children's rights and strong government action on behalf of children. This has been reflected in public attitudes about such issues as corporal punishment, child maltreatment, child sexual health, childcare, and child poverty.

On the issue of the parental use of corporal punishment, public attitudes have been quite different in North America than in most of Europe. Although public support for the practice has declined over time on both continents, support remains much higher in the United States and Canada than it does in Europe, where the practice has been legally banned in many countries. In the United States, for example, where 94 percent of the public in 1969 agreed with the statement "It is sometimes necessary to discipline a child with a good hard spanking," 68 percent agreed in 1994 (Straus and Mathur 1996). Such agreement is significantly higher than the 34 percent conditional agreement in Sweden in 1995 to mild physical punishment. In 2000, a survey found that 62 percent of Americans supported physical punishment as a regular form of punishment (DYG Inc. 2000). And in 2005, 72 percent supported the use of spanking (SurveyUSA 2005). As expected, support has been highest in the red states and lowest in the blue states, ranging from 87 percent support for spanking in Alabama to 55 percent support in Vermont (SurveyUSA 2005). Even in public schools, surveys show that many Americans continue to support the use of corporal punishment, which helps to explain why half of American states, mainly in the south and west, continue to allow its use (Imbrogno 2000).

In Canada, support for the parental use of corporal punishment has not been as high. But it is acceptable to a slight majority of Canadians. As reported in a national survey in 2003, 51 percent do not support changing the law to eliminate the legal defense of physical punishment by parents (Library of Parliament 2007). Support for the legal defense has been found to be strongest in the western provinces and weakest in Quebec. It is interesting to note that although most Canadians approve of the law, they also recognize that corporal punishment is not an effective way of disciplining children and that the practice may have harmful effects (Durrant *et al.* 2004). Nevertheless, a slight majority believes that parents should have the right to use physical force. Given such majority support in both Canada and the United States, it is not unexpected that the law in both countries continues to permit the parental use of corporal punishment.

Similarly, public attitudes toward protecting children from parental maltreatment have also been different in North America than those in northern Europe. As in virtually all countries, Americans and Canadians are repulsed by acts of child abuse or neglect. And most approve of strong measures to deal with the problem. However, citizens in North America have views different from those in Europe on the nature of the problem and how best to deal with it (Furstenberg 1997; Gilbert 1997; Hetherington 2006). Because of a strong cultural belief in individual responsibility, Americans and Canadians tend to see abuse and neglect largely as the problem of individual parents failing to fulfill their responsibilities to their children. Parental maltreatment is understood as largely the product of parental deficiencies and moral failure. When parents act immorally and abuse their children, they are blameworthy and need to be held accountable through child welfare legislation or criminal law. But because of a strong belief in the privacy and autonomy of the family, government responses to maltreatment need to be cautious and restrained. Child welfare authorities should intervene only as a last resort after abuse has been substantiated, only through a strict legal procedure, and only in the least intrusive way, with the aim of keeping families together. Placement in foster care or institutional care should occur only in exceptional circumstances. The general view is that because most parents do a good job in providing for their children, the rights of parents to privacy and autonomy in the raising of their children should be respected. A greater amount of state intervention in the family should be resisted. Such a perspective helps to explain the use of reactive rather than proactive approaches to child protection in North America.

There also has been resistance in North America, especially in the United States, to state intervention in the form of comprehensive sexual health programs in schools. Much of the opposition has been based on social conservatism and the belief that parents—not government or schools—should be responsible for education about sex. And according to the belief, if such education should be necessary in schools, it should be in the form of favoring abstinence from sex before marriage (Luker 2006). According to a nationwide survey of American attitudes to sexual health education conducted in 2003, only a minority of Americans (36%) expressed support for comprehensive sex education (National Public Radio/Kaiser Family Foundation/Kennedy School of Government 2004). Most supported either complete abstinence-only education (15%) or abstinence-plus education (46%), meaning promoting the message that abstinence is best but, in acknowledging that teens do engage in sexual relations, providing basic information about contraception. Although there has been small support for complete abstinence-only education, advocates have been vocal and influential. The federal government, for instance, provides funds to the states for sexual health education only on condition that funds are used for abstinence-only programs. In Canada, although there has been an absence of nationwide surveys, surveys in particular regions of the country—New Brunswick, Nova Scotia, and Ontario—have shown that while most citizens support comprehensive education, a vocal minority object, making the issue controversial (Weaver *et al.* 2002). Given the controversy, many school boards have refused to teach sexual health education, or they have adopted restrictive policies requiring parental permission for children participating in programs (Covell 2007).

On the issue of childcare, there has been much less public support for a strong system of publicly funded care in North America than in Europe. This has been due in part to continuing beliefs in the individual responsibility model or patriarchal model of the family. But it also has been due to lack of concern about quality care from the point of view of the best interests and rights of children. In the United States, as found in a DYG survey (2000), most Americans (65%) did support the principle of government assistance to help parents pay for the costs of childcare and even more (80%) expressed support for paid parental leave. But support for leave was for a short period of time—less than a year—and the support for childcare was in the form of subsidies rather than for a universal or even a comprehensive system. To the extent that there is support for a role by government, the issue is framed in terms of providing limited help for parents rather than of providing quality care in the best interests of the child.

In Canada, there is much wider and deeper public support. In a nationwide survey conducted by Environics Research Group (2006b), almost one half of Canadians (47%) thought it very important and 35 percent believed it somewhat important for government to play a major role in helping parents meet childcare needs. Only 17 percent thought it not very important or not at all important. And over 50 percent favored major funding for a national system while 35 percent supported a modest annual allowance ($1200) to be given directly to parents. However, although those who oppose a strong national system have been in the minority, they have had considerable influence, as reflected in the reluctance of the federal government to develop such a system. And although Canadians are more aware than Americans of quality care being in the best interests of children, the issue is still largely framed in terms of helping parents.

Finally, on the issue of child poverty, there has been much less public support in North America than in Europe for government programs to assist low-income families and children. In the United States, where high value is placed on self-reliance, individual responsibility, and success in the marketplace, the prevailing view has been that parents should work—including heads of single-parent families—and that generous social welfare programs are counterproductive in that they discourage work, encourage dependency, and set a bad example for children (Gilens 1999; Weaver 2000). Although most Americans do approve of modest amounts of social assistance to help poor families, most do not believe that spending should be significantly increased to reduce family and child poverty. According to Martin Gilens (1999), a key reason behind such lack of support is that social welfare is seen to be mainly a program for African-Americans and—due to the influence of the media—that many recipients abuse the system and are undeserving of help. Of particular note here is the fact that very little attention in the United States has been given to the problem of child poverty and the negative outcomes of poverty for children. Similarly, in Canada, where value is also placed on self-reliance and individual responsibility, public support for programs of social assistance have been relatively weak, though not to the same extent as in the United States. Canadians have expressed greater support for social programs such as health care and education than for social assistance. One area where there has been wider support for family assistance is child benefits, which have become increasingly generous over time (Battle 2007). Noteworthy here is that much more attention has been given to the issue of child poverty in Canada, which helps to account for the increasing generosity of child benefits.

To be sure, there have been important variations in public attitudes across North America. Support for child-related policies and programs has been relatively stronger in Canada as compared to the United States, in Quebec as compared to other parts of Canada, and in the American blue states as compared to the conservative red states. The higher degree of support reflects the relative strength of social liberalism and social democratic values, beliefs in the social responsibility model of the family, and beliefs in children as bearers of rights. But in comparison to the Nordic countries and much of Europe, overall public support for strong policies has been lacking because of the relative unfriendliness of American and Canadian political cultures to children and families.

This is not to say that cultural differences are the determining factor in explaining the differing policies. As Gregg Olsen (2002) has pointed out, it is simplistic and implausible to reduce social policy differences between North America and Sweden to a single cause. That Sweden has developed stronger social and family policies has been due to multiple factors, including not only a social democratic culture but also the relative strength of the labor movement and the fact that Sweden is a unitary state with a unicameral legislature and a strong central government. But culture is an important factor, and the relative unfriendliness of North American values and beliefs about children are an important reason that child policies have been relatively weak. Such unfriendliness accounts for why there has been a lack of pressure from public opinion in North America that otherwise would have prodded policy-makers into the making of more serious policies in support of the rights and well-being of children.

A LACK OF RESONANCE

To return to our original question: Why has a greater policy effort not been made in North America on behalf of children and their families? And why, in light of research findings on their importance, have there been relatively weak policies on family supports and early prevention programs? Comparisons between the Nordic countries and North America help provide us with an answer. In the Nordic countries, research findings on risk and protective factors and on the importance of the early years have gained a high degree of acceptance in policy because they have public resonance. Policy-makers are more willing to act on the basis of the research findings because they are backed by supportive public opinion and child-friendly political cultures. But in the United States and Canada, because of the lack of fit between the research evidence, on the one hand, and public attitudes and political culture, on the other, policy-makers are less likely to act. They may be aware of the research but because they are operating in political cultures less friendly to children, without the force of strong public opinion behind them, they are unlikely to put into place aggressive and comprehensive policies in support of children.

The problem is not a lack of research. Although the Nordic nations generally have outperformed the United States and Canada in spending on research and development as a percent of GDP, the United States remains the largest global spender in absolute terms on research. According to data from the OECD (2006a), the United States spent over US$300 billion on research and development in 2005. This was more than the countries of Europe all put together. The United States also did relatively well in research spending as a percent of GDP. Among 32 countries in 2005, it ranked seventh (2.6% of GDP), behind the leaders Sweden, Finland, and Iceland (at 3.9%, 3.5%, and 2.9% respectively). Canada and Norway were well back (at 2.0% and 1.6% respectively). And as part of American spending on research, much funding has been given to universities and institutes for research on how to improve the well-being of children. In 2000, for example, the US Congress authorized the ambitious National Children's Study, a comprehensive longitudinal study of children and youth from before birth to age 21. With projected spending of over US$123 million, the aim was to follow 100,000 children over several years and identify the factors most relevant to improving child health and well-being. In Canada, although not as ambitious, the federal government initiated the National Longitudinal Survey of Children and Youth in 1994, designed to follow 100,000 children (aged 0 to 11 years) for a similar objective. The aim in both countries was to use the data from these studies and other research to guide policies on behalf of children.

The problem also is not a lack of advocacy. In both the United States and Canada, there have been long histories of child welfare and children's rights advocacy (Bottoms, Kovera and McAuliff 2002; Covell and Howe 2001a; Smith and Merkel-Holquin 1996; Stasiulis 2002). Child advocacy organizations and child-focussed professional organizations have not hesitated to use research findings as part of their arsenal in urging governments to develop stronger policies in support of children and their families. In briefs and reports and at hearings, these groups regularly have applied pressure on governments using the latest findings from the research, either in regard to particular issues such as child poverty or childcare, or to the problems confronting particular groups of children such as children with disabilities or minority children. Among the leading groups in the United States have been the Child Welfare League of America (1920), the Annie E. Casey Foundation (1948), and the Children's Defense Fund (1973). Among those in Canada has been the Coalition for the Rights of Children (1989), the Child Welfare League of Canada (1992), and the National Children's Alliance (1996). In addition have been the affiliates of international child advocacy organizations such as UNICEF, Defense for Children, and Save the Children. Together, these and other groups have brought to the attention of policy-makers knowledge of risk factors and early prevention programs. If there is a failure to act, it is not because of the lack of information.

The essential problem is not lack of research or advocacy but the lack of serious listening. In the Nordic countries, there has been more serious listening because the messages conveyed in the research and the policy recommendations have more resonance with public attitudes and in the political cultures. In Sweden, for example, after the Convention on the Rights of the Child was ratified, there was little hesitation in establishing a system of child impact assessments where proposed policies affecting children would be made subject to re-search and evaluation before their acceptance (Sylwander 2001). The reason is that policy-makers in the Nordic world operate in political cultures where value is placed on the use of social research in pol-icy-making and where there is wide support for an active role by gov-ernment in applying research findings to improving social policies (Satka and Eydal 2004). Policy-makers also operate in a context where there is public appreciation of the importance of the early years and of the need for early prevention programs and family supports. So when they are presented with research findings, and with recommen-dations to ban corporal punishment, establish systems of quality childcare, and implement strong programs of parent education and sexual health education, they are more inclined to listen to the re-search, knowing that public opinion is in support. They understand that there are likely to be political benefits. This helps to account for why there has been a relatively close connection in the Nordic countries between research and policies.

But in North America the situation is different. Although there is general awareness of the research and sympathy for children, there is reluctance among policy-makers to act because of ambivalent or divided public attitudes. To be sure, there are segments of public opinion that are relatively supportive of child-friendly policies, partic-ularly in regions such as Quebec and the US blue states. In these areas, because of the relatively friendliness of political cultures to chil-dren and families, policy-makers are more inclined to listen atten-tively to the research and pursue policies that promote healthy child development and steer children away from violent behavior. But over-all, in North America, policy-makers are less inclined to listen be-cause the research findings lack resonance in political cultures that continue to embrace the values of classical liberalism and beliefs in in-dividual freedom, individual responsibility, parental rights, and small government. Given these values and beliefs, together with the lack of belief in children's rights and the social responsibility model of the family, there is suspicion and major doubt about strong policies and programs in support of children, even for apparently worthwhile causes such as preventing violence and crime. From the perspective of many Americans and Canadians, although it is legitimate for govern-ments to support research on the well-being of children and to provide a modest level of assistance to families and children in need, it is not desirable to establish comprehensive policies and programs similar to those in Europe. Besides involving higher taxes, such a nanny impulse would take away from individual responsibility and from parental rights and responsibilities. Aware of this state of public opinion, policy-makers do not act on recommendations for Nordic-style child and family policies. This would be politically unwise.

Furthermore, from the point of view of many in North America, problems such as conduct disorder, childhood aggression, and youth violence do not require Nordic-style child and family policies. There are three main reasons for this viewpoint. First, as noted by James Garbarino (2000) in observing popular beliefs about child aggression, there is the view that the problem of early childhood aggression is exaggerated. Aggression by very young children, especially by boys, is assumed to be quite normal. It is part of growing up. "Boys will be boys." A greater amount of parental or school supervision may be required to ensure that the aggression does not get out of hand. But the problem does require strong programs of family support and early intervention. Moreover, in those rare cases when children act out and become aggressive because of past parental maltreatment or other family problems, there still is no need for major intervention. This is because children are resilient. Early problems will get fixed because children have a great ability to bounce back. Major government programs are therefore unnecessary.

Second is the view that aggression and violence do not result from the lack of government programs but from faulty individuals who need to be held accountable. As discussed by Bernard Schissel (1997) in Canada and Franklin Zimring (1998) in the United States, there is the common view—shaped in part by sensationalistic news coverage by the media—that older children and youth are morally at fault and blameworthy for acts of criminal violence. They may not have full responsibility and culpability as adults do, but they do have an important degree of responsibility. So they deserve to be punished. "If they do the crime they must pay the time." Early childhood problems are not a legitimate excuse. Others blame parents. In cases where parents fail to supervise their children, they say that it is parents who are responsible; this is seen in repeated pressure for parental responsibility laws and youth curfews in the United States (O'Neil 2002) and

Canada (Howe and Covell 2001). The view here is that parents have the responsibility to monitor their children and provide a positive home environment such that their children will not engage in antisocial and criminal behavior. If parents fail to fulfill their responsibilities and this failure is connected to their children becoming involved in crime, the parents need to be held accountable.

Third, and related to the second, is the punitive view that the proper response to children and parents who make wrong choices is tough laws, not strong policies of family support. According to this view, if children and parents know that there will be major consequences and punishment for their irresponsible behavior, they will be less inclined to make the wrong choices. The problem is that systems of youth justice and current laws are too lenient (Cullen, Fisher and Applegate 2000; Sprott 1998). Too much attention is given to rehabilitation and special treatment for young offenders. Rather than working to reduce crime and violence, current laws encourage the problem. If the laws were tougher and if there was greater use of punitive measures such as incarceration, adult sentences, and boot camps, youth would be more likely to refrain from criminal behavior and there would be less crime and violence. And in the case of negligent parents, if they knew they would be held accountable through parental responsibility laws, they would more likely supervise their children and prevent their involvement in crime. Such punitive opinion has had influence. It has helped to account for the recent trend in both the United States and Canada (and other Anglophone countries) toward tougher legal responses to youth in conflict with the law (Roberts *et al.* 2003).

This view that childhood violence and crime is largely the product of faulty individuals rather than inadequate social programs would seem to explain the lack of public pressure for stronger child and family policies in North America. It should be noted, however, that there is a body of research that shows that such punitive opinion is overstated (Roberts *et al.* 2003; Hamilton and Harvey 2004). In the United States, a number of studies have shown that when public opinion is examined more deeply, there is substantial public support for non-punitive approaches such as rehabilitation, treatment programs, and restorative justice sentences such as community service and restitution (Bishop 2006; Nagin *et al.* 2006; Roberts and Stalans 2004;

Scott *et al.* 2006). In Canada, there is similar support for non-punitive approaches (Doob 2000; Hartnagel and Baron 1995). Furthermore, in both countries, there is substantial public support for social programs and early childhood prevention programs as a means of reducing youth crime and violence (Cullen *et al.* 1998; Doob 2000; Doob and Cesaroni 2004; Moon *et al.* 2000). In the words of Julian Roberts and his colleagues, "a considerable body of research indicates that the American and Canadian public believe that government resources should be spent more on early intervention and prevention efforts than on incarcerating offenders" (Roberts *et al.* 2003, p.34).

Why is there this apparent contradiction between this body of research and other indications of punitive public opinion in North America? Roberts and his colleagues explain the issue this way. When people are asked in opinion polls about whether current laws are too lenient, or whether laws need to be tougher, most will say yes. They do this because of simple yes or no questions and because of the influence of sensational media stories of violent young offenders. But in more sophisticated surveys, when they are given more information and when they are given choices about different possible responses to youth crime—incarceration, rehabilitation, early prevention—they are more inclined to support prevention and rehabilitation. It is almost as if the public has two minds—a lower and a higher mind. The lower mind, which is vocal and misinformed, wants to punish children for their antisocial and violent behavior. The higher mind, which is more thoughtful and informed, wants to focus on preventing the behavior through investing in childhood programs and family policies.

Why does this higher mind not have more influence in policy-making? There are several reasons. First, politicians and policy-makers tend to believe that the lower mind is a more dominant political force. This helps to account for the development of policies of what Roberts and his associates call "penal populism." These are policies in which politicians "allow the electoral advantage of a policy to take precedence over its penal effectiveness" (Roberts *et al.* 2003, p.5). Put simply, politicians are more inclined to respond to the lower mind and to the more punitive segment of public opinion because they believe this will spell popularity and votes. And voting patterns suggest it does. So rather than putting major resources into prevention programs and family supports, politicians give attention to toughening the law and creating harsher sentences. Fearful of being seen as "soft on crime," populist politicians compete with each other for being "tough on crime." That their approach has been successful reflects the strength of punitive public attitudes and continuing underlying beliefs in the culture of individual responsibility and retribution.

Second, among those who do believe in the importance of prevention, there is a lack of understanding about what is required. In Canada, Richard Tremblay (2003) conducted a survey to test the extent to which Canadians are aware that physical aggression is most common among very young children, and that early prevention is the best way to prevent or reduce the risk of bullying and later childhood violence. According to the survey results, more than 60 percent of Canadians think that adolescents resort to physical aggression and violence more often than other age groups. Only 2 percent correctly identified preschoolers as those most often using aggression. The results also showed that almost 75 percent of Canadians think that funding and programs should be targeted either to adolescents (41%) or school-aged children. Fewer than 10 percent believed that the focus should be on preschoolers, which is the correct focus, according to the research. As concluded by Tremblay, such lack of education and understanding about the nature of prevention does little to help the cause of public pressure for early prevention programs.

Finally, there is evidence of a relatively high degree of cultural acceptance of violence in North America, particularly in the United States. This also helps to account for the lack of a strong public demand for policies of prevention. In a cross-national study of public attitudes toward violence by Alfred McAlister (2006), a significant relationship was found between attitudes toward killing and the rates of homicides. Compared to citizens in the Nordic countries and Europe, Americans were much more accepting of violence in forms such as killing to defend property or killing someone who has raped your daughter. According to McAlister, this higher level of acceptance is connected to a higher level of homicide in the United States. Michael Adams (2005) finds not only a high level of acceptance but also an increasing normalization of violence in the United States. In response to the statement "a little violent behavior relieves tension," where 15 percent of Americans agreed in 1992, 27 percent agreed in

1997, and 32 percent in 2004. Moreover, 55 percent of males aged 15 and 24 agreed with the statement and almost 40 percent agreed that it was acceptable "to use force to get what you want." What this suggests, at least in the United States, is that violence is increasingly accepted as a normal part of everyday life. In consequence, public demand for violence prevention programs is unlikely to be a significant force.

Politicians and policy-makers are unlikely to develop strong child and family policies and aggressive programs of early prevention unless they are driven to do so by a demanding public. The main focus of politicians in democracies obviously is to win elections in the short term. Thus, although they themselves may be sympathetic to children and to the argument for early prevention and strong family supports, they are unlikely to develop serious policies in this direction without the push from solidly supportive public opinion and child-friendly values, beliefs, and cultures. So in North America, without this push, it is understandable that policy-makers have failed to build strong policies, consistent with the research and with the Convention on the Rights of the Child. Because there has been this failure, and because public attitudes, values, and beliefs have assisted in this failure, child-unfriendly political cultures may be considered as a risk factor for the raising of violent children.

CHAPTER 7

Respecting Children's Rights

*You were not there to protect me as a child, and I'll live with that
damage for the rest of my life. But I vow, as a young person in
this society, to put an end to this violence for the next generation.
You can stand with me, or you can turn your back.*

In his report on violence against children to the UN General
Assembly, Paulo Pinheiro (2006), the independent expert for the UN
Study on Violence Against Children, expressed his hope that there
would be "an end to adult justification of violence against children"
(p.5). Pinheiro attributed much of the violence in children's lives to
societal attitudes that understand it to be inevitable and normal. As a
result, the teenager in the epigraph above stated, children have not
been adequately protected from violence, and they do live with its
consequences through life. Those consequences too often are seen in
the intergenerational transmission of violence.

The pervasive belief in the normality of violence in children's families helps to maintain violence through the following three mechanisms (Pinheiro 2006). One is children's lack of empowerment.
Children often do not know that the violence to which they are exposed is not inevitable, or they may be afraid to report it, or they may
have no one to report to. A second is parental protection of adult family members. Parents tend to stay silent when the perpetrator of violence against the child is a spouse or other relative. The third is
cultural stigma. In many areas not just of the developing world, but
also in industrialized nations, family honour is given higher priority
than is the safety and well-being of children.

In his recommendations, Pinheiro urges quick action to prohibit
by law all forms of violence against children (including corporal

punishment), and urges all countries to work to the prevention of violence against children by addressing the underlying causes of violence. It is imperative, he notes, that adequate resources are committed to address the known risk factors and to strengthen states' implementation of the Convention on the Rights of the Child. We agree. Not only would such action significantly reduce violence against children, but also it would reduce the numbers of violent children. However, such changes in national law, policy, and resource allocation are unlikely to be effected without changes in beliefs, values, and attitudes toward children. A growth in child-friendly cultures is vital. Among his suggestions to gain support for the changes needed to lessen violence against children, Pinheiro suggests (1) sensitizing the public to the harmful effects of violence on child development, (2) educating children and adults on children's rights, and (3) fully respecting the rights of the child, including the child's participation rights. These three suggestions are consistent with the implications that can be drawn from the evidence presented through this book. In this chapter, we provide our thoughts on how these attitude changes may be brought about in child-unfriendly cultures.

In the absence of public attitudes that are supportive of positive parenting and strong child and family policies, we are likely to continue to see the intergenerational transmission of violence. As we have stressed, it is not only families who are responsible for the raising of violent children. It is also public attitudes, values, and beliefs that fail to insist on strong policies on behalf of children and families. Contrary to the Convention on the Rights of the Child, when children are inadequately protected from violence and abuse (Articles 19 and 34), when they are given inadequate childcare, health care, and economic support (Articles 18, 24, and 27), when their best interests are not a primary concern (Article 3), and when there is a lack of public support for the serious implementation of their rights, they are put at risk of a pathway into antisocial and violent behavior. As Pinheiro noted, a major problem is that in many or most parts of the world, children continue to be seen as less important than adults, or as not-yets— not-yet important and not-yet citizens. And importantly, they are not-yet powerful (John 2003). They do not yet have power and they do not yet have respect as bearers of rights, deserving of strong child and family policies. Even in the Nordic countries, there is much more that needs to be done. So the challenges to be addressed are these: how can public attitudes and beliefs be changed such that there is greater public commitment to children and their rights and to strong policies in support of healthy child development?

Social psychologists tell us that attitudes are largely a function of beliefs and the values that are associated with those beliefs (Fishbein and Middlestadt 1995). In turn these beliefs and values are formed through experience and knowledge. Once established, attitudes tend to be somewhat stable and resistant to change (Grant, Button and Noseworthy 1994). But they can be changed. Attitudes are formed through education and experience, and can be changed through education and experience. For example, as discussed in Chapter 6, many members of the public continue to believe that the best way to prevent violence is to punish those who are violent. They see leniency in the law and in the youth justice system as the reason for the problem of violence and criminal behavior among youth. But as pointed out by Julian Roberts and his colleagues (2003), when the public is educated about the characteristic backgrounds of youth in conflict with the law, their attitudes become less punitive and they become more supportive of early prevention and family programs. And the good news is that when attitudes are changed after due consideration of new information such as in the above example, that change is likely to be stable and long-lasting (Olson and Zanna 1993). Moreover, it can gradually permeate the culture. A cogent example here is in the attitudes of Swedish parents to the use of corporal punishment. As a result of the massive public education campaign that accompanied the 1979 no-spanking law, the percentage of those who held attitudes supportive of corporal punishment went from 65 percent prior to the law, to 29 percent by 1981 (Durrant 1995). And by 1994, only 11 percent of the Swedish population held attitudes supportive of corporal punishment (Durrant 1999).

In keeping with the recommendations of Paulo Pinheiro, we see the key means to promoting attitudes supportive of children's rights and child-friendly laws and policies to be the following. First, provision of education about the importance of the early years can be an effective way to sensitize the public to the harmful effects of violence on child development. At this time there does not appear to be widespread awareness of the links between fetal substance exposure and later predisposition to violent behavior, nor of the need for positive parenting and families to lessen the likelihood of the child developing behavioral difficulties reflected in the various forms of violence. Second is provision of widespread education about the rights of the child. Educating children and adults on children's rights is consistent with states' obligations under the Convention. In addition, there is evidence that those who learn about children's rights become more supportive and respectful of children's rights. Third, we believe that respecting the participation rights of the child would provide useful experiential education for adults. Such experience can promote attitudes that reflect a belief in the legitimacy and appropriateness of children as rights-bearing individuals, and a value on respecting those rights. We now briefly address each of these areas as means of promoting a culture of respect for children, reducing the pervasiveness of violence by and against children.

EDUCATION ABOUT THE EARLY YEARS

Public support for early prevention is likely to increase if effective programs of public education are in place that demonstrate the critical importance of the early years, the benefits of family supports as a protective factor against the risks of childhood violence, and the benefits of evidence-based programs such as parent education, home visitation, and quality childcare. The challenge is how to obtain public support for the implementation of such programs. There is no shortage of evidence for best practices in these areas (e.g. Farrington and Welsh 2007; Welsh and Farrington 2006). But concerns about the costs of early prevention and parent education programs may be an obstacle to their implementation. These concerns can be addressed as follows.

First, the financial savings accrued over time from having fewer violent children and a healthier society should more than compensate for initial expenditures. Earlier data from the United States highlight the potential savings. Parenting interventions have been shown to be almost three times as effective as punitive measures at reducing violence and crime (Greenwood *et al.* 1998). Cost-benefit analyses of early programs with children born into high-risk (i.e. rights-violating) circumstances indicate savings to government that exceed costs by a factor of more than seven to one. The savings are calculated on the basis of increased tax revenues from higher employment rates, reductions in the use of social welfare, lower criminal justice system costs, and reduced expenditures in the areas of education and health (Karoly *et al.* 1998). Another way of looking at these data is that the estimated rate of return of effective prevention programs "exceeds the average rate of return on investments in the stock market over the past 30 years" (Barnett 1998, p.206). (And we note here that the stock market did well during this time period.)

Second, governments do spend money on children. However, those funds typically are spent in a haphazard manner with a patchwork of programming that lacks the rights-based framework that would provide a guide to expenditure. Moreover, systematic program evaluation data and child impact assessments are often lacking. The Canadian government, for example, was criticized by the chair of the UN Committee on the Rights of the Child, Jan Doek, during the presentation of its report in 2003. Doek expressed his concern that the government provided only statistics on spending: it failed to provide information on outcomes, goals achieved, and any information that would indicate whether that spending had any useful effect at all. It is possible that much government spending occurs without effecting improvements in children's lives. Without program evaluation or child impact assessments, we cannot know if moneys were well spent or wasted.

Finally, it must be appreciated that there will be a lag between investment in early prevention programs and measurable benefits. Policy-makers, government officials, and the electorate might be disappointed and impatient about the slow pace of change. Policy-makers need to remain evidence-based in their design and funding of interventions. Ongoing education by child advocates may be essential to remind the policy-makers and the public of the ever-growing evidence of the benefits of investing appropriately in children and families.

CHILDREN'S RIGHTS EDUCATION

Beyond showing the benefits of early prevention programs and family supports, education is required to elevate the status and value of children and respect for their rights. This too is a long-term process, but it is a promising means of building child-friendly cultures across generations. The key is to provide children's rights education in schools where children can be educated and empowered through the formal and hidden curriculum (the school's policies and practices) that they are bearers of rights as described in the Convention. The challenge here is to overcome the myths and misperceptions of rights that exist in the absence of knowledge about the Convention. It can be difficult to implement children's rights education when many in the public misunderstand the nature of children's rights. For many parents, teachers, and politicians, "rights" connotes inappropriate entitlements that lead to excessive or untenable demands, and have the potential to promote chaos in our homes, schools, and communities. For example, a British politician, with whom we were discussing the implementation of children's rights education, explained that it was not a good idea to use the discourse of rights because of the public controversy about "travellers arguing for their right to defecate in public areas." Providing knowledge of rights is seen as an impetus for chaos rather than increased respect.

Article 42 of the Convention obligates countries to "make the principles and provisions of the Convention widely known, by appropriate and active means, to adults and children alike." Overall, this has not happened. There has been little evidence of the systematic provision of children's rights education anywhere to children or adults (Howe and Covell 2005). However, there are signs of improvement. For example, Britain appears to be making significant progress in implementing children's rights education in schools.

As described in detail elsewhere (Howe and Covell 2005; Covell 2007), children's rights education is the explicit teaching of the rights of the Convention in an environment that itself models and respects those rights. The overarching goals and content of children's rights education are specified in Articles 29 and 42; the appropriate pedagogy and the basis for school rules and regulations are described in Articles 12–15. In addition, Article 16 protects the child's privacy and has relevance to policies such as locker searches and, under Article 28, children have the right to disciplinary procedures that protect the dignity of the child and are in conformity with the other Convention rights. Consistency with Article 29 requires that teachers provide education that promotes the optimum physical, social, and cognitive development of each child. In addition, it directs the content of education to include teaching respect for the rights of all others, an appreciation of equality, multiculturalism, world peace, and the natural environment. Articles 12–15 obligate teachers to use a democratic pedagogy in the classroom, and obligate school administrators to allow for student input into school decision-making. The Convention rights provide the overarching framework for all school policy and practice, and are incorporated into the school ethos.

To our knowledge, the most comprehensive and Convention-consistent children's rights education initiative at this time is in the county of Hampshire, England. Preliminary evaluation data from that initiative, consistent with earlier data from individual classroom initiatives, indicate that children's rights education can be a very effective tool for increasing respect and support for children's rights (Covell and Howe 2007).

Where such education is practiced, positive outcomes are seen among children, teachers, and parents (Campbell and Covell 2001; Covell and Howe 1999, 2001b, 2007; Covell, O'Leary and Howe 2002; Decoene and De Cock 1996; Howe and Covell 2005; Murray 1999, 2002). Children demonstrate increased respect for the rights of their peers, their families, and their teachers. In addition they show an increased appreciation for children in difficult circumstances. These changes are reflected in increased incidence of responsible, helping, and cooperative behaviors, and in decreased incidence of bullying and defiant behaviors. Interestingly, rights discourse replaces confrontation to settle disagreements. School engagement, confidence, and academic achievement are also increased. Teachers in rights-based classrooms or schools also show increased support for the rights of children. This too is reflected in behavior. Teachers are more democratic in their teachings, providing their students with a rights-consistent balance between guidance and participation. In addition, they listen to their students more, take account of students' thoughts more seriously and are less confrontational with students who misbehave. And contrary to the fears of many, teachers report that when they allow participation in the classroom, they are more listened to and respected by their students. Parent data is primarily anecdotal at this time. However, the pattern reflects that of teachers. Noticing an improvement in their child's behavior, achievement, and self-regulatory skills, parents are embracing the rights-consistent schooling and showing greater respect for children's rights at home.

Were such children's rights education and outcomes widespread, we could predict that over time there would be a significant increase in respect and support for children's rights, and a lessening in violence against and by children. Children one day will become parents, voters, and policy-makers. It is important that they grow up with a deep belief in children's rights so that they will respect children as bearers of rights, adopt rights-consistent parenting practices, and apply pressure on governments for stronger child and family policies. With a wider public belief in children's rights, together with wider public support for early prevention and family supports, the prospects for stronger policies are greatly enhanced.

CHILDREN'S PARTICIPATION

Rights-supportive attitudes can be promoted by respecting children's rights to meaningful participation. For the child, participation can function as a protective factor increasing the likelihood of positive development. For the adult, experience with children as participating members of society can promote attitudes more supportive of respecting the rights of the child. Like children's rights education, participation can make an important contribution to the building of child-friendly cultures by lessening negative stereotypes of adolescents, by promoting respect for children, and by increasing their status.

Article 12 of the Convention requires countries to provide children with a voice in all matters affecting them, with their views being given due weight in accord with their age and maturity. This has yet to be been done to any significant degree. Nonetheless, there have been sufficient initiatives to identify the benefits of child and youth participation. Listening to children and taking their opinions into account has many benefits not only for the individual child but also for society. When children are listened to, their self-worth is increased, their sense of efficacy and decision-making skills are enhanced, and there are improvements in their social relationships and civic involvement (Campbell and Rose-Krasnor 2007). And when children are listened to, policy and program design and functioning are improved and there is increased respect for the participation rights of the child (Zeldin 2004). In turn there is increased respect for children.

Despite evidence of the many benefits of child participation, and of the Convention obligations to provide opportunities for participation, its practice remains relatively rare (e.g. Campbell and Rose-Krasnor 2007; Cavet and Sloper 2004). The lack of respect for the child's participation rights may stem from a misunderstanding about the nature of participation as a right. Participation sometimes is confused with self-determination. The obligation for parents, teachers, and all the adults whose decisions affect children, is to provide opportunities for children to obtain relevant information, to express their thoughts, and to have their voices heard. It is not to ask children simply what they want and then to act on it. A second reason given to explain the paucity of participation is its impracticality—the bureaucratic nature of organizations, meeting times and locations, the difficulty of including marginalized or minority children, and so forth. A third reason is adult distrust. Adults often are uncomfortable sharing power with children and may initially be reluctant to include children in decision-making. Experience can reduce this reluctance. Experience can help clarify the nature of meaningful participation, shatter myths and stereotypes about children, and change fundamental attitudes. When people are induced to act in ways that are inconsistent with their existing attitudes, they change their attitudes (Aronson 1997). The challenge is how to promote that experience and action. Examples of successful youth participation may be helpful.

The United Kingdom is one signatory to the Convention where there is growing respect and support for children's participation rights. As reported by Cavet and Sloper (2004), youth involvement in decisions involving service development is well supported in government policy. For example, the Department of Health has taken steps to involve children in policy-making, service planning, program delivery, and evaluation. In a review of child participation in the United Kingdom, Cavet and Sloper (2004) conclude that there is evidence of more appropriate services as a result. Gerison Lansdown (2001) provides a clear example of how more effective expenditures and services can result from consulting youth on matters that affect them. In a disadvantaged area of London, the local council sought the opinions of four- and five-year-old children in the design of a playground. Much to their surprise, the children expressed a preference for concrete over grass. Grass, they explained, made it too difficult for them to see the discarded needles and broken glass left by local drug addicts. The council was made aware of a very salient issue in the provision of the playground, an issue of which they may have remained unaware had they not asked the children.

That input from youth would be of particular help in reducing the numbers of children raised to be violent is demonstrated in their discussions and recommendations for the *United Nations Secretary General's Study on Violence Against Children*. Some of the youth comments have been presented as epigraphs at the beginnings of the chapters throughout this book. If parents and policy-makers were to listen to the voices of youth, they may be surprised at how insightful and helpful the youth perspective can be. A report on the voices of Canadian children aged 9 to 18 years exemplifies the high level of understanding youth have of violence, its causes and consequences, and the needed interventions (Covell 2006). Children who were representative of general populations of children, Aboriginal children, children in the care of the state, and children who had come into conflict with the law discussed their experiences with violence. They were consistent in their focus on four areas of family functioning and how these contributed to the intergenerational transmission of violence: poor adult role modeling, parental hypocrisy, parental substance abuse, and parental rejection.

Parents were the targets of strong criticism. "Really bad violence happens in homes," the children said (p.9). Parents, they said, are physically violent, they express negative stereotypes, and they hold attitudes supportive of violence. Parents watch televised sports, news shows, and movies that glorify violence, while telling their children not to behave in these ways. Children described the financial and emotional neglect of children that are the consequences of parental substance abuse. Parents "use grocery money to buy drugs," "forgot to feed their children," and "leave their kids home alone all night" (p.9). Concerns were expressed also about child exposure to intimate partner violence and its effects on children "When parents do too much [verbal or physical violence], kids will end up being violent" (p.10). They wanted parents to know what their children see and hear, and they wanted parents to change. The risk factors for violence identified in the social science literature were echoed in the children's comments. Perhaps if youth were listened to more, parents and policy-makers would have a better understanding of what children are being taught, albeit inadvertently, in their homes.

The youth's recommendations to lessen violence also were consistent with the literature as discussed in the preceding chapters. They stressed the need to stop the cycle of violence and suggested the following measures be taken: more accessible supports for child victims of family violence, parenting education, addiction services for parents, a legal ban on the use of corporal punishment, and allowance for youth participation in child-friendly communities. These youth are the experts on the raising of violent children and they need to be heard. It is poignant that violent youth (some who participated in the discussions had such a history) have such clear understanding of where their violence came from and how it could have been prevented. Adults who experience such child participation, even indirectly, have received effective education about the value of respecting children and their rights.

We believe that widespread education and experience in the areas of child participation, children's rights education, and the importance of early prevention would do much, over time, to increase respect for children and support for strong policies that are consistent with children's rights. If parents and families were supported and helped with their child rearing, as called for in the Convention, and children were raised in rights-respecting homes, many of the factors that breed violence—inappropriate socialization styles, poor family functioning, child-unfriendly policies and cultures—would be replaced with factors that promote healthy development and respect. Obviously there would still be problems. The neurological underpinnings of violent behavior are not all preventable or controllable, and even in the most rights-respecting of cultures, not all individuals, practices, and government policies are rights-consistent. However, as respect for children and their rights increases, so the numbers of children raised with predispositions for violence will decrease.

We lost track of Adam and his son. It is hard to be optimistic about their future. It is not that Adam is unaware of his needs. "I need to break the cycle of violence," Adam said; "you don't want your child to live the life you did." The problem is that Adam, like so many others who are parenting in the most difficult of circumstances, is not raising his child in a child-friendly and rights-respecting culture. But perhaps with public support for early prevention, children's rights education, and child participation, Adam's grandchildren will grow in a family and culture that respects their rights. Perhaps that generation will stop the unnecessary raising of children predisposed to violence.

REFERENCES

Abou-Saleh, M.T. and Ghubash, R. (1997) 'The prevalence of early postpartum psychiatric morbidity in Dubai: A transcultural perspective.' *Acta Psychiatrica Scandinavica 95*, 428–32.

Adams, M. (2003) *Fire and Ice: The United States, Canada and the Myth of Converging Values.* Toronto: Penguin Canada.

Adams, M. (2005) *American Backlash: The Untold Story of Social Change in the United States.* Toronto: Viking Canada.

Agoub, M., Moussaoui, D. and Battas, O. (2005) 'Prevalence of postpartum depression in a Morocco sample.' *Archives of Women's Mental Health 8*, 37–43.

Ainsworth, M.D.S., Blehar, M.C., Waters, E. and Wall, S. (1978) *Patterns of Attachment: A Psychological Study of the Strange Situation.* Hillsdale, NJ: Erlbaum.

Alen, A. and Pas, W. (1996) 'The UN Convention on the Rights of the Child's Self-executing Character.' In E. Verhellen (ed.) *Monitoring Children's Rights.* The Hague: Martinus Nijhoff.

Allen, J.P., McElhaney, K.B., Kuperminc, G.P. and Jodl, K.M. (2004) 'Stability and change in attachment security across adolescence.' *Child Development 75*, 6, 1792–805.

Allen, J.P., Moore, C.M. and Kuperminc, G.P. (1997) 'Developmental Approaches to Understanding Adolescent Deviance.' In S. Luthar and J.A. Burack (eds) *Developmental Psychopathology: Perspectives on Adjustment, Risk and Disorder.* New York: Cambridge University Press.

Alltucker, K.W., Bullis, M., Close, D. and Yovanoff, P. (2006) 'Different pathways to juvenile delinquency: Characteristics of early and late starters in a sample of previously incarcerated youth.' *Journal of Child and Family Studies 15*, 4, 479–92.

Almond, G. and Verba, S. (1963) *The Civic Culture.* Princeton NJ: Princeton University Press.

American Bar Association and National Bar Association (2001) *Justice by Gender: The Lack of Appropriate Prevention, Diversion and Treatment Alternatives for Girls in the Justice System.* Washington, DC: American Bar Association and National Bar Association.

American Psychiatric Association (2000) *Diagnostic and Statistical Manual of Mental Disorders* (4th edition). Washington, DC: American Bar Association and National Bar Association.

Anda, R.F., Felitti, V.J., Bremner, D., Walker, J.D. *et al.* (2006) 'The enduring effects of abuse and related adverse experiences in childhood.' *European Archives of Psychiatry and Clinical Neuroscience 256*, 174–86.

Andersen, J., Pettersen, P., Svallfors, S. and Uusitalo, H. (1999) 'The Legitimacy Of The Nordic Welfare States.' In M. Kautto, M. Heikkila, B. Hvinden, S. Marklund and N. Ploug (eds) *Nordic Social Policy*. London: Routledge.

Andersson, G. (2006) 'Child and Family Welfare in Sweden.' In N. Freymond and G. Cameron (eds) *Towards Positive Systems of Child and Family Welfare*. Toronto: University of Toronto Press.

Antecol, H. (2003) 'Why is there cross-country variation in female labor force participation rates?' Claremont, CA: Claremont Colleges Working Papers, number 2003–03.

Antecol, H. and Bedard, K. (2007) 'Does single parenthood increase the probability of teenage promiscuity, substance use, and crime?' *Journal of Population Economics 20*, 55–71.

Archer, J. (2000) 'Sex differences in aggression between heterosexual partners: A meta-analytic review.' *Psychological Bulletin 126*, 651–80.

Aronson, E. (1997) 'The Theory Of Cognitive Dissonance: The Evolution and Vicissitudes of an Idea.' In C. McGarty and S. Haslam (eds) *The Message of Social Psychology: Perspectives on Mind in Society*. Oxford: Blackwell.

Arthur, R. (2005) 'Punishing parents for the crimes of their children.' *The Howard Journal 44*, 3, 233–53.

Ascione, F.R., Weber, C.V. and Wood, D.S. (1997) 'The abuse of animals and domestic violence: A national survey of shelters for women who are battered.' *Society and Animals 5*, 205–18.

Ateah, C.A. and Durrant, J.E. (2005) 'Maternal use of physical punishment in response to child misbehavior: implications for child abuse prevention.' *Child Abuse and Neglect 29*, 169–85.

Autti-Ramo, I. (2000) 'Twelve-year follow up of children exposed to alcohol in utero.' *Developmental Medicine and Child Neurology 42*, 406–11.

Autti-Ramo, I. and Granstrom, M.L. (1996) 'Effects of Fetal Alcohol Exposure on Early Cognitive Development.' In H.L. Spohr and H.C. Steinhausen (eds) *Alcohol, Pregnancy and the Developing Child*. Cambridge: Cambridge University Press.

Babcock, J. C., Waltz, J., Jacobson, N. and Gottman, J. (1993) 'Power and violence: The relation between communication patterns, power discrepancies, and domestic violence.' *Journal of Consulting and Clinical Psychology 61*, 40–50.

Bailey, B.N., Delaney-Black, V., Covington, C.Y., Ager, J. *et al.* (2004) 'Prenatal exposure to binge drinking and cognitive and behavioral outcomes at age 7 years.' *American Journal of Obstetric and Gynecology 191*, 1037–43.

Baker, M. (1995) *Canadian Family Policies: Cross-National Comparisons*. Toronto: University of Toronto Press.

Bakermans-Kranenburg, M.J. and van Ijzendoorn, M.H. (2007) 'Research review: Genetic vulnerability of differential susceptibility in child development: The case of attachment.' *Journal of Child Psychology and Psychiatry 48*, 12, 1160–73.

Baldry, A.C. (2003a) 'Bullying in schools and exposure to domestic violence.' *Child Abuse and Neglect 27*, 713–32.

Baldry, A.C. (2003b) 'Animal abuse and exposure to interparental violence in Italian youth.' *Journal of Interpersonal Violence 18*, 3, 258–81.

Bandura, A. (1973) *Aggression: A Social Learning Analysis*. Englewood Cliffs, NJ: Prentice Hall.

Bandura, A. (1986) *Social Foundations of Thought and Action: A Social Cognitive Theory*. Englewood Cliffs, NJ: Prentice Hall.

Banyard, V.L., Williams, L.M. and Siegel, J. (2003) 'The impact of complex trauma and depression on parenting: An exploration of mediating risk and protective factors.' *Child Maltreatment 8*, 4, 334–49.

Barber, N. (2004) 'Single parenthood as a predictor of cross-national variation in violent crime.' *Cross-Cultural Research 38*, 4, 343–58.

Barnett, W.S. (1998) 'Long-term cognitive and academic effects of early childhood education on children in poverty.' *Preventive Medicine 27*, 2, 204–07.

Barnow, S., Lucht, M., Hamm, A. and Ulrich, J. (2004) 'The relation of a family history of alcoholism, obstetric complications and family environment to behavioral problems among 154 adolescents in Germany: Results from the children of alcoholics study in Pomerania.' *European Addiction Research 10*, 8–14.

Bartz, J.A. and Hollander, E. (2006) 'The neuroscience of affiliation: Forging links between basic and clinical research on neuropeptides and social behavior.' *Hormones and Behavior 50*, 518–28.

Batstra, L., Hadders-Algra, M. and Neelman, J. (2003) 'Effects of antenatal exposure to maternal smoking on behavioural problems and academic achievement in childhood: Prospective evidence from a Dutch birth cohort.' *Early Human Development 75*, 1–2, 21–33.

Battle, K. (2007) 'Child Poverty: The Evolution and Impact of Child Benefits.' In R. Howe and K. Covell (eds) *A Question of Commitment: Children's Rights in Canada*. Waterloo, ON: Wilfrid Laurier University Press.

Baumrind, D. (1967) 'Child care practices anteceding three patterns of preschool behavior.' *Genetic Psychology Monographs 75*, 43–88.

Baumrind, D. (1971) 'Current patterns of parental authority.' *Developmental Psychology Monographs 4*, 1, 1–103.

Bean, C. and Papadakis, E. (1998) 'A comparison of mass attitudes towards the welfare state in different institutional regimes.' *International Journal of Public Opinion 10*, 3, 211–36.

Beck, J.E. and Shaw, D.S. (2005) 'The influence of perinatal complications and environmental adversity on boys' antisocial behavior.' *Journal of Child Psychology and Psychiatry 46*, 1, 35–46.

Beech, A.R. and Mitchell, I.J. (2005) 'A neurobiological perspective on attachment problems in sexual offenders and the role of selective serotonin re-uptake inhibitors in the treatment of such problems.' *Clinical Psychology Review 25*, 153–82.

Bennet, S., Farrington, D.P. and Huesmann, L.R. (2005) 'Explaining gender differences in crime and violence: The importance of social cognitive skills.' *Aggression and Violent Behavior 10*, 263–88.

Bergmark, A. (2000) 'Solidarity in Swedish welfare—standing the test of time?' *Health Care Analysis 8*, 395–411.

Berkowitz, L. (1983) 'Aversively stimulated aggression: Some parallels and differences in research with animals and humans.' *American Psychologist 38*, 1135–44.

Berlin, I. (1969) *Four Essays on Liberty*. Oxford: Oxford University Press.

Bernazzani, O. and Tremblay, R. (2006) 'Early Parent Training.' In B. Welsh and D. Farrington (eds) *Preventing Crime*. Dordrecht, Netherlands: Springer.

Berns, S.B., Jacobson, N. and Gottman, J. (1999) 'Demand-withdraw interaction in couples with a violent husband.' *Journal of Consulting and Clinical Psychology 67*, 666–74.

Bernstein, P. (2003) 'The impact of public opinion on public policy.' *Political Research Quarterly 56*, 29–41.

Beyer, M. (2006) 'Fifty delinquents in juvenile and adult court.' *American Journal of Orthopsychiatry 76*, 2, 206–14.

Bishop, D. (2006) 'Public opinion and juvenile justice policy: Myths and misconceptions.' *Criminology and Public Policy 5*, 4, 653–64.

Bitensky, S.H. (1998) 'Spare the rod, embrace our humanity.' *University of Michigan Journal of Law Reform 31*, 2, 354–91.

Bogaerts, S., Vanheule, S. and Declercq, F. (2005) 'Recalled parental bonding, adult attachment style and personality disorders in child molesters: A comparative study.' *The Journal of Forensic Psychiatry and Psychology 16*, 3, 445–58.

Bogat, G.A., DeJonghe, E., Levendosky, A.A., Davidson, W.S. and von Eye, A. (2006) 'Trauma symptoms among infants exposed to intimate partner violence.' *Child Abuse and Neglect 30*, 109–25.

Bolen, R.M. (2005) 'Attachment and family violence: Complexities in knowing.' *Child Abuse and Neglect 29*, 845–52.

Bolger, K.E. and Patterson, C.J. (2001) 'Developmental pathways from child maltreatment to peer rejection.' *Child Development 72*, 549–68.

Boots, D.P. and Heide, K.M. (2006) 'Parricides in the media. A content analysis of available reports across cultures.' *International Journal of Offender Therapy and Comparative Criminology 50*, 4, 418–45.

Bor, W. and Sanders, M.R. (2004) 'Correlates of self-reported coercive parenting of preschool children at high risk for the development of conduct problems.' *Australian and New Zealand Journal of Psychiatry 38*, 738–45.

Bosmans, G., Braet, C., Van Leeuwen, K. and Beyers, W. (2006) 'Do parenting behaviors predict externalizing behavior in adolescence, or is attachment the neglected third factor?' *Journal of Youth and Adolescence 35*, 3, 373–83.

Bottoms, B., Kovera, M. and McAuliff, B. (2002) *Children, Social Science and the Law.* Cambridge: Cambridge University Press.

Bower-Russa, M.E., Knutson, J.F. and Winebarger, A. (2001) 'Disciplinary history, adult disciplinary attitudes, and risk for abusive parenting.' *Journal of Community Psychology 29*, 3, 219–40.

Bowlby, J. (1969) *Attachment and Loss Vol 1. Attachment.* London: Hogarth Press.

Bowlby, J. (1973) *Attachment and Loss Vol 2. Separation: Anxiety and Anger.* London: Basic Books.

Bowlby, J. (1982) *Attachment: Attachment and Loss* (2nd edition). New York: Basic Books.

Bowlby, J. (1989) 'The Role of Attachment in Personality Development and Psychopathology.' In S.I. Greenspan and G.H. Pollock (eds) *The Course of Life: Vol 1: Infancy.* Madison, CT: International Universities Press.

Bowlus, A., McKenna, K., Day, T. and Wright, D. (2003) *The Economic Costs and Consequences of Child Abuse in Canada.* Report to the Law Commission of Canada. Ottawa: Law Commission of Canada.

Brannigan, A., Gemmell, W., Pevalin, D.J. and Wade, T.J. (2002) 'Self-control and social control in childhood misconduct and aggression: The role of family structure, hyperactivity, and hostile parenting.' *Canadian Journal of Criminology*, 119–42.

Bremner, J.D. and Vermetten, E. (2001) 'Stress and development: Behavioral and biological consequences.' *Development and Psychopathology 13*, 473–89.

Brendgen, M., Vitaro, F., Tremblay, R.E. and Wanner, B. (2002) 'Parent and peer effects of delinquency-related violence and dating violence: A test of two mediational models.' *Social Development 11*, 225–44.

Brennan, P.A., Grekin, E.R. and Mednick, S.A. (1999) 'Maternal smoking during pregnancy and adult male criminal outcomes.' *Archives of General Psychiatry 56*, 125–9.

Brennan, P.A., Grekin, E.R., Mortensen, E.L. and Mednick, S.A. (2002) 'Relationship of maternal smoking during pregnancy with criminal arrest and hospitalization for substance abuse in male and female adult offspring.' *American Journal of Psychiatry 159*, 1, 48–54.

Bretherton, I. (1985) 'Attachment theory: Retrospect and prospect.' *Monographs of the Society for Research in Child Development 50*, 3–35.

Broidy, L.M., Nagin, D.S., Tremblay, R.E., Brame, B. *et al.* (2003) 'Developmental trajectories of childhood disruptive behaviors and adolescent delinquency: A six-site cross-national study.' *Developmental Psychology 39*, 222–45.

Bronfenbrenner, U. (1977) 'Toward an experimental ecology of human development.' *American Psychologist 32*, 513–31.

Bronfenbrenner, U. (1979) *The Ecology of Human Development. Experiments by Nature and Design.* Cambridge: Harvard University Press.

Bronfenbrenner, U. (1986) 'Ecology of the family as a context for human development: Reseach perspectives.' *Developmental Psychology 22*, 6, 723–42.

Brooks, B. and Manza, J. (2006) 'Why do welfare states persist?' *The Journal of Politics 68*, 4, 816–27.

Brown, G. and Moran, P. (1997) 'Single mothers, poverty and depression.' *Psychological Medicine 27*, 21–33.

Brown, S.A., Mott, M.A. and Stewart, M.A. (1992) 'Adolescent Alcohol and Drug Abuse.' In C.E. Walker and M.C. Roberts (eds) *Handbook of Clinical Child Psychology* (2nd edition). New York: Wiley.

Bufkin, J.L. and Luttrell, V.R. (2005) 'Neuroimaging studies of aggressive and violent behavior. Current findings and implications for criminology and criminal justice.' *Trauma, Violence and Abuse 6*, 2, 176–91.

Caesar, P.L. (1988) 'Exposure to violence in the families-of-origin among wife-abusers and maritally non-violent men.' *Violence and Victims 3*, 49–63.

Cameron, G. and Freymond, N. (2006) 'Understanding International Comparisons of Child Protection, Family Service, and Community Caring Systems of Child and Family Welfare.' In In N. Freymond and G. Cameron (eds) *Towards Positive Systems of Child and Family Welfare.* Toronto: University of Toronto Press.

Campaign 2000 (2007) Report card 2006. Available at www.campaign2000.ca/rc/rc06/06_C2000NationalReportCand.pdf, accessed on 21 May 2007.

Campbell, K.M. and Covell, K. (2001) 'Children's rights education at the university level: An effective means of promoting rights knowledge and rights-based attitudes.' *International Journal of Children's Rights 9*, 123–35.

Campbell, K. and Rose-Krasnor, L. (2007) 'The Participation Rights of the Child: Canada's Track Record.' In R.B. Howe and K. Covell (eds) *A Question of Commitment. Children's Rights in Canada.* Waterloo, ON: Wilfrid Laurier University Press.

Canadian Institute for Health Information (2007) *Low Birth Weight*. Available at http://secure.cihi.ca/cihiweb/dispPage.jsp?cw_page=media_25jul2007_e, accessed on 26 July 2007.

Cantwell, N. (1992) 'The Origins, Development and Significance of the United Nations Convention on the Rights of the Child.' In S. Detrick (ed.) *The United Nations Convention on the Rights of the Child*. Dordrecht, Netherlands: Martinus Nijhoff.

Carlton, B.S., Goebert, D.A., Miyamoto, R.H., Andrade, E.S. *et al.* (2006) 'Resilience, family adversity and well being among Hawaian and non-Hawaian adolescents.' *International Journal of Social Psychiatry 53*, 4, 291–308.

Carter, C.S. (2005) 'The chemistry of child neglect: Do oxytocin and vasopressin mediate the effects of early experience.' *Proceedings of the National Academy of Sciences of the United States of America (PNAS) 102*, 18247–8.

Casas, J.F., Weigel, S.M., Crick, N.R., Ostrov, J.M., *et al.* (2006) 'Early parenting and children's relational and physical aggression in the preschool and home contexts.' *Applied Developmental Psychology 27*, 209–27.

Cassidy, J., Kirsh, S.J., Scolton, K.L. and Parke, R.D. (1996) 'Attachment and representations of peer relationships.' *Developmental Psychology 32*, 892–904.

Catalano, R.E. and Hawkins, J.D. (1996) 'The Social Development Model: A Theory of Antisocial Behavior.' In J.D. Hawkins (ed.) *Delinquency and Crime: Current Theories*. New York: Cambridge University Press.

Cavet, J. and Sloper, P. (2004) 'The participation of children and young people in decisions about UK service development.' *Child: Care, Health and Development 30*, 6, 613–21.

Chaaya, M., Campbell, O.M., El Kak, F., Shaar, D., Harb, H. and Kaddour, A. (2002) 'Postpartum depression: Prevalence and determinants in Lebanon.' *Archives of Women's Mental Health 5*, 65–72.

Chaffin, M. (2006) 'The changing focus of child maltreatment research and practice within psychology.' *Journal of Social Issues 62*, 4, 663–84.

Chaffin, M., Hanson, R., Saunders, B.E., Nichols, T., *et al.* (2006) 'Report of the APSAC Task Force on Attachment Therapy, Reactive Attachment Disorder, and Attachment Problems.' *Child Maltreatment 11*, 1, 76–89.

Chance, T. and Scannapieco, M. (2002) 'Ecological correlates of child maltreatment: Similarities and differences between child fatality and nonfatality cases.' *Child and Adolescent Social Work Journal 19*, 139–61.

Chapillon, P., Patin, V., Roy, V., Vincent, A. and Caston, J. (2002) 'Effects of pre- and postnatal stimulation on developmental, emotional, and cognitive aspects in rodents: A review.' *Developmental Psychobiology 41*, 373–87.

Chapin, H.D. (1917) 'Systematized boarding out vs. institutional care for infants and young children.' *New York Medical Journal 22*, 1009–11.

Chapple, C.L. (2003) 'Examining intergenerational violence. Violent role modeling or weak parental controls.' *Violence and Victims 18*, 143–59.

Chase, K.A., Treboux, D. and O'Leary, K.D. (2002) 'Characteristics of high-risk adolescents' dating violence.' *Journal of Interpersonal Violence 17*, 33–49.

Chassin, L., Ritter, J., Trim, K.S. and King, K.M. (2003) 'Adolescent Substance Use Disorders.' In E.J. Mash and R.A. Barkley (eds) *Child Psychopathology* (2nd edition). New York: Guilford.

Child Welfare League of America (2001) *Alcohol, Other Drugs, and Child Welfare*. Pub. No. 0-87868-839-0. Washington: Child Welfare League of America.

Choong, K. and Shen, R. (2004) 'Prenatal ethanol exposure alters the postnatal development of the spontaneous electrical activity of dopamine neurons in the ventral tegmental area.' *Neuroscience 4*, 1083–91.

Chronis, A.M., Lahey, B.B., Pelham Jr., W.E., Williams, S., *et al.* (2007) 'Maternal depression and early positive parenting predict future conduct problems in young children with attention-deficit/hyperactivity disorder.' *Developmental Psychology 43*, 1, 70–82.

Cicchetti, D. and Lynch, M. (1993) 'Toward an ecological/transactional model of community violence and child maltreatment. Consequences for children's development.' *Psychiatry: Interpersonal and Biological Processes 56*, 96–118.

Clarke, R. (1995) 'Situational Crime Prevention.' In M. Tonry and D. Farrington (eds) *Building a Safer Society*. Chicago, IL: University of Chicago Press.

Clarren, S.K., Randels, S.P., Sanderson, M. and Fineman, R.M. (2001) 'Screening for fetal alcohol syndrome in primary schools: A feasibility study.' *Teratology 63*, 3–10.

Cnattingius, S. (2004) 'The epidemiology of smoking during pregnancy: Smoking prevalence, maternal characteristics, and pregnancy outcomes.' *Nicotine and Tobacco Research 6* (Supplement 2), S125–S140.

Coe, C.L., Lulbach, G.R. and Schneider, M.L. (2002) 'Prenatal disturbance alters the size of the corpus callosum in young monkeys.' *Developmental Psychobiology 41*, 178–85.

Cohn, D.A. (1990) 'Child–mother attachment of six-year-olds and social competence at school.' *Child Development 61*, 152–62.

Cole, P.M., Woolger, C., Power, T.G. and Smith, K. (1992) 'Parenting difficulties among adult survivors of father–daughter incest.' *Child Abuse and Neglect 16*, 239–49.

Collins, T., Pearson, L. and Delany, C. (2002) *Rights-Based Approach*. Discussion paper. Office of Senator Pearson, Ottawa, Canada.

Colman, A. (2003) 'Child-abuse reports. Abuse linked to crime.' *Youth Studies Australia 22*, 1, 4–5.

Committee on the Rights of the Child (1994) *UN Doc CRC/C/34 1994*. New York: United Nations.

Committee on the Rights of the Child (2003) *UN Doc CRC/C/15/Add215.2003*. New York: United Nations.

Conners, N.A., Bradley, R.H., Mansell, L.W., Liu, J.Y.*et al.* (2004) 'Children of mothers with serious substance abuse problems: An accumulation of risks.' *American Journal of Drug and Alcohol Abuse 30*, 1, 85–100.

Constantino, J.N., Chackes, L.M., Wartner, U.G., Gross, M. *et al.* (2006) 'Mental representations of attachment in identical female twins with and without conduct problems.' *Child Psychiatry and Human Development 37*, 65–72.

Conway, D. (1995) *Classical Liberalism*. New York: St Martin's Press.

Cooke, C.G., Kelley, M.L., Fals-Stewart, W. and Golden, J. (2004) 'A comparison of the psychosocial functioning of children with drug-versus alcohol-dependent fathers.' *The American Journal of Drug and Alcohol Abuse 30*, 4, 695–710.

Coontz, P.D. and Martin, J.A. (1988) 'Understanding Violent Mothers and Fathers: Assessing Explanations Offered by Mothers and Fathers of Their Use of Control Punishment.' In G.T. Hotaling, D. Finkelho, J. Kirkpatrick and M.A. Straus (eds) *Family Abuse and its Consequences: New Directions in Research*. Newbury Park, CA: Sage.

Cooper, P., Tomlinson, M., Swartz, L., Woolgar, M., Murray, L. and Molteno, C. (1999) 'Postpartum depression and the mother–infant relationship in a South Africa peri-urban settlement.' *British Journal of Psychiatry 175*, 554–8.

Cornia, G. and Danziger, S. (1997) *Child Poverty and Deprivation in the Industrialized Countries, 1945–1995*. Oxford: Clarendon Press.

Covell, K. (2005) *Violence Against Children in North America: United Nations Secretary-General's Study on Violence Against Children*. Toronto: UNICEF Canada.

Covell, K. (2006) *Seen, Heard and Believed. What Youth Say About Violence*. Toronto: UNICEF Canada.

Covell, K. (2007) 'Children's Rights Education: Canada's Best Kept Secret.' In R.B. Howe and K. Covell (eds) *A Question of Commitment. Children's Rights in Canada*. Waterloo, ON: Wilfrid Laurier University Press.

Covell, K. and Howe, R.B. (1999) 'The impact of children's rights education: A Canadian study.' *International Journal of Children's Rights 7*, 171–83.

Covell, K. and Howe, R.B. (2001a) *The Challenge of Children's Rights for Canada*. Waterloo, ON: Wilfrid Laurier University Press.

Covell, K. and Howe, R.B (2001b) 'Moral Education through the 3 Rs: Rights, respect and responsibility.' *Journal of Moral Education 30*, 31–42.

Covell, K. and Howe, R.B. (2007) *Rights, Respect and Responsibility: Year Two Evaluation of the Hampshire County Initiative*. Cape Breton Children's Rights Centre. Available at http://discovery.cbu.ca/children, accessed on 5 June 2008.

Covell, K., O'Leary, J.L. and Howe, R.B. (2002) 'Introducing a new grade 8 curriculum in children's rights.' *The Alberta Journal of Educational Research XLVIII*, 4, 302–13.

Crawford, A. (1998) *Crime Prevention and Community Safety: Politics, Policies and Practices*. London: Longman.

Creeden, K. (2004) 'The neurodevelopmental impact of early trauma and insecure attachment: Re-thinking our understanding and treatment of sexual behavior problems.' *Sexual Addiction and Compulsivity, 11*, 223–47.

Crick, N.R. and Dodge, K.A. (1994) 'A review and reformulation of social information-processing mechanisms in children's social adjustment.' *Psychological Bulletin 115*, 74–101.

Crijnen, A., Achenbach, T. and Verhulst, F. (1999) 'Comparisons of problems reported by parents of children in 12 cultures.' *American Journal of Psychiatry 156*, 4, 569–74.

Criss, M.M., Pettit, G.S., Bates, J.E., Dodge, K.A. and Lapp, A. (2002) 'Family adversity, positive peer relationships, and children's externalizing behavior: A longitudinal perspective on risk and resilience.' *Child Development 73*, 4, 1220–37.

Crnic, K.A., Gaze, C. and Hoffman, C. (2005) 'Cumulative parenting stress across the preschool period: Relations to maternal parenting and child behavior at age 5.' *Infant and Child Development 14*, 117–32.

Crockenberg, S.C. and Leerkes, E.M. (2003) 'Parental acceptance, postpartum depression, and maternal sensitivity: Mediating and moderating processes.' *Journal of Family Psychology 17*, 1, 80–93.

Cross, W. (2001) 'A personal history of childhood sexual abuse: Parenting patterns and problems.' *Clinical Child Psychology and Psychiatry 6*, 4, 563–74.

Cullen, F., Fisher, B. and Applegate, B. (2000) 'Public Opinion about Punishment and Corrections.' In M. Tonry (ed.) *Crime and Justice* (Vol 27). Chicago, IL: University of Chicago Press.

Cullen, F., Wright, J., Brown, S., Blankenship, M. and Applegate, B. (1998) 'Public support for early intervention programs.' *Crime and Delinquency 44*, 187–204.

Cunradi, C., Caetano, R. and Shafer, J. (2002) 'Alcohol-related problems, drug use, and male intimate partner violence severity among US couples.' *Alcoholism: Clinical and Experimental Research 26*, 4, 493–500.

Currie, C.L. (2006) 'Animal cruelty by children exposed to domestic violence.' *Child Abuse and Neglect 30*, 425–35.

Dadds, M.R., Atkinson, E., Turner, C., Blums, G. and Lendich, B. (1999) 'Family conflict and child adjustment: Evidence for a cognitive-contextual model of intergenerational transmission.' *Journal of Family Psychology 13*, 194–208.

Dahinten, V.S., Shapka, J.D. and Willms, J.D. (2007) 'Adolescent children of adolescent mothers: The impact of family functioning on trajectories of development.' *Journal of Youth and Adolescence 36*, 195–212.

Dallaire, D. (2007) 'Children with incarcerated mothers: Developmental outcomes, special challenges and recommendations.' *Journal of Applied Developmental Psychology 28*, 15–24.

Dankoski, M.E., Keiley, M., Thomas, V., Choice, P., Lloyd, S. and Seery, B. (2006) 'Affect regulation and the cycle of violence against women: New directions for understanding the process.' *Journal of Family Violence 21*, 327–39.

Davis, C.A. (2003) *Children Who Kill: Profiles of Pre-teen and Teenage Killers.* London: Allison and Busby, Ltd.

Dawson, G., Ashman, S. and Carver, L.J. (2000) 'The role of early experience in shaping behavioral and brain development and its implications for social policy.' *Development and Psychopathology 12*, 695–712.

Dawson, G., Ashman, S.B., Panagiotides, H., Hessl, D., et al. (2003) 'Preschool outcomes of children of depressed mothers: Role of maternal behavior, contextual risk, and children's brain activity.' *Child Development 74*, 1158–75.

De Bellis, M.D. (2005). 'The psychobiology of neglect.' *Child Maltreatment 10*, 2, 150–72.

De Bellis, M.D., Keshavan, M.S., Shifflet, H., Iyengar, S. et al. (2002) 'Brain structures in pediatric maltreatment-related posttraumatic stress disorder: A sociodemographically matched study.' *Society of Biological Psychiatry 52*, 1066–78.

De Castro, B.O., Merk, W., Koops, W., Veerman, J.W. and Bosch, J.D. (2005) 'Emotions in social information processing and their relations with reactive and proactive aggression in referred aggressive boys.' *Journal of Clinical Child and Adolescent Psychology 34*, 1, 105–16.

Decoene, J. and De Cock, R. (1996) 'The Children's Rights Project in the Primary School "De vrijdagmarkt" in Bruges.' In E. Verhellen (ed.) *Monitoring Children's Rights.* The Hague: Martinus Nijhoff.

Delaney-Black, V., Covington, C., Templin, T., Ager, J. et al. (2000) 'Teacher-assessed behavior of children prenatally exposed to cocaine.' *Pediatrics 106*, 4, 782–91.

Delpisheh, A., Attia, E., Drammond, S. and Brabin, B.J. (2006) 'Adolescent smoking in pregnancy and birth outcomes.' *The European Journal of Public Health 16*, 2, 168–72.

Dembo, R., Williams, L., Wothke, W. and Schmeidler, J. (1992) 'The role of family factors, physical abuse and sexual victimization experiences in high-risk youths' alcohol and other drug use and delinquency: A longitudinal model.' *Violence and Victims 7*, 245–66.

Denenberg, V.H. (1999) 'Is maternal stimulation the mediator of the handling effects in infancy?' *Developmental Psychobiology 34*, 1, 1–3.

Denis, J., Lehoux, P. and Champagne, F. (2004) 'A Knowledge Utilization Perspective on Fine-tuning Dissemination and Contextualizing Knowledge.' In L. Lemieux-Charles and F. Champagne (eds) *Using Knowledge and Evidence in Health Care.* Toronto: University of Toronto Press.

Denov, M.S. (2001) 'A culture of denial: Exploring professional perspectives on female sex offending.' *Canadian Journal of Criminology 43*, 3, 303–29.

Denov, M.S. (2004). 'The long-term effects of child sexual abuse by female perpetrators.' *Journal of Interpersonal Violence 19*, 10, 1137–56.

Dill, V.S. (1998) *A Peaceable School.* Bloomington, IN: Phi Delta Kappa Educational Foundation.

Dishion, T., French, D. and Patterson, G. (1995) 'The Development and Ecology of Antisocial Behavior.' In D. Cicchetti and D. Cohen (eds) *Developmental Psychopathology* (Vol. 2). New York: John Wiley and Sons.

Dishion, T.J., McCord, J. and Poulin, F. (1999) 'When interventions harm: Peer groups and problem behavior.' *American Psychologist 54*, 755–64.

Dodge, K.A., Bates, J.E. and Petit, G.S. (1990) 'Mechanisms in the cycle of violence.' *Science 250*, 1678–83.

Dodge, K.A., Dishion, T.J. and Lansford, J.E. (2006) 'Deviant peer influences in intervention and public policy for youth.' *Social Policy Report*, Vol.XX No. 1. Society for Research in Child Development.

Dodge, K.A., Petit, G.S., McClaskey, C.L. and Brown, M.M. (1986) 'Social competence in children.' *Monographs of the Society for Research in Child Development 51*, 2 Serial # 213.

Dodge, K.A. and Schwartz, D. (1997) 'Social Information Processing Mechanisms in Aggressive Behavior.' In D.M. Stoff, J. Breiling and J. Maser (eds) *Handbook of Antisocial Behavior.* New York: Wiley.

Doek, J. (1992) 'The Current Status of the United Nations Convention on the Rights of the Child.' In S. Detrick (ed.) *The United Nations Convention on the Rights of the Child.* Dordrecht, Netherlands: Martinus Nijhoff.

Dolan, M. and Smith, C. (2001) 'Juvenile homicide offenders: 10 years' experience of an adolescent forensic psychiatry service.' *The Journal of Forensic Psychiatry 12*, 2, 313–29.

Donohue, B., Romero, V. and Hill, H.H. (2006) 'Treatment of co-occurring child maltreatment and substance abuse.' *Aggression and Violent Behavior 11*, 626–40.

Doob, A. (2000) 'Transforming the punishment environment.' *Canadian Journal of Criminology 42*, 323–40.

Doob, A. and Cesaroni, C. (2004) *Responding to Youth Crime in Canada.* Toronto: University of Toronto Press.

Douglas, E.M. (2006) 'Familial violence socialization in childhood and later life approval of corporal punishment: A cross-cultural perspective.' *American Journal of Orthopsychiatry 76*, 1, 23–30.

Downs, W.R., Miller, B.A., Testa, M. and Parek, P. (1992) 'Long-term effects of parent-to-child violence for women.' *Journal of Interpersonal Violence 7*, 365–82.

Drugli, M. (2006) 'Young children treated because of ODD/CD: Conduct problems and social competence in day-care and school settings.' Ph.D. thesis. Norwegian University of Science and Technology, Faculty of Medicine, Trondheim.

Dube, S.R., Anda, R.F., Felitti, V., Edwards, V. and Williamson, D.F. (2002) 'Exposure to abuse, neglect and household dysfunction among adults who witnessed intimate partner violence as children: Implications for health and social services.' *Violence and Victims 17*, 1, 3–18.

Duncan, A., Thomas, J.C. and Miller, C. (2005) 'Significance of family risk factors in development of childhood animal cruelty in adolescent boys with conduct problems.' *Journal of Family Violence 20*, 4, 235–9.

Dunford, F.W. (2000) 'The San Diego Navy Experiment: An assessment of interventions for men who assault their wives.' *Journal of Consulting and Clinical Psychology 68*, 468–76.

Dunn, J. (2004) *Children's Friendships*. Malden, MA: Blackwell.

Dunn, M.G., Tarter, R.E., Mezzich, A.C., Vanyukov, M., Kirisci, L. and Kirillova, G. (2002) 'Origins and consequences of child neglect in substance abuse families.' *Clinical Psychology Review 22*, 1063–90.

Durrant, J.E. (1995) 'Culture, Corporal Punishment and Child Abuse.' In K. Covell (ed.) *Readings in Child Development*. Scarborough, ON: Nelson Canada.

Durrant, J.E. (1999) 'Evaluating the success of Sweden's corporal punishment ban.' *Child Abuse and Neglect 23*, 5, 435–48.

Durrant, J.E. (2000) 'Trends in youth crime and well-being since the abolition of corporal punishment in Sweden.' *Youth and Society 31*, 4, 437–55.

Durrant, J.E. (2003) 'Legal reform and attitudes toward physical punishment in Sweden.' *International Journal of Children's Rights 11*, 2, 147–73.

Durrant, J.E. (2007) 'Corporal Punishment: A Violation of the Rights of the Child.' In R.B. Howe and K. Covell (eds) *A Question of Commitment: Children's Rights in Canada*. Waterloo, ON: Wilfrid Laurier University Press.

Durrant, J.E., Ensom, R. and Coalition on Physical Punishment of Children and Youth (2004) *Joint Statement on Physical Punishment of Children and Youth*. Ottawa: Coalition on Physical Punishment of Children and Youth.

Durrant, J.E. and Janson, S. (2005) 'Law reform, corporal punishment, and child abuse: The case of Sweden.' *International Review of Victimology 12*, 139–58.

Dye, T. (1995) *Understanding Public Policy*. Englewood Cliffs, NJ: Prentice Hall.

DYG Inc. (2000) *What Grown-ups Understand about Child Development: A National Benchmark Survey*. Washington, DC: DYG Inc.

Eamon, M.K. and Mulder, C. (2005) 'Predicting antisocial behavior among Latino young adolescents: An ecological systems analysis.' *American Journal of Orthopsychiatry 75*, 1, 117–27.

Edleson, J.L., Gassman-Pines, J. and Hill, M.B. (2006) 'Defining child exposure to domestic violence as neglect: Minnesota's difficult experience.' *Social Work 51*, 2, 167–74.

Edleson, J.L., Mbilinyi, L.F., Beeman, S.K. and Hagemeister, A.K. (2003) 'How children are involved in domestic violence: Results from a four city telephone survey.' *Journal of Interpersonal Violence 18*, 18–32.

Edlund, J. (2000) 'Public attitudes towards taxation: Sweden 1981–1997.' *Scandinavian Political Studies 23*, 1, 37–65.

Edwards, O.W., Mumford, V.E. and Serra-Roldan, R. (2007) 'A positive youth development model for students considered at-risk.' *School Psychology International 28*, 1, 29–45.

Egeland, B. and Sussman-Stillman, A. (1996) 'Dissociation as a mediator of child abuse across generations.' *Child Abuse and Neglect 20*, 1123–32.

Egeland, B., Yates, T., Appelyard, K. and van Dulmen, M. (2002) 'The long-term consequences of maltreatment in the early years: A developmental pathway model to antisocial behavior.' *Children's Services: Social Policy, Research, and Practice 5*, 4, 249–60.

Ehrensaft, M.K., Cohen, P., Brown, J., Smailes, E., Chen, H. and Johnson, J. (2003) 'Intergenerational transmission of partner violence: A 20-year prospective study.' *Journal of Consulting and Clinical Psychology 71*, 4, 741–53.

Ehrensaft, M.K. and Vivian, D. (1999) 'Adolescent and family predictors of physical aggression, communication, and satisfaction in young adult couples: A prospective analysis.' *Journal of Family Violence 14*, 251–66.

Eichler, M. (1997) *Family Shifts: Families, Policies and Gender Equality*. Toronto: Oxford University Press.

Eklund, J., Alm, P.O. and Klinteberg, B. (2005) 'Monoamine oxidase activity and tri-lodothyronine level in violent offenders with early behavioural problems.' *Neuropsychobiology 52*, 122–9.

Elgar, F.J., McGrath, P.J. and Waschbuch, D.A. (2004) 'Mutual influences on maternal depression and child adjustment problems.' *Clinical Psychology Review 24*, 441–59.

English, D.J., Marshall, D.B. and Orme, M. (1999) 'Characteristics of repeated referrals to child protective services in Washington State.' *Journal of the American Professional Society on the Abuse of Children 4*, 297–307.

Environics Research Group (2006a) 'Fire and ice: The US, Canada, and the myth of converging values.' Toronto: Environics Research.

Environics Research Group (2006b) 'Canadians' attitudes toward national child care policy.' Toronto: Environics Research.

Erikson, E. (1968) *Identity: Youth and Crisis*. New York: Norton.

Ernst, M., Moolchan, E. and Robinson, M. (2001) 'Behavioral and neural consequences of prenatal exposure to nicotine.' *Journal of the American Academy of Child and Adolescent Psychiatry 40*, 630–42.

Esping-Andersen, G. (1990) *The Three Worlds of Welfare Capitalism*. Princeton, NJ: Princeton University Press.

Esping-Andersen, G. (1999) *Social Foundations of Postindustrial Economies*. Oxford: Oxford University Press.

Estrada, F. (1999) 'Juvenile crime trends in post-war Europe.' *European Journal on Criminal Policy and Research 7*, 23–42.

Ethier, L.S., Lemelin, J.P. and Lacharite, C. (2004) 'A longitudinal study of the effects of chronic maltreatment on children's behavioral and emotional problems.' *Child Abuse and Neglect 28*, 1265–78.

European Agency for Development in Special Needs Education (2005) *Early Childhood Intervention: Analysis of Situation in Europe*. Middelfart, Denmark: European Agency for Development in Special Needs Education.

Evans, J., Heron, J., Francomb, H., Oke, S. and Golding, J. (2001) 'Cohort study of depressed mood during pregnancy and after childbirth.' *British Medical Journal 323*, 257–60.

Eydal, G. and Satka, M. (2006) 'Social work and Nordic welfare policies for children—present challenges in the light of the past.' *European Journal of Social Work 9*, 3, 305–22.

Fabian, H.M., Radestad, I.J. and Waldenstrom, U. (2006) 'Characteristics of primiparous women who are not reached by parental education classes after childbirth in Sweden.' *Acta Paediatrica 95*, 1360–9.

Fals-Stewart, W., Kelley, M.L., Fincham, F.D., Golden, J. and Logsdon, T. (2004) 'Emotional and behavioral problems of children living with drug-abusing fathers: Comparisons with children living with alcohol-abusing and non-substance abusing fathers.' *Journal of Family Psychology 18*, 2, 319–30.

Fantuzzo, J., Boruch, R., Beriama, A., Atkins, M. and Marcus, S. (1997) 'Domestic violence and children: Prevalence and risk in five major U.S. cities.' *Journal of the American Academy of Child and Adolescent Psychiatry 36*, 116–22.

Farrington, D.P. (1994) 'Early developmental prevention of juvenile delinquency.' *Criminal Behavior and Mental Health 4*, 209–27.

Farrington, D.P. (1995) 'The development of offending and antisocial behavior from childhood: Key findings from the Cambridge Study in delinquent development.' *Journal of Child Psychology and Psychiatry 36*, 929–64.

Farrington, D.P. (2000) 'Explaining and preventing crime: The globalization of knowledge—The American Society of Criminology 1999 Presidential Address.' *Criminology 38*, 1, 24.

Farrington, D.P., Barnes, G. and Lambert, S. (1996) 'The concentration of offending in families.' *Legal and Criminological Psychology 1*, 47–63.

Farrington, D.P., Gundry, G. and West, D.J. (1975) 'The familial transmission of criminality.' *Medicine Science and the Law 15*, 177–86.

Farrington, D.P., Jolliffe, D., Loeber, R., Stouthamer-Loeber, M. and Kalb, L.M. (2001) 'The concentration of offenders in families, and family criminality in the prediction of boys' delinquency.' *Journal of Adolescence 24*, 579–96.

Farrington, D.P., Lambert, S. and West, D.J. (1998) 'Criminal careers of two generations of family members in the Cambridge Study in Delinquent Development. *Studies on Crime and Crime Prevention 7*, 85–106.

Farrington, D.P., Langan, P. and Tonry, M. (2004) *National Crime Rates Compared 1981–1999.* Washington, DC: U.S. Department of Justice: Bureau of Justice Statistics.

Farrington, D.P. and Welsh, B. (2003) 'Family-based prevention of offending: A meta-analysis. *The Australian and New Zealand Journal of Criminology 36*, 2, 127–51.

Farrington, D.P. and Welsh, B. (2006) 'Improved Street Lighting.' In B. Welsh and D. Farrington (eds) *Preventing Crime.* Dordrecht, Netherlands: Springer.

Farrington, D.P. and Welsh, B. (2007) *Saving Children from a Life of Crime: Early Risk Factors and Effective Interventions.* New York: Oxford University Press.

Farrington, D.P. and West, D. (1981) 'The Cambridge Study in Delinquent Behavior (United Kingdom).' In S. Mednick and A. Beart (eds) *Prospective Longitudinal Research: An Empirical Basis for Primary Prevention.* Oxford: Oxford University Press.

Fast, D.K. and Conry, J. (2004) 'The challenge of fetal alcohol syndrome in the criminal legal system.' *Addiction Biology 9*, 161–6.

Federal Bureau of Investigation (2007) *Crime in the United States 2005.* Available at www.fbi.gov/ucr/05cius, accessed on 20 March 2007.

Feiring, C. and Furman, W.C. (2000) 'When love is just a four letter word: Victimization and romantic relationships in adolescence.' *Child Maltreatment 5*, 293–98.

Feldman, S. and Zaller, J. (1992) 'The political culture of ambivalence: Ideological responses to the welfare state.' *American Journal of Political Science 36*, 268–307.

Felthous, A.R. and Yudowitz, B. (1997) 'Approaching a comparative typology of assaultive female offenders.' *Psychiatry 40*, 270–6.

Ferguson, T. (1952) *The Young Delinquent in His Social Setting.* London: Oxford University Press.

Fergusson, D.M. and Horwood, L. (1996) 'The role of adolescent peer affiliations in the continuity between childhood behavioral adjustment and juvenile offending.' *Journal of Abnormal Child Psychology 24*, 2, 205–21.

Fergusson, D.M. and Horwood, L.J. (1998) 'Exposure to interparental violence in childhood and psychosocial adjustment in young adulthood.' *Child Abuse and Neglect 22*, 339–57.

Fergusson, D.M., Horwood, L.J. and Ridder, E.M. (2005) 'Partner violence and mental health outcomes in a New Zealand Cohort.' *Journal of Marriage and the Family 67*, 1103–19.

Fergusson, D.M., Woodward, L.J. and Horwood, L. (1998) 'Maternal smoking during pregnancy and psychiatric adjustment in late adolescence.' *Archives of General Psychiatry 55*, 721–7.

Ferrarini, T. (2006) *Families, States and Labour Markets.* Cheltenham: Edward Elgar.

Finkelhor, D., Ormrod, R.K. and Turner, H.A. (2007) 'Poly-victimization: A neglected component in child victimization.' *Child Abuse and Neglect 31*, 7–26.

Fishbein, M. and Middlestadt, S. (1995) 'Noncognitive effects on attitude formation and change: Fact or artifact?' *Journal of Consumer Psychology 4*, 2, 181–202.

Flekkoy, M. (1991) *A Voice for Children.* London: Jessica Kingsley Publishers.

Flekkoy, M. and Kaufman, N. (1997) *The Participation Rights of the Child: Rights and Responsibilities in Family and Society.* London: Jessica Kingsley Publishers.

Flouri, E. and Buchanan, A. (2002) 'Father involvement in childhood and trouble with the police in adolescence.' *Journal of Interpersonal Violence 17*, 6, 689–701.

Floyd, R.L., O'Connor, M.J., Sokol, R.J., Bertrand, J. and Cordero, J.F. (2005) 'Recognition and prevention of fetal alcohol syndrome.' *Obstetrics and Gynecology 106*, 1059–64.

Floyd, R.L., Sobell, M., Velasquez, M.M., Ingersoll, K. *et al.* (2007) 'Preventing alcohol-exposed pregnancies. A randomized controlled trial.' *American Journal of Preventive Medicine 32*, 1, 1–10.

Foley, D.L., Eaves, L.J., Wormley, B., Silberg, J.L. *et al.* (2004) 'Childhood adversity, monoamine oxidase A genotype, and risk for conduct disorder.' *Archives of General Psychiatry 61*, 738–44.

Fontaine, R.G. (2006) 'Evaluative behavioral judgments and instrumental antisocial behaviors in children and adolescents.' *Clinical Psychology Review 26*, 956–67.

Forbes, E.E., Shaw, D.S., Fox, N.A., Cohn, J.F., Silk, J. and Kovacs, M. (2006) 'Maternal depression, child frontal asymmetry, and child affective behavior as factors in child behavior problems.' *Journal of Child Psychology and Psychiatry 47*, 1, 79–87.

Forth, A.E. and Burke, H.C. (1998) 'Psychopathy in Adolescence: Assessment, Violence and Developmental Precursors. In D.J. Cooke, A.E. Forth and R.D. Hare (eds) *Psychopathy: Theory, Research and Implications for Society.* Dordrecht, Netherlands: Kluwer Academic Publishing.

Frankel, K. and Bates, J. (1990) 'Mother–toddler problem solving: Antecedents in attachment, home behavior and temperament.' *Child Development 61*, 810–19.

Freeman, M. (1992) 'Taking children's rights more seriously.' *International Journal of Law and the Family 6*, 52–71.

Freeman, M. (1996) 'Introduction: Children as Persons.' In M. Freeman (ed.) *Children's Rights: A Comparative Perspective.* Aldershot: Darmouth Publishing.

Freeman, M. (2007) 'Why it remains important to take children's rights seriously.' *International Journal of Children's Rights 15*, 5–23.

Friedman, M. (1962) *Capitalism and Democracy*. Chicago, IL: University of Chicago Press.

Friendly, M. (2007) 'Early Learning and Child Care: Is Canada on Track?' In R.B. Howe and K. Covell (eds) *A Question of Commitment: Children's Rights in Canada*. Waterloo, ON: Wilfrid Laurier University Press.

Fryxell, D. (2000) 'Personal, social and family characteristics of angry students.' *Professional School Counseling 4*, 2, 86–95.

Furstenberg, F. (1997) 'State–family alliances and children's welfare.' *Childhood 4*, 2, 183–92.

Galindo, R., Zamudio, P.A. and Valenzuela, C.F. (2005) 'Alcohol is a potent stimulant of immature neuronal networks: Implications for fetal alcohol spectrum disorder.' *Journal of Neurochemistry 94*, 1500–11.

Garbarino, J. (2000) *Lost Boys*. New York: Anchor Books.

Geist, C. (2005) 'The welfare state and the home: Regime differences in the domestic division of labour.' *European Sociological Review 21*, 1, 23–41.

Gelfand, D.M. and Drew, C.J. (2003) *Understanding Child Behavior Disorders*. Belmont, CA: Thompson.

Gelles, R. (1996) *The Book of David: How Preserving Families Can Cost Children Their Lives*. New York: Basic Books.

George, C., Herman, K.C. and Ostrander, R. (2006) 'The family environment and developmental psychopathology: The unique and interactive effects of depression, attention and conduct disorder.' *Child Psychiatry and Human Development 37*, 163–77.

Gershoff, E.T. (2002) 'Corporal punishment by parents and associated child behaviors and experiences: A meta-analytic and theoretical review.' *Psychological Bulletin 128*, 4, 539–79.

Gibson, C.L., Piquero, A.R. and Tibbetts, S.G. (2000) 'Assessing the relationship between maternal cigarette smoking during pregnancy and age at first police contact.' *Justice Q 17*, 519–42.

Gil, D.G. (1970) *Violence Against Children: Physical Abuse in the United States*. Cambridge, MA: Harvard University Press.

Gilbert, N. (1997) 'Conclusion: A Comparative Perspective.' In N. Gilbert (ed.) *Combatting Child Abuse: International Perspectives and Trends*. New York: Oxford University Press.

Gilens, M. (1999) *Why Americans Hate Welfare*. Chicago, IL: University of Chicago Press.

Glasser, M., Kolvin, I., Campbell, D., Glasser, A., Leitch, I. and Farrelly, S. (2001) 'Cycle of child sexual abuse: Links between being a victim and becoming a perpetrator.' *British Journal of Psychiatry 179*, 482–94.

Global Peace Index (2007) Available at http://global-culture.org/blog/2007/06/04/global-peace-index/, accessed on 12 August 2007.

Glynn, C., Herbst, S., O'Keefe, G. and Shapiro, R. (1999) *Public Opinion*. Boulder, CO: Westview Press.

Gould, C. (1988) *Rethinking Democracy*. Cambridge: Cambridge University Press.

Graham-Bermann, S.A. and Levendosky, A.A. (1998) The social functioning of preschool-age children whose mothers are emotionally and physically abused.' *Journal of Emotional Abuse 1*, 59–84 .

Grant, M.J., Button, C.M. and Noseworthy, J. (1994) 'Predicting attitude stability.' *Canadian Journal of Behavioural Science 26*, 68–84.

Graves, K.N. (2007) 'Not always sugar and spice: Expanding theoretical and functional explanations for why females aggress.' *Aggression and Violent Behavior 12*, 131–40.

Gray, R.F., Indurkhya, A. and McCormick, M.C. (2004) 'Prevalence, stability, and predictors of clinically significant behavior problems in low birth weight children at 3, 5 and 8 years of age.' *Pediatrics 114*, 3, 736–43.

Gray, T. (1991) *Freedom*. London: Macmillan.

Graydon, S. (1999) *Bad Girls*. Available at Media Awareness Network, www.media-awareness.ca/english/resources/articles/stereotyping/bad_girls.cfm, accessed on 12 April 2007.

Greenberg, M.T. (1999) 'Attachment and Psychopathology in Childhood.' In J. Cassidy and P. Shaver (eds) *Handbook of Attachment: Theory, Research and Clinical Applications*. New York: Guilford Press.

Greenberg, M.T., Speltz, M.L., DeKlyen, M. and Endriga, M. (1991) 'Attachment security in preschoolers with and without externalizing behavior problems: A replication.' *Development and Psychopathology 3*, 413–30.

Greenwood, P.W., Model, K.E., Hydell, C.P. and Chiesa, J. (1998) *Diverting Children from a Life of Crime: Measuring Costs and Benefits*. Santa Monica, CA: Rand Corporation.

Grogan-Kaylor, A. (2004) 'The effect of corporal punishment on antisocial behavior in children.' *Social Work Research 28*, 3, 153–62.

Gunnar, M.G., Fisher, P.A. and The Early Experience, Stress, and Prevention Network (2006) 'Bringing basic research on early experience and stress neurobiology to bear on preventive interventions for neglected and maltreated children.' *Development and Psychopathology 18*, 651–77.

Guttmann-Steinmetz, S. and Crowell, J. (2006) 'Attachment and externalizing disorders: A developmental psychopathology perspective.' *Journal of the American Academy of Child and Adolescent Psychiatry 54*, 440–51.

Habbick, B., Nanson, J., Snyder, R., Casey, R. and Schulman, A.L. (1996) 'Foetal alcohol syndrome in Saskatchewan: Unchanged incidence in a 20-year-period.' *Canadian Journal of Public Health 87*, 3, 204–7.

Halpern, C.T., Oslak, S.G., Young, M.L., Martin, S. and Kupper, L. (2001) 'Partner violence among adolescents in opposite sex romantic relationships: Findings from the National Longitudinal Study of Adolescent Health, *American Journal of Public Health 91*, 1679–85.

Hamarman, S. and Bernet, W. (2000) 'Evaluating and reporting emotional abuse in children.' *Journal of the American Academy of Child and Adolescent Psychiatry 39*, 7, 928–30.

Hamilton, C. and Harvey, R. (2004) 'The role of public opinion in the implementation of international juvenile justice standards.' *International Journal of Children's Rights 11*, 369–90.

Hammarberg, T. (1990) 'The U.N. Convention on the Rights of the Child—and how to make it work.' *Human Rights Quarterly 12*, 97–105.

Hanlon, T.E., O'Grady, K.E., Bennerr-Sears, T. and Callaman, J.M. (2005) 'Incarcerated drug-abusing mothers. Their characteristics and vulnerability.' *American Journal of Drug and Alcohol Abuse 1*, 59–77.

Hanson, R.K. and Harris, A.J. (2000) 'Where should we intervene? Dynamic predictors of sexual assault recidivism.' *Criminal Justice and Behavior 27*, 6–35.

Hantrais, L. (2004) *Family Policy Matters: Responding to Family Change in Europe.* Bristol: The Polity Press.

Harden, B.J.,Winslow, M.B., Kenziora, K.T., Shahinfar, A. *et al.*(2000) 'Externalizing problems in Head Start children: An ecological exploration.' *Early Education and Development 11*, 357–85.

Harlow, H.F., Harlow, M.K. and Suomi, S.J. (1971) 'From thought to therapy: Lessons from a primate laboratory.' *American Scientist 59*, 538–49.

Harris, G.T., Rice, M.E. and Cormier, C.A. (1991) 'Psychopathy and violent recidivism.' *Law and Human Behavior 15*, 625–37.

Harris, G.T., Rice, M.E. and Lalumiere, M. (2001) 'Criminal violence. The roles of psychopathy, neurodevelopmental insults, and antisocial parenting.' *Criminal Justice and Behavior 28*, 4, 402–26.

Harris, W.M., Lieberman, A.F. and Marans, S. (2007) 'In the best interests of society.' *Journal of Child Psychology and Psychiatry 48*, 3–4, 392–411.

Hart, S.N. (1991) 'From property to person status: Historical perspective on children's Rights.' *American Psychologist 46*, 1, 53–9.

Hartnagel, T.F. and Baron, S.W. (1995) 'It's Time to Get Serious: Public Attitudes Toward Juvenile Justice in Canada.' In J.H. Creechan and R.A. Silverman (eds) *Canadian Delinquency.* Scarborough: Prentice-Hall.

Hartz, L. (1964) *The Founding of New Societies.* New York: Harcourt, Brace and World.

Haskett, M.E. and Willoughby, M. (2006) 'Paths to child social adjustment: Parenting quality and children's processing of social information.' *Child: Care, Health and Development 33*, 1, 67–77.

Hastings, R. (2005) 'Issues and challenges.' *Canadian Journal of Crime and Criminology and Criminal Justice 47*, 2, 209–19.

Haugland, B.S.M. (2003) 'Paternal alcohol abuse: Relationship between child adjustment, parental characteristics, and family functioning.' *Child Psychiatry and Human Development 34*, 2, 127–46.

Headey, B., Scott, D. and de Vauss, D. (1999) 'Domestic violence in Australia: Are women and men equally violent?' Available at www.fact.on.ca/Info/dom/heady99.pdf, accessed on 11 April 2007.

Heide, K.M. (2003) 'Youth homicide: A review of the literature and a blueprint for action.' *International Journal of Offender Therapy and Comparative Criminology 47*, 1, 6–36.

Heidelise, A., Duffy, F.H., McAnulty, G., Rivkin, M.J., *et al.* (2004) 'Early experience alters brain function and structure.' *Pediatrics 113*, 4, 846–57.

Henderson, T., Monroe, P., Garand, J. and Burts, D. (1995) 'Explaining public opinion toward government spending on child care.' *Family Relations 44*, 1, 37–45.

Herrenkohl, R., Egolf, B. and Herrenkohl, E. (1997) 'Preschool antecedents of adolescent assaultive behavior: A longitudinal study.' *American Journal of Orthopsychiatry 6*, 3, 422–32.

Herrenkohl, T.I., Hill, K.G., Chung, I.J., Guo, J., Abbott, R.D. and Hawkins, J.D. (2003) 'Protective factors against serious violent behavior in adolescence: A prospective study of aggressive children.' *Social Work Research 27*, 3, 179–91.

Herrera,V.M. and McCloskey, L.A. (2001) 'Gender differences in the risk for delinquency among youth exposed to family violence.' *Child Abuse and Neglect 25*, 1037–51.

Hetherington, R. (2006) 'Learning from Difference: Comparing Child Welfare Systems.' In N. Freymond and G. Cameron (eds) *Towards Positive Systems of Child and Family Welfare.* Toronto: University of Toronto Press.

Heymann, S., Penrose, K. and Earle, A. (2006) 'Meeting children's needs: How does the United States measure up?' *Merrill-Palmer Quarterly 52,* 2, 189–215.

Highet, N. and Drummond, P. (2004) 'A comparative evaluation of community treatments for post-partum depression: Implications for treatment and management practices.' *Australian and New Zealand Journal of Psychiatry 38,* 212–18.

Hildyard, K.L. and Wolfe, D.A. (2002) 'Child neglect: Developmental issues and outcomes.' *Child Abuse and Neglect 26,* 679–95.

Hill, J. (2002) 'Biological, psychological and social processes in the conduct disorders.' *Journal of Child Psychology and Psychiatry 43,* 1, 133–64.

Hill, M. and Tisdall, K. (1997) *Children and Society.* London: Addison Wesley Longman.

Hindberg, B. (2001) *Ending Corporal Punishment.* Stokholm: Ministries of Health and Social Affairs and Foreign Affairs.

Hines, D.A., Brown, J. and Dunning, E. (2007) 'Characteristics of callers to domestic abuse helpline for men.' *Journal of Family Violence 22,* 63–72.

Holden, G.W. and Ritchie, K.L. (1998) 'The Development of Research into Another Consequence of Family Violence.' In G.W. Holden, R. Geffner and E.N. Jouriles (eds) *Children Exposed to Marital Violence: Theory, Research and Applied Issues.* Washington, DC: American Psychological Association.

Holmes, W.C. and Sammel, M.D. (2005) 'Physical abuse of boys and possible associations with poor adult outcomes.' *Annals of Internal Medicine 143,* 8, 581–9.

Holtzworth-Munroe, A. (2005) 'Female perpetration of physical aggression against an intimate partner: A controversial new topic of study.' *Violence and Victims 20,* 253–61.

Hook, B., Cederblad, M. and Berg, R. (2006) 'Prenatal and postnatal maternal smoking as risk factors for preschool children's mental health.' *Acta Pediatrica 95,* 6, 671–7.

Howe, R.B. (2001) 'Do parents have fundamental rights?' *Journal of Canadian Studies 36,* 3, 61–78.

Howe, R.B. (2007) 'Introduction: A Question of Commitment.' In R.B. Howe and K. Covell (eds) *A Question of Commitment: Children's Rights in Canada.* Waterloo, ON: Wilfrid Laurier University Press.

Howe, R.B. (2008) 'Children's rights as crime prevention.' *International Journal of Children's Rights 16* (in press).

Howe, R.B. and Covell, K. (2001) 'Juvenile curfews: A Canadian perspective.' *Children's Legal Rights Journal 21,* 12–20.

Howe, R.B. and Covell, K. (2005) *Empowering Children: Children's Rights Education as a Pathway to Citizenship.* Toronto: University of Toronto Press.

Howe, R.B and Covell, K. (2007) 'Conclusion: Canada's Ambivalence Toward Children.' In R.B. Howe and K. Covell (eds) *A Question of Commitment: Children's Rights In Canada.* Waterloo, ON: Wilfrid Laurier University Press.

Huefner, J.C., Ringle, J.L., Chmelka, M.B. and Ingram, S.D. (2007) 'Breaking the cycle of intergenerational abuse: The long term impact of a residential care program.' *Child Abuse and Neglect 31,* 187–99.

Huesmann, L.R., Eron, L.D. and Dubow, E.F. (2002) 'Childhood predictors of adult criminality: Are all risk factors reflected in childhood aggressiveness?' *Criminal Behavior and Mental Health 12,* 185–208.

Huizink, A.C., Mulder, E.J.H. and Buitelaar, J.K. (2004) 'Prenatal stress and risk for psychopathology: Specific effects of induction of general susceptibility.' *Psychological Bulletin 130*, 115–42.

Hummel, P., Thomke, V., Oldenburger, H. and Specht, F. (2000) 'Male adolescent sex offenders against children: Similarities and differences between those offenders with and without a history of sexual abuse.' *Journal of Adolescence 23*, 305–17.

Ierley, A. and Claassen-Wilson, D. (2003) 'Making Things Right. Restorative Justice for School Communities.' In T.S. Jones and R. Compton (eds) *Kids Working It Out*. San Francisco, CA: Jossey-Bass.

Imbrogno, A. (2000) 'Corporal punishment in America's public schools and the U.N. Convention on the Rights of the Child.' *Journal of Law and Education 29*, 2, 125–47.

Inglehart, R. (1988) 'The renaissance of political culture.' *American Political Science Review 82*, 4, 1203–30.

International Centre for Crime Prevention (1999) *Crime Prevention Digest II: Comparative Analysis of Successful Community Safety*. Montreal: International Centre for Crime Prevention.

Jackson, A.P., Brooks-Gunn, J., Huang, C. and Glassman, M. (2000) 'Single mothers in low wage jobs: Financial strain, parenting, and preschoolers' outcomes.' *Child Development 71*, 1409–23.

Jaffee, P., Wolfe, D. and Wilson, S. (1990) *Children of Battered Women*. Newbury Park, CA: Sage.

Jaffee, S.R., Caspi, A., Moffitt, T. and Taylor, A. (2004) 'Physical maltreatment victim to antisocial child: Evidence of an environmentally mediated process.' *Journal of Abnormal Psychology 113*, 44–55.

Jellen, L.K., McCarroll, J.E. and Thayer, L.E. (2001) 'Child emotional maltreatment: A 2 year study of US army cases.' *Child Abuse and Neglect 25*, 623–39.

John, M. (2003) *Children's Rights and Power: Charging up for a New Century*. London: Jessica Kingsley Publishers.

Johnson, M.P. (1995) 'Patriarchal terrorism and common couple violence: Two forms of violence against women.' *Journal of Marriage and the Family 57*, 283–94.

Johnson, M.P. and Ferraro, K.J. (2000) 'Research on domestic violence in the 1990s: Making distinctions.' *Journal of Marriage and the Family 62*, 948–63.

Johnston, D. (2006) 'The wrong road: Efforts to understand the effects of parental crime and incarceration.' *Criminology and Public Policy 5*, 4, 703–19.

Johnstone, S.J., Boyce, P.M., Hickey, A.R., Morris-Yatees, A. and Harris, M. (2001) 'Obstetric risk factors for postnatal depression in urban and rural community samples.' *Australian and New Zealand Journal of Psychiatry 35*, 69–75.

Jones, K.L., Chambers, C.D., Hill, L.L., Hull, A.D. and Riley, E.P. (2006) 'Alcohol use in pregnancy: Inadequate recommendations for an increasing problem.' *British Journal of Obstetrics and Gynaecology 113*, 967–8.

Jones, K.L. and Smith, D.W. (1973) 'Recognition of the fetal alcohol syndrome in early infancy.' *The Lancet 2*, 999–1001.

Josefsson, A., Angelsioo, L., Berg, G., Ekstrom, C. *et al.* (2002) 'Obstetric, somatic and demographic risk factors for postpartum depressive symptoms.' *Obstetrics and Gynecology 99*, 223–8.

Joseph, R. (1999) 'Environmental influences on neural plasticity, the limbic system, emotional development and attachment: A review.' *Child Psychiatry and Human Development 29*, 3, 189–208.

Jung, J. (2001) *Psychology of Alcohol and Other Drugs*. Newbury Park, CA: Sage.

Junger-Tas, J. and Decker, S. (2006) (eds) *International Handbook of Juvenile Justice*. Dordrecht, Netherlands: Springer.

Kadushin, A. and Martin, J.A. (1981) *Child Abuse: An Interactional Event*. New York: Columbia University Press.

Kangas, O. and Rostgaard, T. (2007) 'Preferences or institutions?' *Journal of European Social Policy 17*, 3, 240–56.

Karoly, L. (2005) *Early Childhood Interventions: Proven Results, Future Promise*. Santa Monica, CA: Rand Corporation.

Karoly, L.A., Greenwood, P.W., Everingham, S.S., Hoube, J. *et al.* (1998) *Investing in Our Children: What we Know and Don't Know about the Costs and Benefits of Early Childhood Interventions*. Santa Monica, CA: Rand Corporation.

Karp, J. (1999) 'The Convention on the Rights of the Child: Protecting children's human dignity.' Paper presented to the Conference 'Children are Unbeatable', London, England, 2 March.

Kautto, M., Heikkila, M., Hvinden, B., Marklund, S. and Ploug, N. (1999) 'Introduction: The Nordic Welfare States in the 1990s.' In M. Kautto, M. Heikkila, B. Hvinden, S. Marklund and N. Ploug (eds) *Nordic Social Policy*. London: Routledge.

Kearney, C.A. (2003) *Casebook in Child Behavior Disorders*. Toronto: Wadsworth/Thompson.

Keiley, M.K. (2002) 'Attachment and affect regulation: A framework for family treatment of conduct disorder. *Family Processes 41*, 3, 477–93.

Keller, P.S., Cummings, E.M. and Davies, P.T. (2005) 'The role of marital discord and parenting in relations between parental problem drinking and child adjustment.' *Journal of Child Psychology and Psychiatry 46*, 9, 943–51.

Kellermann, A., Dawna, S., Rivera, F. and Mercy, J. (1998) 'Preventing youth violence: What works?' *Annual Review of Public Health 19*, 271–92.

Kelly, K. and Totten, M. (2002) *When Children Kill: A Social-Psychological Study of Youth Homicide*. Peterborough: Broadview Press.

Kernic, M.A., Wolf, M.E., Holt, V.L., McKnight, B., Huebner, C.E. and Rivara, F. (2003) 'Behavioral problems among children whose mothers are abused by an intimate partner.' *Child Abuse and Neglect 27*, 1231–46.

Khaleque, A. and Rohner, R.P. (2002) 'Perceived parental acceptance-rejection and psychological adjustment: A meta-analysis of cross-cultural and intracultural studies.' *Journal of Marriage and the Family 64*, 54–64.

Khoo, E., Hyvonen, U. and Nygren, L. (2002) 'Child welfare or child protection.' *Qualitative Social Work 1*, 4, 451–71.

Kids Count Database (2007) 'Poverty.' Available at www.kidscount.org/datacenter/compare_results.jsp?i=210, accessed on 3 April 2007.

Kildal, N. and Kuhnle, S. (2005) 'The Nordic Welfare Model and the Idea of Universalism.' In N. Kildal and S. Kuhnle (eds) *Normative Foundations of the Welfare State: The Nordic Experience*. London: Routledge.

King, M.L. (1963) 'Letter from Birmingham Jail.' *The Christian Century* No. 80 (12 June), 767–73.

Kingree, J.B., Phan, D. and Thompson, M. (2003) 'Child maltreatment and recidivism among adolescent detainees.' *Criminal Justice and Behavior 30*, 6, 623–43.

Kitzmann, K.M., Gaylord, N.K., Holt, A.R. and Kenny, E.D. (2003) 'Child witnesses to domestic violence: A meta-analytic review.' *Journal of Consulting and Clinical Psychology 71*, 2, 339–52.

Knutsson, K.E. (1997) *Children: Noble Causes or Worthy Citizens?* Florence: UNICEF.

Koblinsky, S.A., Kuvalanka, K.A. and Randolph, S.M. (2006) 'Social skills and behaviour problems of urban African American preschoolers: Role of parenting practices, family conflict, and maternal depression.' *American Journal of Orthopsychiatry 76*, 4, 554–63.

Kodituwakku, P.W. (2007) 'Defining the behavioral phenotype in children with fetal alcohol spectrum disorders: A review.' *Neuroscience and Behavioral Reviews 31*, 192–201.

Kodituwakku, P.W., Coriale, G., Fiorentino, D., Aragon, A.S. *et al.* (2006) 'Neurobehavioral characteristics of children with fetal alcohol spectrum disorders in communities from Italy: Preliminary results.' *Alcoholism: Clinical and Experimental Research 30*, 9, 1551–61.

Kolko, D.J. (2002) 'Child Physical Abuse.' In J.E.B. Myers (ed.) *APSAC Handbook on Child Maltreatment.* Thousand Oaks, CA: Sage.

Korpi, W. (2000) 'Fear of inequality: Gender, class, and patterns of inequality in different types of welfare states.' *Social Politics: International Studies in Gender, State, and Society 7*, 2, 127–91.

Langstrom, N., Grann, M. and Lindblad, F. (2000) 'A preliminary typology of young sex offenders.' *Journal of Adolescence 23*, 319–29.

Lansdown, G. (2001) *Promoting Children's Participation in Democratic Decision Making.* Florence: UNICEF Innocenti Centre.

Lansford, J.E., Chang, L., Dodge, K., Malone, P.S. *et al.* (2005) 'Physical discipline and children's adjustment: Cultural normativeness as a moderator.' *Child Development 76*, 6, 1234–46.

Lansford, J.E., Malone, P.S., Dodge, K.A., Crozier, J.C., Pettit, G. S. and Bates, J.E. (2006) 'A 12-year prospective study of patterns of social information processing problems and externalizing behaviors.' *Journal of Abnormal Child Psychology 34*, 715–24.

Larsson, B. and Frisk, M. (1999) 'Social competence and emotional/behaviour problems in 6–16-year-old Swedish school children.' *European Child and Adolescent Psychiatry 8*, 24–33.

Lavis, J. (2004) 'A Political Science Perspective on Evidence-based Decision-making.' In L. Lemieux-Charles and F. Champagne (eds) *Using Knowledge and Evidence in Health Care.* Toronto: University of Toronto Press.

Lavoie, F., Herbert, M., Tremblay, R., Vitaro, F., Vezina, L. and McDuff, P. (2002) 'History of family dysfunction and perpetration of dating violence by adolescent boys: A longitudinal study.' *Journal of Adolescent Health 30*, 375–83.

Le Bordais, C. and Marcil-Gratton, N. (1994) 'Quebec's Pro-active Approach to Family Policy: Thinking and Acting Family.' In M. Baker (ed.) *Canada's Changing Families: Challenges to Public Policy.* Ottawa: The Vanier Institute of the Family.

Leonard, K.E. (2002) 'Alcohol and Substance Abuse in Marital Violence and Child Maltreatment.' In C. Wekerle and A. Wall (eds) *The Violence and Addiction Equation: Theoretical and Clinical Issues in Substance Abuse and Relationship Violence.* New York: Brunner-Routledge.

Leschied, A.W., Chiodo, D., Whitehead, P.C. and Hurley, D. (2005) 'The relationship between maternal depression and child outcomes in a child welfare sample: Implications for treatment and policy.' *Child and Family Social Work 10*, 281–91.

Leve, L.D. and Chamberlain, P. (2004) 'Female juvenile offenders: Defining an early-onset pathway for delinquency.' *Journal of Child and Family Studies 13*, 4, 439–52.

Levendosky, A.A., Bogat, G.A., von Eye, A. and Davidson, W.S. (2004) 'The social networks of women experiencing domestic violence.' *American Journal of Community Psychology 34*, 1–2, 95–109.

Levendosky, A.A., Huth-Bocks, A.C., Shapiro, D.L. and Semel, M.A. (2003) 'The impact of domestic violence on the maternal–child relationship and preschool-age children's functioning.' *Journal of Family Psychology 17*, 3, 275–87.

Levendosky, A.A., Leahy, K.L., Bogat, G.A., Davidson, W.S. and von Eye, A. (2006) 'Domestic violence, maternal parenting, maternal mental health and infant externalizing behavior.' *Journal of Family Psychology 20*, 4, 544–52.

Leventhal, J. (2005) 'Getting prevention right: Maintaining the status quo is not an option.' *Child Abuse and Neglect 29*, 209–13.

Levine, S. (2005) 'Stress: An Historical Perspective.' In T. Steckler, N. Kalin and J.M. Reuls (eds) *Handbook on Stress, Immunology and Behavior*. Amsterdam: Elsevier.

Levitt, P., Reinoso, B. and Jones, L. (1998) 'The critical impact of early cellular environment on neuronal development.' *Preventive Medicine 27*, 180–4.

Library of Parliament. (2007) 'The "spanking" law: Section 43 of the criminal code.' Available at www.parl.gc.ca/information/library/PRBpubs/prb0510-e.htm, accessed on 13 August 2007.

Linares, L.O., Heeren, T., Bronfman, E., Zuckerman, B., Augustyn, M. and Tronick, E. (2001) 'A mediational model for the impact of exposure to community violence on early childhood behavior problems.' *Child Development 72*, 639–52.

Lipset, S.M. (1990) *Continental Divide: The Values and Institutions of the United States and Canada*. New York: Routledge.

Lipset, S.M. (1996) *American Exceptionalism: A Double-Edged Sword*. New York: Norton.

Locke, T.F. and Newcomb, M.D. (2003) 'Childhood maltreatment, parental alcohol/drug related problems, and global parent dysfunction.' *Professional Psychology: Research and Practice 34*, 73–9.

Locke, T.F. and Newcomb, M.D. (2004) 'Child maltreatment, parent alcohol- and drug-related problems, polydrug use and parenting practices: A test of gender differences and four theoretical perspectives.' *Journal of Family Psychology 18*, 1, 120–34.

Loeber, R. and Farrington, D.P. (2000) 'Young children who commit crime: epidemiology, developmental origins, risk factors, early interventions, and policy implications.' *Development and Psychopathology 12*, 737–62.

Loeber, R. and Hay, D. (1997) 'Key issues in the development of aggression and violence from childhood to early adulthood.' *Annual Review of Psychology 48*, 371–410.

Lomas, J. (1990) 'Finding audiences, changing beliefs: The structure of research use in Canadian health policy.' *Journal of Health Politics, Policy and Law 15*, 3, 525–42.

Loney, B.R., Huntenberg, A., Counts-Allan, C. and Schmeelk, K.M. (2007) 'A preliminary examination of the intergenerational continuity of maternal psychopathic features.' *Aggressive Behavior 33*, 14–25.

Losel, F., Bliesener, T. and Bender, D. (2007) 'Social information processing experiences of aggression in social contexts and aggressive behavior in adolescents.' *Criminal Justice and Behavior 34*, 3, 330–47.

Luker, K. (2006) *When Sex Goes to School*. New York: W.W. Norton.

Lukes, S. (1973) *Individualism*. New York: Harper and Row.

Lundy, B.L., Jones, N.A., Field, T., Nearing, G. *et al.* (1999) 'Prenatal depression effects on neonates.' *Infant Behavior and Development 22*, 119–29.

Luthar, S., Cicchetti, D. and Becker, B. (2000) 'The construct of resilience: A critical evaluation and guidelines for future work.' *Child Development 71*, 543–62.

Lyons-Ruth, K., Wolfe, R., Lyubchik, A. and Steingard, R. (2002) 'Depressive Symptoms in Parents of Children under 3. Sociodemographic Predictors, Current Correlates, and Associated Parenting Behaviors.' In N. Halfon, K.T. McLearn and M.A. Schuster (eds) *Child Rearing in America: Challenges Facing Parents With Young Children*. New York: Cambridge University Press.

Maccoby, E.E. (2000) 'Parenting and its effects on children: On reading and misreading behavior genetics.' *Annual Review of Psychology 51*, 1–27.

MacKenzie, D., Wilson, D. and Kidder, S. (2001) 'Effects of correctional boot camps on offending.' *Annals of the American Academy of Political and Social Science 578*, 1, 126–43.

Mackintosh, V.H., Myers, B.J. and Kennon, S.S. (2006) 'Children of incarcerated mothers and their caregivers: Factors affecting the quality of their relationship.' *Journal of Child and Family Studies 15*, 5, 581–96.

Magdol, L., Moffitt, T.E., Caspi, A. and Silva, P.A. (1998) 'Developmental antecedents of partner abuse: A prospective-longitudinal study.' *Journal of Abnormal Psychology 107*, 375–89.

Main, M. and Hesse, E. (1990) 'Parents' Unresolved Traumatic Experiences are Related to Infant Disorganization Status: Is Frightened or Frightening Behavior the Linking Mechanism?' In M. T. Greenberg, D. Cicchetti and E.M. Cummings (eds) *Attachment in the Preschool Years*. Chicago, IL: University of Chicago Press.

Manly, J.T., Cicchetti, D. and Barnett, D. (1994) 'The impact of subtype, frequency, chronicity, and severity of child maltreatment on social competence and behavior problems.' *Development and Psychopathology 6*, 121–43.

Manzer, R. (1985) *Public Policies and Political Development in Canada*. Toronto: University of Toronto Press.

Mapp, S.C. (2006) 'The effects of sexual abuse as a child on the risk of mothers physically abusing their children: A path analysis using systems theory.' *Child Abuse and Neglect 30*, 1293–310.

Martens, P. (1997) 'Immigrants, crime, and criminal justice in Sweden.' *Crime and Justice 21*, 183–255.

Mash, E.J. and Wolfe, D.A. (1999) *Abnormal Child Psychology*. New York: Wadsworth.

Maslow, A.H. (1970) *A Theory of Human Motivation*. New York: Harper Row.

Masotti, P., George, M.A., Szala-Meneok, K., Morton, M. *et al.* (2006) 'Preventing fetal alchohol spectrum disorder in Aboriginal communities.' *PLOS Medicine 3*, 1, 24–9.

Maughan, B., Rowe, R., Messer, J., Goodman, R. and Meltzer, H. (2004) 'Conduct disorder and oppositional defiant disorder in a national sample: Developmental epidemiology.' *Journal of Child Psychology and Psychiatry 45*, 3, 609–21.

Maughan, B., Taylor, C., Taylor, A., Butler, N. and Bynner, J. (2001) 'Pregnancy smoking and childhood conduct problems: A causal association?' *Journal of Child Psychology and Psychiatry 42*, 1021–8.

May, P.A., Fiorentino, D., Gossage, J.P., Kalberg, W.O. *et al.* (2006) 'Epidemiology of FASD in a province in Italy: Prevalence and characteristics of children in a random sample of schools.' *Alcoholism: Clinical and Experimental Research 30*, 9, 1562–75.

Mayes, L.C., Swain, J.E. and Leckman, J.F. (2005) 'Parental attachment systems: neural circuits, genes and experiential contributions to parental engagement.' *Clinical Neuroscience Research 4*, 301–13.

McAlister, A. (2006) 'Acceptance of killing and homicide rates in nineteen countries.' *European Journal of Public Health 16*, 3, 260–6.

McCain, M., Mustard, J.F. and Shanker, S. (2007) *Early Years Study 2: Putting Science into Action.* Toronto: Council for Early Child Development.

McCann, J. (2002) *Threats In Schools. A Practical Guide for Managing Violence.* New York: Haworth Press

McCartney, K., Owen, M.T., Booth, C.L., Clarke-Stewart, A. and Vandell, D.L. (2004) 'Testing a maternal attachment model of behavior problems in early childhood.' *Journal of Child Psychology and Psychiatry 45*, 4, 765–78.

McClosky, H. and Zaller, J. (1984) *The American Ethos.* Cambridge, MA: Harvard University Press.

McElhaney, K.B., Immele, A., Smith, F.D. and Allen, J.P. (2006) 'Attachment organization as a moderator of the link between friendship quality and adolescent delinquency.' *Attachment and Human Development 8*, 1, 33–46.

McFarlane, J.M., Groff, J.Y., O'Brien, J.A. and Watson, K. (2003) 'Behaviors of children who are exposed and not exposed to intimate partner violence: an analysis of 330 black, white, and Hispanic children.' *Pediatrics 113*, 3:1, 202–7.

McGillivray, A. (1997) 'Therapies of Freedom: The Colonization of Aboriginal Childhood.' In A. McGillivray (ed.) *Governing Childhood.* Aldershot: Dartmouth.

McGroder, S.M. (2000) 'Parenting among low-income, African American single mothers with preschool age children. Patterns, predictors and developmental correlates.' *Child Development 71*, 752–71.

McGuigan, W.M. and Pratt, C.C. (2001) 'The predictive impact of domestic violence on three types of child maltreatment.' *Child Abuse and Neglect 25*, 869–83.

McKee, T.E., Harvey, E.M., Danforth, J.S., Ulaszek, W.R. and Friedman, J.L. (2004) 'The relation between parental coping styles and parent–child interactions before and after treatment for children with ADHD and Oppositional Behavior.' *Journal of Clinical Child and Adolescent Psychology 33*, 1, 158–68.

McLoyd, V.C. (1998) 'Socioeconomic disadvantage and child development.' *American Psychologist 53*, 2, 185–204.

Melton, G. (2002) 'Starting a New Generation of Research.' In B. Bottoms, M. Kovera and B. McAuliff (eds) *Children, Social Science and the Law.* Cambridge: Cambridge University Press.

Merez-Perez, L., Heide, K.M. and Silverman, I.J. (2001) 'Childhood cruelty to animals and subsequent violence against humans.' *International Journal of Offender Therapy and Comparative Criminology 45*, 5, 556–73.

Meyers, M., Gornick, J. and Peck, L. (2001) 'Packaging support for low-income families: Policy variation across the United States.' *Journal of Policy Analysis and Management 20*, 3, 457–83.

Meyers, J. and Wilcox, B. (1998) 'Public Policy Applications of Research on Violence and Children.' In P. Trickett and C. Schellanbach (eds) *Violence Against Children in the Family and the Community.* Washington, DC: American Psychological Association.

Miller, K. (2006) 'The impact of parental incarceration on children: An emerging need for effective interventions.' *Child and Adolescent Social Work Journal 23*, 4, 472–86.

Miller, L.C., Chan, W., Litvinova, A., Rubin, A. *et al.* (2006) 'Fetal alcohol spectrum disorders in children residing in Russian orphanages: A phenotypic survey.' *Alcoholism: Clinical and Experimental Research 30*, 3, 531–8.

Moffitt, T.E. (1993) 'Adolescence-limited and life-course persistent antisocial behavior: A developmental taxonomy.' *Psychological Review 100*, 674–701.

Moffitt, T.E., Caspi, A., Rutter, M. and Silva, P. (2001) *Sex Differences in Antisocial Behavior.* Cambridge: Cambridge University Press.

Monuteaux, M.C., Blacker, D., Biederman, J., Fitzmaurice, G. and Buka, S.L. (2006) 'Maternal smoking during pregnancy and offspring overt and covert conduct problems: a longitudinal study.' *Journal of Child Psychology and Psychiatry 47*, 9, 883–90.

Moon, M., Sundt, J., Cullen, F. and Wright, J. (2000) 'Is child saving dead? Public support for juvenile rehabilitation.' *Crime and Delinquency 46*, 1, 38–60.

Moore, C.G., Probst, J.C., Tompkins, M., Cuffe, S. and Martin, A.B. (2007) 'The prevalence of violent disagreements in US Families: Effects of residence, race/ethnicity, and parental stress.' *Pediatrics 119*, Supplement 1, 568–76.

Moreira, J., de Fatima Silva, M., Moleiro, C., Aguiar, P. *et al.* (2003) 'Perceived social support as an offshoot of attachment style.' *Personality and Individual Differences 34*, 485–501.

Morgan, R. (1997) 'Imprisonment: Current Concerns and a Brief History since 1945.' In M. Maguire, R. Morgan and R. Reiner (eds) *The Oxford Handbook of Criminology* (2nd edition). Oxford: Oxford University Press.

Morrell, J. and Murray, L. (2003) 'Parenting and the development of conduct disorder and hyperactive symptoms in childhood: A prospective longitudinal study from 2 months to 8 years.' *Journal of Child Psychology and Psychiatry 44*, 4, 489–508.

Morse, B.J. (1995) 'Beyond the conflict tactics scale: Assessing gender differences in partner violence.' *Violence and Victims 10*, 251–72.

Moss, E., Smolla, N., Cyr, C., Dubois-Comtois, K., Mazzarello, T. and Berthiaume, C. (2006) 'Attachment and behavior problems in middle childhood as reported by adult and child informants.' *Development and Psychopathology 18*, 425–44.

Moss, K. (2004) 'Kids witnessing family violence.' *Canadian Social Trends.* Statistics Canada, Catalogue No. 11–008.

Moss, P. and Petrie, P. (2002) *From Children's Services to Children's Spaces: Public Policy, Children and Childhood.* London: Routledge-Falmer.

Mulligan, C.J., Robin, R.W., Osier, M.V., Sambuughin, N. *et al.* (2003) 'Allelic variation at alcohol metabolism genes (ADH1B, ADH1C, ALDH2) and alcohol dependence in an American Indian Population.' *Human Genetics 113*, 325–36.

Mullis, R.L., Cornille, T.A., Mullis, A.K., and Huber, J. (2004) 'Female juvenile offending: A review of characteristics and contexts.' *Journal of Child and Family Studies 13*, 2, 205–18.

Mumola, C.J. (2000) *Bureau of Justice Statistics Bulletin: Incarcerated Parents and their Children.* Washington, DC: US Department of Justice.

Murray, E. (1999) 'Exploring children's emerging conceptions of their participation rights and responsibilities.' Unpublished dissertation, University of Victoria, British Columbia.

Murray, E. (2002) 'Impact of children's rights education on primary-level children.' Unpublished paper, Mount Royal College, Calgary, Alberta.

Murray, L. and Cooper, P.J. (2003) 'Intergenerational Transmission of Affective and Cognitive Processes Associated with Depression: Infancy and the Preschool Years.' In I.M. Goodyer (ed.) *Unipolar Depression: A Lifespan Perspective*. Oxford: Oxford University Press.

Murray, J. and Farrington, D.P. (2005) 'Parental imprisonment: Effects on boys' antisocial behavior and delinquency through the life-course.' *Journal of Child Psychology and Psychiatry 46*, 12, 1269–78.

Myers, B., Smarsh, T., Amlund-Hagen, K. and Kennon, S. (1999) 'Children of incarcerated mothers.' *Journal of Child and Family Studies 8*, 11–25.

Nager, A., Johnsson, L.M. and Sundquist, K. (2005) 'Are sociodemographic factors and year of delivery associated with hospital admission for postpartum psychosis? A study of 500,000 first-time mothers.' *Acta Psychiatrica Scandinavica 112*, 47–53.

Nagin, D., Piquero, A., Scott, E. and Steinberg, L. (2006) 'Public preferences for rehabilitation versus incarceration of juvenile offenders.' *Criminology and Public Policy 5*, 4, 627–52.

Nas, C.N., de Castro, B.O. and Koops, W. (2005) 'Social information processing in delinquent adolescents.' *Psychology, Crime and Law 11*, 4, 363–75.

Nash, K., Rovet, J., Greenbaum, R., Fantus, E., Nulman, I. and Koren, G. (2006) 'Identifying the behavioural phenotype in fetal alcohol spectrum disorder: Sensitivity, specificity and screening potential.' *Archives of Women's Mental Health 9*, 181–6.

National Public Radio/Kaiser Family Foundation/Kennedy School of Government (2004) 'Sex education in America: General public/parents survey.' Available at www.npr.org/templates/story/story.php?storyId=1622610, accessed on 14 April 2007.

Newman, J.P., Schmitt, W.A. and Voss, W.D. (1997) 'The impact of motivationally neutral cues on psychopathic individuals: Assessing the generality of the response modulation hypothesis.' *Journal of Abnormal Psychology 106*, 4, 563–75.

Nicholas, K.B. and Rasmussen, E.H. (2006) 'Childhood abusive and supportive experiences, inter-parental violence and parental alcohol use: Prediction of young adult depressive symptoms and aggression.' *Journal of Family Violence 21*, 1, 43–61.

Niehoff, D. (2003) 'A vicious circle: The neurobiological foundations of violent behavior.' *Modern Psychoanalysis 28*, 2, 235–45.

Nilsson, K.W., Sjoberg, R.L., Damberg, M., Leppert, J. *et al.* (2005) 'Role of monoamine oxidase A genotype and psychosocial factors in male adolescent criminal activity.' *Biological Psychiatry 59*, 121–7.

Noble, C. (1997) *Welfare As We Knew it: A Political History of the American Welfare State*. New York: Oxford University Press.

Nolan, J. (1998) *The Therapeutic State*. New York: New York University Press.

O'Brien, L.M., Heycock, E.G., Hanna, M., Jones, P.W. and Cox, J.L. (2004) 'Postnatal depression and faltering growth: A community study.' *Pediatrics 113*, 5, 1242–7.

O'Brien, M., John, R.S., Margolin, G. and Erel, O. (1997) 'Reliability and diagnostic efficacy of parents' reports regarding children's exposure to marital aggression.' *Violence and Victims 9*, 45–52.

O'Connor, M.J. (1996) 'The Implications of Attachment Theory for the Socioemotional Development of Children Exposed to Alcohol Prenatally.' In H.L. Spohr and H.C. Steinhausen (eds) *Alcohol, Pregnancy and the Developing Child*. Cambridge: Cambridge University Press.

OECD (2006a) *OECD Health Data 2006*. Available at http://ocde.p4.siteinternet.com/publications/doifiles/01200606IT02.xls, accessed on 21 March 2007.

OECD (2006b) *Starting Strong II: Early Childhood Education and Care*. Paris: OECD.

OECD (2007) *Family Database: Family Policies*. Available at www.oecd.org/els/social/family/database, accessed on 20 March 2007.

Office of Sweden's Children's Ombudsman (2007) 'The Swedish corporal punishment ban.' Available at www.bo.se/Adfinity.aspx?pageid=90, accessed on 3 August 2007.

O'Hara, K. (1998) *Comparative Family Policy*. Ottawa: Canadian Policy Research Networks.

O'Keefe, M. (1998) 'Factors mediating the link between witnessing interparental violence and dating violence.' *Journal of Family Violence 13*, 39–57.

O'Leary, C.M. (2004) 'Fetal alcohol syndrome: Diagnosis, epidemiology, and developmental outcomes.' *Journal of Paediatric Child Health 40*, 1–2, 8–10.

Olds, D., Henderson, C., Kitzman, H., Eckenrode, J., Cole, R. and Tatelbaum, R. (1999) 'Prenatal and infancy home visitation by nurses: Recent findings.' *The Future of Children 9*, 1, 44–65.

Olds, D., Pettit, L., Robinson, J., Henderson, C. *et al.* (1998) 'Reducing risks for antisocial behavior with a program of prenatal and early childhood home visitation.' *Journal of Community Psychology 26*, 1, 65–83.

Olney, F.W. (2004) 'Fetal alcohol syndrome at the cellular level.' *Addiction Biology 9*, 137–49.

Olsen, G. (2002) *The Politics of the Welfare State*. Toronto: Oxford University Press.

Olson, J.M. and Zanna, M.P. (1993) 'Attitudes and attitude change.' *Annual Review of Psychology 44*, 117–54.

Ondersma, S.J., Delaney-Black, V., Covington, C.Y., Nordstrom, B. and Sokol, R.J. (2006) 'The association between caregiver substance abuse and self-reported violence exposure among young urban children.' *Journal of Traumatic Stress 19*, 1, 107–18.

O'Neil, M. (2002) 'Youth curfews in the United States.' *Journal of Youth Studies 5*, 1, 49–67.

Orlebeke, J.F., Knol, D.L. and Verhulst, F.C. (1997) 'Increase in child behavior problems resulting from maternal smoking during pregnancy.' *Archives of Environmental Health 52*, 317–21.

Osofsky, J.D. (1995) 'Children who witness domestic violence: The invisible victims.' *Social Policy Report, 1X (3) Society for Research in Child Development*, 1–16.

Osofsky, J.D. (2003) 'Prevalence of children's exposure to domestic violence and child maltreatment: Implications for prevention and intervention.' *Clinical Child and Family Psychology Review 6*, 3, 161–70.

Ozawa, M. (2004) 'Social welfare spending on family benefits in the United States and Sweden: A comparative study.' *Family Relations 53*, 3, 301–9.

Pardini, D.A. (2006) 'The callousness pathway to severe violent delinquency.' *Aggressive Behavior 32*, 590–8.

Patel, V., Rahman, A., Jacob, K.S. and Hughes, M. (2004) 'Effect of maternal health on infant growth in low income countries: New evidence from South Asia.' *British Medical Journal 328*, 820–3.

Patel, V., Rodrigues, M. and de Souza, N. (2002) 'Gender, poverty, and postnatal depression: A study of mothers in Goa, India.' *American Journal of Psychiatry 159*, 43–7.

Patterson, G.R. (1982) *A Social Learning Approach: Coercive Family Process*. Eugene: Castalia.

Patterson, G.R., Reid, J.B. and Dishion, T.J. (1998) *Human Emotions: A Reader*. Malden: Blackwell.

Patterson, G.R. and Yoerger, K. (1999) 'Intraindividual growth in covert antisocial behavior: A necessary precursor to chronic juvenile and adult arrests?' *Criminal Behavior and Mental Health 9*, 24–38.

Perera, F.P., Rauh, V., Whyatt, D., Tang, D. *et al.* (2005) 'A summary of recent findings on birth outcomes and developmental effects of prenatal ETS, PAH, and pesticide exposures.' *Neurotoxicology 26*, 573–87.

Peters, R., Peters, J., Laurendeau, M., Chamberland, C. and Peirson, L. (2001) 'Social Policies for Promoting the Well-being of Canadian Children and Families.' In I. Prilleltensky, G. Nelson and L. Peirson (eds) *Promoting Family Wellness and Preventing Child Maltreatment.* Toronto: University of Toronto Press.

Pettersen, P. (2001) 'Welfare state legitimacy: Ranking, rating, paying.' *Scandinavian Political Studies 24*, 1, 27–49.

Pettit, G. and Dodge, K. (2003) 'Violent children: Bridging development, intervention, and public policy.' *Developmental Psychology 39*, 2, 187–8.

Phillips, B. and Alderson, P. (2003) 'Beyond "anti-smacking": Challenging violence and coercion in parent–child relations.' *International Journal of Children's Rights 115*, 175–97.

Phillips, S.D., Barth, R.P., Burns, B.J. and Wagner, H.R. (2004) 'Parental arrest and children involved with child welfare agencies.' *American Journal of Orthopsychiatry 74*, 2, 174–86.

Phillips, S.D., Burns, B.J., Wagner, H.R., Kramer, T.L. and Robbins, J.M. (2002) 'Parental incarceration among adolescents receiving mental health services.' *Journal of Child and Family Studies 11*, 4, 385–99.

Pinheiro, P.S. (2006) *Summary Report of the Independent Expert for the United Nations Study on Violence Against Children*. A/61/299. Presented to the General Assembly 61st session (October)

Poehlmann, J. (2005) 'Representations of attachment relationships in children of incarcerated mothers.' *Child Development 76*, 679–96.

Price, C. (1996) 'Monitoring the United Nations Convention on the Rights of the Child in a Non-party State: The United States.' In E. Verhellen (ed.) *Monitoring Children's Rights*. The Hague: Martinus Nijhoff.

Pridemore, W.A. (2002) 'Social problems and patterns of juvenile delinquency in transitional Russia.' *Journal of Research in Crime and Delinquency 39*, 2, 187–213.

Pritchard, C. and Butler, A. (2003) 'A comparative study of children and adult homicide rates in the USA and the major western countries 1974–1999.' *Journal of Family Violence 18*, 6, 341–50.

Proctor, L.J. (2006) 'Children growing up in a violent community: The role of the family.' *Aggression and Violent Behavior 11*, 558–76.

Public Safety Canada (2007) 'Factsheet: Crime prevention through social development.' Available at http://ww4.ps-sp.gc.ca/en/library/publications/fact_sheets/cpsd/index.html, accessed on 27 July 2007.

Rahman, A., Iqbal, Z. and Harrington, R. (2003) 'Life events, social support and depression in childbirth: Perspectives from a rural community in the developing world. *Psychological Medicine 33*, 1161–7.

Raikes, A.H., Green, B., Atwater, J., Kisker, E., Constantine, J. and Chazan-Cohen, R. (2006) 'Involvement in Early Head Start home visiting services.' *Early Childhood Research Quarterly 21*, 2–24.

Raikes, A.H. and Thompson, R.A. (2005) 'Links between risk and attachment security: Models of influence.' *Applied Developmental Psychology 26*, 440–55.

Ravndal, E., Lauritzen, G., Frank, O., Jansson, I. and Larsson, J. (2001) 'Childhood maltreatment among Norwegian drug abusers in treatment.' *International Journal of Social Welfare 10*, 142–7.

Regmi, S., Sligl, W., Carter, D., Grut, W. and Seear, M. (2002) 'A controlled study of postpartum depression among Nepalese women: Validation of the Edinburgh Postpartum Depression Scale in Katmandu.' *Tropical Medicine and International Health 7*, 4, 378–82.

Retz, W., Retz-Junginger, P., Supprian, T.,Thome, J. and Rosler, M. (2004) 'Association of serotonin transporter promoter gene polymorphism with violence: Relation with personality disorders, impulsivity, and childhood ADHD pathology.' *Behavioral Sciences and the Law 22*, 415–25.

Retz, W., Rosler, M., Supprian, T., Retz-Junginger, P. and Thome, J. (2003) 'Dopamine D3 receptor gene polymorphism and violent behavior: Relation to impulsiveness and ADHD-related psychopathology.' *Journal of Neural Transmission 110*, 561–72.

Rhule, D.M., McMahon, R.J. and Spieker, S.J. (2004) 'Relation of adolescent mothers' history of antisocial behavior to child conduct problems and social competence.' *Journal of Clinical Child and Adolescent Psychology 33*, 3, 524–35.

Richters, J.E. and Martinez, P. (1993) 'The NIMH Community Violence Project.1. Children as victims of and witnesses to violence.' *Psychiatry 56*, 7–21.

Richters, J. and Waters, E. (1991) 'Attachment and Socialization: The Positive Side of Social Influence.' In M. Lewis and L. Feinman (eds) *Social Influences and Socialization in Infancy*. New York: Plenum Press.

Ristock, J.L. (2003) 'Exploring dynamics of abusive lesbian relationships: Preliminary analysis of a multisite, qualitative study.' *American Journal of Community Psychology 31*, 3–4, 329–41.

Roberts, J. (2000) 'Changing public attitudes towards corporal punishment.' *Child Abuse and Neglect 24*, 8, 1027–35.

Roberts, J. and Stalans, L. (2004) 'Restorative sentencing: Exploring the views of the public.' *Social Justice Research 17*, 3, 315–34.

Roberts, J., Stalans, L., Indermaur, D. and Hough, M. (2003) *Penal Populism and Public Opinion: Lessons from Five Countries*. Oxford: Oxford University Press.

Roberts, R., O'Connor, T., Dunn, J. and Golding, J. (2004) 'The effects of child sexual abuse in later family life: Mental health, parenting and adjustment of offspring.' *Child Abuse and Neglect 28*, 525–45.

Roberts, S.L., Bushnell, J.A., Collings, S.C. and Purdie, G.L. (2006) 'Psychological health of men with partners who have postpartum depression.' *Australian and New Zealand Journal of Psychiatry 40*, 704–11.

Robins, L.N., West, P.A. and Herjanic, B.L. (1975) 'Arrests and delinquency in two generations: A study of black urban families and their children.' *Journal of Child Psychology and Psychiatry and Allied Disciplines 16*, 2, 125–40.

Rodriquez, A. and Bohlin, G. (2005) 'Are maternal smoking and stress during pregnancy related to ADHD symptoms in children?' *Journal of Child Psychology and Psychiatry 46*, 3, 246–54.

Roelofs, J., Meesters, C., ter Huurne, M., Bamelis, L. and Muris, P. (2006) 'On the links between attachment style, parental rearing behaviors, and internalizing and externalizing problems in non-clinical children.' *Journal of Child and Family Studies 15*, 3, 331–44.

Rohner, R.P. (1986) *The Warmth Dimension: Foundations of Parental Acceptance–Rejection Theory.* Thousand Oaks, CA: Sage.

Rohner, R.P. and Britner, P.A. (2002) 'Worldwide mental health correlates of parental acceptance–rejection: Review of cross-cultural and intercultural evidence.' *Cross-Cultural Research 36*, 1, 16–47.

Roisman, G.I., Collins, W.A., Sroufe, L.A. and Egeland, B. (2005) 'Predictors of young adults' representations of and behavior in their current romantic relationship: Prospective tests of the prototype hypothesis.' *Attachment and Human Development 7*, 2, 105–21.

Romano, E., Tremblay, R.E., Boulerice, B. and Swisher, R. (2005) 'Multilevel correlates of childhood physical aggression and prosocial behavior.' *Journal of Abnormal Child Psychology 33*, 5, 565–78.

Romito, P., Saurel-Cubizolles, M.J. and Lelong, N. (1999) 'What makes new mothers unhappy: Psychological distress one year after birth in Italy and France.' *Social Science and Medicine 49*, 1651–61.

Room, R. (2005) 'Public health policy on alcohol: An international perspective.' *Addiction 100*, 1562–3.

Rosenbaum, D., Lurigio, A. and Davis, R. (1998) *The Prevention of Crime: Social and Situational Strategies.* Belmont, CA: Wadsworth.

Rosenblum, L.A. and Andrews, M.W. (1994) 'Influences of environmental demand on maternal behavior and infant development.' *Acta Paediatrica Supplement 397*, 57–63.

Rosenblum, L.A., Coplan, J.D., Friedman, S., Bassoff, T., Gorman, J.M. and Andrews, M.W. (1994) 'Adverse early experiences affect noradrenergic and serotonergic functioning in adult primates.' *Biological Psychiatry 35*, 4, 221–7.

Rosenstein, D.S. and Horowitz, H.A. (1996) 'Adolescent attachment and psychopathology.' *Journal of Consulting and Clinical Psychology 64*, 244–53.

Rossow, I. (2001) 'Alcohol and homicide: A cross-cultural comparison of the relationship in 14 European countries.' *Addiction 96*, 77–92.

Roy, T.S., Andrews, J.E., Seidler, F.J. and Slotkin, T. (1998) 'Nicotine evokes cell death in embryonic rat brain during neuralation.' *The Journal of Pharmacology and Experimental Therapeutics 287*, 1136–44.

Roy, T.S., Seidler, F.J. and Slotkin, T. (2002) 'Prenatal nicotine exposure evokes alterations of cell structure in hippocampus and somatosensory cortex.' *The Journal of Pharmacology and Experimental Therapeutics 300*, 124–33.

Rubertsson, C., Wickberg, B., Gustavsson, P. and Radestad, I. (2005) 'Depressive symptoms in early pregnancy, two months and one year postpartum-prevalence and psychosocial risk factors in a national Swedish sample.' *Archives of Women's Mental Health 8*, 97–104.

Rutter, M., Giller, H. and Hagel, A. (1998) *Antisocial Behavior by Young People.* Cambridge: Cambridge University Press.

Saltaris, C. (2002) 'Psychopathy in juvenile offenders. Can temperament and attachment be considered as robust developmental precursors?' *Clinical Psychology Review 22*, 729–52.

Salter, D., McMillan, D., Richards, M., Talbot, T. *et al.* (2003) 'Development of sexually abusive behavior in sexually victimised males: A longitudinal study.' *The Lancet 361*, 471–6.

Satka, M. and Eydal, G. (2004) 'The History of Nordic Welfare Policies for Children.' In H. Bremback, B. Johansson and J. Kampmann (eds) *Beyond the Competent Child:*

Exploring Contemporary Childhoods in the Nordic Welfare States. Roskilde: Roskilde University Press.

Savage, J. and Vila, B. (2002) 'Changes in child welfare and subsequent crime rate trends: A cross-national test of the lagged nurturance hypothesis.' *Applied Developmental Psychology 23*, 51–82.

Scaramella, L.V. and Conger, R.D. (2003) 'Intergenerational continuity of hostile parenting and its consequences: The moderating influence of children's negative emotional reactivity.' *Social Development 12*, 3, 420–39.

Schene, P. (2006) 'Forming and Sustaining Partnerships in Child and Family Welfare: The American Experience.' In N. Freymond and G. Cameron (eds) *Towards Positive Systems of Child and Family Welfare.* Toronto: University of Toronto Press.

Schissel, B. (1997) *Blaming Children.* Halifax: Fernwood.

Schneider, M.L., Clarke, A.S. Kraemer, G.W., Roughton, E.C. *et al.* (1998) 'Prenatal stress alters brain biogenic amine levels in primates.' *Development and Psychopathology 10*, 427–40.

Schneider, S. and Jacoby, W. (2005) 'Elite discourse and American public opinion.' *Political Research Quarterly 58*, 3, 367–79.

Schwartz, J.P., Hage, S.M., Bush, I. and Burns, L.K. (2006) 'Unhealthy parenting and potential mediators as contributing factors to future intimate violence.' *Trauma, Violence and Abuse 7*, 3, 206–21.

Scott, E., Reppucci, N.D., Antonishak, J. and DeGennaro, J. (2006) 'Public attitudes about the culpability and punishment of young offenders.' *Behavioral Sciences and the Law 24*, 815–32.

Scott, S. (1998) 'Aggressive behavior in childhood.' *British Medical Journal 316*, 202–6.

Seelau, S.M. and Seelau, E.P. (2005) 'Gender-role stereotypes and perceptions of heterosexual, gay and lesbian domestic violence.' *Journal of Family Violence 20*, 6, 363–71.

Semidei, J., Radel, L.F. and Nolan, C. (2001) 'Substance abuse and child welfare: Clear linkages and promising responses.' *Child Welfare League of America LXXX*, 2, 109–28.

Serin, R.C., Peters, R.D. and Barbaree, H.E. (1990) 'Predictors of psychopathy and release outcome in a criminal population.' *Psychological Assessment 2*, 419–22.

Shaw, D.S., Gilliom, M., Ingoldsby, E.M. and Nagin, D.S. (2003) 'Trajectories leading to school-age conduct problems.' *Developmental Psychology 39*, 2, 189–200.

Shaw, D.S., Owens, E.B., Vondra, J., Keenan, K. and Winslow, E.B. (1996) 'Early risk factors and pathways in the development of early disruptive behavioural problems.' *Development and Psychopathology 8*, 679–700.

Shaw, M., van Dijk, J. and Rhomberg, W. (2003) 'Determining trends in global crime and justice.' Available at www.unodc.org/pdf/crime/forum/forum3_Art2.pdf, accessed on 29 July 2007.

Shonkoff, J.P. and Phillips, D.A. (eds) (2000) *From Neurons to Neighborhoods. The Science of Early Childhood Development.* Washington, DC: National Academy Press.

Shulman, S., Elicker, J. and Sroufe, L.A. (1994) 'Stages of friendship growth in preadolescence as related to attachment history.' *Journal of Social and Personal Relationships 11*, 341–61.

Shumaker, D.M. and Prinz, R.J. (2000) 'Children who murder: A review.' *Clinical Child and Family Psychology Review 3*, 2, 97–115.

Sigelman, C.K., Berry, C.J. and Wiles, K.A. (1984) 'Violence in college students' dating relationships.' *Journal of Applied Social Psychology 5*, 530–48.

Simons, R.L., Lin, K.H. and Gordon, L.C. (1998) 'Socialization in the family of origin and male dating violence: A prospective study.' *Journal of Marriage and the Family 60,* 467–78.

Skondras, M., Markianos, M., Botsis, A., Bistolaki, E. and Christodoulou, G. (2004) 'Platelet monoamine oxidase activity and psychometric correlates in male violent offenders imprisoned for homicide or other violent acts.' *European Archives of Psychiatry and Clinical Neuroscience 254,* 380–6.

Slavkin, M.L. (2001) 'Enuresis, fire-setting, and cruelty to animals: Does the ego triad show predictive validity?' *Adolescence 36,* 143, 461–6.

Small, M. and Limber, S. (2002) 'Advocacy for Children.' In B. Bottoms, M. Kovera and B. McAuliff (eds) *Children, Social Science and the Law.* Cambridge: Cambridge University Press.

Smith, E. and Merkel-Holquin, L. (1996) *A History of Child Welfare.* New Brunswick, NJ: Transaction Publishers.

Smith-Khuri, E., Iachan, R., Scheidt, P., Overpeck, M. *et al.* (2004) 'A cross-national study of violence-related behaviors in adolescents.' *Archives of Pediatrics and Adolescent Medicine 158,* 539–44.

Snyder, J. and Patterson, G.R. (1986) 'The effects of consequences on patterns of social interaction: A quasi-experimental approach to reinforcement in natural interaction.' *Child Development 57,* 1257–68.

Sood, B., Delaney-Black, V., Covington, C., Nordstrom-Klee, B. *et al.* (2001) 'Prenatal alcohol exposure and childhood behavior at age 6 to 7 years: I. Dose-dependent effect.' *Pediatrics 108,* 2, e34.

Sorkhabi, N. (2005) 'Applicability of Baumrind's typology to collective cultures: Analysis of cultural explanations of parent socialization effects.' *International Journal of Behavioral Development 29,* 6, 552–63.

Speltz, M.L., DeKlyen, M. and Greenberg, M.T. (1999) 'Attachment in boys with early onset conduct problems.' *Development and Psychopathology 11,* 269–86.

Spitz, R.A. (1945) 'Hospitalism: An inquiry into the genesis of psychiatric conditions in early childhood.' *Psychoanalytic Study of the Child 1,* 53–74.

Spohr, H.L. (1996) 'Fetal Alcohol Syndrome in Adolescence: Long-term Perspective of Children Diagnosed in Infancy.' In H.L. Spohr and H.C. Steinhausen (eds) *Alcohol, Pregnancy and the Developing Child.* Cambridge: Cambridge University Press.

Sprott, J. (1998) 'Understanding public opposition to a separate youth justice system.' *Crime and Delinquency 44,* 399–411.

Stanley, J.L., Bartholomew, K., Taylor, T., Oram, D. and Landolt, M. (2006) 'Intimate violence in male same-sex relationships.' *Journal of Family Violence 21,* 1, 31–41.

Starzyk, K.B. and Marshall, W.L. (2003) 'Childhood family and personological risk factors for sexual offending.' *Aggression and Violent Behavior 8,* 93–105.

Stasiulis, D. (2002) 'The active child citizen: Lessons from Canadian policy and the children's movement.' *Citizenship Studies 6,* 4, 507–39.

Statistics Canada (2007a) 'Infant mortality rates, by province and territory.' Available at www.40.statcan.ca1/01/cst01/health21a.htm, accessed on 22 May 2007.

Statistics Canada (2007b) *Health Reports* (82-003-XWE). Available at: www.statcan.ca/bsolc/ english/bsolc?catno=82-003-x, accessed on 27 July 2007.

Statistics Canada (2007c) *Homicide Offenses.* Available at www40.statcan.ca/101/cst01/legal12ahtm?sdi=homicide%20offenses, accessed on 30 July 2007.

Steinberg, L. (2001) 'We know some things: Parent–adolescent relationships in retrospect and prospect.' *Journal of Research in Adolescence 11*, 1–19.

Steinhausen, H.C. (1996) 'Psychopathology and Cognitive Functioning in Children with Fetal Alcohol Syndrome.' In H.L. Spohr and H.C. Steinhausen (eds) *Alcohol, Pregnancy and the Developing Child*. Cambridge: Cambridge University Press.

Steinhausen, H.C. and Spohr, H.L. (1998) 'Long-term outcome of children with fetal alcohol syndrome: Psychopathology, behavior and intelligence.' *Alcohol: Clinical and Experimental Research 22*, 334–8.

Sternberg, K.J., Baradaran, L.P., Abbott, C.B., Lamb, M.E. and Guterman, E. (2006) 'Type of violence, age, and gender differences in the effects of family violence on children's behavior problems: A mega-analysis.' *Developmental Review 26*, 89–112.

Sternberg, K.J., Lamb, M.E., Guterman, E., Abbott, C.B. and Dawud-Noursi, S. (2005) 'Adolescents' perceptions of attachments to their mothers and fathers in families with histories of domestic violence: A longitudinal perspective.' *Child Abuse and Neglect 29*, 853–69.

Stevens, S. and Arbiter, N. (1995) 'A therapeutic community for substance-abusing pregnant women and women with children: Process and outcome.' *Journal of Psychoactive Drugs 27*, 49–56.

Stewart, E.A., Simons, R.L. and Conger, R.D. (2002) 'Assessing neighborhood and social psychological influences on childhood violence in an African-American sample.' *Criminology 40*, 4, 801–29.

Straus, M.A. (1994) *Beating the Devil Out of Them: Corporal Punishment in American Families*. New York: Lexington Books.

Straus, M.A. and Kaufman-Kantor, G.K. (1994) 'Corporal punishment by parents: A risk factor in the epidemiology of depression, suicide, alcohol abuse, child abuse, and wife beating.' *Adolescence 29*, 543–61.

Straus, M.A. and Mathur, A. (1996) 'Social Change and the Trends in Approval of Corporal Punishment by Parents from 1969 to 1994.' In D. Frehsee, W. Horn and K.-D. Bussmann (eds) *Family Violence Against Children*. New York: Walter de Gruyter.

Straus, M.A., Sugarman, D. and Giles-Sims, J. (1997) 'Spanking by parents and subsequent antisocial behavior of children.' *Archives of Pediatric and Adolescent Medicine 151*, 761–7.

Straus, M.A. and Yodanis, C.L. (1996) 'Corporal punishment in adolescence and physical assaults on spouses later in life. What accounts for the link?' *Journal of Marriage and the Family 58*, 825–41.

SurveyUSA (2005) 'Disciplining a child.' Available at www.surveyusa.com/50StateDisciplineChild0805SortedbySpank.htm, accessed on 14 August 2007.

Sutton, S.E., Cowen, E.L., Crean, H.F. and Wyman, P.A. (1999) 'Pathways to aggression in young, highly stressed urban children.' *Child Study Journal 29*, 1, 49–68.

Svallfors, S. (1995) 'The end of class politics? Structural cleavages and attitudes to Swedish welfare policies.' *Acta Sociologica 38*, 53–74.

Svallfors, S. (1997) 'Worlds of welfare and attitudes to redistribution: A comparison of eight Western nations.' *European Sociological Review 13*, 3, 283–304.

Svallfors, S. (2004) 'Class, attitudes, and the welfare state.' *Social Policy and Administration 38*, 2, 119–38.

Swain, J.E., Lorberbaum, J.P., Kose, S. and Srathearn, L. (2007) 'Brain basis of early parent-infant interactions: Psychology, physiology, and *in vivo* functional neuroimaging studies.' *Journal of Child Psychology and Psychiatry 48*, 3–4, 262–87.

Swedish National Council for Crime Prevention (2001) *Crime Prevention in the Nordic Context: The Nordic Model.* Stockholm: Sewdish National Council for Crime Prevention.

Swift, K. and Callahan, M. (2006) 'Problems and Potential of Canadian Child Welfare.' In N. Freymond and G. Cameron (eds) *Towards Positive Systems of Child and Family Welfare.* Toronto: University of Toronto Press.

Swinford, S.P., Demaris, A., Cernovich, S.A. and Giordano, P.C. (2000) 'Harsh physical discipline in childhood and violence in later romantic involvements: The mediating role of problem behaviors.' *Journal of Marriage and the Family 62*, 2, 508–20.

Sylwander, L. (2001) *Child Impact Assessments.* Stockholm: Ministry of Health and Social Affairs, Sweden.

Tackett, J.L., Krueger, R.F., Iacono, W.G. and McGue, M. (2005) 'Symptom-based subfactors of DSM-defined conduct disorder: Evidence for etiologic distinctions.' *Journal of Abnormal Psychology 114*, 483–87.

Takala, H. (2004) 'Nordic cooperation in criminal policy and crime prevention.' *Journal of Scandinavian Studies in Criminology and Crime Prevention 5*, 2, 131–47.

Taylor, C. (1979) 'What's Wrong with Negative Liberty?' In A. Ryan (ed.) *The Idea of Freedom.* London: Oxford University Press.

Teicher, M.H. (2002) 'Scars that won't heal: The neurobiology of child abuse.' *Scientific American 286*, 3, 68–76.

Teicher, M.H., Andersen, S.L., Polcari, A., Anderson, C.M., Navalta, C.P. and Kim, D. (2003) 'The neurobiological consequences of early stress and childhood maltreatment.' *Neuroscience and Biobehavioral Reviews 27*, 33–44.

Theodore, A.D., Chang, J.J., Runyan, D. K., Hunter, W.M. *et al.* (2005) 'Epidemiologic features of the physical and sexual maltreatment of children in the Carolinas.' *Pediatrics 115*, 3, 331–7.

Theodore, A.D., Runyan, D. K. and Chang, J.J. (2007) 'Measuring the risk of physical neglect in a population-based sample.' *Child Maltreatment 12*, 1, 96–105.

Therborn, G. (1993) 'The Politics of Childhood: The Rights of the Children in Modern Times.' In F. Castles (ed.) *Families of Nations: Patterns of Public Policy in Western Democracies.* Aldershot: Dartmouth.

Thomas, A., Chess, S. and Birch, H.G. (1968) *Temperament and Behaviour Disorders in Children.* New York: New York University Press.

Thompson, R. (1999) 'Early Attachment and Later Development.' In J. Cassidy and P. Shaver (eds) *Handbook of Attachment: Theory, Research and Clinical Applications.* New York: Guilford Press.

Thormaehlen, D.J. and Bass-Field, E.R. (1994) 'Children: The secondary victims of domestic violence.' *Maryland Medical Journal 43*, 355–9.

Tolan, P.H., Gorman-Smith, D. and Henry, D.B. (2003) 'The developmental ecology of urban males' youth violence.' *Developmental Psychology 39*, 2, 274–91.

Tomlinson, M., Cooper, P.J., Stein, A., Swartz, L. and Molteno, C. (2006) 'Post-partum depression and infant growth in a South Africa peri-urban settlement.' *Child: Care, Health and Development 32*, 1, 81–6.

Tremblay, R. E. (2003) 'Public opinion and violence prevention.' *Bulletin of the Centre of Excellence for Early Childhood Development 2*, 1, 1.

Tremblay, R.E. (2006) 'Prevention of youth violence: Why not start at the beginning?' *Journal of Abnormal Child Psychology 34*, 481–7.

Tremblay, R.E., Japel, C., Perusse, D., Boivin, M. *et al.* (1999) 'The search for the age of "onset" of physical aggression: Rousseau and Bandura revisited.' *Criminal Behaviour and Mental Health 9*, 8–23.

Trocme, N., MacLaurin, B., Fallon, B., Daciuk, J. *et al.* (2001) *Canadian Incidence Study of Reported Child Abuse and Neglect: Final Report.* Ottawa: Minister of Public Works and Government Services, Canada.

Turner, J. and Turner, F. (2005) *Canadian Social Welfare.* Toronto: Pearson Education Canada.

Tyler, S., Allison, K. and Winsler, A. (2006) 'Child neglect: Developmental consequences, intervention, and policy implications.' *Child and Youth Care Forum 35*, 1, 1–20.

UNICEF (2003) *Child Maltreatment Deaths in Rich Countries.* Available at www.unodc/en/data-and-analysis/United-Nations-Surveys-on-Crime-Trends-and-t he-Operations-of-Criminial-Justice-Systems.html, accessed on 21 May 2007.

UNICEF (2004) *Summary Report of the Study of the Impact of the Implementation of the Convention on the Rights of the Child.* Florence: UNICEF Innocenti Research Centre.

UNICEF (2007) *Child Poverty in Perspective: An Overview of Child Well-Being in Rich Countries.* Innocenti Report Card 7. Florence: UNICEF Innocenti Research Centre.

United Nations (2006) *World Report on Violence Against Children.* New York: The United Nations Secretary General's Study on Violence Against Children. Available at www.violencestudy.org/a553, accessed on 5 June 2007.

United Nations Office on Drugs and Crime (2007) *United Nations Survey of Crime Trends, Seventh Survey, Eighth Survey, Ninth Survey.* Available at www.unodc.org, accessed on 29 July 2007.

United Nations Treaty Body Database (2007)*Committee on the Rights of the Child: State Party Report.* Available at www.unhchr/ch/tbs/doc.nsf, accessed on 24 July 2007.

United Nations (2007) *United Nations Secretary General's Study on Violence Against Children.* Available at www.violencestudy.orgIMG/pdf/English-2-2.pdf, accessed on 5 June 2007.

US Department of Justice (2000) *Investing Wisely in Crime Prevention.* Washington, DC: US Department of Justice.

VanDeMark, N.R., Russell, L.A., O'Keefe, M., Finkelstein, N., Noether, C.D. and Gampel, J. (2005) 'Children of mothers with histories of substance abuse, mental illness and trauma.' *Journal of Community Psychology 33*, 4, 445–59.

Van Goozen, S.H.M. and Fairchild, G. (2006) 'Neuroendocrine and neurotransmitter correlates in children with antisocial behavior.' *Hormones and Behavior 50*, 647–54.

Van Goozen, S.H.M., Fairchild, G., Snoek, H. and Harold, G.T. (2007) 'The evidence for a neurobiological model of childhood antisocial behavior.' *Psychological Bulletin 133*, 1, 149–82.

Verhellen, E. (1994) *Convention on the Rights of the Child.* Kessel-Lo: Garant.

Verhellen, E. (1996) 'Monitoring Children's Rights.' In E. Verhellen (ed.) *Monitoring Children's Rights.* The Hague: Martinus Nijhoff.

Vittrup, B., Holden, G.W. and Buck, J. (2006) 'Attitudes predict the use of physical punishment: A prospective study of the emergence of disciplinary practices.' *Pediatrics 117*, 6, 2055–64.

Vuijk, P., van Lier, P.A.C., Huizink, A.C., Verhulst, F.C. and Crijnen, A.A. (2006) 'Prenatal smoking predicts non-responsiveness to an intervention targeting attention-deficit/hyperactivity symptoms in elementary schoolchildren.' *Journal of Child Psychology and Psychiatry 47*, 9, 891–901.

Waddell, C., Lavis, J., Abelson, J., Lomas, J. *et al.* (2005) 'Research use in children's mental health policy in Canada.' *Social Science and Medicine 61*, 1649–57.

Waddell, C., Lomas, J., Offord, D. and Giacomini, M. (2001) 'Doing better with "bad kids": Explaining the policy-research gap with conduct disorder in Canada.' *Canadian Journal of Community Mental Health 20*, 2, 59–76.

Wakschlag, L.S., Gordon, R.A., Lahey, B., Loeber, R., Green, S. and Leventhal, B. (2000) 'Maternal age at first birth and boys' risk for conduct disorder.' *Journal of Research on Adolescence 10*, 417–41.

Wakschlag, L. and Hans, S. (2002) 'Maternal smoking in pregnancy and conduct problems in high risk youth: A developmental framework.' *Development and Psychopathology 14*, 351–69.

Wakschlag, L., Leventhal, B., Pine, D.S., Pickett, K. and Carter, A.S. (2006) 'Elucidating early mechanisms of developmental psychopathology: The case of prenatal smoking and disruptive behavior.' *Child Development 77*, 4, 893–906.

Wakschlag, L., Pickett, K., Cook, E., Benowitz, N. and Leventhal, B. (2002) 'Maternal smoking during pregnancy and severe antisocial behavior in offspring: A review.' *American Journal of Public Health 92*, 966–74.

Waller, M.A. (2001) 'Resilience in ecosystemic context: Evolution of the concept.' *American Journal of Orthopsychiatry 71*, 3, 290–7.

Walrath, C.M., Ybarra, M.L., Sheehan, A.K., Holden, E.W. and Burns, B.J. (2006) 'Impact of maltreatment on children served in community mental health programs.' *Journal of Emotional and Behavioral Disorders 14*, 3, 143–56.

Walsh, A., Beyer, J.A. and Petee, T.A. (2001) 'Violent Delinquency: An examination of psychopathic typologies.' *Journal of Genetic Psychology 148*, 3, 385–92.

Ward, T., Hudson, S.M. and Marshall, W.L. (1996) 'Attachment style in sex offenders: A preliminary study.' *The Journal of Sex Research 33*, 17–26.

Ward, T. and Siegert, R. (2002) 'Toward a comprehensive theory of child sexual abuse: A theory knitting perspective.' *Psychology, Crime and Law 8*, 319–51.

Waterston, T. and Goldhagen, J. (2006) 'Why children's rights are central to international child health.' *Archives of Disease in Childhood 92*, 176–80.

Wattendorf, D.J., Usaf, M.C. and Muenke, M. (2005) 'Fetal alcohol spectrum disorders.' *American Family Physician 72*, 2, 279–85.

Watts-English, T., Fortson, B., Gibler, N., Hooper, S.R. and De Bellis, M.D. (2006) 'The psychobiology of maltreatment in childhood.' *Journal of Social Issues 62*, 4, 717–36.

Weaver, A., Byers, E.S., Sears, H., Cohen, J. and Randall, H. (2002) 'Sexual health education at school and at home.' *Canadian Journal of Human Sexuality 11*, 1, 129–41.

Weaver, R.K. (2000) *Ending Welfare as We Know It.* Washington, DC: Brookings Institution Press.

Weissman, M.M., Pilowsky, D.J., Wickramaratane, P.J., Talati, A. *et al.* (2006) 'Remissions in maternal depression and child psychopathology.' *Journal of the American Medical Association 295*, 1389–98.

Weissman, M.M., Warner, V., Wickramaratne, P. and Kandel, D. (1999) 'Maternal smoking during pregnancy and psychopathology in offspring followed to adulthood.' *Journal of the American Academy of Child and Adolescent Psychiatry 38*, 892–9.

Welsh, B. and Farrington, D. (2004) 'Effective Programmes to Prevent Delinquency.' In J. Adler (ed.) *Forensic Psychology: Concepts, Debates and Practices.* Cullompton: Willan.

Welsh, B. and Farrington, D. (2006) *Preventing Crime: What Works for Children, Offenders, Victims, and Places.* Dordrecht, Netherlands: Springer.

West, D.J. and Farrington, D.P. (1977) *The Delinquent Way of Life.* London: Heinemann.

West, M. and Prinz, R.J. (1987) 'Parental alcoholism and childhood psychopathology.' *Psychological Bulletin 102,* 2, 204–18.

Whitaker, R.C., Orzol, S.M. and Kahn, R.S. (2006) 'Maternal mental health, substance use, and domestic violence in the year after delivery and subsequent behavior problems in children at age 3 years.' *Archives of General Psychiatry 63,* 551–60.

White, H.R. and Chen, P. (2002) 'Problem drinking and intimate partner violence.' *Journal of Studies in Alcohol 63,* 2, 205–14.

Widom, C.S. (2000) 'Childhood victimization: Early adversity, later psychopathology.' *National Institute of Justice Journal 242,* 2–9.

Wiklund, S. (2007) 'United we stand? Collaboration as a means for identifying children and adolescents at risk.' *International Journal of Social Welfare 16,* 3, 202–11.

Williams, G.M., O'Callaghan, M., Najman, J.M., Bor, W., Andersen, M.J. and Richards, D. (1998) 'Maternal cigarette smoking and child psychiatric morbidity: A longitudinal study.' *Pediatrics 102,* 1, e11.

Williams, J. and Van Dorn, R. (1999) 'Delinquency, Gangs, and Youth Violence.' In J. Jenson and M. Howard (eds) *Youth Violence.* Washington, DC: National Association of Social Workers Press.

Wisensale, S. (2006) 'California's paid leave law: A model for other states?' *Marriage and Family Review 39,* 1, 177–95.

Wolfe, D.A. (1998) *Child Abuse: Implications for Child Development and Psychopathology* (2nd edition). Thousand Oaks, CA: Sage.

Wolfe, D.A., Crooks, C.V., Lee, V., McIntyre-Smith, A. and Jaffe, P.G. (2003) 'The effects of children's exposure to domestic violence: A meta-analysis and critique.' *Clinical Child and Family Psychology Review 6,* 3, 171–87.

Wolfe, D.A., Wekerle, C., Scott, K., Straatman, A. and Grasley, C. (2004) 'Predicting abuse in adolescent dating relationships over 1 year: The role of child maltreatment and trauma.' *Journal of Abnormal Psychology 113,* 3, 406–15.

Wolff, S. and McCall Smith, A. (2001) 'Children who kill.' *British Medical Journal 322,* 61–2.

Wood, J.J., Cowan, P.A. and Baker, B.L. (2002) 'Behavior problems and peer rejection in preschool boys and girls.' *Journal of Genetic Psychology 163,* 72–88.

Wood, J.J., Emmerson, N.A. and Cowan, P.A. (2004) 'Is early attachment security carried forward into relationships with preschool peers?' *British Journal of Developmental Psychology 22,* 245–53.

World Health Organization (2000) *World Health Report.* Available at www.who.int/whr/2000/en/annex01_en.pdf, accessed on 19 July 2007.

World Health Organization (2002a) 'Moving towards a tobacco-free Europe.' Available at www.euro.who.intmediacentre/PR/2002/20020214_1, accessed on March 2007.

World Health Organization (2002b) *World Report on Violence and Health.* Available at http://who.int/hq/2002/9241545615.pdf, accessed on 20 May 2007.

World Health Organization (2005) *Multi-country Study on Women's Health and Domestic Violence Against Women.* Geneva: WHO.

World Health Organization (2007) 'Third milestones of a global campaign for violence prevention report.' Available at http://whqlibdoc.who.int/publications/2007/9789241595476_eng.pdf, accessed on 18 July 2007.

Wright, L.E. and Seymour, C.B. (2000) *Working With Children and Families Separated by Incarceration.* Washington, DC: Child Welfare League of America.

Ybarra, G.Y., Wilkens, S.L. and Lieberman, A.F. (2007) 'The influence of domestic violence on preschooler behavior and functioning.' *Journal of Family Violence 22,* 33–42.

Zeldin, S. (2004) 'Youth as agents of adult and community development: Mapping the processes and outcomes of youth engaged in organizational governance.' *Applied Developmental Science 8,* 2, 75–90.

Zeskind, P.S. and Stephens, L.E. (2004) 'Maternal selective serotonin reuptake inhibitor use during pregnancy and newborn neurobehavior.' *Pediatrics 113,* 2, 368–75.

Zielinski, D.S. and Bradshaw, C.P. (2006) 'Ecological influences on the sequelae of child maltreatment: A review of the literature.' *Child Maltreatment 11,* 1, 49–62.

Zimmerman, S. (1992) *Family Policies and Family Well-being: The Role of Political Culture.* Newbury Park, CA: Sage.

Zimring, F. (1998) *American Youth Violence.* New York: Oxford University Press.

SUBJECT INDEX

ADHD and maternal depression
  121
advocacy for children 221
aggression 13
  and authoritarian parenting
    68–9
  and corporal punishment 75–8
  and cortisol levels 39–40
  and exposure to intimate partner
    violence (IPV) 105–7
  gene expression and early
    adversity 35–6
  link to childhood physical abuse
    86, 118
  link to fetal tobacco exposure
    42–6
  modeling of 74, 95, 97, 103,
    104, 107–8
  and serotonin dysregulation
    38–9
  and social information
    processing deficits 92–3
alcohol use
  effects on children's behavior
    117–18
  link to high homicide rate,
    Finland 157
  prenatal exposure to, effects of
    46–52
amygdala, negative emotion
  regulation 40
animal cruelty, link with exposure
  to intimate partner violence
  (IPV) 104
antisocial behaviors 12
  cross-cultural variations 178
  peer influences 16, 58, 127
  prevention 207–8
  risk factors 124
    coercive parenting 70–1
    parental criminality 107–14
    parenting quality 65, 66,
      117–18
    physical abuse 85–6, 106–7
    use of corporal punishment
      76, 77

attachment relationship
  importance of 53, 55–6
  insecure, impact of 54–5, 58,
    59–62
  quality of 53, 56, 58–9
  role of oxytocin 56–7
  theory of 53–4
attitudes
  changing to respect children's
    rights 229–31
  see also public opinion
authoritarian parenting style 68–9,
  71–2
authoritative parenting style 66–7

beliefs about children
  Nordic countries 201–8
  North America 213–19
binge drinking 47, 51
brain development 32–41
  effects of tobacco and alcohol
    47–52
  neglect leading to adverse 85
bullying 93, 104, 154–5, 178–9

child abuse 80–90
  see also child maltreatment
child deaths from maltreatment
  147–8, 169
child-friendly policies 136–40
  and reduced violence 153–8
  see also Nordic countries, policies
child health
  Nordic policies 149–50
  North American policies 171–3
child impact assessments 25,
  141–2, 221–2
child maltreatment 86–7
  brain structure, effects on 64–5
  and child killers 88–90
  chronicity and outcome of 87
  deaths from 147–8, 169
  and deficits in social information
    processing 90–4
  IPV predicting likelihood of 105

and parental criminality 109–10
and parental substance abuse
  115–16
predictor of later interpersonal
  violence 87–8, 98, 101
responses to by governments
  145–7, 153, 167–8, 205–6,
  216
child neglect 84–5
child physical abuse 80
  corporal punishment as primary
    risk factor 79–80
  and history of sexual abuse 82
  and intimate partner violence
    (IPV) 105–7
  predicting violence in adulthood
    85–6
child poverty
  Nordic countries
    low levels of 145
    public support to reduce 207
  North America
    higher levels of 166–7
    less public support to reduce
      218–19
  see also poverty
child rearing styles see parenting
  styles
child sexual abuse 80
  chronicity and outcomes 81–2
  female perpetrators 83–4
  intergenerational transmission
    82
  male victims, impact on 83
  and subsequent harsh parenting
    82
child-unfriendly policies 159–60
  and increased violence 177–82
  see also North America, policies
child welfare
  Nordic policies 145–8
  North American policies 167–9
childcare 139
  accessibility of 32
  Nordic policies 142–3
  North American policies 162–5

Children's rights approach 18–26,
195, 228–31
    children's participation 235–9
    early prevention, benefits of
        231–2
    providing education about
        232–5
classical liberalism 209–11
coercive parenting 70–1
conduct disorder 12
    genetic factors 36
    and insecure attachment 59
    and maternal depression 119,
        121
    and maternal smoking 45
    North America 177–8
    parental rejection 69
    and parental substance abuse
        115, 116–17
corporal punishment
    attitudes supporting use of 78–9
    criticism of by UN Committee
        64
    legal ban on 25–6, 148–9, 158,
        170–1, 202–3
    modeling aggression in children
        74
    and mothers with history of
        sexual abuse 82
    Nordic countries 148–9, 204–5
    North America 170–1, 215–16
    predictor of later aggressive
        behaviors 75–8, 140
    prevalence of 72–3, 171
    public education campaigns
        against 139–40, 148–9,
        202–3, 230
    risk factor for child physical
        abuse 79–80
cortisol levels and childhood
    aggression 39–40
crime prevention
    Nordic countries 152–3
    North America 174–7
criminal violence 13, 14
    children with FASD 50
    comparisons across countries
        155–6, 180–1
    Nordic countries 155, 158, 180
    North America 179–82
    and severe child maltreatment
        88–9
    see also homicide rates
criminality, parental 107–14
cultural contexts 183–4
    cross-cultural similarities
        corporal punishment and
            child aggression 77–8
        outcome of parenting styles
            71–2
    policy-making in North America
        constraints on 184–9
        reasons for lack of 220–8
    political cultures 189–96
        in the Nordic countries
            196–208
        in North America 208–19
cycle of violence 9–10, 238–9

dating violence 87–8
deaths of children
    from maltreatment 147–8, 169
    infant mortality rates 150,
        172–3
democratic parenting style 66–8,
    71
depression see maternal depression
disruptive behavior disorders
    and insecure attachment 58–9
    link to fetal alcohol exposure
        49–50
    link to fetal exposure to tobacco
        42–3
    and maternal depression 120–1
domestic violence 95–6
    and early coercive parenting 71
    politicization of 96–7
    rates of perpetration 96
    see also intimate partner violence
        (IPV)

early environmental adversity,
    effects of 35–8
early prevention programs 137–8
    cost-benefits of 231–2
    Nordic countries 146–7, 150–3
    North America 173–7
    public support, need for 221–7
ecological approaches 17–18, 76,
    155
education
    about the early years, benefits of
        231–2
    childcare/early childhood 139,
        142–3, 151, 173
    children's rights 232–5
    parent programs 25–6, 138–9
    public education programs
        139–40, 148–9, 230
    sexual health education 140,
        151, 174–5, 206, 216–17
emotion regulation
    and abusive parenting 93, 98
    and attachment 55–6, 57–8
    neural underpinnings 34–5,
        38–40
emotional abuse 80–1, 101, 118
equality of opportunity 190–2
ethnic differences
    child poverty 167
    infant mortality rates 172–3

families
    clustering of problems in 124–5
    intimate partner violence (IPV)
        97–107
    maternal depression 119–24
    models of 192–4
    parental criminality 107–14
    parental substance abuse by
        114–18
    resilience to adverse
        circumstances 125–8
    risk factors for violence in
        13–15
family policy 130–1, 192–4
    characteristics of child-friendly
        136–40

characteristics of
    child-unfriendly 159–60
    models of 133–4
    Nordic countries 140–58,
        199–201
    North America 160–9, 211–13
fathers, effects of maternal
    depression on 120
female delinquency 110–11
female incarceration 111–12
female violence 96–101
fetal alcohol spectrum disorder
    (FASD) 47–51
fetal alcohol syndrome (FAS) 47–8
fetal rights and health 30–2

gender differences
    dating violence, predictors of 88
    intimate partner violence (IPV)
        100–1
    prenatal smoking and aggression
        45–6
    social information processing
        93–4
gender equality 99, 133–4, 193,
    201, 212–13
genetic influences 15
    MAO gene, early adversity and
        risk of aggression 35–6
    physical abuse and violence in
        adulthood 86
    problem drinking, genetic
        predisposition to 50–1,
        118
    substance abuse, heritability of
        27, 118
government role 20
    in family policy, public opinion
        199–201
    and individualism 190–2
    Nordic countries 196–9
    North America 208–11
    providing child-rearing support
        127–8
    see also policy interventions

health care see child health
heritability see genetic influences
hippocampus
    adverse effects of alcohol 48
    vulnerability to stress 40
home visitation programs 138
homicide rates
    for children 88–9
    cross-country comparisons
        179–80
    Nordic countries 157–8
    North America 179–80
        and attitudes toward killing
            226–7
        variation within 181–2
    sources of data on 156–7
hostile parenting 70
HPA axis functioning, disrupted by
    adverse early rearing 39–40

incarceration of parents, effects on
    children 110–14

income support
Nordic policies 144–5
North American policies 165–7
individual responsibility model
191, 193, 209, 212, 216–19
individualism 190–2
infant mortality rates 150, 172–3
insecure attachment 54–6
risk factor for violence 57–62
intergenerational transmission
attachment quality 57
childhood sexual abuse 82
cortisol secretion and aggression
39–40
criminal behavior 107–9, 111
fetal alcohol spectrum disorder
(FASD) 50–1
partner violence 88
substance abuse 114–15
internal working model 56, 59, 60
interventions
alcohol reduction during
pregnancy 51
programs promoting resilience
127–8
for sexual abuse victims 82
social information processing 94
see also policy interventions
intimate partner violence (IPV)
96–7
corporal punishment as a
predictor of 76–7
and early insecure attachment
60–1
effects of childhood exposure to
81, 103–4, 106–7
in same-sex relationships 101
link to child physical abuse
105–6
men as victims of 100–1
prevalence of 102–3
as a relationship characteristic
101–2
and substance abuse 116
subtypes of 99–100
traditional definition of 98–9

justice, children's rights as first
principle of 22–3
juvenile offending 53–4, 60
link to hostile parenting 70
and parental criminality 110–12
and parental substance abuse
114

"lagged nurturance hypothesis"
155, 156, 179
limbic system, role in emotion
regulation 38, 40

maltreatment see child
maltreatment
MAO (monoamine oxidase) gene,
effects of low levels 36
maternal depression 119–20
and behavior problems in
children 120–1
effects on fathers 120

medication during pregnancy,
adverse effects of 121–2
and poor parenting 121, 123–4
postpartum 121–4
maternal deprivation 36–7, 53–4,
85
maternal prenatal smoking (MPS),
link to child aggression 42–6
mega-analysis, IPV studies 106–7
minimum age controversy 31
modeling of parental behavior by
children 65, 97, 103, 113,
118, 237

nature and nurture, interaction
between 17–18, 30–1, 32–41
needs perspective 23–4, 194–5,
204
neglect 81, 84–5
neurological perspectives
and attachment 52–62
brain development 32–41
effects of prenatal alcohol use
46–52
effects of prenatal smoking 41–6
neurotransmitters 33–4, 38–9
Nordic countries
policies 141–2
child health 149–50
child welfare 145–8
childcare 142–3
corporal punishment 148–9
early prevention 150–3
income support 144–5
and reduced violence 153–8
political culture 196
beliefs about children 201–8
family policy 199–201
role of government 196–9
North America
policies 160–2
child health 171–3
child welfare 167–9
childcare 162–5
corporal punishment 170–1
early prevention 173–7
income support 165–7
and increased violence
177–82
political culture 208
beliefs about children
213–19
family policy 211–13
role of government 208–11
research
disconnection from policy
184–9
reasons for rejection of
220–8

ombudsman for children, Norway
141, 203, 204
oxytocin, link to maternal caring
behavior 56–7

parent education programs 25–6,
138–9
cost savings of 231–2

parental acceptance, importance of
69–70
parental criminality
and child welfare system
involvement 109–10
effects of incarceration 111–14
and greater delinquency in
children 110–11
predictive of child criminality
107–9
parental rejection, effects of 69–70,
78, 117–18
parental responsibility 223–4
parental substance abuse see alcohol
use; substance abuse
parenting styles 63–4
child abuse 80–1
maltreatment 86–90
neglect 84–5
physical abuse 85–6
sexual abuse 81–4
corporal punishment 72–80
effect on brain development 37
importance of positive parenting
64–6
influence of 17–18
social information processing
90–4
see also attachment relationship
parents, criticism of by children
237–8
parricide 89–90
participation, children's 235–9
patriarchal model of the family
192–3, 194, 196, 212
"patriarchal terrorism" 99–100
peer relationships
impact of child maltreatment
98, 127
link to attachment quality 58,
59
and parental acceptance 69
"penal populism" 225–6
permissive parenting 67–8
physical abuse see child physical
abuse
physical aggression 13, 68
policy interventions 129–30
child and family policy 130–6
child-friendly policies 136–40
advantages of 153–4
and reduced violence 154–8
child-unfriendly policies 159–60
and greater violence 177–82
Nordic policies 141–2
child health 149–50
child welfare 145–8
childcare 142–3
corporal punishment 148–9
early prevention 150–3
income support 144–5
North American policies 160–2
child health 171–3
child welfare 167–9
childcare 162–5
corporal punishment 170–1
early prevention 173–7
income support 165–7
policy process, "inherent
ambiguity" in 185–6

political culture and children
      189–90
   children's status, views on
      194–6
   individualism and role of
      government 190–2
   views on family and family
      policy 192–4
positive parenting, importance of
      64–6
postpartum depression 120, 121–4
postpartum psychosis 122
poverty 125
   aims by Sweden to eliminate
      132–3
   income support 144–5, 165–7
   and parental stress 32, 62
   and public support for reducing
      207, 218–19
   single teenaged mothers 66, 119
pregnancy
   and fetal exposure to drugs
      41–52
   health care, Nordic countries
      150
   in teenagers, efforts to prevent
      140, 151, 174–5, 206,
      216–17
   rights of the fetus 30–2
   treatment for depression during
      121–2
prevention programs
   financial savings from 231–2
   see also early prevention
      programs
primary caregiver, importance of
      infant's attachment to 52–62
proactive interventions 25, 127–8
protective factors 17, 65, 121,
      126–8, 136–7
psychopaths, emotional detachment
      of 59–60
public education campaigns
      139–40, 148–9, 230
public opinion 188–9, 200
   Nordic countries 198–9, 200–1,
      221–2
   against corporal punishment
      202–3
   North America 211–13, 222–4
   cultural acceptance of
      violence 226–7
   punitive attitudes 224–6
   on government intervention in
      the family 200
   public support for reducing
      poverty 207, 218–19
public spending 231–2
   Nordic countries 132–3, 142–3,
      150, 198, 199
   North America 132, 162, 165,
      174, 213
punitive attitudes 224–6

rejection, parental 69–70, 78
relational aggression 68–9
research
   bias in IPV studies 96–7
   disconnection with policy 184–9

findings
   policy-makers acting on 220,
      221–2
   policy-makers' reluctance to
      act on 222–7
   spending on 220–1
resilience, factors promoting 125–8
rights of children see children's
      rights approach
romantic relationships, link to early
      attachment quality 59
Russia, effects of social changes 18

same-sex relationships, violence in
      101
school killings 10–11
secure attachment, benefits of
      53–4, 55, 57–8
self-control, development of 74–5
serotonin (5-HT) neurotransmitter
      system and aggression 38–9
sexual abuse see child sexual abuse
sexual health education 140, 151,
      174–5, 206, 216–17
sexual offenders
   professionals' views of female
      83, 84
   risk factors 61, 81, 93
single parents
   clustering of problems 125, 140
   depressive symptoms 119–20
   incarceration of, effects on
      children 111–12
   and poor parenting practices 66
   teen pregnancies, efforts to
      prevent 140, 151, 174–5,
      206, 216–17
smoking 41
   during pregnancy
      and childhood behavior
      problems 42–6
   effects on fetal brain 42, 43
social deficits, children with FASD
      49, 50
social democracy
   Canada 210, 218–19
   Nordic countries 196–9, 219
social information processing 90–1
   and aggression subtypes 92–3
   gender differences 93–4
   and hostile parenting 70
   theory of 91–2
social responsibility model 192–5,
      199–201
socialization see parenting styles
"Strange Situation" experiment,
      attachment quality 54, 56, 59
stress 125
   and attachment difficulties 62
   low cortisol levels and childhood
      aggression 39–40
   maternal, neurobehavioral
      effects of 36–7
   neural mechanisms 38–41
   and poverty 32, 62
substance abuse
   comorbidity with child neglect
      115–16

effects on children's behavior
      116–17
   heritability of 118
   and intimate partner violence
      (IPV) 116
   and poor parenting 115
   prevalence rates 114
   see also alcohol use; smoking
success, measuring 25–6

targeted programs 127, 132, 140
teen pregnancies, efforts to prevent
      140, 151, 174–5, 206,
      216–17
temperament, infant's 15–16, 53
tobacco, effects of prenatal
      exposure to 41–6
trust, infant's development of 32,
      53, 54

UN Convention on the Rights of
      the Child 18–19
   categories of rights and guiding
      principles 19–20
   and child protection 64
   and childcare provision 32
   endorsement by Nordic
      countries 141, 201–4
   and fetal rights, minimum age
      controversy 31
   implementation and
      enforcement of 21–2,
      141–2
   and parental responsibilities
      95–6
   resilience promoting programs
      127–8
   unratified by the United States
      19, 160, 177, 213–14
UN Secretary General's Global Study
      on Violence Against Children
      11, 12, 63, 95, 228, 237
universal vs. reactive programs
      127–8, 132–3, 140

violence
   definitions of types of 12–13
   mechanisms maintaining 228
   neural mechanisms 34–5
   North American acceptance of
      226–7
   problem of 10–12
   views of children 237–8
   ways of reducing 228–9
   see also criminal violence

welfare states 131–3
   Nordic countries 196–9
   North America 208–11
World Report on Violence Against
      Children (United Nations)
      27, 29, 137

AUTHOR INDEX

Abou-Saleh, M.T. 122
Achenbach, T. 154
Adams, M. 212–13, 226–7
Agoub, M. 122, 123
Ainsworth, M.D.S. 54
Alen, A. 24
Allen, J.P. 59
Allison, K. 84
Alltucker, K.W. 111
Alm, P.O. 36
Almond, G. 189
American Bar Association and
    National Bar Association 111
American Psychiatric Association
    12, 80
Anda, R.F. 34, 40, 64
Andersen, J. 198
Andersson, G. 146
Andrews, M.W. 36
Antecol, H. 66, 201
Applegate, B. 224
Arbiter, N. 116
Archer, J. 99, 100
Aronson, E. 236
Arthur, R. 65
Ascione, F.R. 104
Ashman, S. 37
Ateah, C.A. 72, 78
Autti-Ramo, I. 47, 49

Babcock, J.C. 60
Bailey, B.N. 49
Baker, B.L. 58
Baker, M. 200
Bakermans-Kranenburg, M.J. 15,
    53
Baldry, A.C. 102, 104
Bandura, A. 74, 91
Banyard, V.L. 82
Barbaree, H.E. 59
Barber, N. 71
Barnes, G. 108
Barnett, D. 87
Barnett, W.S. 232
Barnow, S. 117
Baron, S.W. 225

Bartz, J.A. 56
Bass-Field, E.R. 104
Bates, J. 58
Bates, J.E. 90
Batstra, L. 44
Battas, O. 122
Battle, K. 165, 219
Baumrind, D. 66, 71
Bean, C. 207
Beck, J.E. 37
Becker, B. 126
Bedard, K. 66
Beech, A.R. 56, 57
Bender, D. 91
Bennet, S. 94
Berg, R. 44
Bergmark, A. 207
Berkowitz, L. 75
Berlin, I. 190, 191
Bernazzani, O. 138
Bernet, W. 81
Berns, S.B. 60
Bernstein, P. 188
Berry, C.J. 77
Beyer, J.A. 89
Beyer, M. 14
Birch, H.G. 15
Bishop, D. 224
Bitensky, S.H. 170
Bliesener, T. 91
Bogaerts, S. 61
Bogat, G.A. 98, 103, 119, 121
Bohlin, G. 45
Bolen, R.M. 53
Bolger, K.E. 87
Boots, D.P. 13, 14, 89, 90
Bor, W. 71
Bosmans, G. 65
Bottoms, B. 221
Bower-Russa, M.E. 72, 78, 79
Bowlby, J. 53–4, 55, 56, 57, 59, 60,
    70
Bowlus, A. 80
Bradshaw, C.P. 87, 126, 127
Brannigan, A. 70, 125
Bremner, J.D. 39

Brendgen, M. 110
Brennan, P.A. 43–4, 45
Bretherton, I. 58
Britner, P.A. 69
Broidy, L.M. 11
Bronfenbrenner, U. 17, 126
Brooks, B. 133, 198, 211
Brown, G. 119
Brown, J. 98
Brown, S.A. 118
Buchanan, A. 66
Buck, J. 72
Bufkin, J.L. 34, 35, 38, 39, 40
Burke, H.C. 59, 60
Butler, A. 88
Button, C.M. 230

Caesar, P.L. 77
Callahan, M. 168, 169, 174
Cameron, G. 167
Campaign 2000 167
Campbell, K.M. 234, 235, 236
Canadian Institute for Health
    Information 172, 173
Cantwell, N. 31
Carlton, B.S. 126
Carter, C.S. 57
Carver, L.J. 37
Casas, J.F. 65, 68–9
Cassidy, J. 58
Catalano, R.E. 16
Cavet, J. 236
Cederblad, M. 44
Cesaroni, C. 225
Chaaya, M. 122
Chaffin, M. 61, 81, 86, 124, 125
Chamberlain, P. 111
Champagne, F. 185
Chance, T. 116
Chang, J.J. 84
Chapillon, P. 35
Chapin, H.D. 84
Chapple, C.L. 60
Chase, K.A. 87
Chassin, L. 118
Chen, P. 116

Chess, S. 15
Child Welfare League of America 117, 221
Choong, K. 48
Chronis, A.M. 119, 120, 121, 126
Cicchetti, D. 17, 87, 126
Claassen-Wilson, D. 12
Clarke, R. 152
Clarren, S.K. 47
Cnattingius, S. 41, 42
Coe, C.L. 36
Cohn, D.A. 58
Cole, P.M. 82
Collins, T. 23, 25
Colman, A. 11
Committee on the Rights of the Child 64
Conger, R.D. 70, 71
Conners, N.A. 48, 114, 115
Conry, J. 50, 52
Constantino, J.N. 53
Conway, D. 191, 192
Cooke, C.G. 115, 117
Coontz, P.D. 79
Cooper, P. 122
Cooper, P.J. 123
Cornia, G. 145
Covell, K. 9, 19, 20, 32, 43, 68, 71, 72, 75, 79, 80, 95, 96, 127, 161, 166, 171, 194, 214, 217, 221, 224, 233, 234, 237
Cowan, P.A. 58
Crawford, A. 152
Creeden, K. 34, 65
Crick, N.R. 91
Crijnen, A. 154, 178
Criss, M.M. 126, 127
Crnic, K.A. 125
Crockenberg, S.C. 122, 123
Cross, W. 82
Crowell, J. 53, 56, 57
Cullen, F. 224, 225
Cunradi, C. 116
Currie, C.L. 98, 102, 103, 104

Dadds, M.R. 104
Dahinten, V.S. 66, 119, 121, 125
Dallaire, D. 111, 128
Dankoski, M.E. 62
Danziger, S. 145
Davis, C.A. 89
Davis, R. 152
Dawson, G. 34, 37, 120
De Bellis, M.D. 33, 34, 36, 38, 64, 65, 85
de Castro, B.O. 92, 93
De Cock, R. 234
de Souza, N. 122
de Vauss, D. 100
Decker, S. 208
Declercq, F. 61
Decoene, J. 234
DeKlyen, M. 58
Delaney-Black, V. 49
Delany, C. 23
Delpisheh, A. 41, 42
Dembo, R. 114
Denenberg, V.H. 35
Denis, J. 185

Denov, M.S. 81, 83–4
Dill, V.S. 12
Dishion, T.J. 12, 70, 178
Dodge, K.A. 12, 70, 90, 91, 184
Doek, J. 21, 232
Dolan, M. 14
Donohue, B. 115, 116
Doob, A. 225
Douglas, E.M. 78
Downs, W.R. 77
Drew, C.J. 14
Drugli, M. 154, 178
Drummond, P. 119, 122–3, 124
Dube, S.R. 116
Dubow, E.F. 11
Duncan, A. 103, 104
Dunford, F.W. 87
Dunn, J. 55, 57, 58, 114, 115, 117
Dunning, E. 98
Durrant, J.E. 72, 73, 75, 78–9, 80, 139–40, 142, 148–9, 158, 170, 202, 205, 216, 230
Dye, T. 130

Eamon, M.K. 76
Earle, A. 162
Edleson, J.L. 96, 102
Edlund, J. 207
Edwards, O.W. 126
Egeland, B. 86, 116
Egolf, B. 75
Ehrensaft, M.K. 60, 80, 88, 103, 104
Eichler, M. 192, 193, 194
Eklund, J. 36
Elgar, F.J. 120
Elicker, J. 58
English, D.J. 116
Environics Research Group 212, 218
Erikson, E. 16, 53, 54
Ernst, M. 42
Eron, L.D. 11
Esping-Andersen, G. 131–2, 196–7, 208–9, 210
Estrada, F. 158
Ethier, L.S. 87
European Agency for Development in Special Needs Education 151
Evans, J. 121
Eydal, G. 142, 197, 202, 204, 205, 206, 222

Fabian, H.M. 122
Fals-Stewart, W. 116.17
Fantuzzo, J. 102
Farrington, D.P. 11, 65, 88, 94, 108, 109, 111, 112, 113, 137, 138, 139, 140, 152–3, 173, 176, 231
Fast, D.K. 50, 52
Federal Bureau of Investigation 181
Feiring, C. 98
Feldman, S. 213
Felthous, A.R. 104
Ferguson, T. 107

Fergusson, D.M. 16, 43, 44, 45, 100, 102, 104, 125
Ferrarini, T. 144, 145, 165, 166
Ferraro, K.J. 99
Finkelhor, D. 125
Fishbein, M. 230
Fisher, B. 224
Flekkoy, M. 20, 141, 195, 203
Flouri, E. 66
Floyd, R.L. 46, 51
Foley, D.L. 36
Fontaine, R.G. 90, 92
Forbes, E.E. 119
Forth, A.E. 59, 60
Frankel, K. 58
Freeman, M. 19, 22, 23
French, D. 178
Freymond, N. 167
Friedman, M. 191
Friendly, M. 162, 163
Frisk, M. 154, 178
Fryxell, D. 14
Furman, W.C. 98
Furstenberg, F. 205, 216

Galindo, R. 48
Ganstrom, M.L. 49
Garbarino, J. 161, 223
Gassman-Pines, J. 96
Gaze, C. 125
Geist, C. 201
Gelfand, D.M. 14
Gelles, R. 128
George, C. 71
Gershoff, E.T. 72, 73, 74–5, 77, 78, 140
Ghubash, R. 122
Gibson, C.L. 45
Gil, D.G. 79
Gilbert, N. 145, 167, 205, 216
Gilens, M. 218
Giles-Sims, J. 140
Giller, H. 15
Glasser, M. 82
Global Peace Index 158, 181
Glynn, C. 188
Goldhagen, J. 20
Gordon, L.C. 77
Gorman-Smith, D. 16
Gornick, J. 135
Gottman, J. 60
Gould, C. 191, 192
Graham-Bermann, S.A. 103
Grann, M. 82
Grant, M.J. 230
Graves, K.N. 97, 103, 125, 126
Gray, R.F. 43, 46
Gray, T. 191
Graydon, S. 97
Greenberg, M.T. 58
Greenwood, P.W. 231
Grogan-Kaylor, A. 140
Gundry, G. 108
Gunnar, M.G. 34, 35, 37, 39
Guttmann-Steinmetz, S. 53, 56, 57

Habbick, B. 50
Hadders-Algra, M. 44

Hagel, A. 15
Halpern, C.T. 87
Hamarman, S. 81
Hamilton, C. 224
Hammarberg, T. 19
Hanlon, T.E. 110
Hans, S. 45
Hanson, R.K. 93
Hantrais, L. 200
Harden, B.J. 103, 120
Harlow, H.F. 36
Harlow, M.K. 36
Harris, A.J. 93
Harris, G.T. 14, 15, 59
Harris, W.M. 104, 105
Hart, S.N. 19, 194, 195
Hartnagel, T.F. 225
Hartz, L. 209
Harvey, R. 224
Haskett, M.E. 70
Hastings, R. 176
Haugland, B.S.M. 116, 117, 154, 178
Hawkins, J.D. 16
Hay, D. 65
Headey, B. 100, 101, 102
Heide, K.M. 13, 14, 89, 90, 104
Heidelise, A. 37
Henderson, T. 213
Henry, D.B. 16
Herjanic, B.L. 108
Herman, K.C. 71
Herrenkohl, E. 75
Herrenkohl, R. 75–6, 140
Herrenkohl, T.I. 11, 14
Herrera, V.M. 98, 99
Hesse, E. 55
Hetherington, R. 205, 216
Heymann, S. 162, 163, 164, 165
Highet, N. 119, 122–3, 124
Hildyard, K.L. 81, 84, 85, 86
Hill, H.H. 115
Hill, J. 14, 15
Hill, M. 20
Hill, M.B. 96
Hindberg, B. 205
Hines, D.A. 98, 99, 100–1
Hoffman, C. 125
Holden, G.W. 72, 100
Hollander, E. 56
Holmes, W.C. 86
Holtzworth-Munroe, A. 100
Hook, B. 44, 45, 46
Horowitz, H.A. 59
Horwood, L. 16, 43, 100, 104
Howe, R.B. 19, 20, 32, 68, 71, 75, 79, 127, 161, 166, 182, 194, 195, 213, 214, 221, 224, 233, 234
Hudson, S.M. 61
Huefner, J.C. 87
Huesmann, L.R. 11, 68, 94
Huizink, A.C. 37
Hummel, P. 82
Hyvonen, U. 146

Ierley, A. 12
Imbrogno, A. 170, 215
Indurkhya, A. 43

Inglehart, R. 189
International Centre for Crime Prevention 152

Jackson, A.P. 65
Jacobson, N. 60
Jacoby, W. 213
Jaffee, P. 80, 86, 102
Janson, S. 148, 149, 202
Jellen, L.K. 102
John, M. 229
Johnson, M.P. 99
Johnsson, L.M. 122
Johnston, D. 112
Johnstone, S.J. 123
Jones, K.L. 46, 47, 48
Jones, L. 30
Josefsson, A. 123
Joseph, R. 33
Jung, J. 118
Junger-Tas, J. 208

Kadushin, A. 79
Kahn, R.S. 14, 15
Kangas, O. 201
Karoly, L. 138, 232
Karp, J. 80
Kaufman-Kantor, G.K. 77
Kaufman, N. 20, 195
Kautto, M. 196, 198
Kearney, C.A. 16
Keiley, M.K. 59
Keller, P.S. 116
Kellermann, A. 138, 139, 140
Kelly, K. 89
Kennon, S.S. 112
Kernic, M.A. 104, 105
Khaleque, A. 69, 70
Khoo, E. 146
Kidder, S. 12
Kids Count Database 167, 172, 175
Kildal, N. 197
King, M.L. 22
Kingree, J.B. 85, 87
Kitzmann, K.M. 106, 107
Klinteberg, B. 36
Knol, D.L. 45
Knutson, J.F. 72
Knutsson, K.E. 19
Koblinsky, S.A. 65, 66, 103, 119, 120, 126
Kodituwakku, P.W. 46, 49
Kolko, D.J. 86
Koops, W. 92
Korpi, W. 133–4
Kovera, M. 221
Kuhnle, S. 197
Kuperminc, G.P. 59
Kuvalanka, K.A. 65

Lacharite, C. 87
Lalumiere, M. 14
Lambert, S. 108
Langan, P. 158
Langstrom, N. 82, 158
Lansdown, G. 236

Lansford, J.E. 12, 77, 91, 94
Larsson, B. 154, 178
Lavis, J. 185
Lavoie, F. 77
Le Bordais, C. 135, 213
Leckman, J.F. 56
Leerkes, E.M. 122, 123
Lehoux, P. 185
Lelong, N. 122
Lemelin, J.P. 87
Leonard, K.E. 116
Leschied, A.W. 119, 120
Leve, L.D. 111
Levendosky, A.A. 98, 102, 103, 120, 121
Leventhal, J. 169, 174
Levine, S. 35
Levitt, P. 30
Library of Parliament 215
Lieberman, A.F. 98, 104
Limber, S. 214
Lin, K.H. 77
Linares, L.O. 103
Lindblad, F. 82
Lipset, S.M. 210
Locke, T.F. 115, 116, 118
Loeber, R. 65, 111
Lomas, J. 185
Loney, B.R. 103
Losel, F. 91, 92, 93
Luker, K. 151, 175, 206, 217
Lukes, S. 190
Lulbach, G.R. 36
Lundy, B.L. 37
Lurigio, A. 152
Luthar, S. 126
Luttrell, V.R. 34, 35, 38, 39, 40
Lynch, M. 17
Lyons-Ruth, K. 121

Maccoby, E.E. 65
MacKenzie, D. 12
Mackintosh, V.H. 112
Magdol, L. 60, 104
Main, M. 55
Manly, J.T. 87
Manza, J. 133, 198, 211
Manzer, R. 210
Mapp, S.C. 82, 123
Marans, S. 104
Marcil-Gratton, N. 135, 213
Marshall, D.B. 116
Marshall, W.L. 14, 58, 61, 62
Martens, P. 158
Martin, J.A. 79
Martinez, P. 102
Mash, E.J. 40
Maslow, A.H. 70
Masotti, P. 47, 48
Mathur, A. 215
Maughan, B. 11, 45, 178
May, P.A. 11, 47, 49
Mayes, L.C. 56
McAlister, A. 226
McAuliff, B. 221
McCain, M. 162, 164, 169, 173, 174
McCall Smith, A. 14, 89
McCann, J. 12

McCarroll, J.E. 102
McCartney, K. 62, 119, 124
McCloskey, L.A. 98, 99
McClosky, H. 189, 210
McCord, J. 12
McCormick, M.C. 43
McElhaney, K.B. 59
McFarlane, J.M. 98, 104
McGillivray, A. 161
McGrath, P.J. 120
McGroder, S.M. 65
McGuigan, W.M. 102, 105
McKee, T.E. 68
McLoyd, V.C. 66
McMahon, R.J. 111
Melton, G. 214
Merez-Perez, L. 104
Merkel-Holquin, L. 221
Meyers, M. 135, 163, 166, 184, 187
Middlestadt, S. 230
Miller, C. 103
Miller, K. 111, 112, 113
Miller, L.C. 47
Mitchell, I.J. 56, 57
Moffitt, T.E. 13, 16, 98
Monuteaux, M.C. 42, 45
Moolchan, E. 42
Moon, M. 225
Moore, C.G. 103
Moore, C.M. 59
Moreira, J. 56
Morgan, R. 111
Morrell, J. 66, 124
Morse, B.J. 100
Moss, E. 58
Moss, K. 104
Moss, P. 134, 143, 204, 206
Mott, M.A. 118
Moussaoui, D. 122
Muenke, M. 47
Mulder, C. 76
Mulligan, C.J. 50
Mullis, R.L. 11
Mumford, V.E. 126
Mumola, C.J. 112
Murray, E. 234
Murray, J. 112, 113
Murray, L. 66, 123, 124
Mustard, J.F. 162
Myers, B.J. 110, 112

Nager, A. 122
Nagin, D. 224
Nas, C.N. 92
Nash, K. 49
National Public Radio/Kaiser
    Family Foundation/Kennedy
    School of Government 217
Neelman, J. 44
Newcomb, M.D. 115, 116, 118
Newman, J.P. 59
Nicholas, K.B. 117, 118
Niehoff, D. 33, 34, 40
Nilsson, K.W. 15
Noble, C. 132
Nolan, C. 115
Nolan, J. 115, 209
Noseworthy, J. 230

Nygren, L. 146

O'Brien, L.M. 122
O'Brien, M. 102
O'Connor, M.J. 48
O'Hara, K. 135, 143, 200, 201, 211, 212, 213
O'Keefe, M. 104
O'Leary, K.D. 47, 87, 234
O'Neil, M. 223
OECD 144, 150, 162, 165, 171, 174
Office of Sweden's Childrens
    Ombudsman 205
Olds, D. 138, 173
Olney, F.W. 50
Olsen, G. 132, 134, 135, 143, 144, 162, 164, 165, 166, 169, 174, 197, 198, 211, 219
Olson, J.M. 230
Ondersma, S.J. 114
Orlebeke, J.F. 45
Orme, M. 116
Ormrod, R.K. 125
Orzol, S.M. 14, 15
Osofsky, J.D. 102, 105
Ostrander, R. 71
Ozawa, M. 144

Papadakis, E. 207
Pardini, D.A. 49, 60
Pas, W. 24
Patel, V. 122, 123
Patterson, C.J. 87
Patterson, G.R. 16, 70-1, 75, 178
Pearson, L. 23
Peck, L. 135
Penrose, K. 162
Perera, F.P. 42, 46
Peters, R. 134, 163, 164, 166, 167
Peters, R.D. 59
Petit, G.S. 90
Petrie, P. 134, 143, 204, 206
Pettersen, P. 199
Pettit, G. 184
Phan, D. 85, 87
Phillips, B. 72
Phillips, D.A. 14, 17, 33, 38, 138, 139, 161, 173
Phillips, S.D. 109, 110, 112
Pinheiro, P.S. 228-9, 230
Piquero, A.R. 45
Poehlmann, J. 110
Poulin, F. 12
Pratt, C.C. 102, 105
Price, C. 160, 214
Pridemore, W.A. 11, 18
Prinz, R.J. 14, 88, 117
Pritchard, C. 88
Proctor, L.J. 16
Public Safety Canada 176

Radel, L.F. 115
Radestad, I.J. 122
Rahman, A. 122
Raikes, A.H. 62, 138
Randolph, S.M. 65

Rasmussen, E.H. 117, 118
Ravndal, E. 114
Regmi, S. 122
Reid, J.B. 70
Reinoso, B. 30
Retz, W. 34, 39
Rhomberg, W. 156
Rhule, D.M. 111, 125
Rice, M.E. 14
Richters, J.E. 58, 102
Ridder, E.M. 100
Ristock, J.L. 101
Ritchie, K.L. 100
Roberts, J. 81, 82, 120, 122, 202, 205, 224, 225, 230
Robins, L.N. 108
Robinson, M. 42
Rodrigues, M. 122
Rodriquez, A. 45
Roelofs, J. 65, 69
Rohner, R.P. 69, 70, 78
Roisman, G.I. 59
Romano, E. 120
Romero, V. 115
Romito, P. 122, 123
Room, R. 47
Rose-Krasnor, L. 235, 236
Rosenbaum, D. 152
Rosenblum, L.A. 36
Rosenstein, D.S. 59
Rossow, I. 157
Rostgaard, T. 201
Roy, T.S. 42
Rubertsson, C. 122, 123
Runyan, D.K. 84
Rutter, M. 15

Saltaris, C. 59, 60
Salter, D. 81, 82, 83
Sammel, M.D. 86
Sanders, M.R. 71
Satka, M. 142, 197, 202, 204, 205, 206, 222
Saurel-Cubizolles, M.J. 122
Savage, J. 155, 156
Scannapieco, M. 116
Scaramella, L.V. 70, 71
Schene, P. 168, 169, 174
Schissel, B. 223
Schmitt, W.A. 59
Schneider, M.L. 36
Schneider, S. 213
Schwartz, D. 91
Schwartz, J.P. 71
Scott, D. 100
Scott, E. 225
Scott, S. 65
Seelau, E.P. 99, 101
Seelau, S.M. 99, 101
Seidler, F.J. 42
Semidei, J. 115, 116
Serin, R.C. 59
Serra-Roldan, R. 126
Seymour, C.B. 109
Shanker, S. 162
Shapka, J.D. 66
Shaw, D.S. 11, 47, 58, 157, 180
Shaw, M. 155-6
Shen, R. 48

Shonkoff, J.P. 14, 17, 33, 38, 138, 139, 161, 173
Shulman, S. 58
Shumaker, D.M. 14, 88
Siegel, J. 82
Siegert, R. 61
Sigelman, C.K. 77
Silverman, I.J. 104
Simons, R.L. 77
Skondras, M. 36
Slavkin, M.L. 104
Sloper, P. 236
Slotkin, T. 42
Small, M. 214
Smith, C. 14
Smith, D.W. 46
Smith, E. 221
Smith-Khuri, E. 154, 178
Snyder, J. 75
Sood, B. 49, 51
Sorkhabi, N. 67, 71, 78
Speltz, M.L. 58
Spieker, S.J. 111
Spitz, R.A. 85
Spohr, H.L. 47, 49, 51
Sprott, J. 224
Sroufe, L.A. 58
Stalans, L. 224
Stanley, J.L. 101, 102
Starzyk, K.B. 14, 58, 62
Stasiulis, D. 221
Statistics Canada 172, 175, 181
Steinberg, L. 71
Steinhausen, H.C. 47, 49, 50
Stephens, L.E. 121
Sternberg, K.J. 53, 102, 105
Stevens, S. 116
Stewart, E.A. 11, 14, 16
Stewart, M.A. 118
Straus, M.A. 73, 77, 106, 140, 215
Sugarman, D. 140
Sundquist, K. 122
Suomi, S.J. 36
SurveyUSA 215
Sussman-Stillman, A. 116
Sutton, S.E. 11
Svallfors, S. 198, 199, 207, 211
Swain, J.E. 56, 122, 123
Swedish National Council for Crime Prevention 152
Swift, K. 168, 169, 174
Swinford, S.P. 74, 77
Sylwander, L. 24, 142, 222

Tackett, J.L. 15
Takala, H. 152
Taylor, C. 191
Teicher, M.H. 40, 41, 65, 93
Thayer, L.E. 102
Theodore, A.D. 84, 86
Therborn, G. 202
Thomas, A. 15
Thomas, J.C. 103
Thompson, M. 85, 87
Thompson, R. 58
Thompson, R.A. 62
Thormaehlen, D.J. 104
Tibbetts, S.G. 45
Tisdall, K. 20

Tolan, P.H. 16
Tomlinson, M. 122, 123
Tonry, M. 158
Totten, M. 89
Treboux, D. 87
Tremblay, R.E. 13, 138, 226
Trocme, N. 73, 79
Turner, F. 135
Turner, H.A. 125
Turner, J. 135
Tyler, S. 84, 115

UNICEF 141, 145, 148, 150, 151, 154, 156, 169, 172, 175, 178, 207
United Nations 11, 27, 29, 63, 138, 140, 148, 237
United Nations Office on Drugs and Crime 157, 180
United Nations Treaty Body Database 141
US Department of Justice 176
Usaf, M.C. 47

van Dijk, J. 155–6
Van Dorn, R. 138
Van Goozen, S.H.M. 14, 33, 34, 35, 36, 37, 38, 39–40
van Ijzendoorn, M.H. 15, 53
VanDeMark, N.R. 114, 115, 117
Vanheule, S. 61
Verba, S. 189
Verhellen, E. 19, 21, 24, 194
Verhulst, F.C. 45, 154
Vermetten, E. 39
Vila, B. 155, 156
Vittrup, B. 72, 78
Vivian, D. 60
Voss, W.D. 59
Vuijk, P. 46

Waddell, C. 184, 185, 186, 187, 188
Wakschlag, L.S. 42, 44, 45, 111
Waldenstrom, U. 122
Waller, M.A. 126
Walrath, C.M. 81, 86
Walsh, A. 89, 90
Ward, T. 61
Waschbuch, D.A. 120
Waters, E. 58
Waterston, T. 20
Wattendorf, D.J. 47, 50
Watts-English, T. 34, 38, 65, 93
Weaver, A. 217
Weaver, R.K. 218
Weber, C.V. 104
Weissman, M. 45, 124
Welsh, B. 137, 138, 139, 140, 152–3, 173, 176, 231
West, D.J. 88, 108
West, M. 117
West, P.A. 108
Whitaker, R.C. 14, 15
White, H.R. 116
Widom, C.S. 117
Wiklund, S. 147

Wilcox, B. 184, 187
Wiles, K.A. 77
Wilkens, S.L. 98
Williams, G.M. 44
Williams, J. 138
Williams, L.M. 82
Willms, J.D. 66
Willoughby, M. 70
Wilson, D. 12
Wilson, S. 102
Winebarger, A. 72
Winsler, A. 84
Wisensale, S. 165
Wolfe, D.A. 40, 81, 84, 85, 86, 87, 88, 98, 102, 105, 107, 126
Wolff, S. 14, 89
Wood, D.S. 104
Wood, J.J. 58
Woodward, L.J. 43
World Health Organization 41, 98–9, 137, 138, 139, 140, 150, 154, 157, 171, 178–9
Wright, L.E. 109

Ybarra, G.Y. 98, 102
Yodanis, C.L. 77
Yoerger, K. 16
Yudowitz, B. 104

Zaller, J. 189, 210, 213
Zanna, M.P. 230
Zeldin, S. 236
Zeskind, P.S. 121
Zielinski, D.S. 87, 126, 127
Zimmerman, S. 213
Zimring, F. 223

Printed in the United States
152082LV00001BB/2/P